Making the
Americas Modern

Hemispheric Art, 1910-1960

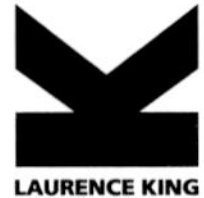

Published in 2018
by Laurence King Publishing Ltd
361–373 City Road
London EC1V 1LR
Tel +44 20 7841 6900
Fax +44 20 7841 6910
E enquiries@laurenceking.com
www.laurenceking.com

A catalogue record for this book is available from the
British Library.

ISBN 978 1 78627 155 6
Designed by John Round Design
Printed in China

Acknowledgments

I am very grateful to those people directly concerned with the
writing and production of this book. Tim Barringer, editor of the
series in which this volume appears, has been an encouraging
and inspiring colleague and friend for many years. At Laurence
King I am indebted to the expert staff, whose patience and
kindness are gratefully acknowledged. They include Laurence
King, Kara Hattersley-Smith, Melissa Danny, Julia Ruxton, Simon
Walsh, and Ana Machado. Much of the content of this volume
is the result of many years of teaching, lecturing, and research
on the subjects considered here, and the stimulation I have
received through the interactions with my many students has
been deeply rewarding. I have learned more from them than
from any other source.

Making the Americas Modern

Hemispheric Art, 1910-1960

Edward J. Sullivan

Laurence King Publishing

Global Perspectives series

Contents

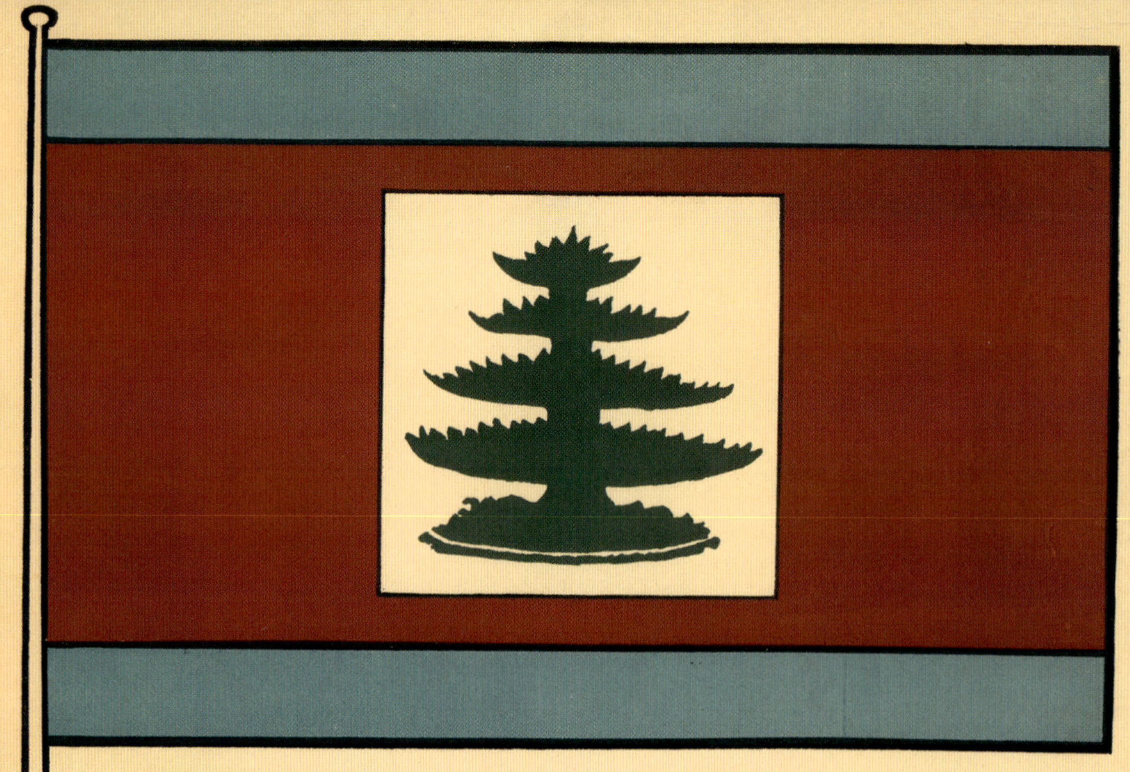

INTERNATIONAL EXHIBITION OF MODERN ART

ASSOCIATION OF AMERICAN PAINTERS AND SCULPTORS

69th INF'T'Y REG'T ARMORY, NEW YORK CITY
FEBRUARY 15th TO MARCH 15th 1913
AMERICAN & FOREIGN ART.

AMONG THE GUESTS WILL BE — INGRES, DELACROIX, DEGAS, CÉZANNE, REDON, RENOIR, MONET, SEURAT, VAN GOGH, HODLER, SLEVOGT, JOHN, PRYDE, SICKERT, MAILLOL, BRANCUSI, LEHMBRUCK, BERNARD, MATISSE, MANET, SIGNAC, LAUTREC, CONDER, DENIS, RUSSELL, DUFY, BRAQUE, HERBIN, GLEIZES, SOUZA-CARDOZO, ZAK, DU CHAMP-VILLON, GAUGUIN, ARCHIPENKO, BOURDELLE, C. DE SEGONZAC.

LEXINGTON AVE.–25th ST.

Fragmentary Histories of Hemispheric Art, 1910–1960

This book tells an unconventional story. It does not contain a linear narrative and does not allow for a hegemony of either chronology or geography, even though it is bound by a specific, albeit broad, span of time and place. This text consists of a divergent approach from the widely accepted and now-canonical stories of modernity, such as those suggested by Alfred H. Barr, founding director of New York's Museum of Modern Art, in his organization of the museum's collection and his schematic drawing for the cover of the landmark exhibition *Cubism and Abstract Art* (1936). Many of the artists whose works I analyze are not in the category of "famous art stars," and some of them may not be familiar to the audience of this volume. I have particular interest in the accomplishments of women and artists who belong to any number of communities that are usually un- or under-represented in mainstream and even smaller arts institutions. I argue, in this text, against the sovereignty of "influence" and the long-held but now mostly disparaged notions of peripheries versus centers. In virtually all chapters of this book, "sources" are fluid and drift simultaneously from south to north and vice versa, and from west to east.

When embarking on this project I chose to investigate a wide variety of interconnected phenomena about art and forms of visuality throughout the Americas. This having been said, the question of how to define "the Americas" is an obvious one. This book looks at artists and works of art from virtually all parts of the western hemisphere: the Americas in my estimation is a broad rather than a narrow terrain, encompassing North,

Unidentified artist
Poster from the 1913 Armory Show.
See fig. 1.

Central, and South America as well as the island nations of the Caribbean, some of which still form parts of the old networks of colonialist domination. This is, however, neither a survey of art, nor an encyclopedia of artists and their achievements.

Certain readers might find some of my juxtapositions bizarre, or at least unorthodox. And they may indeed be, as they often do not conform to conventional or widely accepted hierarchies of artistic value in terms of images, media, or technique but, rather, to my own. In *Making the Americas Modern* the lion's share of attention is paid to painting (in formats large and small, from modest canvases to monumental murals). Nonetheless, photography, sculpture, and various forms of graphic art are here as well when they best illustrate separate but interrelated histories. There are many places in the hemisphere that do not appear in this book, and many forms of art that go unmentioned. This is both deliberate and inevitable. And it is one of the many reasons that the title of this preliminary essay includes the term "fragmentary histories." Not wishing this to be either a survey of art or a proposal for a new canon, but rather a series of essays on larger themes, I acknowledge that the omissions (which may be more obvious to some readers than to others) are part of a process of "natural selection" and not a dismissal or a signal of condescension for any place, artist, or form of artistic production. What I have tried to do, instead, is attempt to "read between the lines," and sometimes enter the liminal borders of arts and ideas to suggest a mode of seeing and apprehension of the arts in the first half of the twentieth century in the greater Americas that might serve to stimulate debate and other ways of thinking.

Many of the works discussed here are figurative, but I also dedicate considerable space to varying forms of non-figuration, or arts that stand in an in-between space, straddling representational and abstract art. And two chapters of the book are dedicated to a variety of options taken by artists interested in paths leading to obliteration of conventional form.

Exhibiting Modern Art, 1910–1960

The discussions herein are situated between 1910 and 1960. This choice is by no means arbitrary. Among the key events at the beginning and end points of this era are many related to dramatic shifts in the American aesthetic consciousness, combined with events in the societal and political realms that helped to shape the artistic directions taken by practitioners across the region.

At either end of this spectrum we have the organization of major exhibitions that heralded a change in the ways artists made their decisions, created their work, and marketed it to a large public. In 1913 the *International Exhibition of Modern Art* was held, more popularly known as the Armory Show (for its venue in the 69th Infantry Regiment Armory, one of several military arsenals and training sites used for the instruction of soldiers, on Lexington Avenue, between 25th and 26th streets in Manhattan—a building still in existence and the home of New York's National Guard) (FIG. 1). This event represented an important step forward in the introduction to the United States of the latest avant-garde achievements of European and American artists.

The poster, designed by an unknown artist, includes the names of solely European artists from earlier phases of modern art history (Delacroix, Ingres, Cézanne, Renoir) as well as contemporary artists (Constantin Brancusi, Wilhelm Lehmbruck, Albert Gleizes) whose art heralded new approaches. None of the Americans is listed here, and none of the more audacious non-U.S. contributors to the exhibition (Marcel Duchamp, Francis Picabia) is present. The Armory Show, as I will discuss in the body of the book, was a curious and stimulating mixture of old and new. Some examples of the most advanced art were mocked in the press, and the still-conservative audiences in New York and beyond undoubtedly had a difficult time assimilating some

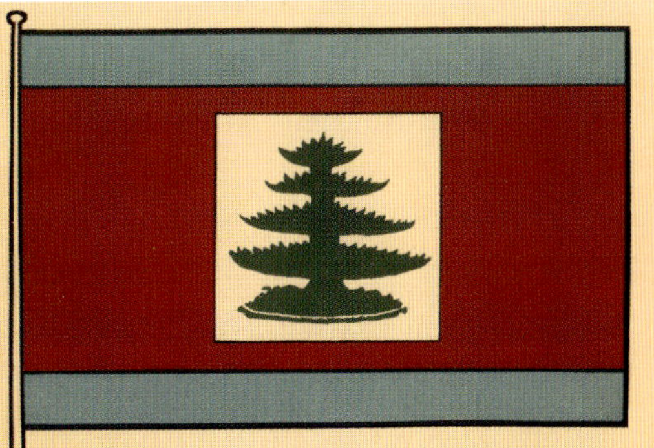

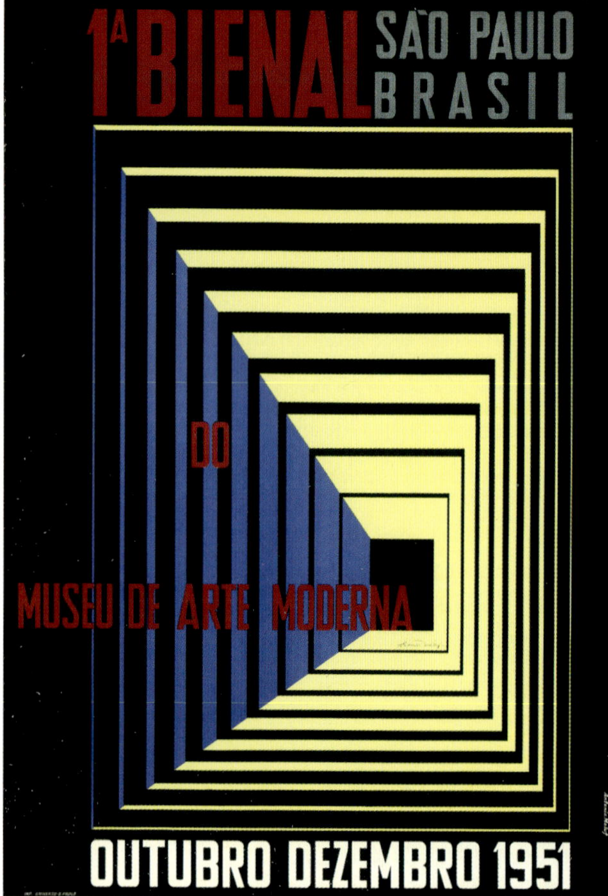

of the most outrageous contributions. Yet the exhibition was groundbreaking in promoting the experimental in art in a way that had not existed before.

Almost 40 years later and about 5,000 miles to the south, the first Bienal de São Paulo was organized. Graphic designer Antônio Maluf's poster for this 1951 event (FIG. 2) vividly suggests some of the directions that art in Brazil (and many other countries of South America and the Caribbean) would take in the 1950s and beyond, when geometric art as well as Kineticism and other forms of Constructivist nonobjectivity assumed pride of place, if only briefly (as in the case of Venezuela, where government support of geometric abstract and kinetic art elicited deep dissatisfaction from younger artists by the early 1960s). Like the Armory Show in a U.S. context, the São Paulo Biennial played a crucial role, stimulating artists from all parts of the hemisphere to take their work in new directions. This oldest biennial of the Americas (still in existence) showcased the most advanced forms of art from around the world to its thousands of visitors, who came to Brazil's largest city to witness the latest in experimental artistic trends. In a pre-Internet age the biennial was a much-awaited bellwether of the "new," especially for South American artists, collectors, and curators.

Between these two exhibitions there were, of course, many other landmark shows that represented important steps on the road to artistic regeneration and originality. Many of the artists in this book participated in, or were acutely aware of, the trends that these exhibitions represented. Just to cite some of the most consequential markers of artistic shifts, we might turn our attention to exhibitions like the first show of the Canadian Group of Seven at the Art Gallery of Toronto in May 1920 (see my discussion of the work of Lawren Harris in Chapter 2, dedicated to landscape). The *Semana de Arte Moderna* (Week of Modern Art) was held in São Paulo's Teatro Municipal in February 1922. Organized by or including the work of Brazilian Vanguard artists Anita Malfatti, Tarsila do Amaral, and Emiliano Di Cavalcanti (among many other painters, sculptors, industrial designers, and architects), it famously heralded a new regime in the visual arts of Brazil (even though the majority of visitors, as well as those artists who responded to the avant-garde sensibility, represented the local elites). The year 1927 witnessed the organization of the *Exposición de Arte Nuevo* at the Havana headquarters of the Association of Painters and Sculptors, an anti-conservative group of young artists. The show included members of the first generation of the Cuban Vanguard (Carlos Enríquez, Victor Manuel García, and Amelia Peláez, among many others) as well as foreign artists who went on to have substantial careers outside of Cuba, including Alice Neel and the Latvian-born future New York School Abstract Expressionist Adja Yunkers.

Time Frames

Even more weight was given to my choice of chronological markers for this book, flagging the sociopolitical as well as climactic events that shaped the "space" of the time period under question and led to artistic experimentation and transformation. The year 1910 witnessed the beginning of the Mexican Revolution, a series of civil wars that ended only in 1920. It heralded changes in virtually every way and had marked consequences for the political and artistic futures of other nations in Latin America. By 1960 the Cuban Revolution, which had, in local parlance, "triumphed" at the beginning of 1959, was well on its way to consolidating its reverberations in every aspect of Cuban life—including the arts. Cuba's shift to socialism and its ultimate alliances with the Soviet Union had profound implications for the political—and cultural/artistic—lives not only of Cubans but for people across the hemisphere and around the world who, at least during its early phases, looked to Cuba as a beacon of inspiration for resistance to the supremacy of the capitalist system as represented by the United States. In a pan-Caribbean format, the 1950s also represents a time of increased anti-colonialist sentiment as independence movements marked the histories of such Anglophone nations as Jamaica, Trinidad, and Barbados. These struggles bore fruit in the following decade, with Jamaican independence being declared in 1962, and that of Trinidad and Barbados in 1966. And for the United States, the mid-1950s also marked the beginning of the two-decade-long national trauma of the Vietnam War.

Much of the art in this book responds to social situations in a time of ongoing crises that included the two world wars, the worldwide economic Depression, and labor unrest throughout the Americas (miners' strikes throughout the Andes in the 1930s, violent confrontations of labor versus management at the Ford Motor Company's River Rouge plant near Detroit, Michigan in 1932, and countless other examples). The rise of dictatorships in places like Cuba and the Dominican Republic in the 1920s and 30s and beyond (Gerardo Machado and, later, Fulgencio Batista in Cuba; Rafael Trujillo in the Dominican Republic) were followed by the regime of Juan Perón in Argentina, starting in 1946. These latter-day *caudillos* ("strong men," to use the Latin American term for autocratic leader) prefigured the rise of the right-wing military dictatorships in South America of the 1960s. All of these phenomena had their consequences in the arts discussed here—as did natural occurrences like the Dust Bowl in the central United States in the 1930s, tropical hurricanes such as the San Zenón Cyclone that virtually leveled the city of Santo Domingo in 1930, or the ferocious droughts in Brazil in the 1940s.

Major architectural achievements also mark the beginning and end points of this book and, at the same time, stand for aesthetic shifts in their respective countries. The year 1910 witnessed the creation of what was then the world's tallest structure, New York's Woolworth building in lower Manhattan, one of the culminating moments in the skyscraper boom that had started approximately 30 years earlier. In Buenos Aires, the *Exposición del Centenario* celebrated both the beginning of the independence movement from Spain and the announcement of the city as a thoroughly modern metropolis. Many of its structures (the most prominent of them in the Art Nouveau manner) represented the commencement of the careers of both native-born and foreign architects whose careers would flourish in the decades after the *Exposición* and lend to the city, especially the upscale neighborhoods of Palermo and Recoleta, the elegant, Europeanizing character that is still to be appreciated today.

On the other side of the chronological spectrum, the most outstanding socio-architectural project, the creation of Brasília, a new capital for Brazil in a barely inhabited part of the interior, was undertaken over a five-year period in the late 1950s. President Juscelino Kubitschek, the architects Lúcio Costa and Oscar Niemeyer, and the garden designer Roberto Burle Marx collaborated on this initiative, which was officially inaugurated on April 22, 1960, marking a new moment in Brazilian art and culture and establishing a model for other would-be utopian cities.

In the epilogue I indicate further turns of the art worlds of the western hemisphere which, in themselves, represented responses to new phases of social engagement that included the many projects of resistance and self-determination embodied by the hemisphere-wide civil rights movements by people of color and indigenous peoples of virtually every nation, as well as those who campaigned for feminist rights and gay liberation.

Divisions of the Story
I begin and end this series of eight histories of visuality in the first half of the twentieth century with what I will call "visionary art." This insufficient term refers not to one specific phenomenon but to the plethora of options open to artists who wished to create imagery evocative not of quotidian realities of the observable world and its accessories, but capable of transporting the viewer into other aesthetic, imaginary, or personal realms.

The book opens with a discussion of artworks that might be loosely associated with Symbolism and other related philosophical, literary, theoretical, musical, and visual forms of expression. Symbolism may be associated with a nineteenth-century sensibility in Europe, and indeed, there are manifestations of a Symbolist aesthetic in various parts of the Americas around 1900, but the greater impact of this mode of thought and vision took place in the 1910s and 20s, thus illustrating that the chronological patterns of the development of the arts and other forms of expression are never synchronically aligned on either side of the Atlantic (or the Pacific) oceans.

Landscape as a metaphor for both rural and urban circumstances, national sentiments, indicators of progress, or metaphors for stability takes on a poignancy in the western hemisphere in the period under consideration here and is examined in the second chapter of this text. Following upon the achievements of nineteenth-century landscape painters throughout the Americas, the twentieth century witnessed dramatic departures (and some continuations) of the heroic mode as exemplified by, for example, the Hudson River School painters or the late Romantic depicters of nature in Mexico or Brazil. Mechanized landscapes and industrial cityscapes share the stage with images of more pastoral forms of the countryside.

Chapter 3 concerns "blackness." This is perhaps the most problematic story to consider within my context, as its meanings are obviously multivalent and filled with subtle complexities that have to be considered on many levels. I introduce this story by looking at artists in several centers of the Americas where images of persons of color were used as reminiscences of things and time that had ceased to exist. Other artists employed the image of the black body in art as a signal of modernity. This is especially true in representations of performative activities by black bodies—or the representation of people of color as indicators of a sense of place. In the Caribbean and Brazil (and elsewhere), blackness and "national authenticity" are sometimes conflated (usually by white artists) in a questionable formation of images that border on racist visualizations.

Blackness as depicted by black artists is another, albeit related, theme that appears not only in this chapter, which I call "Visualizing Blackness in the Americas," but throughout the book as a whole. Phenomena like the U.S. Harlem Renaissance in the 1920s and 30s, and the use by black artists in the Spanish- and Portuguese-speaking Americas of subjects related to either the history of enslavement or themes gleaned from a more generalized interest in expressing a black sensibility are discussed here.

There are two chapters in this text devoted to what I would call "social engagements." Chapters 4 and 5 constitute not simply a disquisition on the large-scale artistic movements of the pre-World War II era that deal with social realism. Rather, I attempt to look at a broad spectrum of artists who treat the challenges presented by the economic and social circumstances of a world turned upside down, as it were, by such phenomena as the Depression of the 1930s, the onslaught of nationalist sensibilities in the face of hostile political situations abroad, or the effects of exile, migration, and poverty occasioned by climactic conditions throughout North and South America.

A modern social consciousness (especially in the 1930s and into the 40s) was expressed through large-scale artistic projects. We note the rise of the (often) symbolically potent products of the mural painters in Mexico who, inspired by official support in the 1920s and public acclaim until the 40s (when enthusiasm for their art waned), were able to create panoramic representations of historic or contemporary slices of life or metaphoric dramas in both public and private settings. The Mexican example, discussed in Chapter 4, had serious consequences for public arts elsewhere. Its effects were felt in Brazil, Argentina, Cuba, and elsewhere, but muralism was especially influential for artists in the United States who, during the 1930s (with government financing), covered vast walls in city halls, post offices, municipal headquarters, and other official structures, as well as in schools, colleges, and universities throughout the country.

Beginning in the 1910s in many artistic centers of North, South, and Central America and the Caribbean, there was an increasingly marked tendency to simplify and, in fact, to abstract space and form in painted, drawn, photographed, or sculpted compositions. Segmented space became of interest to many artists who were attracted to or otherwise engaged with European Cubist and Constructivist-related form. The importance of specifically Brazilian, Uruguayan, Argentinean, American, or Canadian modes of geometry in art contrast compellingly with one another and, in certain cases, anticipate visual phenomena that characterize artistic production in other parts of the world, especially Europe. Geometrically based art, as well as forms of abstraction that rely on more fluid ways of creating a composition—gestural, organic, or biomorphic abstraction, including various permutations of Abstract Expressionism within and outside the United States—are given equal attention in Chapters 6 and 7 of this book. However, the reader should not look to this volume for yet another recounting of the often-told saga of the New York School and its consecrated heroes.

The last story, told in Chapter 8, brings us back to various forms of visionary art. Here I consider Surrealists as well as some of the so-called "intuitive" or self-trained artists and their participation in the ongoing development of a modern art. While conventional narratives often exclude or minimize the achievements to modernity of artists who are outside the conventional circuits of dealer/gallery/collector/critic networks, works by "naïve" artists have, in the past, been considered unique components of the emerging modernization of art, judging, for example, by a series of exhibitions in the early days of New York's Museum of Modern Art that featured either individual "primitive" artists like Morris Hirshfield, or group showings of "American Primitives."

Furthermore, Surrealism and intuitive art are often separated in discussions of a modern sensibility in art. I argue for their intimate relationship. Jean Dubuffet (whose own work in the mode of *art brut*, or "raw art," bore the marks of his affinities for untrained artists) lent his substantial collection of over 1,200 works of art by the insane, children, and other individuals far from the conventional art circles of Europe, to his Filipino-American artist friend Alfonso Ossorio in New York for some 15 years. Beginning in 1952 it was on view in Ossorio's home in East Hampton, Long Island, where it was seen and admired, and had a serious impact on the imaginations of many of the well-known "stars" of the mid-twentieth-century art world, from Surrealists to Abstract Expressionists.

End of the Story
The book's chronology terminates at around 1960—just at the time when dramatically new forms of art were taking hold in the Americas, Europe, and Asia (especially Japan). Pop Art, Conceptualism, Minimalism, installation art, video art, and performance art constitute some of the myriad of manifestations of "the new," and they all form integral components of the post-1960 visual landscape that arguably marks the dissolution of "the frame"—a word I use here in a metaphorical rather than a literal sense. The epilogue to this book seeks to suggest only a

few of the options that preoccupied the imaginations of artists throughout the Americas, as elsewhere. Obviously I can only offer the briefest hints at new perspectives that heralded a further phase of "contemporaneity" in many fields of visuality.

The series of essays or stories told here represent liberal blendings and juxtapositions of artworks within individual thematic contexts. There has been no attempt to categorize the works I use either as the best or most representative examples, something that would be essentially antithetical to my project. In many ways each example could be changed for another. However, each work of art makes a specific point that in aggregate forms a comprehensive series of statements leading to the clarification of the overall theme of each segment. I seek to engage and compare works and artists from a wide variety of locales. I am fully aware that this geographic eclecticism runs the risk of flattening or erasing the many differences and local variations on the subjects I am investigating, as well as the cultures they represent, but I hope that this is not the impression gleaned by the reader. Rather, I have attempted to locate examples of art that share affinities and open up the arguments presented. Throughout the Americas, local specificity, distinct visual languages, and aesthetic and political concerns differ widely. In realizing the imperative of cultural distinctness, I also offer examples that, while by no means proposing anything that resembles "American-ness" in art (there is no such thing) or anything approaching hemispheric unity, still serve to underscore the existence of criteria, patterns, and forms of historical development whose parallels (and sometimes, intersections) may serve as illustrations of both the diversity and common currents of expression that make such an approach understandable—and even acceptable.

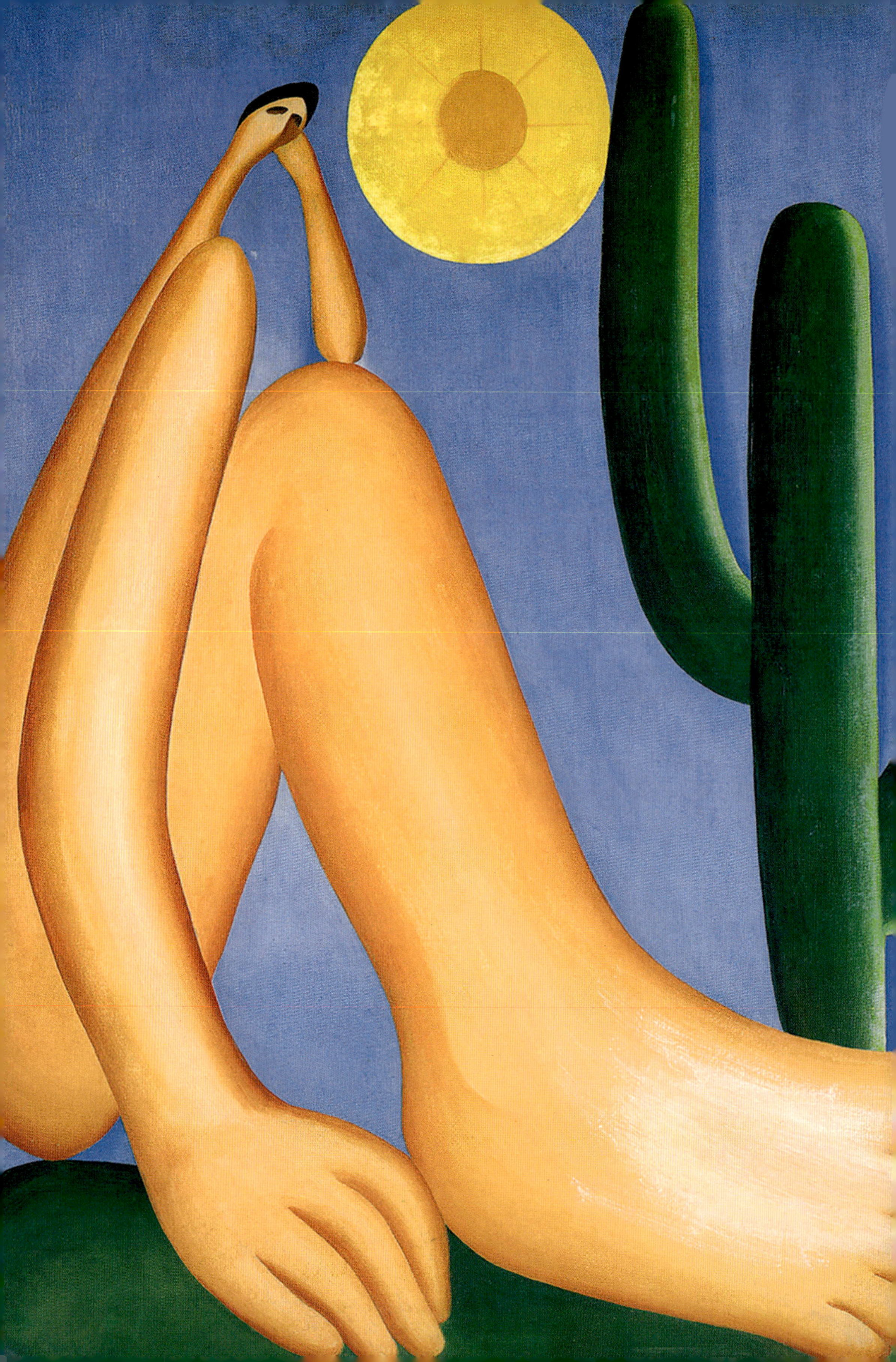

Chapter 1

The Expanding Mind:
Symbolist Imagery in the Americas

We begin the first story of these fragmentary histories of modernity in the Americas with a subject that, at first glance, might seem antithetical to our theme. "Decadence" is a general, and generally unsatisfactory, term. It is nonetheless useful as a trope to conjure up a mood of inner reverie and, in terms of art, a move away from the spirit of academicism. The word evokes specific stylistic trends related to arts such as Symbolism and Art Nouveau and their parallels in architecture, sculpture, and design (ceramics, mosaics, textiles, furniture). Ask any new art-history student to place decadent Symbolism within a chronological time frame and they will probably mention the decades between around 1890 and 1910—precisely the era before the present account begins.

Nonetheless, assumptions about the chronological specificity of artistic or literary movements are invariably predicated on the long-accepted canons of works that are thought to speak, as it were, as representatives of the most often-discussed manifestations of a certain mode of thought or visual expression. Thus, an 1899 entrance to a Paris Métro station by Hector Guimard (1867–1942), the 1893 painting *The Scream* by Edvard Munch (1863–1944), or Paul Verlaine's (1844–1896) *Élégies* (Elegies), composed in the same year as Munch painted his iconic image of inner torment, would stand among the principal contenders for the most representative examples of "decadent" art of the Symbolist movement.

Tarsila do Amaral
Abaporu, 1928 (detail).
See fig. 1.12.

American Decadence and Redemption, c.1910–1930

Let's begin our assessment of an American mode of Symbolism with a fairly unassuming yet powerfully suggestive object—a small bronze plaque from about 1918 by the Colombian artist Marco Tobón Mejía (1876–1933) (FIG.1.1). While diminutive in size, it is a richly revealing work of art, not only for its delicate sensuality but also for its historical resonances. The artist created a niche for the figure of a long-haired female form. Her knees are drawn up to her chest and her arms are spread horizontally and affixed by straps to the outer "frame" of the construction. Is she a dead or a captured creature? Is she on display, arrested as if in full flight, but attached to a structure that presents her to the public as an object of wonder—or repulsion? This woman possesses the form of a bat; her forelimbs are highly elongated to support the bat-wing membranes that allow her to fly. The lines describing this apparition are sinuous and curvilinear. The edges of the wings curl up at the bottom of the plaque, and the creature's hair is a twisting mass of curls that reaches halfway down the length of the relief. Here, the artist has entered into the realm of Art Nouveau patterning, even though there is a

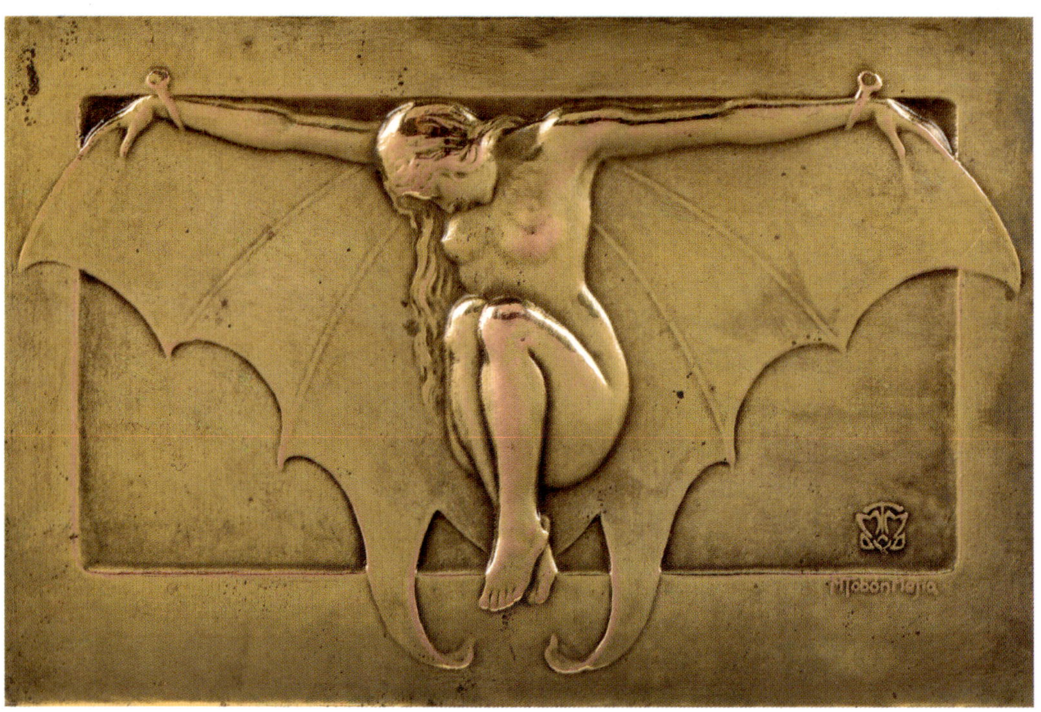

20

certain restraint that distances the work's forms from the most audacious examples of this style of decoration.

The bat is the quintessential creature of the night, like owls and cats; a mammal, a devourer of insects and beings harmful to the natural environment. The bat has been portrayed in the mythologies of many world cultures as malevolent, associated with pestilence. In the print series "Los Caprichos" (1799) by Francisco de Goya (1746–1828), bats often hover over the nefarious activities of the human participants playing out their satirical dramas. Later, Bram Stoker's novel *Dracula* (1897) associated bats with vampires and thus with evil. In nineteenth- and early twentieth-century art and literature, bats inevitably accompany vampires and embody the many-layered legends of the Transylvanian monster.[1] Bats are connected with death, too. And, as bloodsuckers, their image fed into the misogynistic concept of women as devourers of men—they are linked to the image of the castrating woman, the femme fatale who quintessentially defines the "decadent" aspects of fin de siècle art and literature.

Yet here in Tobón Mejía's bronze plaque we have not a German, Austrian, or French artist engaging in depictions of a bat, but one from Colombia, whose work was in part dictated by his academic training both in Bogotá and in Paris. It was in Paris, in the thrall of such artists as Auguste Rodin (1840–1917) and Eugène Carrière (1849–1906), that Tobón Mejía created other similar reliefs of famous or infamous female figures of the past, like Judith and Salomé, all of which have, according to Colombian art historian Álvaro Medina, a touch of Freudian urgency and anxiety.[2]

Tobón Mejía was born in Santa Rosa de Osos, a small town near the major intellectual and commercial capital of Medellín, at a time when Colombia was a highly divided nation, with communications between cities being extremely difficult. The country described in the novels of Gabriel García Márquez as isolated and retrograde was even more remote in parts in the late nineteenth century. From 1905 to 1909 Tobón Mejía worked as an illustrator for periodicals in Havana before making his way to Paris, where he lived for the rest of his life. His work in sculpture (almost all of it done in the French capital) can be divided into two genres: intimate reliefs and small sculptures like *Murciélago*, in which he was able to exercise a freedom from his earlier academic training; and large-scale public monuments in major Colombian cities that attest to his lingering attachment to a highly conservative mode of art that dominated in official and academic Latin American circles until well into the first and second decades of the twentieth century.

The fact that *Murciélago* was created in Paris also speaks to the importance of that city as a magnet for Latin American artists, as it had been since at least the second half of the nineteenth century. For Colombians—and, indeed, for artists from virtually all parts of Latin America whose careers were formed in the late 1800s—Paris (and, to a lesser extent, other European capitals) was critical to the configuration of their modern aesthetic. The Argentinean art historian Marta Traba summarized the conundrum faced by many artists of varying degrees of talent in this first generation of modern painters and sculptors of the Americas who, in their search for new forms of expression, flourished in places far from home. While not mentioning Tobón Mejía (whose work falls into the category Traba described), she does cite Andrés de Santa María (1860–1945), another Colombian who worked in Paris, first in a mode reminiscent of the Impressionists and, later, in a peculiarly original amalgam of Postimpressionism, Expressionism, and visionary art in his religious and secular paintings, especially after about 1920. Traba states that these artists

are recognized as forerunners of the art to come, owing to the exceptional quality and innovative character of their work. They were, however, the product of the same milieu as their less-talented colleagues, they received the same poor academic instruction, they struggled with similar problems, and they encountered the same lack of understanding on the part of a conservative and unreceptive public.[3]

Santa María's 1934 painting of the Annunciation (FIG. 1.2) creates an unsettling and otherworldly atmosphere in which two female figures, who look more like contemporary women from the privileged classes of Paris or Bogotá, confront each other in an airless red chamber. The dove representing the Holy Spirit lends a nominal sacred air to the scene, but we are left wondering about the real content of the conversation in this seraphic tête-à-tête.[4]

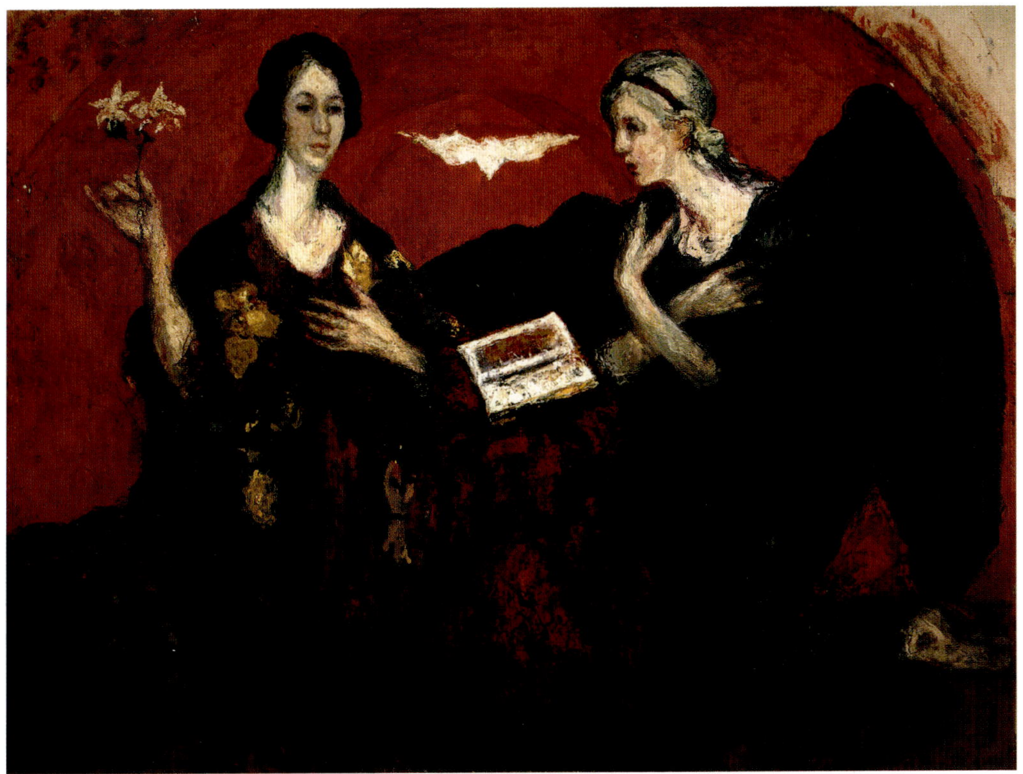

We might take Traba's observation further and examine the place of the contributions of people like Tobón Mejía in Colombia, Leopoldo Romañach (1862–1951) in Cuba, Martín Malharro (1865–1911) in Argentina (the latter two both highly respected artists and teachers in their respective cities), and many others who developed forms of art that derived from modes that had long before fallen out of fashion (Impressionism and various permutations of Postimpressionism) in the "mainstream" artistic capitals of Europe, and introduced them to the art schools, ateliers, galleries, and museums of their home countries, thus creating a pathway for a gradual rejection of retardataire academicism and the possibility of new modes of expression in the Americas. Impressionism, a radical and even scandalous art form in Paris in the 1870s, played an analogous role in cities like Havana, Buenos Aires, or Lima much later, in the years after 1900. The same could be said for any number of other trends, all of which were embraced in one form or another by artists of the Americas, both to revitalize them, using them as tools for

Fig. 1.2
Andrés de Santa María
La Anunciación (The Annunciation), c.1934, oil on canvas, 51½ x 67⅞ in. (131 x 172.2 cm). Museo Nacional de Colombia, Bogotá.

23

artistic innovation and reformulation, and to establish them as points of stimulus for younger artists who would then go on to represent the more audacious vanguards of the 1920s and later.

The North American (Anglophone) art scene in the first two decades of the century followed a similar path. Anyone studying the art exhibited in the 1913 Armory Show in New York, or the first exhibition of the Group of Seven in Canada, also confronts a heterogeneous grouping of art forms that, conventionally, could be judged as derivative. But it is my contention that the struggles that occurred throughout the Americas to transform the artistic profile of individual cities—including grappling with local adaptations of forms observed abroad (on artists' individual journeys, in exhibitions, or through reproductions in magazines and newspapers)—constituted an incipient form of modernity and rebellion against the status quo.

In a European context Symbolism represented one of the last steps in a series of revival styles that embraced neo-medieval spirituality and evocative visual form to suggest other-worldly values in art, literature, and music. On the other hand, Symbolism also accorded with the late nineteenth-century desire for understanding the inner workings of the mind, and a coming to terms with the weight of the unconscious in the wake of Sigmund Freud's writings on dreams and Carl Jung's explorations into archetypes to explain human actions, both conscious and inadvertent. Symbolism represented, paradoxically, a rejection of traditional religious and societal values, and the exaltation of the urges and desires that are present just under the surface of the rational human psyche.

All of this was true in an American (especially a Latin American) context, and Symbolism and Art Nouveau were not without a significant presence in the American visual and literary landscape in the late nineteenth century. In North America, such a literary work as Edgar Allan Poe's "The Raven" (first published in 1845) could be considered a harbinger of Symbolist poetry. Perhaps the most outstanding contribution to Symbolist letters was the lengthy series of sonnets and other forms of poetry as well as narrative tales collectively entitled *Azul* (Blue) by the Nicaraguan poet and essayist Rubén Darío (1867–1916). Darío was a peripatetic writer whose influence on literary forms throughout the Spanish-speaking Americas as well as in Spain was notable.

Azul was composed in 1888 by the acknowledged creator of the genre known as *Modernismo* (the literary equivalent of Symbolism, as well as the Spanish term for Art Nouveau). It relied heavily on illusion and manipulation of the reader's mood through the evocation of colors, especially blue and white. This use of synesthesia, or the linking of tones with human temperament, became a hallmark of Symbolism in all of its forms, on both sides of the Atlantic. Darío had close relationships with French and Spanish Symbolists, and his later works, such as the 1905 *Cantos de vida y esperanza* (Songs of Life and Hope), are clearly indebted to Paul Verlaine. In terms of the visual arts, there were a number of distinctly American versions of Art Nouveau, especially in the architecture of the most culturally developed cities such as Havana, Mexico City, and Buenos Aires. In painting and sculpture there was a greater presence of Symbolist-related art after 1900.

The present "story" of arts related to nonconformist visual and psychic experiences comes at the beginning of a series of inquiries into the nature of modernity in the western hemisphere, and I suggest that within the context of what we could call the greater Americas, these visionary art forms are as revolutionary, and go as much against the established norm, as other forms of "the new" that are also discussed herein.

In conventional art-historical as well as literary narratives of modernity in Latin American art, the time period around 1920 is usually cited as the starting point of a turn toward a greater inventiveness, openness to experimental forms, and the appropriation and transformation of models from abroad to create a "new" and "modern" art that would be most representative of the nations emerging onto the avant-garde scene.[5] Such phenomena as the initiation of the Mexican mural movement in the early 1920s or the 1922 Week of Modern Art in São Paulo are seen as the beginning of the foundation myths of modernity in the Spanish- and Portuguese-speaking Americas. In the United States, the Armory Show is the predictable epicenter for the "new" in New York. But if we examine these phenomena closely it becomes clear that things are not as straightforward as the chroniclers would like them to be. Mexican muralism, as it was practiced in the 1920s and 30s, relied heavily, in certain cases, on artistic conventions that had found their way into Mexican art several decades before. And the art shown in São Paulo in 1922 or in New York in 1913 was much more eclectic than is generally acknowledged. In both of those exhibitions, conservative, classicizing works were often exhibited side by side with the most audaciously innovative paintings or sculptures.

Art Nouveau and Symbolism played a major role in the modernization of the art world of Mexico City. The start of the Mexican Revolution in 1910, one of the events that determined the chronological borders of this book, marked the end of the more than three-decade-long presidency of Porfirio Díaz, who held considerable personal power in virtually all aspects of Mexican government. In addition he was instrumental in establishing a new artistic outlook, especially in the capital city. Many of the streets of downtown Mexico City still attest to the strong attraction that Art Nouveau had for Mexicans, and the undulations of its design motifs often compete on a single street, with the neocolonial (or, in the historic center, *original* colonial) structures for prominence. The Palacio de Bellas Artes (Palace of Fine Arts), not far from the Metropolitan Cathedral, was the city's most outstanding architectonic monument of its time. Begun in 1904 during the so-called *Porfiriato* (Porfirian era), its eclectic combinations of ornamental details on the facade attest to a sophisticated taste for Art Nouveau, Beaux Arts, and, eventually, Art Deco details (the building was not completed until 1934). In the theater of the Palacio, a monumental stained-glass curtain, executed by the Tiffany workshop, was designed in 1911 by the painter Gerardo Murillo (1875–1964), also known as "Dr. Atl." It depicts the two prominent volcanoes outside of Mexico City, Popocatépetl and Ixtacíhuatl. Their forms are defined by thousands of individual pieces of glass that create a unique example of Art Nouveau decorative arts.

From the turn of the twentieth century, Symbolist painting and graphic arts were a hallmark of the shift toward modernity in the arts in Mexico. Mexico City was the capital of the publishing world in the Spanish-speaking Americas and many journals, such as *Azul* (1894–96, its name inspired by the Darío *modernista* poems described above), the *Revista Moderna* (published between 1898 and 1903), and the *Revista Moderna de México* (1903–11), became immensely important organs for the dissemination of information about the arts in all their manifestations, not only for Mexicans but for literate audiences throughout the Spanish-speaking world in the Americas, Spain, and the Philippines. The artists who created the many prints that accompanied the articles in these journals preferred the mode of Art Nouveau illustration that shared many links with their European counterparts, such as Aubrey Beardsley (1872–1898) or Alfonse Mucha (1860–1939). The sensuous lines and often erotic subject matter of the work of artists like Julio Ruelas (1870–1907) constituted outstanding examples of Mexican *Modernismo* or Art Nouveau illustration. Ruelas was also a highly distinguished painter whose experiences in Germany (Munich and Karlsruhe) and Switzerland at the end of his short career were definitive for him and, in his connections to the style and subject matter of painters such as Arnold Böcklin (1827–1901), link him to one of the principal forms of modernity during the first decade of the twentieth century.[6]

None of the early twentieth-century illustrators of Mexican magazines and broadsheets is as familiar to a large public as José Guadalupe Posada (1852–1913). Famous for his political caricatures in the form of skeletons, or *calaveras*, Posada took on an immense variety of topics in the zinc prints created in his workshops, first in his native city of Aguascalientes, and later in Mexico City. Satirical commentary on every level of society, as well as illustrations for chapbooks, short plays, and compilations of popular expressions, were among the genres undertaken by Posada. Despite his association with scenes of the Mexican Revolution and popular customs (as well as his predilection for the skeleton), Posada was an artist whose modernity was unquestioned. He absorbed the pictorial vocabulary of Art Nouveau and radically transformed it in his drawing, which more often than not relied on undulating, serpentine lines. He also served as a spiritual mentor for several of the younger artists who came to define a spirit of modernity in Mexican art. These included José Clemente Orozco (1883–1949), whose own career began as a magazine illustrator in the Art Nouveau mode, and Diego Rivera (1886–1957), who claimed Posada as a virtual father of modern art in Mexico.[7] The French-Mexican painter, printmaker, and muralist Jean Charlot (1898–1979) was in part responsible for the "rediscovery" and placement of this turn-of-the-century artist at the head of the pantheon of modern art pioneers in

Fig. 1.3
José Guadalupe Posada
El Jarabe en Ultratumba
(Dance Beyond the
Grave), c.1913,
engraving on lead, 5½
x 7⅞ in. (14 x 20 cm).
Private collection.

Mexico. His writings about Posada in the 1920s returned this graphic artist to his place among the great figures of modern Mexican art.[8]

A classic example of the type of Posada work that is virtually universally recognized is the undated (probably around 1912–13) zinc print called the *El Jarabe en Ultratumba* (Dance Beyond the Grave) (FIG. 1.3). This small yet powerful image, originally printed as the central focus of a larger broadsheet sold for pennies on street corners and in news kiosks in Mexico, incorporates the expressive linear quality that bears witness to a relationship with graphic traditions throughout the Western world at the turn of the twentieth century. Eight skeletons attend a festive gathering, eating and drinking. This activity is set in a cantina, or *pulquería* (a local bar where *pulque*, a liquor made from the fruit of the maguey cactus, is consumed). The central figures are a *calavera* couple engaged in a lively dance and observed with attention by the others. The celebratory air of this picture seems to conflict with its self-consciously macabre subject matter, yet this is perfectly in accord with the Symbolist fascination with death imagery on both sides of the Atlantic. This example, like almost all of Posada's other single-sheet broadsides, evinces a specifically Mexican reference. Many of these prints refer to contemporary political events in Mexico City and throughout the country, while others are of a satirically symbolic nature, caricaturing types or customs of the nation's peoples.

Skeleton imagery relates this work to several traditions of the past in Mexico, including the predilection for the grotesque and, particularly, death iconography common in pre-Hispanic Mexican art (especially Aztec). It also relates Posada to the often-exaggerated depictions of death that are common in Mexican colonial images of the dead Christ or the martyrdoms of saints. On the other hand, Posada's work comments on warfare (the imminent Mexican Revolution) and the impending destruction of society in a way that removes it from the specific details of time and place (not unlike the model of Goya in his antiwar prints of the early nineteenth century) and makes it even more powerful for the dread that is mixed with the inevitable humor produced by seeing a group of skeletons feasting and dancing.

The art historian Ramón Favela, who charted the career of Diego Rivera during the crucial years of its initial formation, described his youthful years as "restless."[9] From 1907 to 1910 Rivera traveled through Europe (Spain, France, Holland, and Belgium) on a scholarship he had received from the state government of Veracruz. Throughout his travels Rivera experimented with various modes of painting, from Monet-like Impressionism to compositions reminiscent of the proto-Cubist still lifes of Paul Cézanne (1839–1906). However, the impact of his experiences in Belgium, a veritable vortex of Symbolist activity in all the arts, was definitive for at least a brief time in his career. A painting such as the 1909 *House over the Bridge* (FIG. 1.4) represents a well-known structure in Bruges, a city that had captured the imagination of artists and writers for its ancient structures and its faded place in the history of Flanders.

The Belgian novelist and poet Georges Rodenbach published a monument of Symbolist literature in 1892 entitled *Bruges-La-Morte* (with a cover illustration by Symbolist painter Fernand Khnopff [1858–1921] showing the same buildings painted by

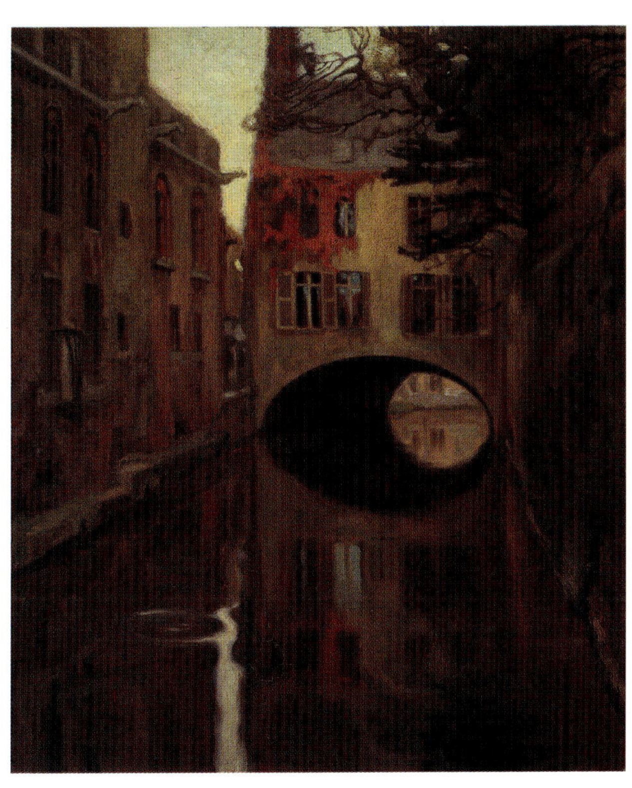

Rivera), evoking the quasi-mystical emotions provoked by his wanderings through the city. The plot focuses on the deaths of the wife and mistress of the protagonist, Hugues Viane, and eerily situates the reader in the misty, ethereal atmosphere of what he deems a crumbling city.[10] Rodenbach's work was certainly known to Rivera, and the Mexican artist linked his imagination to Rodenbach's haunting evocation of place in this and many of the other 44 paintings that were exhibited in Mexico City in 1910 at his first one-artist show, organized on the eve of the outbreak of the revolution.

Only a few years after Rivera painted his eerie version of Bruges, his friend Ángel Zárraga (1886–1946) created a series of pictures that attest to his thorough assimilation of Symbolist imagery. Zárraga's famous 1910 painting entitled *Ex Voto de San Sebastián* (Votive Offering to St. Sebastian) (FIG. 1.5) displays the form of a highly sexualized, mostly nude young man confronted by a kneeling female supplicant. The veiled young woman kneels at the left of the composition. Her head is bowed and she does not communicate directly with the saint who appears almost as a living (yet wounded) presence before her. An inscription appears at the lower right, as it would in a nineteenth-century popular ex-voto image, stating, "My Lord: I do not know how to laud you in complex verses as the poets would do, but accept Lord this humble and rough work that I have made with my mortal hands. Angel Zárraga." The *Votive Offering* has been called "perhaps one of the most Freudian paintings that exists" (even though the writings of Sigmund Freud would not be widely known in Mexico for another decade).[11]

Another of Zárraga's works that plays with the tropes of Symbolist imagery is his earlier (1909) *Woman and Puppet* (FIG. 1.6). The scene takes place in a fantastical landscape with cypress trees (usually associated with death) in the left background, and a lake and mountains at the right. A woman, nude except for an intricately embroidered shawl (*mantón de Manila*) draped around her arms, holds a huge, grotesque puppet of a male harlequin in her left hand. The puppet appears deflated, defeated, and, with its hideously scowling face staring out at us, radiates both fear and hopelessness. The manipulations of a demonic woman with a faux-sweet, insouciant expression on her face immediately thrust the viewer into the realm of the vampire-like creature, a

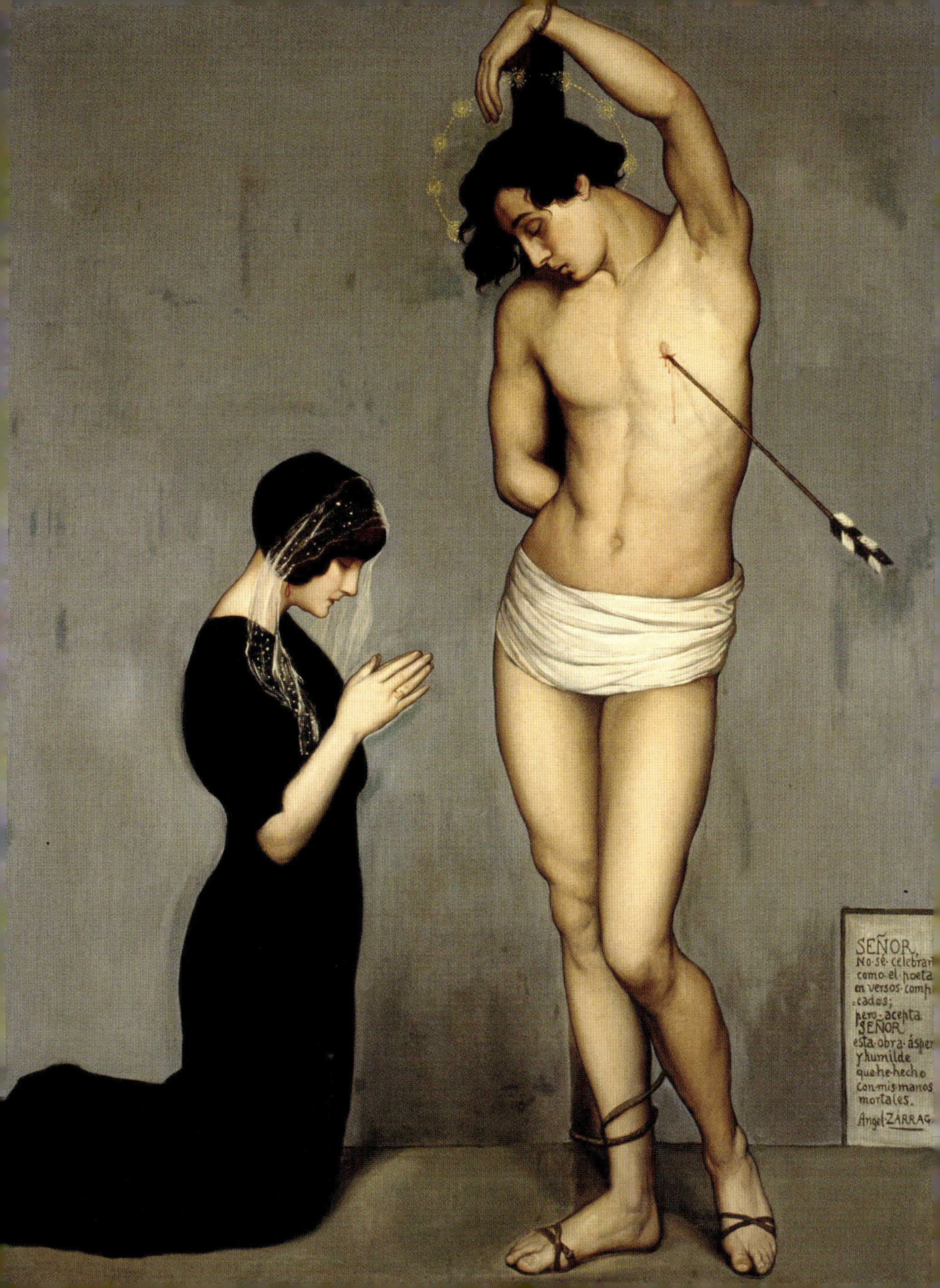

SEÑOR,
No sé celebrar
como el poeta
en versos compli
cados;
pero acepta
SEÑOR
esta obra áspera
y humilde
que he hecho
con mis manos
mortales.
Angel ZARRAGA

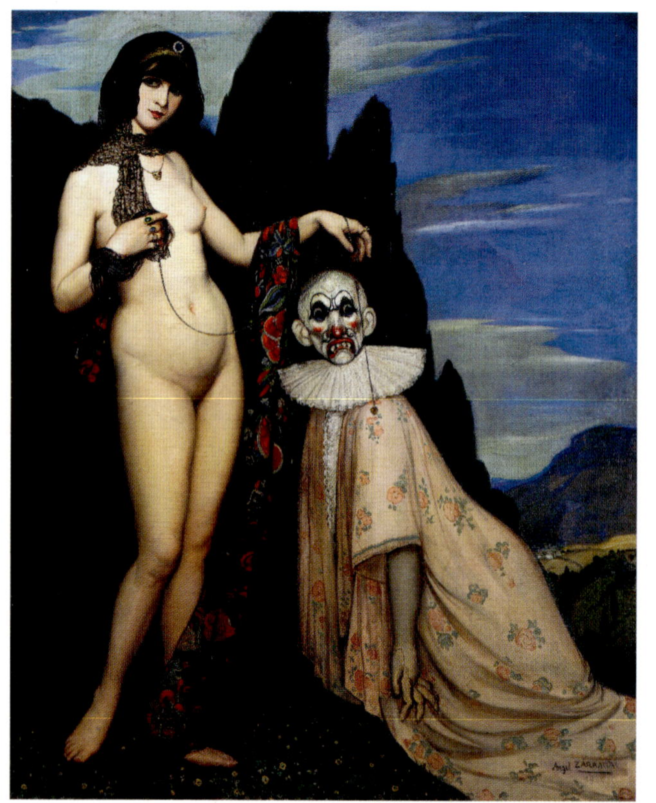

devouring female who inhabits the dreams and nightmares of men. This painting is, in fact, a manifestation of Symbolist imagery by a Mexican artist who was surely sensitized to and interested in Freud's texts, which he had read in Paris.[12] Most of Zárraga's career developed in Europe where he, like the young Rivera, flirted with a wide variety of modern art forms. While Rivera ultimately settled on his characteristic indigenous classicism after 1922, Zárraga spent most of his career investigating a wider variety of artistic options, from Cubism, to neoclassical monumentalism, to a late-career variety of religious neo-Symbolism.

The 1916 painting *Our Gods* (FIG. 1.7) by Saturnino Herrán (1887–1918) is an independent canvas based on smaller watercolor sketches that served as studies for a major, unfinished monument of Mexican muralism. This work depicts a friezelike disposition of five figures—four scantily dressed males and one female (only partially seen at the left of the composition)—all painted in muted colors, splayed out along the surface of the picture. They hold vessels for ritual offerings and appear in poses ultimately derived from Greco-Roman conventions of narrative stone carving. Beginning in 1914, Herrán, a native of Aguascalientes (also the hometown of José Guadalupe Posada), began work on a project for what was then known as the Teatro Nacional (National Theatre) and is today called the Palacio de Bellas Artes (discussed above). The series of proposed panels (unfinished owing to the artist's early death) was to depict, in symbolic terms, the merging of both indigenous and European peoples into what the contemporary philosopher, politician, and art patron José Vasconcelos (1882–1959) would later call *La Raza cósmica* (the cosmic race) in a text of the same name, published in 1925, that quickly became a veritable proclamation of national identity.[13] In the mural planned by Herrán (which, had it been executed, would have stood as one of the first examples of what became the Mexican mural movement that continued well into the mid-twentieth century), Spaniards and representatives of the Indian races of the country progress toward a figure of the Aztec god Coatlicue, merged with a depiction of the crucified Christ. Herrán created a number of preparatory drawings that have been commented upon as studies in ethnicity as well as symbols of an incipient nationalism that came to fruition in the later, post-1922 murals by artists like Rivera, Orozco, or David Alfaro Siqueiros (1896–1974), among many others.[14]

In the context of this discussion, it is the connections of Herrán's painting, done in shades of brown, gray, and muted

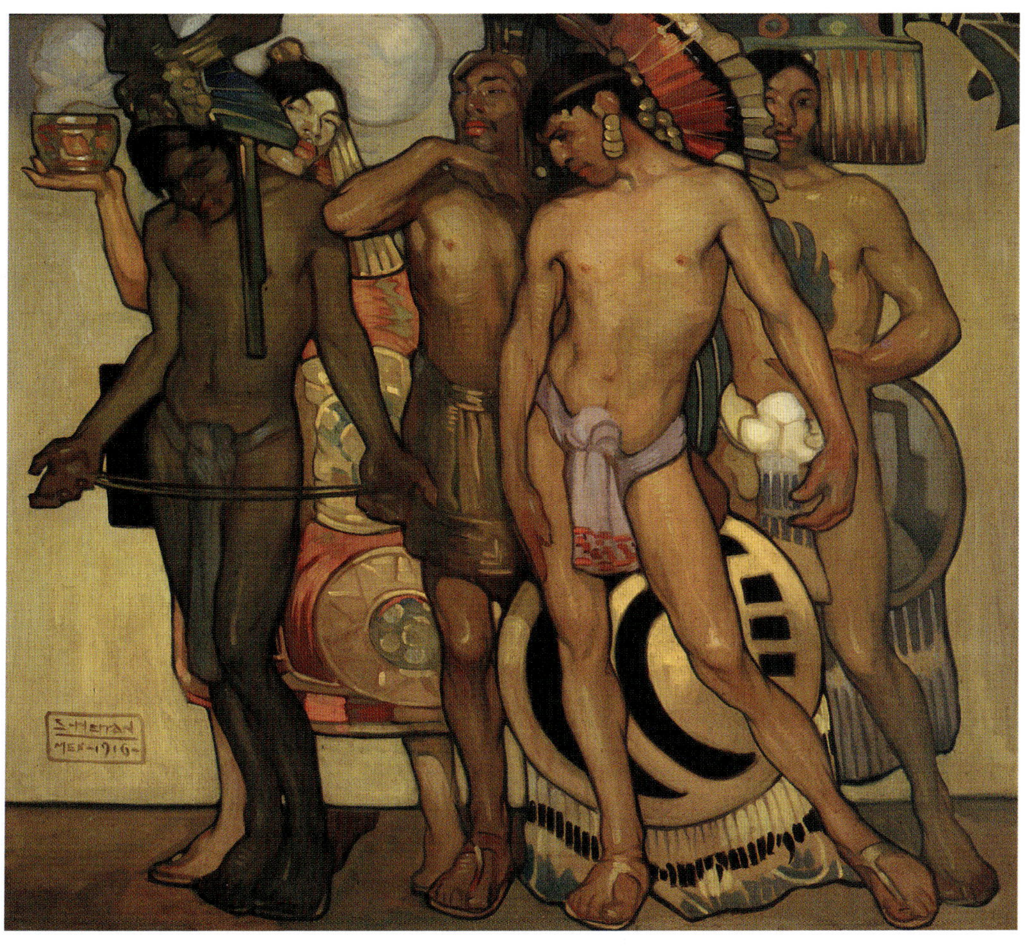

blues and greens, to Symbolism that link it with the works described thus far, and to the larger trends within the Americas, to create a "new" art of both seeming decadence and internally oriented poetic expression. These male figures are depicted as heroic, youthful, and muscular. They appear lost in reverie and their bodies are exposed for the delectation of the viewer. Other studies for *Our Gods* depict similarly homoerotic figures, yet this painting monumentalizes the sensuality and dreamlike quality of their apparition and, indeed, the availability of these men to enter our repertory of erotic fantasies. While much of the art that adheres to the codes of Symbolist sexual suggestivity employs the female body as the subject of the gaze, Herrán's paintings are noteworthy examples of a clear tendency that runs throughout many instances of Mexican modernism in which the male nude or semi-nude figure is the focus of attention. The irony of this attentiveness to the sensual potential of the male form in the art of a nation that, like many others in the Iberian Americas, exalted the values of heteronormativity is both surprising and compelling.[15]

North American Visionaries

Although much of the North American art examined in this book and produced in the first half of the twentieth century is rooted in either avant-garde experimentation or realistic depictions of historical or social events, there is a pronounced strain of the spiritual and aesthetic that corresponds to a taste for concretizing mystical events that developed in the United States and Canada throughout the nineteenth century. These culminated in the development and proliferation of a variety of religious sects in the later decades of the century, some of them conforming to a growing millennialist anxiety as the 1880s and 90s advanced. To understand the strong undercurrent of spiritually oriented painting, sculpture, and photography in the post-1910 era it is important to consider the afterlife of the aesthetic trends in American art and literature of the last quarter of the nineteenth century. Landscape is the area in which this is most obviously observed, and in Chapter 2 we will briefly discuss the legacy of transcendentalist emotional content in a wide variety of approaches to landscape, from the painters who defined what art historians Andrew Wilton and Tim Barringer have termed "the American Sublime," to the artists associated with Tonalism (or experiments in suggesting mood through nuanced color), such as George Inness (1825–1894), a follower of the philosophy of Emanuel Swedenborg (1688–1772), who asserted the spiritual connectedness of all things within the natural realms.[16] That chapter will also touch upon members of Canada's Group of Seven, especially Lawren Harris (1885–1970) as well as Emily Carr (1871–1945) in Western Canada, who embodied strong spiritualist tendencies in their art.

In figurative arts of around 1900, the spiritual often merges with a sense of both visual and emotional experimentation. Artists tend to embed a moral urgency in scenes with either overt or surreptitious religious or philosophical sensibilities. Painters such as Arthur B. Davies (1862–1928), Louis M. Eilshemius (1864–1941), or the Lebanese-born American poet-philosopher-artist Kahlil Gibran (1883–1931), who became something of a cult figure later in the twentieth century for his 1923 book *The Prophet,* may all be classified as American Symbolists.[17] Each was highly successful and provided stimulus for younger mystically oriented artists.

Philosophical and literary sources for visual symbolism in the United States are of considerable significance after 1910. At the turn of the century, interest in a wide variety of quasi-mystical religions or forms of philosophical practice became enormously important in American intellectual and popular circles. The Ukrainian-born philosopher, spiritualist, and medium Helena Petrovna Blavatsky (1831–1891) had a considerable impact in this realm, both in Europe and in the United States (where she arrived in 1873), as well as in Latin America. Theosophy, her philosophical mode of communication of spiritual values and mystical leanings, was a combination of ideas culled from many forms of world transcendental teachings from both the West (including pre-Columbian civilizations) and Asia. The impact of Theosophy was immense, especially after Blavatsky co-founded the Theosophical Society in 1875, which succeeded in spreading the ideas of universal harmony and brotherhood through spiritual intervention throughout Western Europe and the Americas.

The Russian painter Wassily Kandinsky (1866–1944) was influenced by the values of Theosophy and employed many of its concepts in writing his influential 1910 text *Concerning the Spiritual in Art*. Blavatsky had spent considerable time in the United States and Latin America (Mexico and Peru) as well as in Europe. After her death, some of her disciples—in particular, the British-born mystic and political activist (and member of the Theosophical Society) Annie Besant (1847–1933), and the Austrian writer and theosophist Rudolf Steiner (1861–1925)—carried on her work.

For our purposes, the impact of theosophical principles as they were applied to the visual arts was most perfectly embodied by the publication, in 1901, of *Thought-Forms*, the book that Besant co-wrote with Charles W. Leadbeater (1854–1934).[18] This volume, which had great success on both sides of the Atlantic and has been continuously in print since its original publication, prefigured many of the ideas later expressed in Kandinsky's 1910 book. As the reader understands from Besant and Leadbeater's volume, thoughts may be made manifest through color; the will to create form will result in the manifestation of the humors or "ethers" within a work of art. One of the major topics touched upon throughout is the synesthetic blending of color and music to create works of art that carry with them specific spiritual auras and moods.

These books and the vogue for mystical thought in the last years of the nineteenth and the first several decades of the twentieth century served as portents for the popularity of neo-mystical literature and art as well as self-help movements that arose again throughout the West in the 1960s and beyond, when the legacy of psychedelic imagery blended with the popularity of South Asian mysticism, Sufism, and other forms of non-Western religion. As these ideas would have an impact, both direct and indirect, on the visual arts in North America in the 1920s and 30s (their influence in certain parts of Latin America, such as Argentina, was especially strong), we might examine several works of art that bear witness to an interest in the spiritual, mystical, and mythical elements present in the American psyche at the time.

Arthur B. Davies's painting *Cloud of Change* (c.1920) (FIG. 1.8) epitomizes the transcendental bent of many artists in North

America whose imaginations compelled them to integrate the human form with nature. The four nude women in this picture inhabit a forest in which they appear to merge with the trees, air and light surrounding them as they emerge from a bath in an unseen pool. This work pays homage to the tradition of late nineteenth-century American Tonalism—a mode of landscape painting in which a light and misty atmosphere sets a mood of contemplation. Nonetheless, Davies was hardly a retrograde artist. He was, in fact, one of the chief proponents of a variety of modern styles of art, and admired the European Cubists and their contemporaries. The figures in *Cloud of Change* do indeed seem to breathe the same air as the monumental nudes created by Cézanne, although in a much more conservative manner. Davies's admiration for all forms of progressive art manifested itself in his energetic promotion of the 1913 Armory Show in New York, one of the jumping-off points for the further establishment of visual modernity in the United States.

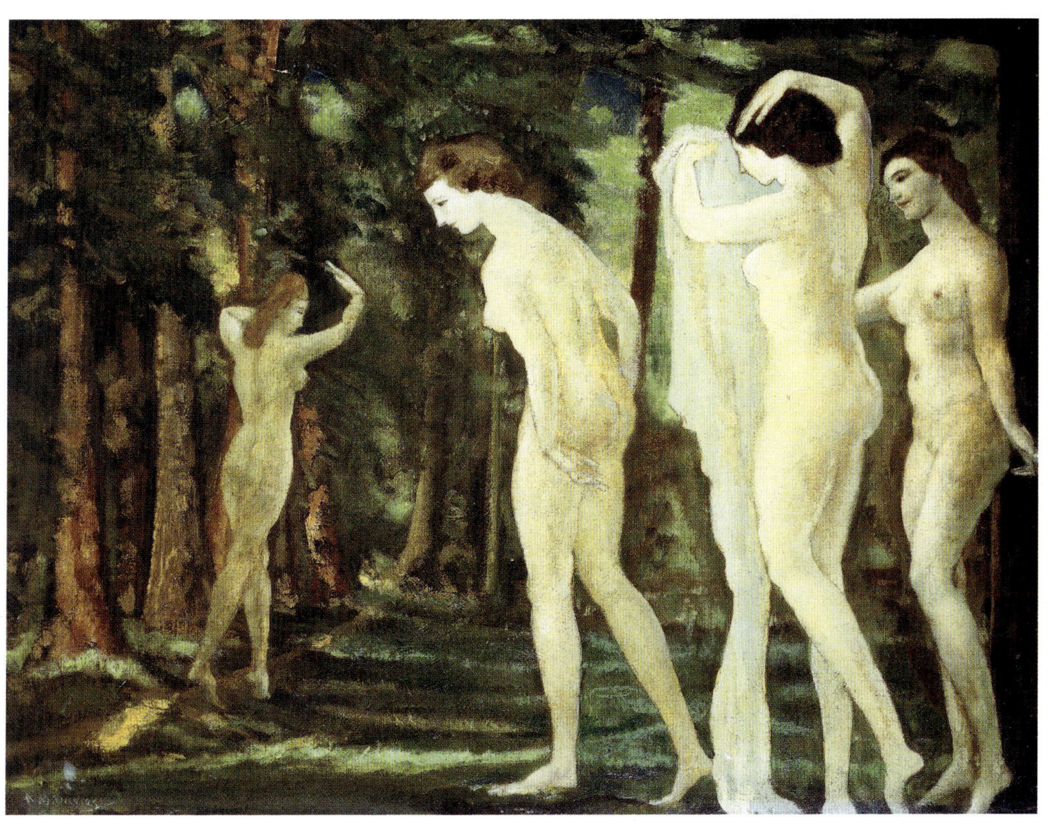

The title of *Diana at the Bath* (FIG. 1.9) by Lorser Feitelson (1898–1978) may suggest a classical narrative yet it is, in fact, a study of sinuous form and suggestive gestures. Indeed, the viewer is hard put to recognize any specific individual in this concatenation of figures. Painted in 1922, this work, which at first blush may not appear to be based upon any specific reminiscence or evocation of the mystical tendencies of American art, is, nonetheless, an important document of the awareness on the part of artists of many stylistic tendencies, of the weight of spirituality that pervaded the American artistic consciousness in the pre- and post-World War I period. Feitelson employs shades of pale blue, green and gray to create a somewhat out-of-focus landscape for the activity undertaken by a group of women in a natural setting. Their clothing hangs on a tree whose branches assume almost human pro-

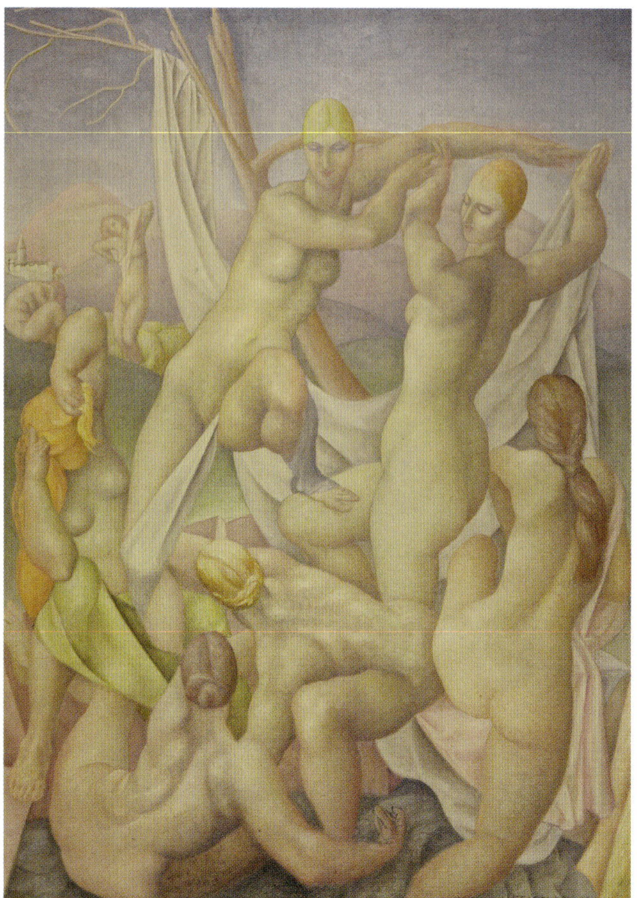

portions, complementing the confusion of human limbs that twist and turn in every possible direction. Feitelson, who much later in life became known for his championing of hard-edge abstract painting in Southern California, painted this work during his youthful sojourn in Paris. On one hand its Michelangelesque Mannerist reverberations relate this picture to the between-the-wars taste throughout Europe for classicizing art (this being a rather extreme example of what has been called the "return to order" after the chaos of World War I). Nonetheless, I would prefer to see Feitelson's work as an equal product of a distinctly American sensibility linked to spirituality. If at first viewing of *Diana* we may be reminded of the writhing figures of the

Gates of Hell by Auguste Rodin (1840–1917) we may also relate Feitelson's visionary tableau with the hundreds of idealistic or even quasi-religious evocations of the American Symbolists who were the immediate predecessors of this artist who trained in his youth in New York.

In the 1930s Feitelson became one of the leaders of a group of artists who turned Los Angeles into a center of visionary and Surrealist art production. Feitelson, his wife—the painter Helen Lundeberg (1908–1999)—and his students, including Philip Guston (1913–1980) and Reuben Kadish (1913–1992), broke with the strict admonitions of Surrealist leader André Breton (1896–1966) regarding the importance of using the unconscious as a basis for the creation of their works. During this period, Feitelson and his colleagues "based their symbolic tableaux … not on random dream images, but on conscious rational associations."[19] Alfred H. Barr called Feitelson the "leader of the California Post-Surrealists," and included him in his landmark MoMA 1936–37 exhibition *Fantastic Art, Dada, Surrealism.*[20] (For more on Surrealism in the Americas see Chapter 8.)

The work of Agnes Pelton (1881–1961) embodies more directly than that of Feitelson the intimate connections held by many North American artists with Theosophy and related spiritual movements and philosophies popular in the 1920s and 30s. This German-born, New York-trained painter felt the impact of mystically directed art from her earliest years of study at Manhattan's Art Students League with Arthur Wesley Dow (1857–1922), a painter, photographer, and pedagogue (teacher of, among others, Georgia O'Keeffe [1887–1986] and Charles Sheeler [1883–1965]) whose own work, mainly landscapes, could be described as "visual music." Dow was intensely interested in Asian art and attempted to instill in his students an appreciation of the spiritual qualities of traditional Chinese and Japanese painting. Pelton responded eagerly to her teacher's instruction (as well as to the art of Eilshemius), and the two works she exhibited at the Armory Show attest to her sensitivity to the otherworldly.[21]

In early 1932, Pelton, who had prior knowledge of the Southwest from trips she had made to New Mexico in the late 1910s, moved to the tiny community of Cathedral City, in the southern California desert near Palm Springs. Pelton worked in solitude (as she had done for the previous ten years, living in an abandoned nineteenth-century windmill on the eastern end of Long Island, New York) and created a compelling body of work that was a direct expression of her study of Agni Yoga, an Asian form of meditation related to Theosophy. Pelton read Besant and Leadbeater's book *Thought-Forms* and put into practice its connections between colors, music, and natural elements. Her 1933 painting *The Primal Wing* (FIG. 1.10) presents a highly abstracted landscape, with the intensely blue-gray-black sky serving as a backdrop for the stylized red mountains and pale blue lagoon of the lower part of the canvas. The principal focus is a large bird's wing that slowly floats through this landscape of the imagination. It becomes the quintessence not only of avian nature but also of the forces of life itself. It is a delicately veined object with its pinkish-white feathers creating a fanlike form that resembles a bird in flight. The wing, a synecdoche of the bird, thus becomes the bird itself, dominating the air, enlivening and literally conquering the space it occupies.

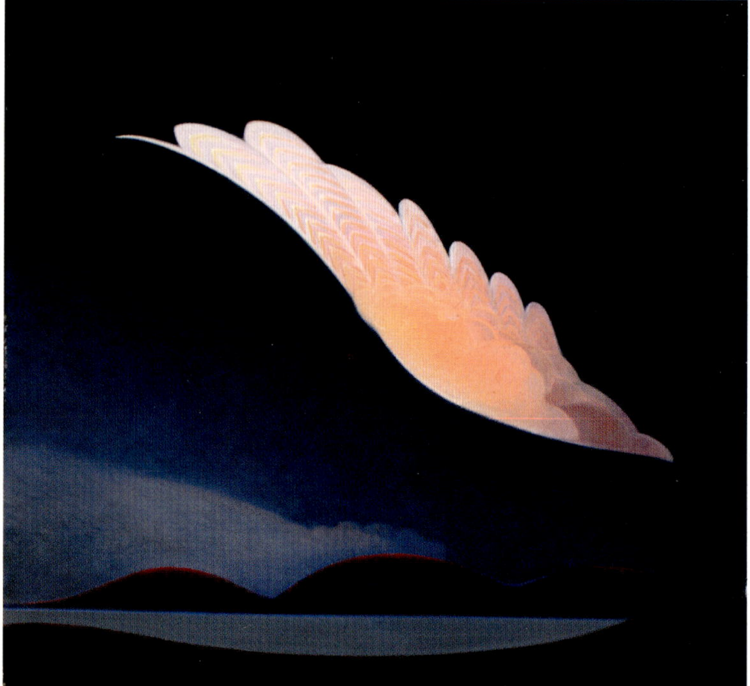

Cannibals in the Southern Cone:
Alejandro Xul Solar and Tarsila do Amaral

The title of this section refers to the cultural trope of cannibalism that has been used to refer to Brazil since the 1500s. Among the first accounts of life in the New World came from the German explorer Hans Staden (c.1525–c.1576), who in 1556 spent some ten months in captivity with the Tupinambá of Brazil. He wrote a description of his time there and discussed their propensity for cooking and eating their captives. Staden's text was of great interest to the European public and codified the image of the New World "savage." According to Brazilian art historian Ana Maria Belluzzo, Staden occupies "the central place in the structure of mythic narratives: he is the traveling hero that breaks his ties with the world he knows and oscillates between the uncontrollable forces of the universe."[22]

In the early twentieth century the trope of cannibalism was revived in Brazilian cultural theory when the critic and essayist Oswald de Andrade (1890–1954) wrote the 1928 "Manifesto Antropófago" (Cannibalist Manifesto), which argued for a new definition of modern art for his country. The gist of the innovations he called for included ingesting and digesting foreign forms of culture to conform to a "new" look and an innately Brazilian (and, by extension, Latin American) manner of artistic (visual, literary, and musical) expression.[23] The perfect distillation of Andrade's call for a Brazilian reconfiguration of art appears in the painting called *Abaporu*, created by Tarsila do Amaral (1886–1973) in 1928, discussed below. The work's title derives from the words meaning "one who eats" in the indigenous Tupi language. I am taking this metaphor and using it on a broader scale to discuss visionary art in Brazil and Argentina as represented by the work of two painters from the 1920s and 30s.

No artist encapsulates the fascination with the spiritual, an interest in the occult, and a reliance on all aspects of the emotional over the empirical more than Argentinean artist, mystic, linguist, and astrologer Alejandro Xul Solar (1887–1963). His paintings, especially the watercolors of the 1920s and 1930s, constitute perfect expressions of the dream-like worlds he created to illustrate universal archetypes, ancient mythology, and esoteric symbolism. With jewel-like colors Xul (the son of German and Italian immigrant parents; his given name was Oscar Agustín

Alejandro Schulz Solari) manifests a variety of expressions of a universe of symbols, creatures, and fantastic landscapes. Xul is, at the same time, a representative (as is Tarsila do Amaral) of one of the most audacious and experimental modernist movements of the moment. The entire body of Xul's art was, in fact, viewed by contemporary audiences in Argentina as rule-breaking, innovative, and the height of modernist experimentation in Buenos Aires.

Xul was friendly with Emilio Pettoruti (1892–1971) (discussed in Chapter 6) and they encountered each other in Europe, where Xul lived (in England, France, Germany, and Italy) between 1912 and 1924. While there he may well have studied the work of Paul Klee (1879–1940), and indeed there is a somewhat superficial similarity between the production of the Swiss–German and the Argentinean artists, especially in their mutual attraction to motifs derived in part from folk idioms and the art of children. Yet the impact of Xul's travels resided more in the area of spirituality and philosophy. His life-long interest in Theosophy as well as many forms of esoteric thought developed during his journeys and conversations with friends of a similar mystical disposition.

In Paris, Xul met Aleister Crowley (1875–1947), the famous British occultist, whose interest in Spiritism partly developed in Mexico City where he moved in 1900 and where he was initiated into Freemasonry. Crowley (whose astrological chart was done by Xul) introduced him to the *I Ching* and guided him in his own writings on esoteric subjects. By this time Xul had started writing his *San Signos* notebooks, which recorded the artist's imagined astral voyages. All of these mystical experiences made their way into his painting and defined it as representing a fundamental departure from art as it had been practiced in Argentina, or, for that matter, in South America, up until that time.

Xul's friend Emilio Pettoruti gives us a good picture of Xul's character and interests in his autobiography, stating that he was at his happiest "when discussing the signs of the Zodiac or Egyptian mummies."[24] Both artists returned to Argentina in 1924, where they formed integral components of a small circle of painters and writers who constituted the founding parents of vanguard art and literature in Buenos Aires. The journal *Martín Fierro* (named after the hero of the 1872 eponymous epic poem by José Hernández [1834–1886] concerning nineteenth century gaucho life which had come to be the principal literary expression of national identity) served as the chief mode of distribution to an elite public of information and analysis of the latest artistic achievements of artists who had, for the most part, absorbed new forms of art in Europe and made it their mission to re-formulate them into a local idiom.

The issue dated May 15, 1924 (published shortly after the return of Xul and Pettoruti from Europe) contains the *Martín Fierro Manifesto* (FIG. 1.11). Authored by the poet Oliverio Girondo (1891–1967), this manifesto, of equal importance to the myriad such declarations by artists, poets, and philosophers of the period, lays out the aesthetic tenets of a major faction of the Buenos Aires avant-garde of the era. *Martín Fierro* was one of several other influential (although often short-lived) journals to promote literary and artistic experimentation in Argentina in the early 1920s. Others included *Prisma* and *Proa*. Among other movements promoted by these magazines was that of *Ultraísmo*, a philosophy of progress and experimentation that had originated in Spain, with roots in such other international trends as Futurism.

The so-called Martín Fierro Group included the renowned writer Jorge Luis Borges (1899–1986). The friendship between the writer and Xul Solar, and their collaborations on texts and their illustrations, was long-lasting and became strained only when General Juan Perón (1895–1974) came to power in the 1950s. Borges disagreed virulently with Perón's nationalistic policies while they were tolerated by Xul. Nonetheless, in public Xul and Borges remained close friends. Borges compared the spirit of Xul's writings and art to that of William Blake (1757–1827),

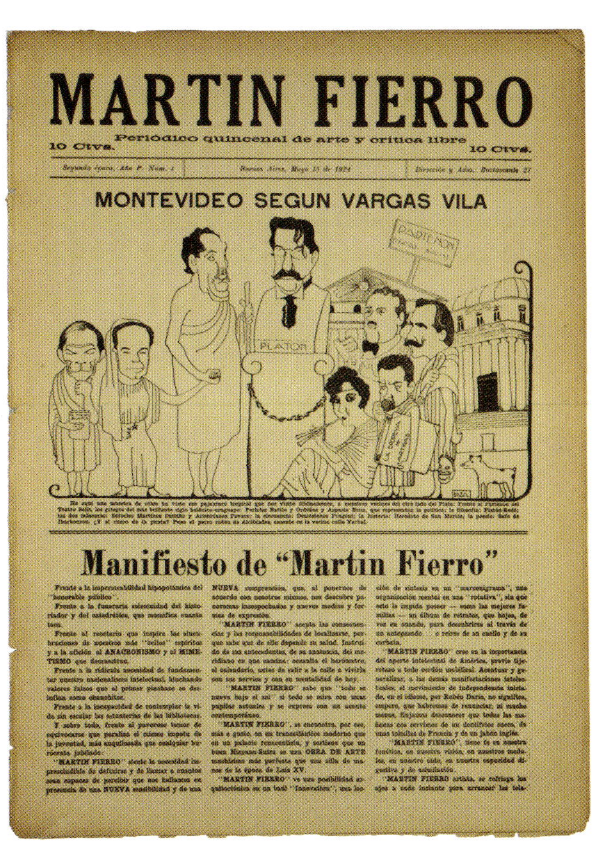

the visionary English poet and printmaker. This was an apt association because, among other things, ethereal images and evocative texts were inextricably intertwined in both artists' sensibilities.[25]

Tarsila do Amaral is one of the key figures in the modernization of Latin American art in the early twentieth century and, arguably, Brazil's most distinguished artist of the period. While her career was very long (she began showing her art in the early 1920s and was still active into the early 1970s), the intensity of her creativity and her impact on fellow Brazilian artists may be limited to a brief period of some ten years, starting in 1923.[26] The paintings she produced between around 1924 and 1927 represent her "Pau Brasil" phase, after the name of a manifesto by her husband, Oswald de Andrade. The 1924 "Pau Brasil Manifesto" (like the later Cannibalist Manifesto mentioned above) referenced a traditional product (Brazil wood) that served as one of the nation's first exports. Andrade referred to the distinctive qualities of Brazilian culture, prompting Tarsila to create images that exploited some of the autochthonous aspects of the Brazilian rural landscape or visual definitions of the modern Brazilian city (see Chapter 2 for Tarsila and the modern landscape). These paintings attested to Tarsila's early training in Paris (a city to which she returned many times in the 1920s and beyond) in the Cubist modes of her friends and colleagues André Lhote (1885–1962), Fernand Léger (1881–1955), and Constantin Brancusi (1876–1957).

By 1927, Tarsila's artistic personality had taken on a different cast. While she was never as deeply concerned with the occult or mystical philosophies as her Argentine contemporary Xul Solar (born only one year after her), she was nonetheless touched with the spirit of symbolic and visionary art, and in several of her most characteristic and best-known works from the last three years of the 1920s her interest in creating an oneiric worldscape was manifest. Before the decade was up (and before she turned to a uniquely personal form of social realism prompted by a visit to the Soviet Union in 1932) Tarsila created several images that stand as landmarks of Brazilian—and American—art of their period. The years 1927 to 1929 constitute her "Anthropophagic" or Cannibalist phase, again referring to the manifesto published by Andrade (the couple separated in the last months of 1929).

Abaporu (The One Who Eats) (FIG. 1.12) is one of the hall-marks of modernist art of the western hemisphere. It, along with a contemporaneous and equally powerful painting also by Tarsila from 1928 called *Antropofagia* (Cannibalism), pertains directly to a Brazilian sensibility; both use Brazilian indigenous and folk mythologies as their base while, at the same time, sharing stylistic characteristics with contemporary art on both sides of the

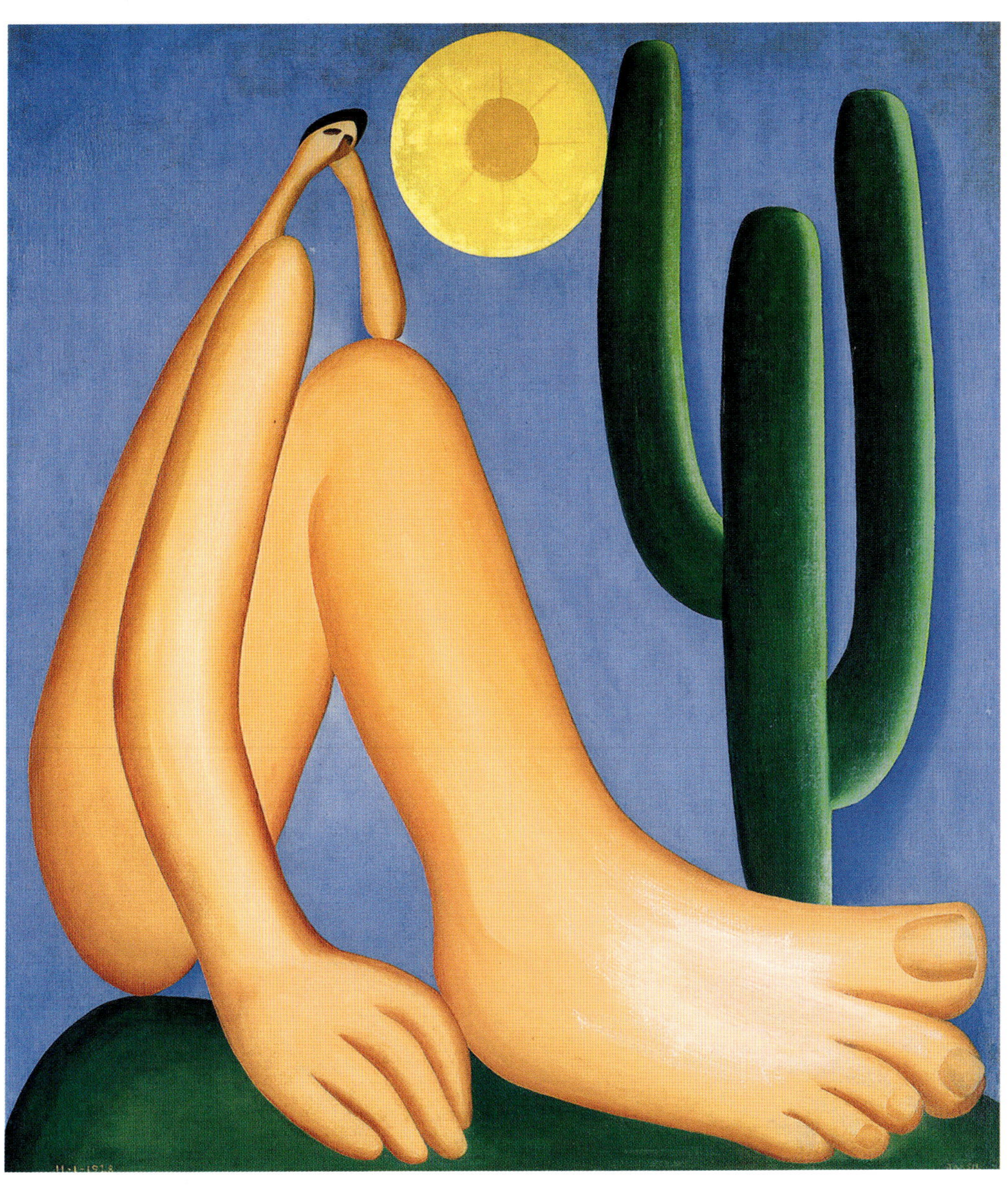

Fig. 1.12
Tarsila do Amaral
Abaporu (The One Who Eats), 1928, oil on canvas, 34 x 29 in. (86.4 x 73.7 cm). Museo de Arte Latinoamericano de Buenos Aires, Fundación Costantini.

Atlantic, north and south. In this painting an enormous figure sits in a barren landscape. Its form is distended and disturbing. With a pinlike head, snakelike neck, and outsized right arm and single leg, this creature embodies a disturbing sense of dread, while also appearing strangely benign, like a gentle Cyclops who would harm no one after a generous meal. The principal element of the entire canvas is the foot occupying the entire lower-right portion of the picture. It juts out as far as possible from the picture plane, almost at the point of entering the space of the viewer. Only the hand that reaches down to the same level rivals its immensity. This figure, who appears to contemplate its curious life, with head resting on the other (tiny) hand, is taken from the wealth of Brazilian legend that derived from tales handed down by rural peoples and members of the nation's indigenous tribes, from pre-Portuguese times. The fantastically proportioned cannibal in Tarsila's painting is directly related to some of the creatures evoked in the novel *Macunaíma* (1928) by Mário de Andrade (1893–1945; no relation to Oswald, but a close friend of the couple), a book that has been called the forerunner of the magical realist tendencies in Latin American literature.[27]

Landscape plays an almost equally salient role in this picture. The artist uses only three colors to define the creature's amorphous habitat. The sky, taking up most of the background, is a flat medium-tone blue; the lemonlike, completely round sun is composed of two shades of yellow; and the ground on which the devouring creature rests is an intense emerald-green. This is also the color used for the cactus, which is as simply defined and as strangely compelling as the composition's main figure. The cactus itself is an odd plant. It is not a conventional cactus as seen in most tropical climates, but rather a saguaro cactus noted for its large "arms." This vegetal form grows only in the Sonoran Desert of the Southwest United States and the northern Mexican border state of Sonora. Tarsila never traveled there, but seems to have been attracted to its otherworldly "exotic" nature.

Evoking the word "exotic" in connection with works by Tarsila, and indeed many of the Latin American Surrealists or surrealizing artists we are considering here, begs examination. One of the key points of contention for critics and historians of Latin American art, especially in the late 1980s and 90s, was the concentration on its perceived "folkloric" and "exotic" elements.

This is certainly an important and valid point of discussion, and the exoticizing of Latin American culture—a phenomenon that has been observed since at least the nineteenth century (and, in fact, much earlier) on the part of writers who have traveled to the region—is a contested area of critical discourse. Nonetheless, we must balance these views with considerations of images such as Tarsila's *Abaporu*, which utilizes, in a completely self-conscious way, an "exotic" or strange, and specifically Brazilian, form as a modernizing, self-aware appropriation of a national myth or icon for the purposes of creating a work of art that speaks directly to a form of resistance against older, established models, and a strong assertion of individuality, alongside a spirit of artistic and national self-projection.[28]

Tarsila's painting thus evidences, in addition, an engagement with a type of fantastical imagery that links it, and her, with Surrealism. Tarsila's many European trips and periods of residence in Paris in the 1920s put her in direct contact with artists in the canonical circle of Breton, as well as many others on the periphery of this movement. But Tarsila was also drawn to the large, rounded proportions of the work of painters associated with between-the-wars classicism throughout Western Europe, including Pablo Picasso (1881–1973) in France and Mario Sironi (1885–1961) in Italy, among many others. The biomorphic forms of artists like Joan Miró (1893–1983) are also recalled in Tarsila's definition of each component of *Abaporu*.

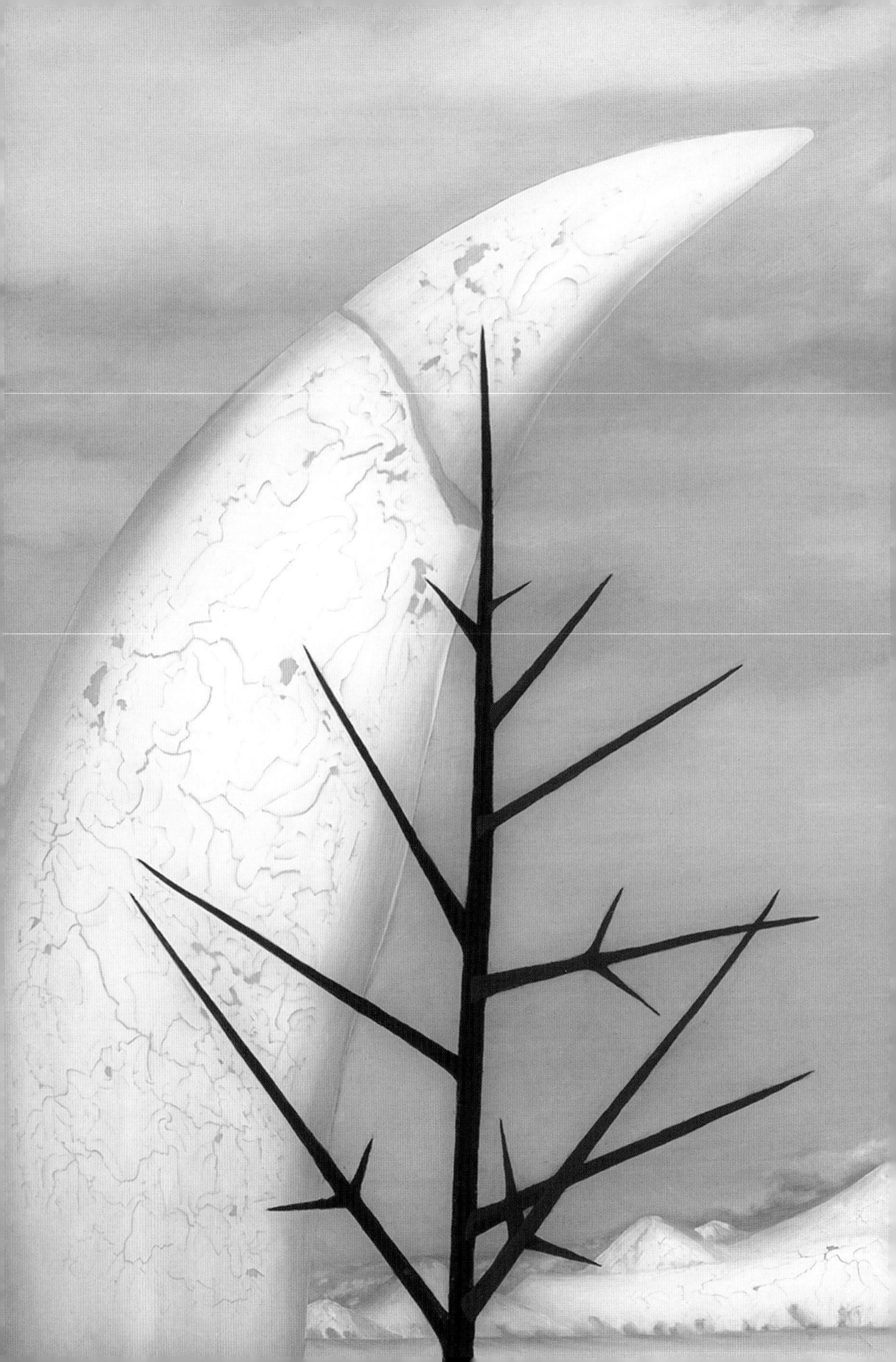

A Sense of Place:
Landscapes, Cityscapes, and Topographies of the Self

Artists create unique impressions of locales they observe through the mediation of the self. Specific places can be suggested by images, but never truly represented, as they are infused with personal decisions; choices derived from individual sensibility, and reactions to the momentary circumstances in which the artist finds herself at the moment of conception of a painting, drawing, or photograph. At the same time, landscapes (and within this category I include representations of both rural and urban venues) may also encapsulate a spirit of time, a sense of communal feeling regarding the land and its development (or preservation), changes in the cityscape (which, during the period under scrutiny in this book, includes depictions of often-dramatic transformations reflecting rapid modernization), and, in the broadest terms, manifestations of collective identities.[1]

In this chapter a variety of approaches to establishing a sense of individual locations are examined, with a view to analyzing how the depictions of American places evolved through the space of some 50 years. In addition, as is the case throughout this volume, the implicit question of shared or collective sensibilities is present. This collectivity may be seen from a regional, national, or continental sense, or it may not exist at all. Such is the fundamental challenge of writing a book like this, and such is the experiment presented to the reader.

Rebecca Salsbury James
Winter in Taos, 1948
(detail). See fig. 2.6.

The Year 1916

This chapter opens with an examination of three works of art, all painted in 1916. The first is a dramatic landscape by Uruguayan painter Pedro Blanes Viale (1878–1926) entitled *Iguazú Falls* (FIG. 2.1), depicting one of the quintessential natural wonders of South America in a way that recalls both earlier representations of the grandeur of nature and, stylistically, looks forward to an avant-garde concept of how to illustrate the geological and aquatic phenomena of a specific place. The other two works that represent a year of progress and change, as well as deeply troubling trauma throughout the hemisphere, are both cityscapes. New York-based artist Childe Hassam (1859–1935) painted *The Fourth of July, 1916* (FIG. 2.2) in his Manhattan studio, depicting an event that recalled both celebratory and disturbing nationalistic sentiments on the part of U.S. citizens. *El Riachuelo* (FIG. 2.3) is a view of the newly developed and bustling port of Buenos Aires by Pío Collivadino (1869–1945). Each of these works

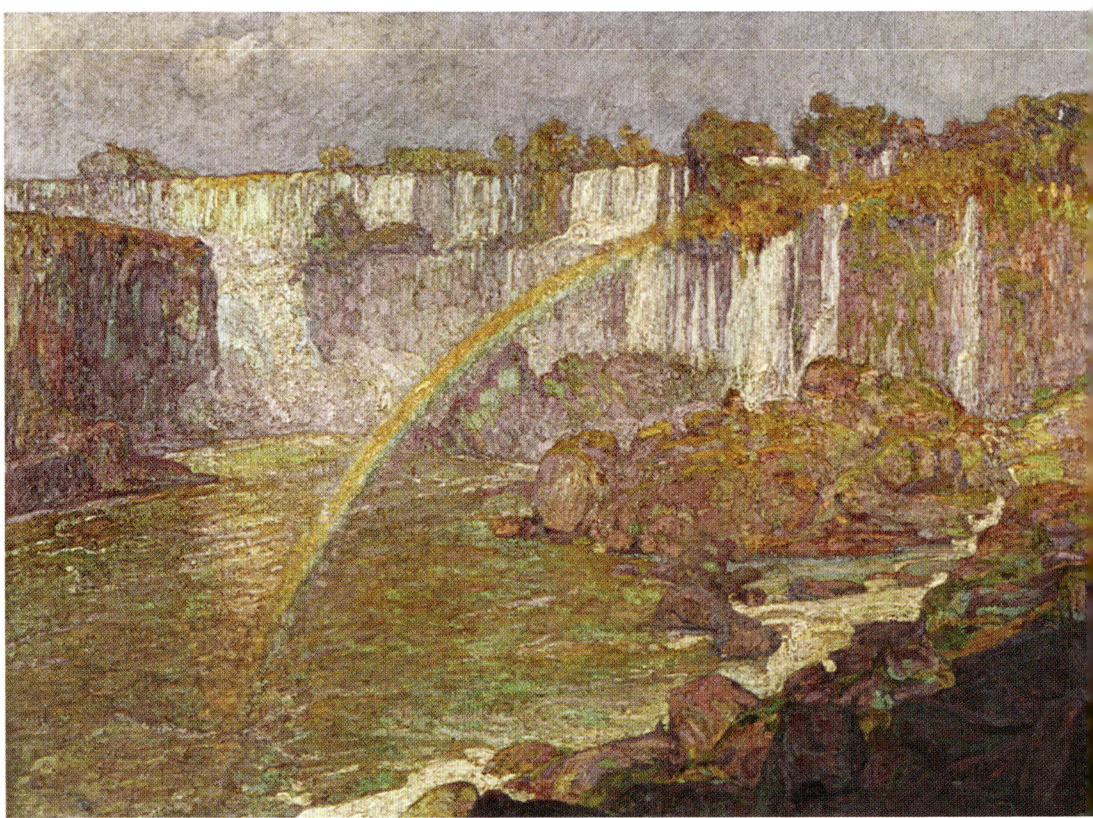

encapsulates the disparate (or eclectic) qualities of the comparisons and contrasts inherent in this text, and they are illustrative of some of the major themes in this chapter. The first image celebrates the grandeur of nature in a way that refers directly to debated South American theories of the countryside. The two cityscapes include one in which we see a politically motivated depiction of a triumphant metropolis, and another in which we are shown a vista of industrial development in a rapidly transforming city, populated mostly by immigrants.

The year 1916 proved to be a crucial one in the early history of the twentieth century in the Americas. World War I was in its third year in Europe. Although the fighting did not have direct consequences on American soil it had an immense impact on the future social and economic fortunes of virtually every country in the hemisphere. The United States became actively involved in 1917. When the United States declared war on Germany, a number of its allies, including Cuba, Guatemala, Haiti, Honduras,

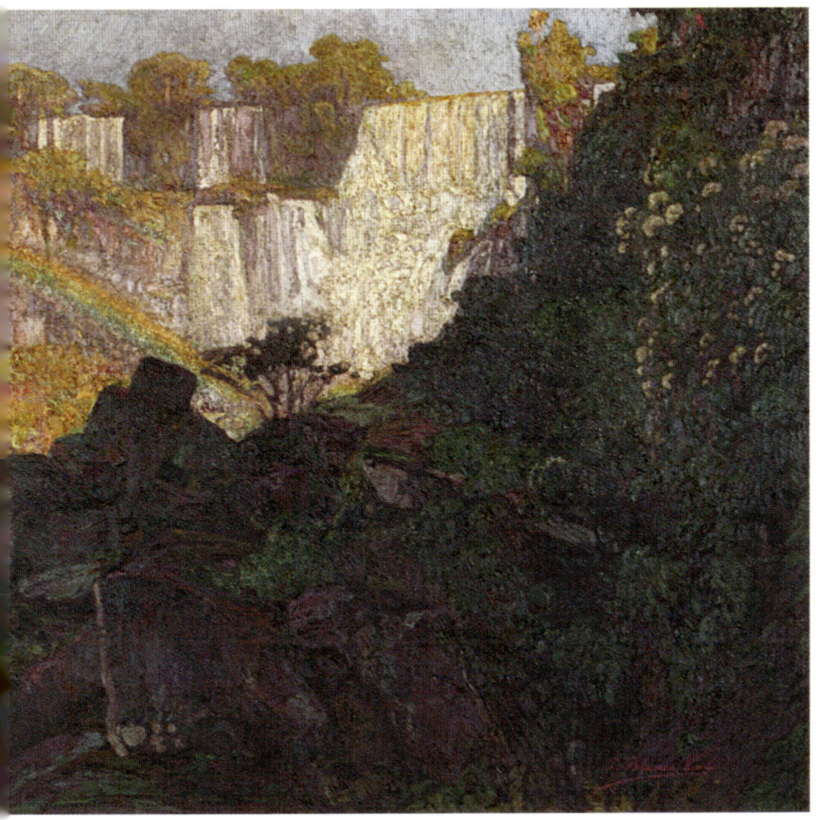

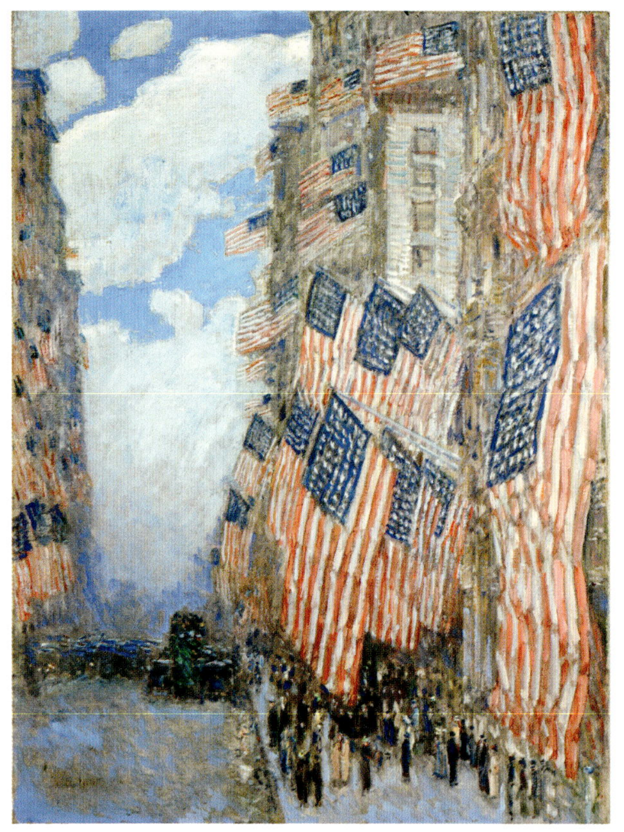

Nicaragua, and Panama (all de facto economic dependencies of the United States), did the same. Canadian soldiers and sailors were conscripted by the thousands into the British war effort as part of a Commonwealth nation. In 1916, Brazil (having expressed pro-German sentiments throughout the early part of the war) was directly affected when a German submarine sank the merchant ship *Rio Branco*. Brazil countered by declaring war on Germany the following year.

Mexico was neutral, but then the Mexican Revolution was raging, having entered its sixth chaotic year. During the presidency of Venustiano Carranza (1859–1920), the leader of the rebel forces of the north, Francisco (Pancho) Villa (1878–1923), declared war on the United States and crossed the border at Columbus, New Mexico, in early March 1916, prompting U.S. President Woodrow Wilson (1856–1924) to send the so-called Punitive Expedition into the Mexican state of Chihuahua to hunt Villa down.

The Great War, as it was known to much of the world, also heralded an economic boom throughout the Americas. The Cuban sugar industry realized its most dramatic ascent while the productivity of European sugar beet fields collapsed. Argentina had a lively and lucrative trade with Germany during the war years while never formally siding with Emperor Wilhelm II.

In terms of landscape and the increased interest in depictions of the wilderness or the rapidly developing countryside throughout the Americas, we may also look to 1916 as a definitive year. In the United States the National Park Service was created in August under the presidency of Wilson. Prior to this date Theodore Roosevelt (1858–1919), for whom conservation and

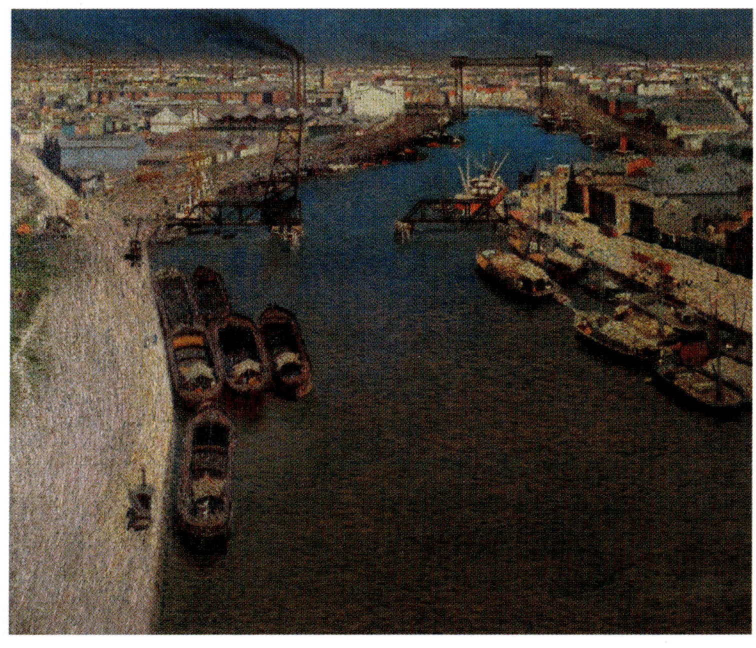

preservation of large swaths of undeveloped land (especially in the west of the country) was a major desideratum, had declared a series of National Monuments that included many natural sites, the first of which was the Devils Tower in Wyoming. Canada passed the National Parks Act in 1930, although the first of such parks, Banff, was created as early as 1885.

A new system of interstate roadways was begun in the United States in 1916 with the passage of the Federal Aid Road Act, providing five years of funding for the establishment of a network of highways that would replace the unwieldy, unsystematic grid of local roads that prevailed throughout the 48 contiguous states. With more access came greater ease of tourism, which accounted for an increased interest in documenting the landscape in visual images. Fascination with the less-charted portions of the country had, of course, stimulated the public imagination since at least the mid-nineteenth century, with a huge interest in the works of landscape painters like Frederic Edwin Church (1826–1900), Thomas Moran (1837–1926), and Albert Bierstadt (1830–1902), among dozens of others who created visual likenesses of the far west and uninhabited regions of the northeast. Road networks stretched across other American nations, too. While the Trans-Canada Highway was not created until much later in the twentieth century, a nationwide road system was part of the modernization project of Cuban President Gerardo Machado (governed 1925–33), who intended to link the length and breadth of the island nation directly to the roadway system in the United States by connecting Cuban highways with a system of ferries to Florida and thence to the rest of the country.[2] This ideal of Pan-Americanism was only partially realized. Ambitious networks of roads did not become a phenomenon in most other Latin American countries until later in the century. Countries like Brazil and Colombia, for example, were notoriously difficult to navigate by automobile until at least the 1950s.

The year 1916 was also important in the Latin American imaginary as a time to reflect on 100 years of independence from Spain. In July of that year Argentina celebrated the centenary of the signing of its declaration of independence at the Congress of Tucumán. It should be noted that 1916 also witnessed the Easter Uprising in Ireland and the eventual development of the rebellion leading to its independence from Britain. Countries like Argentina, Chile, the United States, and Canada, with their large populations of Irish immigrants, observed the progress of these events with keen interest.

Pedro Blanes Viale's monumental composition *Iguazú Falls* is a panoramic canvas that depicts the spot where the Iguazú River is divided into the upper and lower regions, forming a series of cascades that represents the most extensive waterfall system in the world. Iguazú Falls creates a natural border between Brazil and Argentina. Blanes Viale chose a site on the Argentine side of the falls, dramatically illuminated by bright sunlight, casting the foreground in the lower right into darkness and creating a convincing sense of depth to the picture. The falls, with its raging waters, takes up the majority of this horizontal composition, with a middle and left foreground of rocks and the rushing river. The inherent drama of this natural spectacle is enlivened by the presence of a rainbow that stretches virtually the length of the picture, increasing the sense of awe and wonderment felt by the viewer and relating this work to earlier nineteenth-century traditions of painting of the Sublime. The artist's short, choppy brushwork adds to the excitement of this scene, as it appears to echo the intensity of the natural elements portrayed.

Blanes Viale spent some six months at Iguazú in 1916, producing a corpus of work based on a variety of physical viewing points of the falls. He sketched and painted on site and worked up the larger canvases in his studio.[3] This picture reminds us clearly of the artistic consequences of the "long nineteenth century" as it continues the hemispheric-wide tradition of romanticizing landscapes of dramatic natural marvels such as towering mountain ranges (from the Adirondacks to the Rockies, and the Sierra Madre range in Mexico to the Andes), gorges, cataracts, and other testimonies to the power of nature and, by extension, the power of the deity. Viewers aware of artistic traditions in Canada and the United States might recollect the popularity of scenes depicting the wilderness of the west, including depictions by Paul Kane (1810–1871) of the dramatic mountain ranges in Western Canada or, in a closer comparison to Blanes Viale's subject, the many scenes of Niagara Falls on the Canadian–U.S. border between Ontario and New York State by Frederic Edwin Church, William Morris Hunt (1824–1879), and others.

Nineteenth-century traveler artists to Latin America, such as the German painter Johann Moritz Rugendas (1802–1858), who worked throughout the region in the 1820s and 1830s, or native-born landscapists like Mexican painter José María Velasco (1840–1912), are all artistic cousins to Blanes Viale. His plein air painting, a mode of art-making that he introduced to Uruguay, is a continuation of traditions first established earlier in the nineteenth century. Nonetheless, in an Uruguayan context Blanes Viale's art created a new link in the chain of events that led away from the conservative, academic realism of the 1890s and early 1900s to the establishment of an avant-garde sensibility in Montevideo with the arrival there of Joaquín Torres-García (1874–1949) and his unique Cubist and Constructivist-related vision, which would mark the Uruguayan capital as one of the epicenters of South American modernist culture in the later phase of the century's first half (see Chapter 7).

Blanes Viale spent much of his mature career in Spain, and especially the Balearic Islands (his father was from Mallorca), where he associated with the more conservative contemporaries of the young Pablo Picasso, such as the landscapists Joaquin Mir (1873–1940) and Hermen Anglada Camarasa (1871–1959). Collectively they influenced Blanes Viale's style, which has been characterized as an amalgamation of Impressionism, Neo-Impressionism, and Art Nouveau—a further instance of a departure on the part of an artist from the Americas, from the clichéd canonicity of the process of art's history.

Iguazú Falls is a product of Blanes Viale's late career in South America. His associations with contemporaneous European styles of art are less important to an understanding of what this painting represents in a specifically American context than an articulation of some of the associations with the circumstances of "American-ness" inherent in it. It is difficult to analyze this painting without examining its allusions to time and place. The grandiosity of the falls begs the question of Blanes Viale's intention when creating this depiction of American splendor. The rainbow creates a bridge uniting the darker foreground with the glowing light of the background, unifying the composition. The falls itself unites two parts of the continent—Spanish-speaking Argentina with Portuguese-speaking Brazil.

Only a decade and a half lay behind the creation of this symbol-laden painting and the Spanish-American War (1898). The tensions and misunderstandings inherent in the relationship between the nations of Latin America and the United States (sometimes referred to as the Colossus of the North) were articulated in a famous essay by José Martí (1853–1895). Martí was a Cuban writer, political activist, art critic, poet, journalist, and translator whose death in the armed struggle for his country's independence from Spain earned him the status of national hero. Martí's tract *Our America* first appeared in *La Revista Ilustrada* (published in New York) in January 1891. Republished often after that and known throughout the Americas, this lengthy essay served as a warning to the populace of the Spanish-speaking Americas against the expansionist tendencies of the United States.[4] Any lettered person of the time would have both known the text itself and understood the sentiments that it expressed. The painting by Blanes Viale could easily be interpreted as a distillation of the points of strength needed by the land south of the U.S. border to resist North American desires for expansion and annexation.

In 1905 the highly influential poet and essayist Rubén Darío (1867–1916) wrote his famous verses entitled "A Roosevelt" (To [Theodore] Roosevelt). Roosevelt represented for Latin

Americans the epitome of both the power and the threat of the United States within a hemispheric context. Roosevelt had championed the building of the Panama Canal after supporting a 1903 revolution in that country, paving the way for American intervention. The early history of the twentieth century was, in fact, a continuation of the interventionist policies whereby the United States invaded and established a long-standing military and economic presence in Mexico, Central America, and throughout the Caribbean. South America was not directly affected by the latter-day implementations of the theories of the nineteenth-century Monroe Doctrine, which sanctioned U.S. exceptionalism and theoretically authorized territorial expansion. Nonetheless, an acute sensitivity and resistance to U.S. policies was a constantly evolving reality within Latin America. Darío encapsulated these sentiments in his poem, which begins with the following verse:

> *It is with the voice of the Bible, or the verse of Walt Whitman*
> *That I should come to you, Hunter,*
> *Primitive and modern, simple and complicated,*
> *With something of Washington and more of Nimrod!*
> *You are the United States*
> *You are the future invader*
> *Of the naïve America that has Indian blood*
> *That still prays to Jesus Christ and still speaks Spanish.*[5]

Darío died in 1916 in his native Nicaragua, having attained immense popularity as a spokesperson for the Spanish-speaking Americas and defender of the integrity of Hispanic culture before the threat of U.S. imperialism. Four years prior to his death he visited Montevideo, invited by several local businessmen to participate in the publication of the periodicals *Mundial Magazine* and *Elegancias*. In the Uruguayan capital Darío lectured and made the acquaintance of various intellectuals, writers, and artists. Blanes Viale almost certainly met Darío there, and would undoubtedly have been familiar with his writing and the tenor of his expression of support for the primacy of Spanish America. That Blanes Viale created one of his most enduring compositions in a mode that speaks of the physical and spiritual grandeur of the region, in a representation of the most inspiring of wonders of the continent, is a clear reflection of the impact of the Nicaraguan poet's inspiration and a palpable indication of the spirit of the times.

We now change our focus to examine a cityscape showing a festival day in New York, thousands of miles away from the South American hinterlands. While this may indeed appear to be an abrupt shift of gears, there are, in fact, many points of intersection—some visual, but most thematic—between the Blanes Viale view of Iguazú Falls and the 1916 Manhattan street scene painted by the American Impressionist Childe Hassam. Hassam's picture has a complex title that refers to the specific historical events behind its creation. *The Fourth of July, 1916 (The Greatest Display of the American Flag Ever Seen in New York, Climax of the Preparedness Parade in May)* is set on Fifth Avenue, the city's traditional parade boulevard. Both the presence of the green omnibus and the tall buildings on either side of the street, of almost uniform height, identify this thoroughfare. There is no specific monument included to give us a clue as to which cross streets are portrayed by Hassam, although since he had a studio just off Fifth Avenue on West 57th Street, it is most likely that he had chosen a nearby venue for this depiction of a sun-drenched national holiday.

Hassam was a native of the Boston area and his early career developed there. His 1886–89 voyage to Paris was of great importance in that it afforded him first-hand access to the French painters of the later phases of the Impressionist movement that he most admired. This pioneer of American Impressionism remained faithful throughout his career to the techniques of both objects and perspective dissolving in sunlight, enhanced by the use of short, often-choppy strokes of the brush. In this painting the dominant images are the flags fluttering on both sides of the street. Those at the lower right, closest to the viewer, move almost violently in the breeze. Their colors contrast with the blue and white of the cloud-filled sky. The crowd attending the parade is composed of hundreds of individuals who are barely suggested by a few summary daubs of color.

This painting was one of the first of over 30 flag pictures done by Hassam. All of them are set on the streets of New York City, both uptown and downtown, during the years just preceding and concurrent with the entry of the United States into World

War I in April 1917.[6] I mentioned above the links that bind this painting with the work by Blanes Viale, beyond the simple coincidence of their dates of creation. The *Iguazú Falls* image (which, like the Hassam, is done in a technique reminiscent of the Impressionists, a viable avant-garde form of visuality in the Americas in the first decades of the twentieth century) is redolent of indications of national or regional identity and the visual projection of the grandeur of the Iberian Americas. Hassam's painting makes similar claims and describes a specific moment of nationalist fervor.

The Preparedness Day parade took place on Fifth Avenue on May 13, 1916, between 23rd and 58th Streets. Lasting for over 12 hours and including more than 100,000 marchers, this event was the popular culmination of a pro-war sentiment that had been growing precipitously throughout the United States since the Great War had begun in Europe two years earlier. Former president Theodore Roosevelt, Rubén Darío's antagonist in the poem quoted above, wrote several tracts in favor of the entry of the country into war. His 1916 book *Fear God and Take Your Own Part* (along with the 1915 *America and the World War*) articulated the principles of what became known as the Preparedness Movement, a drive to counter the neutrality and isolationist sentiments of the presidency of Woodrow Wilson. Wilson subsequently had a change of heart and urged the passing of the National Defense Act in 1916, paving the way for the army and navy's expansion and ultimate entrance into the theater of war.[7] Less than two months after the Preparedness Day manifestations, the parade to celebrate the U.S. national holiday on July 4 served as a reiteration of the fervor of bellicose sentiments. Hassam, a proponent of U.S. intervention in the war, evokes the tenor of the times in this work. He employs the city with its newly erected skyscrapers, facilitated by the industrial-era economic prosperity, as a powerful metaphor for a place (New York) that represented the heart of a nation fully cognizant of its aggressive pride and nationalistic fervor at a critical moment in its history, and not embarrassed to express it.[8]

Pío Collivadino's 1916 *El Riachuelo* (The Little River) is an urban view, like the Fifth Avenue depicted by Childe Hassam, and like Hassam's picture, it offers intimations of a city on the move. The title of this work by Collivadino (son of Italian immigrants from Lombardy) refers to the river that runs from Buenos Aires province to the city itself, merging with the great Río de la Plata to form the Port of Buenos Aires, which in Collivadino's day had become one of the busiest in the hemisphere. The painting shows the port at the sector of the Argentine capital known as La Boca, a neighborhood that had witnessed impressive growth since the last third of the nineteenth century, owing to the large-scale immigration of Italian working-class families who arrived in Argentina after an immigration reform act was passed in 1876. Collivadino shows the scene from a high vantage point. The artist favored such panoramic views and, in this case, he presents the dockside *barrio* as seen from a bridge opposite the Puente Transbordador (Transporter Bridge) of La Boca. Collivadino traveled throughout the city in his *carro-taller* (mobile workshop), making sketches and taking photographs for use in finished paintings that, at this point in his career, demonstrate his affinities with a latter-day form of Neo-Impressionism.[9]

The day is bright and the industrial landscape is seen as a clean environment, not yet polluted by the effluvium of later years. The river itself is the protagonist of this image and human activity is limited to tiny specks of shadow. The factories, networks of scaffolding, smokestacks, and transport boats all tell a story of movement, commerce, and progress. Collivadino portrays a scene in which the results of toil are evident in the city/riverscape but the laborers themselves are all but absent. The impact of photography is apparent in the detailed renderings of the buildings, construction cranes, and boats, creating the aura of a modern, fast-growing city. Modernist cityscapes were soon to appear on the artistic horizon where such elements as factories, automobiles, railroad cars, or high-tension wires are all transformed into quasi-abstracted metaphors of "progress." For the moment, however, we are still within the midst of a visual program that favors factual renditions of observed reality to project a sense of stability and development. Such socioeconomic solidity, however, would prove to be merely illusory. Shortly after this and other views of Buenos Aires under its most ambitious early twentieth-century phase of construction by Collivadino and others, the Tragic Week of 1919 occurred, with its prolonged riots, murders, and widespread manifestation of

social unrest among workers protesting the abuses of big industry (particularly foreign investment) in the Argentine capital.[10]
Acute racial tension that existed among the many groups of
immigrants in Argentina's capital exacerbated the viciousness
of the Tragic Week.

Landscapes of the Mind

Uruguayan painter José Cúneo (1887–1977) sometimes signed
his works with his full surname "Cúneo Perinetti." His 1914 *La
Cañada* (The Stream) (FIG. 2.4) is a premonitory painting, antic-
ipating the later images of the Uruguayan countryside bathed
in moonlight for which he became most famous. Cúneo's *lunas*
(moons) with their sometimes tortured skies and expressionistic landscapes below are highly spiritualized and represent
an approach to nature painting that is more reflective of inner

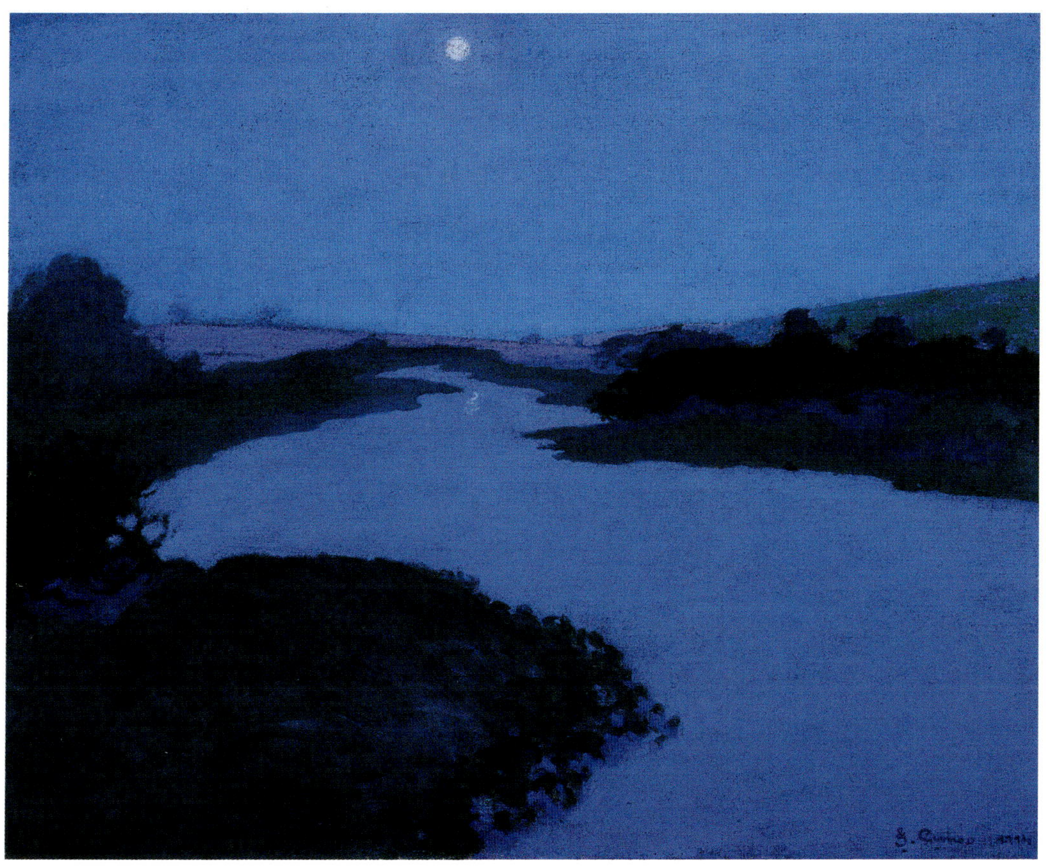

Chapter 2 · A Sense of Place

61

anxieties and preoccupations and less concerned with straight-forward renditions of topographic or climatic circumstances. We may use this picture as the beginning point to discuss a series of landscapes that depart from the essentially nineteenth-century heroic approach and depend instead on the artist's evocation of a state of mind or a mood. Cúneo's paintings have been compared to landscapes by the U.S. artist Albert Pinkham Ryder (1847–1917) as well as the nocturnal views by Russian-born Expressionist Chaim Soutine (1893–1943), both of whose striking pictures often represent quasi-abstract and tumultuous views of swirling clouds of moonlit places painted in dark colors, evocative of an atmosphere somewhere between exaltation and despair.[11] It is improbable, however, that Cúneo knew Ryder's work, so this may be taken as an example of the pervasive popularity throughout the hemisphere in the 1910s of a neo-Romantic sensibility that characterized much landscape art of the Americas.

This painting by Cúneo (a friend and admirer of his fellow Uruguayan Blanes Viale[12]) establishes a mood of contemplation and meditation, principally by its liberal use of a single color; the entire composition is bathed in various hues of blue or bluish gray. It also evokes quasi-abstract patterns through its description of topography. This riverscape defines a meandering body of water that opens wide at the lower right of the composition. The vegetation along its banks is cast in dark shadow and the land beyond—the empty, flat pampa of the Uruguayan outback—fades into the distance below the blue evening sky that dominates the upper third of the painting. A pale moon, a small white disk with subtle pulsations of light emanating from it, is visible at the uppermost center part of the composition.

Uruguayan art historian Gabriel Peluffo Linari states that Cúneo is a "pioneer in the lyrical treatment of rural landscapes, an approach that was later adopted by other painters and by those involved in the Nativist literary movement of the 1920s."[13] *La Cañada* plays a significant role in the development of landscape art in Uruguay and, by extension, the Southern Cone countries of Argentina and Chile. While this painting is visually related to Symbolism, with its mood-creating color and undulating lines, it also plays a role within the debates about what virgin landscape represented in the national consciousness. Nineteenth-century attitudes to "the rural" in the South American countries just mentioned were dramatically different from those of North American artists, who conceived of landscape painting as grand backdrops for the "positive" pursuits of expansion and settling (with all of the depredations that we now know were integrally linked to those activities) of western territories.

The pampas, or the wilderness regions of Argentina, Chile, and Uruguay, were viewed with suspicion, while their native populations (considerably smaller than in North America and in more northerly regions of Latin America) were considered barbaric. Native peoples in this part of South America (the Mapuche, Charrúa, and many other tribes) suffered mistreatment at the hands of white settlers and federal and local governments analogous to their North American indigenous counterparts. Other inhabitants included (in Argentina, Uruguay, and southern Brazil) the gauchos, the mixed-race (white and indigenous) equivalents of the North American cowboys (or the vaqueros in Mexico), individuals who had rebelled against the society of urban centers and moved to inhabit the outback regions. The gauchos were fabled as free spirits who tamed the wilderness and they were often lionized as the embodiments of freedom against the constructions of both colonialism and the domination of urban progress.

The 1872–79 Argentinean poem *Martín Fierro*, by José Hernández (1834–1886), describes the adventures of its eponymous gaucho hero; it became a pan-national epic that was thought to embody the spirit of the region's autonomy.[14] But the gauchos were also mistrusted and sometimes feared, and the land they inhabited was seen as the backdrop for fiendish activities— places to be ignored or forgotten. Such sentiments were fostered by the writings of Argentina's seventh president, the writer and philosopher Domingo Faustino Sarmiento (1811–1888), whose 1845 book *Facundo. Civilización y barbárie* (*Facundo: Civilization and Barbarism*) proved to be a deep and lastingly influential investigation into the nature of progress in the region, arguing that the city represented advancement and improvement, while the countryside epitomized all the negative connotations of the new nations of the south.[15]

Cuneo's painting turns away from this aspect of the Uruguayan imaginary, creating a placid yet still somewhat mysterious countryside view of an oneiric landscape that exists more within the realm of the personal imagination and bears no relationship to previous conceptualizations of the southern South American wilderness as either threatening or devoid of positive substance. The place he paints becomes a repository of, or background for, individual reveries. It is a landscape of potential for the projection of the inner vision and, as such, connects with similar approaches to parts of the countryside that had formerly been untamed, wild, or threatening, such as the deserts of the western United States, or the forests or glaciers of northern Canada, to which we will turn our attention now.

Southwest Reveries

The malaise prompted by the end of World War I and the realization of the extent of its mass destruction motivated many U.S. artists to leave their urban environments in search of a less pressured and more "authentic" atmosphere in which to produce their art. This was not a new phenomenon, of course, as artists over many generations had become disaffected from their native terrain at a time of wholesale self-questioning. Yet the travels on the part of Marsden Hartley (1877–1943) and his fellow New York-based artists within the circle of the photographer and arts entrepreneur Alfred Stieglitz (1864–1946) were not akin to those of, say, Paul Gauguin (1848–1903), who fled to the South Pacific in order to escape the decadent urbanization of France and immerse himself in the "exotic." A desire to be free from the dominance of European modernism and to discover a path to making "real" American art was the principal factor driving U.S. artists westward.[16]

New Mexico became the venue, in many cases, for this search for an authentic American form of expression. Taos and Santa Fe, ancient cities in the north of what had recently become (in 1912) the forty-seventh state, captured the attention of artists, both professional and amateur, who flocked there in the 1920s. They sought something they could not find in the industrialized East and desired to encounter what some writers described as the roots of Americanism. This very notion is ironic, given the fact that the population of indigenous peoples and those of Spanish and Mexican descent were, and continue to be, the subjects of severe racial and economic discrimination. The visiting artists were often considered by the long-settled local populations to be eccentric interlopers, there to profit from the undeniable attractions of the rugged landscape, the distinctive colors of the terrain, and the culture of non-white inhabitants.[17]

New Mexico was a key element in the development of Marsden Hartley's career. He first visited Taos in 1918 and remained in the state, traveling later to Santa Fe, until the following year. The many pastels he did at that time were testimonies to his fascination with the landscape. Done in a fairly representational style, they show a range of places as well as moods. He later continued his meditations on the New Mexico landscape in New York in 1920, and returned to it as a subject for a series of highly transformed, often disturbing paintings while living in Berlin in 1923.

Berlin was a city that Hartley knew well before and during the first days of World War I. It carried an emotional weight analogous to that which New Mexico had produced in his imagination. The trauma of the recently ended war was palpable in early 1920s Berlin and it made a distinctive mark on his psyche. Hartley translated this anxiety into a series of landscape paintings with New Mexico (and other American venues such as Maine) as their subject, producing images of singularly evocative power. He called these ruminations on the southwest landscape his "New Mexico Recollections." *New Mexico Recollection* of c.1923 (FIG. 2.5) could be described as a distillation of a tortured imagination. This picture is dramatically different in spirit from the optimistic, wondrously inquisitive pastels of the same locale done five years earlier. Under a threatening sky punctuated by white clouds that appear more leaden than puffy, mountains defined by blacks, deep browns, and rust reds reach almost to the top of the composition. The land itself reminds us of churning magma, unstable and intimidating, arid and deathly. Two trees rise up symmetrically on the left and right foregrounds of the composition. As in other similar Berlin-created New Mexico paintings, these trees resemble, according to the art historian Heather Hole, "asparagus spears or, more symbolically, phallic forms. They certainly do not resemble any trees commonly seen in New Mexico."[18]

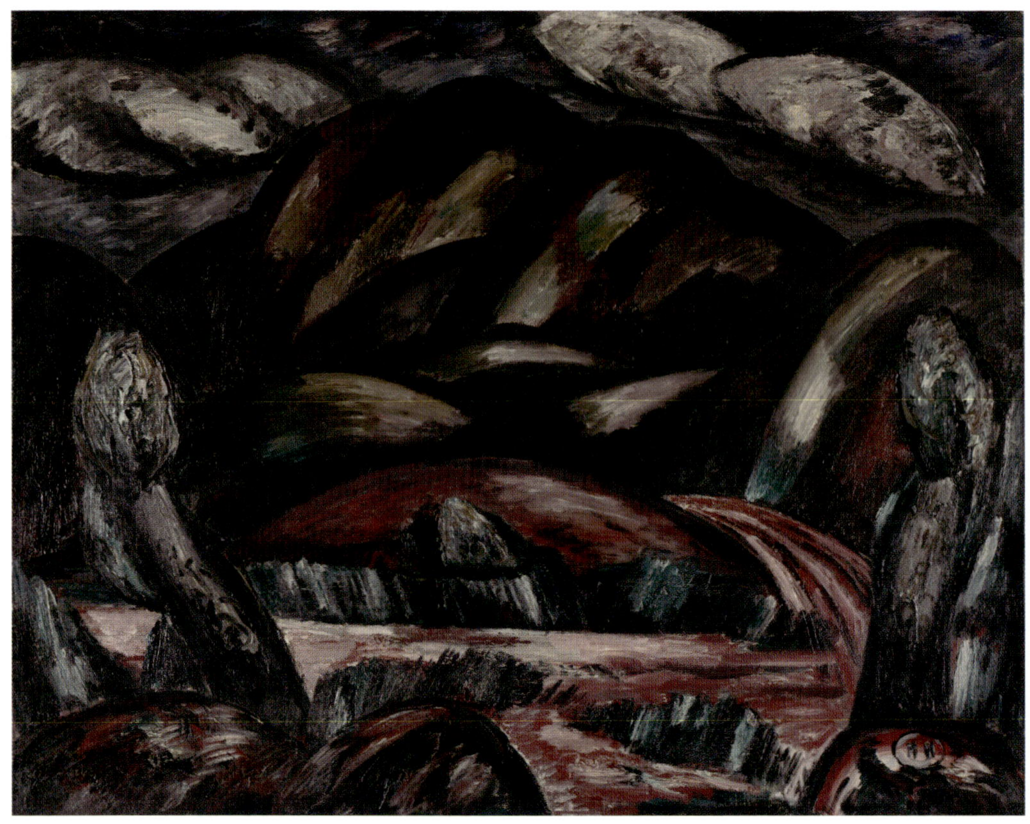

Hartley continued throughout his career to invest his land-scapes with the same urgent, and often darkly disturbing, mood. His late-period landscapes of the coast and interior of his home state of Maine (an interest in which was reignited upon encountering the transcendental nature writings of Ralph Waldo Emerson and Henry David Thoreau, as well as the poetry of Walt Whitman) propel us, as do the New Mexico pictures, into an atmosphere of wonder before the overwhelming forces of nature and despair for the fragility of humanity.[19]

The art world of Taos was galvanized by the dynamic person-ality of Mabel Dodge (1879–1962, later known as Mabel Dodge Luhan after her marriage to the Native American artist Antonio [Tony] Luhan of the Taos Pueblo tribe). By 1912 Dodge Luhan had become something of a guru for artists in New York with her artistic and literary salons. She shifted her attention to the Southwest in 1919 when she went to Taos and established an artists' colony there. This ever-changing gathering of painters

Fig. 2.5
Marsden Hartley
New Mexico Recollection,
c.1923, oil on canvas,
40 x 31⅞ in. (101.6 x
80.9 cm). Cleveland
Museum of Art.

66

and writers, including Hartley, O'Keeffe, D. H. Lawrence (1885–1930), and the Irish writer and Republican army officer Ernie O'Malley (1897–1957), among many others, would come and go between Taos and New York and elsewhere. The photographer Paul Strand (1890–1976) was another early arrival and he lived on and off in Dodge Luhan's Taos compound over the course of 20 or more years (during which time he executed his famous series of photographs of the parish church in the village of Ranchos de Taos made even more famous by O'Keeffe's painting of the same subject). In 1926 Strand traveled to Taos with his wife, Rebecca Salsbury, a self-taught artist who would divorce Strand in 1933 and settle permanently in the town, becoming a fixture of the growing coterie of painters.

Rebecca Salsbury James (1891–1968), as she came to be known after her marriage to the Taos-based businessman William James, worked in close proximity to Georgia O'Keeffe and created a body of work that, like Hartley's during his Taos years and his post-Taos experience in Berlin, used the dramatic landscape for highly expressive purposes.[20] Unlike Hartley, however, Salsbury James utilized the high desert terrain of northern New Mexico to evoke dreamy scenarios of comforting and intriguingly intimate sentiments. Her 1948 *Winter in Taos (Brown Bear Tooth and Honey Locust Thorns)* (FIG. 2.6) is a prime example of her emblematic reveries on her adopted town. The brown bear's tooth, evoking rituals of Native American peoples, takes up the bulk of the space. Bear symbolism is pervasive within Native American cultures. A necklace of bear claws, for instance, both offers protection from evil and evidences

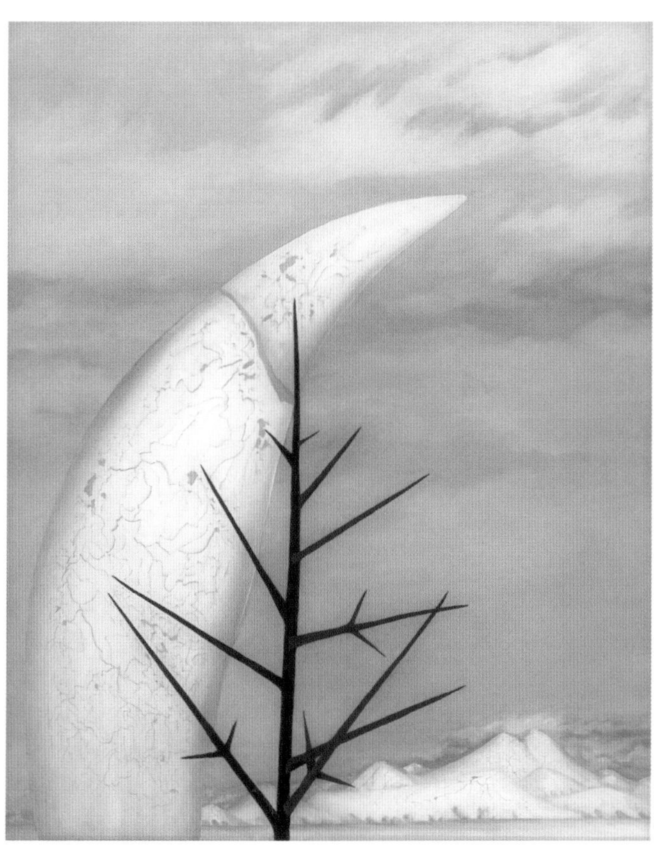

Chapter 2 · A Sense of Place

the power and strength of the wearer. Located in front of it in this picture is a branch of the honey locust (also called a thorny locust) dividing the lower portion of the image into two roughly equal halves. The honey locust tree (generally considered native to the eastern part of the United States but found as well in New Mexico) provided food for Native Americans with the pulp from its branches.

A chilly, windy winterscape, with snow-covered hills in the far distance at lower right, creates an aura of frigidity that is representative of the snowy atmosphere of this part of the world from December through early spring. Salsbury James's picture is considerably different from Hartley's *New Mexico Recollection* discussed above, but it is no less powerful in its ability to evoke a place that has entered the popular North American imagination as a land of the myth of dreams.

It is significant to note that Salsbury James painted most of her works on glass (a technique also used to great advantage by Hartley on several occasions early on in his career). The reverse glass process is an ancient one and there are examples from medieval and Byzantine traditions in Europe. In the New World, reverse glass painting found particular favor in Ibero-America; it became part of the repertory of forms employed by the creators of sacred imagery in New Mexico in the eighteenth century, and this continues today. Salsbury James appropriated this form of art (examples of which she had undoubtedly seen in private collections of her artist-collector friends and colleagues, or at such public institutions as the Spanish Colonial Arts Society in Santa Fe, or the Harwood Museum in Taos[21]), stripping it of its traditional Catholic connotations and infusing it with an equally, or even more, powerful reminder of the authority of the forces of nature, which had been revered by native populations for millennia before the coming of Europeans to the Americas. Salsbury James created images that may be read as landscapes of intimate association and identification of herself with the place—New Mexico—that became the backdrop for her entire creative career.

Canadian Wilderness

A key link between New Mexico as a generative force for emotionally charged landscape and the modernist landscape tradition in Canada is provided by the art of Lawren Stewart Harris (1885–1970). Harris is well known as one of the founders of the Group of Seven, the Toronto-based artists' collective that flourished from 1920 (when they had their first exhibition at the Art Gallery of Toronto, now the Art Gallery of Ontario) to 1933. This alliance produced for both Canadians and audiences abroad a vision of the grandeur of nature as equivalent to the authority of both God and nation.[22] All of the Group of Seven, as well as other artists associated in one way or another with them, including Tom Thomson (1877–1917) and Emily Carr (1871–1945), were deeply immersed in forms of transcendental philosophy and the poetry of Walt Whitman, among other sources of spiritual nourishment.[23] The Theosophy of Helena Blavatsky influenced Harris and, during his residency in Santa Fe, New Mexico, beginning in 1938, he helped to found the Transcendental Painting Group, which counted among its members Agnes Pelton, whose work was discussed in Chapter 1.[24]

Harris's 1928 painting *Lake and Mountains* (FIG. 2.7) is representative of his mature landscape art as it developed in Ontario, with many forays into the north and west of the country.[25] After 1934 he gave up figuration altogether and dedicated his later career to creating abstract compositions reminiscent of Wassily Kandinsky's geometrically infused paintings of the 1920s and 30s. Kandinsky's *Concerning the Spiritual in Art* was as much of a model of inspiration for Harris as it had been for his colleagues in the Group of Seven. In this work we sense the artist's urge to simplify and to abstract forms in his monumental picture, the result of a sketching trip the year of its creation to Lake Superior and the Canadian Rockies. While Harris does not

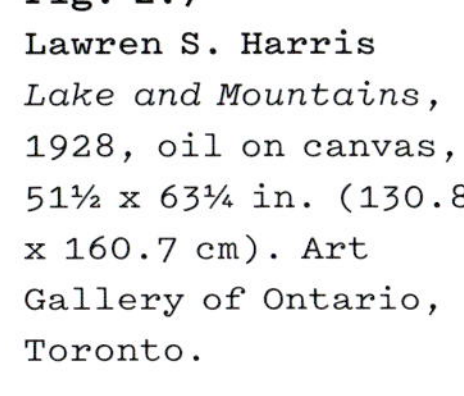

Fig. 2.7
Lawren S. Harris
Lake and Mountains,
1928, oil on canvas,
51½ x 63¼ in. (130.8
x 160.7 cm). Art
Gallery of Ontario,
Toronto.

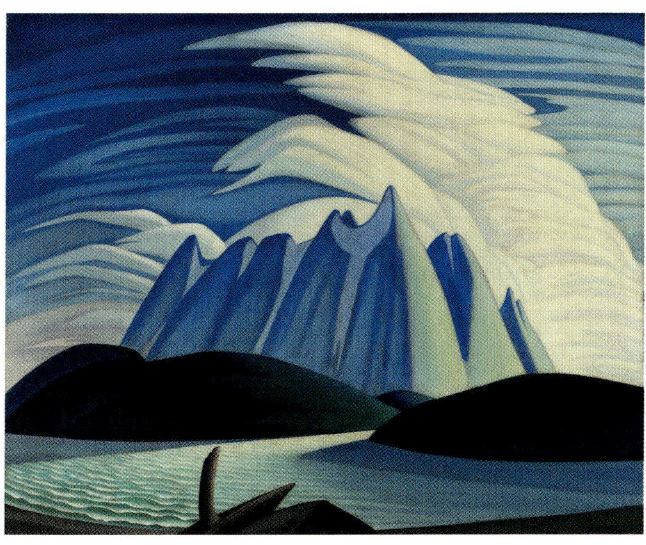

Fig. 2.8
Emily Carr
Trees in the Sky, 1939,
oil on canvas, 44 x 27
in. (111.6 x 68.7 cm).
Art Gallery of Ontario,
Toronto.

present a specific place, he compresses into a grand whole the quintessential qualities of water and mountains beneath a sky filled with looming white clouds. The infinity of the forces of northern nature is present in a composition that relies on a limited range of icy blues and gray greens, contrasted with brilliant whites of the clouds. The waters of the lake are elliptical and the hills of the foreground are uniformly round, serving as foils to the upsweeping, jagged peaks of the Rocky Mountains, which dominate the center portion of the image. The overall impression is of vast horizontality. This vaporous, stony landscape is a wide-angle synecdoche of the vastness of the Canadian wilderness, a quality that contrasts drastically with the verticality and creepy aliveness of the 1939 *Trees in the Sky* by Harris's friend and fellow Canadian landscapist Emily Carr (FIG. 2.8), painted in the far more verdant and more temperate climes of the Pacific coast province of Carr's native British Columbia.

Carr was not a member of the Group of Seven but she sought them out in Toronto after having read the first study of their art published in 1926 by Fred B. Housser, a book that represented an early statement of the concept of "Canadian-ness" in landscape painting.[26] Her affinities with the group's investment in their art of a sense of place and transcendence are well known. Walt Whitman's poetry was, as the artist claimed in her voluminous journals, one of the main sources of inspiration—as it was for the Eastern Canadian painters—and Carr became, under her friend Lawren Harris's influence, a participant in the affinities for Theosophy (a philosophy she later renounced to return to a non-church-based form of Christianity).

Trained in London and Paris, Carr spent almost her entire career in Victoria on Vancouver Island.[27] By the time of her death she had entered the national imaginary as representing the artist who best embodied a sense of Canadian identity, bound up with a sometimes-evanescent spirituality. Yet in recent times her art—especially the large body of paintings and drawings of First Nation villages and their outstanding features, including totem poles, that characterized her subject matter until around 1930—has been the subject of potent criticism on the part of postcolonial critics who have accused her of the voyeuristic opportunism of a non-indigenous "settler" with a limited understanding of native traditions and the meanings of their material culture.[28]

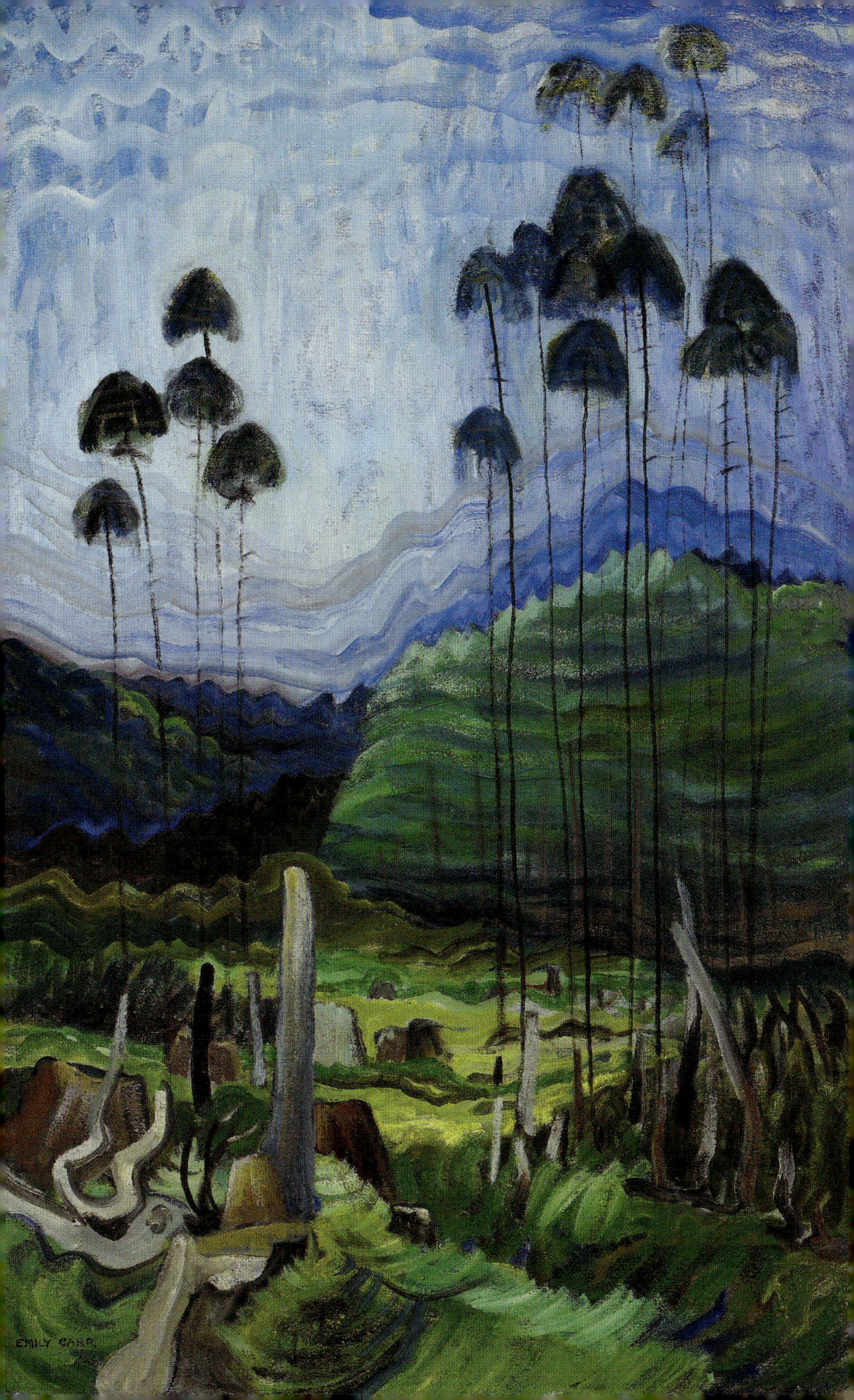
EMILY CARR

Trees in the Sky is a late work by Carr. Painted six years before her death it demonstrates a deep personal meditation on the constant change and transformation of nature. It is not a picture that consciously functions as an emblem of place but it is nonetheless a testimony to the artist's intense engagement with the temperate rain forests of Vancouver Island. The canvas is divided into two parts. The upper depicts the vaporous blue sky painted in the artist's characteristic liquefied oils (diluted with gasoline) to create the streaky effect of a cloudy atmosphere redolent of gloom. The enormous trees, with spindly trunks and mushroom-like crowns, reach up to the topmost portions of the composition, connecting the upper and lower halves of the image. The mountains dominate the center and appear striated; the nearer ones are green, while those farther away are painted in a darker shade of blue than that of the sky. The lower foreground is the most intriguing part of this picture. In some ways it is not unlike Marsden Hartley's dreamscape of New Mexico, recreated in his imagination years after witnessing it and reimagining it as something of a nightmare scenario.

Carr wrote profusely. Her journals were posthumously published in 1966 under the title *Hundreds and Thousands*.[29] Many of the entries deal directly with her experiences of sketching in the forest, which she did regularly. A representative passage gives us a sense of her visceral connection to the leaves, trees, rocks, and moss as living entities:

Everything is green. Everything is waiting and still. Slowly things begin to move, to slip into their places … Colors you had not noticed come out, timidly or boldly … Nothing is crowded; there is living space for all. Air moves between each leaf. Sunlight plays and dances. Nothing is still now. Life is sweeping through the spaces. Everything is alive. The air is alive. The silence is full of sound. The green is full of color … Tender youthfulness, laughing at gnarled oldness. Moss and ferns, and leaves and twigs … You must be still in order to see and hear it.[30]

Mexican Volcanoes

The last work of art considered in this category alluding to the symbolic potential of landscape is the *Self-Portrait* of 1958 (FIG. 2.9) by Mexican artist Gerardo Murillo, also known as Dr. Atl (a name he gave himself, referring to the Nahuatl or Aztec word for "water"). If references to integration of the self into the land were implicit in the works discussed above, this image shows the two subjects of the painting—the artist and the volcanic landscape of Mexico's central high plateau—as virtually one and the same. The aged artist, with long flowing beard, appears in the foreground holding a paintbrush. His voluminous robe covers most of his body and, with his penetrating gaze, he appears like a sage from some other time, or an aged master of the Renaissance in the midst of a moment of inspiration. As in the painting of Iguazú Falls by Blanes Viale with which I started this chapter, there is a grand panoramic vista unified by the presence of a rainbow, a mitigating feature that somewhat softens this troubled scene of a rain- and cloud-obscured terrain. The surface of this picture, like many others by Dr. Atl, is mottled and textured. It was done on wood panel with oil and the artist's own invented materials, which he called Atl Colors, consisting of a bar made of pigments, kerosene, and wax that he rubbed across the surfaces of his paintings like an oily pastel, creating a streaky, almost three-dimensional effect.

Atl was a key figure in the development of Mexican painting from the 1920s onward. Active in and promoter of the early phases of the Mexican mural movement, he was also a great supporter of folk customs, music, and arts as part of the nationalist agenda following the end of the Mexican Revolution in

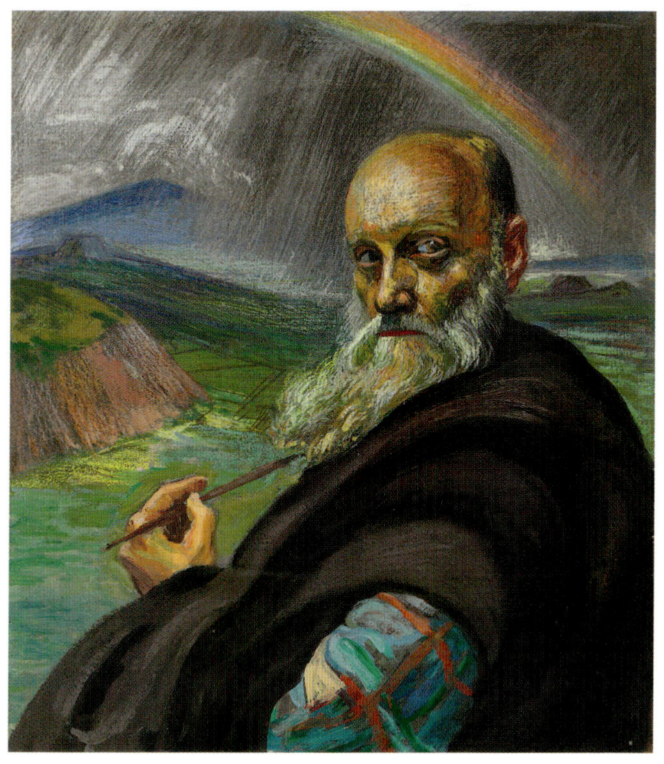

Fig. 2.9
Dr. Atl (Gerardo
Murillo)
Self-Portrait, c.1958,
oil and tempera on
wood, 28 x 24 in. (71
x 61 cm). Private
collection.

1920. In 1921 he published a lengthy compendium of information on popular arts, representing traditions whose revival was promoted by the government.[31] Dr. Atl was also instrumental in the organization of exhibitions of this material at home and abroad.[32] While many of his portraits are arresting, he became best known for his landscapes, especially those of the volcanoes outside of Mexico City, Popocatépetl and Ixtacíhuatl. After 1943 and the spontaneous eruption of Paricutín in the state of Michoacán, this geological phenomenon virtually took over the imagination of the artist. His landscapes bear heavily weighted messages of solidarity with the Mexican nation. The most violent depictions of volcanoes such as Paricutín may also be understood as symbolic of the aggression and brute force that he admired in the articulation of mid-century philosophies of Fascism and National Socialism, much to the detriment of his career, even though he enjoyed popular exoneration in the last stages of his life.[33]

Cityscapes

Let us now investigate visual representations of some of the swiftly developing cities throughout the hemisphere. Through such factors as increased immigration from Europe and Asia (especially in South America and the Caribbean), improvements in transportation both on land and in the air (following the achievements in aviation of the Wright Brothers in the United States in 1903, and the Brazilian Alberto Santos-Dumont in Paris in 1906) as well as massive industrialization following World War I, places like São Paulo, Buenos Aires, Mexico City, Havana, and New York were on their way to new phases of expansion and material well-being—at least for the privileged and wealthy who benefitted from the toil of the vast mass of meagerly compensated working-class citizens and non-citizens laboring in urban centers. The representation of cities became the quintessential vehicle to express—in concrete or symbolic terms—the "new" and the "modern."

We started this chapter with several prototypical works from 1916. Among them were two urban scenes, the festive view of Fifth Avenue, New York, by Childe Hassam, and the Buenos Aires port scene by Pío Collivadino. Both represented

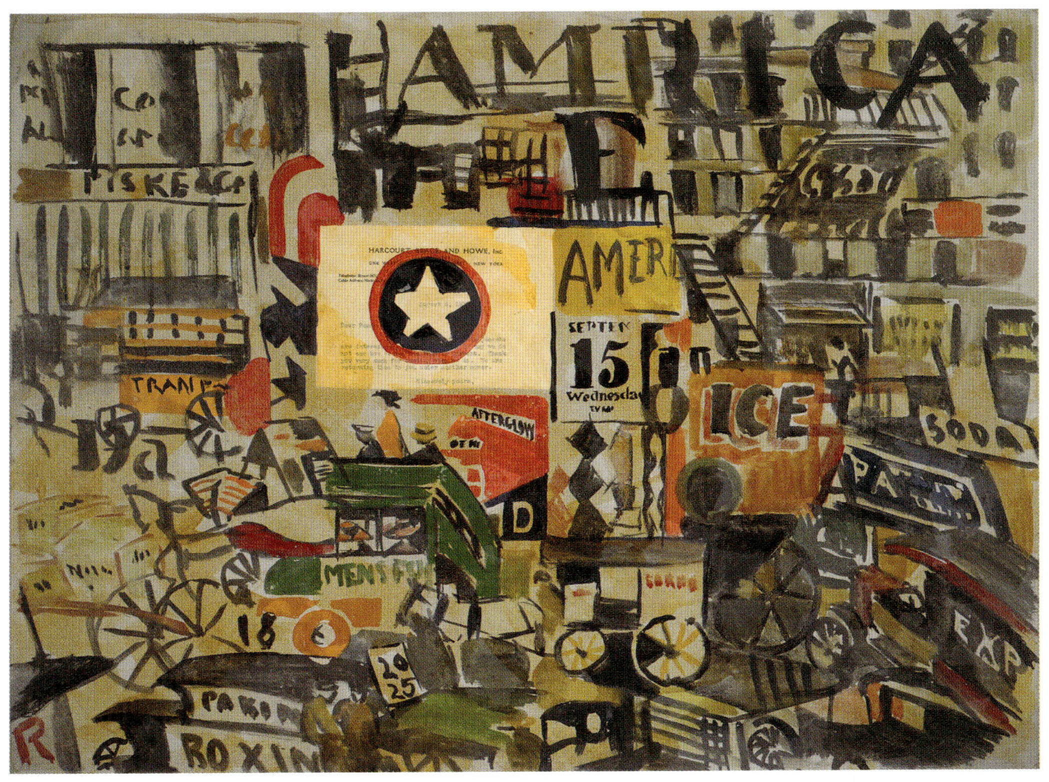

attempts to capture the excitement of movement and progress, or, in the case of the Hassam, the impetus to join a worldwide warfare movement (which would, in itself, ultimately promote prosperity in its aftermath). Those two paintings, however, represented, in their use of Impressionist and Neo-Impressionist modes of spatial construction and stylistic techniques, a survival of the artistic approaches of the previous century. Created only four years later, the *New York Street Scene* by Uruguayan artist Joaquín Torres-García (FIG. 2.10) presents a radically different view of the metropolis from that of his somewhat older contemporary, Hassam.

In *New York Street Scene* we find a chaotic evocation of the noise, commerce, and traffic of downtown Manhattan, where Torres-García and his family lived and worked from 1920 to 1922. We also observe an exemplar of the materiality of modernism. The artist created this work with oil and collage on board. The imposition of words on the surface plays a major role and suggests pieces of torn paper. "America" is emblazoned

Fig. 2.10
Joaquín Torres-García
New York Street Scene,
c.1920, oil and collage
on academy board coated
in gray paint, 18 x 24
in. (45.7 x 60.8 cm).
Yale University Art
Gallery, New Haven.
Gift of the Collection
Société Anonyme
(1941.723).

at the upper right. Other words, either in their entirety or in fragmentary form, appear throughout a picture that recalls the artist's engagement with Futurism and Cubism, and also adumbrates his later creation of a personal form of Constructivism. Torres-García termed this mode *Universalismo Constructivo* (Constructive Universalism), consisting of paintings and sculptures based on the grid, with individual niches for archetypal symbols that have held meaning for societies from ancient to modern times (see Chapter 7).

New York Street Scene, however, aims to present a multilayered snapshot of the city's topography and iconography. It is an evocation of postwar vitality and increased economic stability (even though thousands of the newly arrived immigrants were living in conditions of dire poverty throughout Manhattan and other parts of New York). Movement is represented by people (summarily sketched) walking through a maze of traffic comprised of horse-drawn peddlers' carts, motorcars, and trams. Buildings on the opposite sides of a narrow street are suggested by awnings, fire escapes, facades, and the words of the products sold in the shop interiors. The lower portion of the canvas is a virtual symphony of the rounded forms of wheels. All of them are attached to wagons or other modes of transportation, but it is their distinctive shapes that add a sense of back-and-forth movement to the picture, as if it were a fluid entity, about to move at any moment. In the center of the composition is a white star with a field of black encircled in red. This is painted atop a fragment of a letter from the New York publisher Harcourt, Brace and Howe, advising Torres-García that they have declined to give the struggling artist a job. As the art historian Geaninne Gutiérrez-Guimarães states, "The superimposition of the letter over images of America's booming industrial and commercial economy points to the incongruity between the country's promises and the reality of his own situation."[34]

When he painted this picture Torres-García was living in Manhattan with his family. He had come more for financial reasons than any other; his career in Barcelona (where he had lived since his youth) had dried up and he had not yet become a part of the Parisian avant-garde that marked the next phase of his development. Thinking he could become a manufacturer of toys (a venture that proved financially unviable) he settled in New York. While Torres-García did not prosper in the new environment of Manhattan he made many artistic contacts that would influence him for the rest of his life. He was aligned with the Société Anonyme, an organization founded by the collector and arts promoter Katherine Dreier (1877–1952) that organized shows of advanced art by the likes of Marcel Duchamp (1887–1968), Joseph Stella (1877–1946), Man Ray (1890–1976), Marsden Hartley, and many others who became friends and acquaintances of the Uruguayan painter and sculptor. Dreier purchased *New York Street Scene* along with several other works by Torres-García that eventually passed into the collection of Yale University along with the rest of her holdings of modernist paintings and sculpture. Torres-García also participated in exhibitions of the Whitney Studio Club, a forerunner to the Whitney Museum of American Art, and the Pennsylvania Academy of the Fine Arts in Philadelphia, among others. By the time he returned to Europe he was undoubtedly invigorated by the artistic and intellectual life of New York (as this street scene and other related paintings demonstrate), and he channeled this stimulus into even more experimental work that continued to manifest the vigor of the youthful milieu in which he had lived and worked during his brief stint in the largest city of the Americas.

Manhattan in the 1920s was in a frenzy of building and commercial activity. The construction of Grand Central Terminal, finally completed in 1927, could be understood as representing the new face of midtown. Skyscrapers were going up all up and down Fifth, Madison, and Park avenues. These were office buildings as well as hotels and private apartments. The "look" of modern New York, which continues in one form or another to this day, had been established by the late 1920s. Even during the darkest moments of the Depression (which began with what came to be known as Black Tuesday, October 29, 1929, and continued well into the later years of the following decade), construction in New York persisted. This is attested to by many visual images in all media. Diego Rivera spent parts of 1931 and 1932 in New York where he had a major one-man show at the Museum of Modern Art (founded in 1929). It consisted of a series of portable murals of both rural scenes of Mexico and the skyline of Manhattan, which took on a new aspect virtually

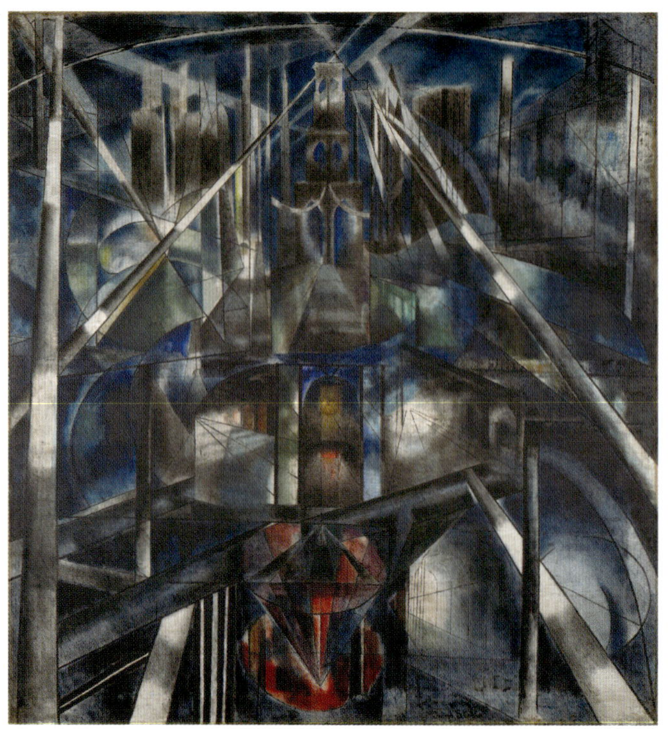

every day with so many construction projects underway, even during the nadir of the Depression.[35]

Within the iconography of the industrialized hemisphere during the 1920s, cityscapes of New York become the inevitable symbols of transformation and optimism (although an optimism not without a tinge, in many instances, of skepticism). Just at the cusp of the new decade, Torres-García's friend and colleague the Italian immigrant artist Joseph Stella created his *Brooklyn Bridge* (1919–20) (FIG. 2.11). This heralds, in semi-abstract, Futurist terms,[36] the figurative arrival into the realm of Gotham (the oldest nickname for New York, originating in the early nineteenth century), and provides a metaphor for the dizzying dynamism of the rising city. This painting, which creates its virtually overwhelming visual excitement through the use of shimmering color, energetic orthogonal lines, and evocations of the bridge structure's stately arches and spandrels, was purchased (like the Torres-García street scene discussed above) by Katherine Dreier for the Société Anonyme. It presents itself to us as an emblem of the present state of optimistic entry into a new glittering land, such as that imagined in 1900 by the novelist L. Frank Baum in his wildly popular novel *The Wonderful Wizard of Oz.*

Straight lines, clean, clear light, cuboid forms, a "machine aesthetic," and depictions of the products of industry, innovation, and capitalism are all inherent concepts within the uniquely North American form of art that used some of the visual vocabulary of Cubism and Futurism to local ends. Factories, assembly lines, stockyards, docks, railroad yards, airplanes, steamship decks, and even views of burgeoning suburbs are all integral parts of the visual vocabulary of Precisionism, but the downtown views

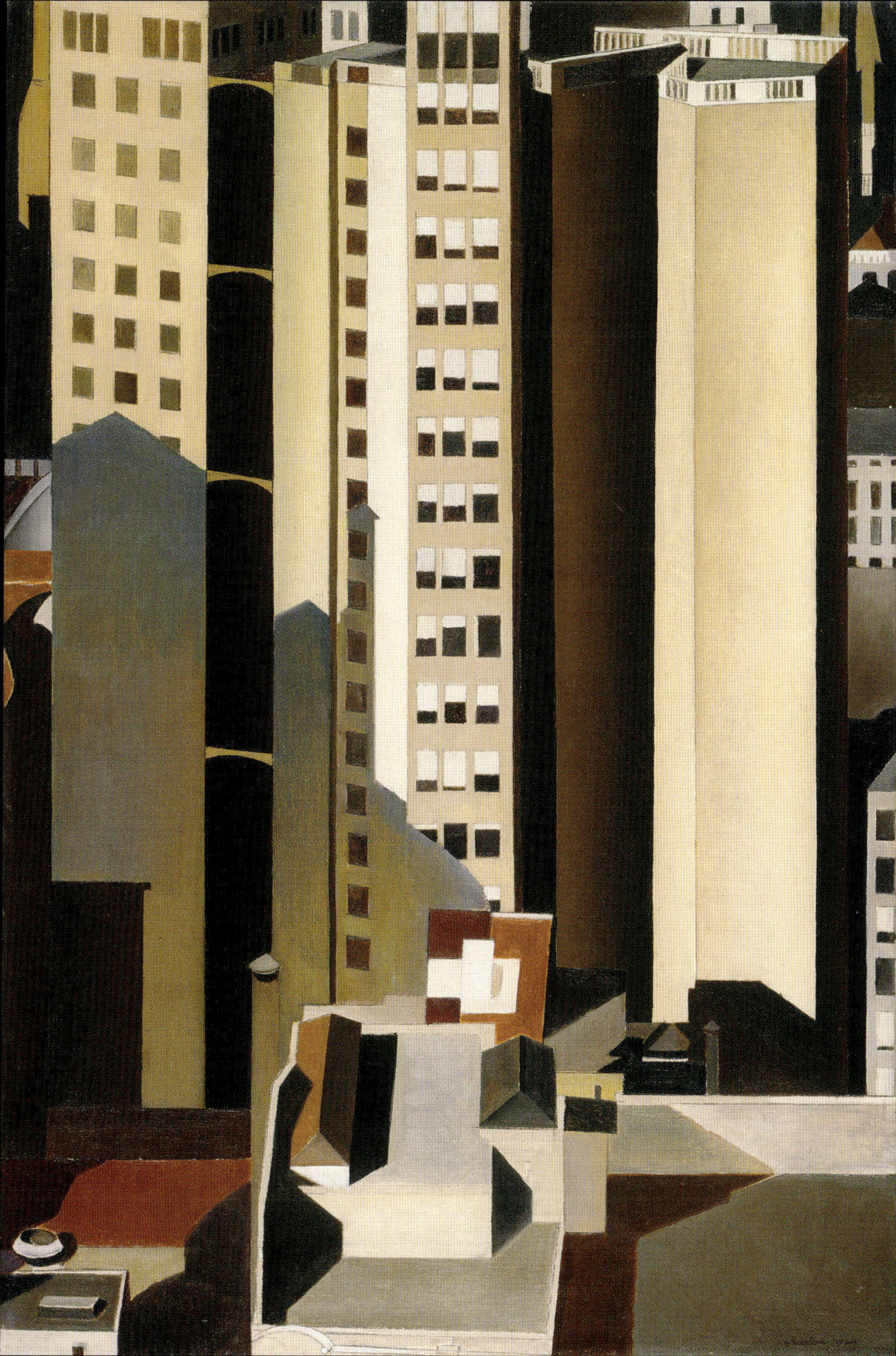

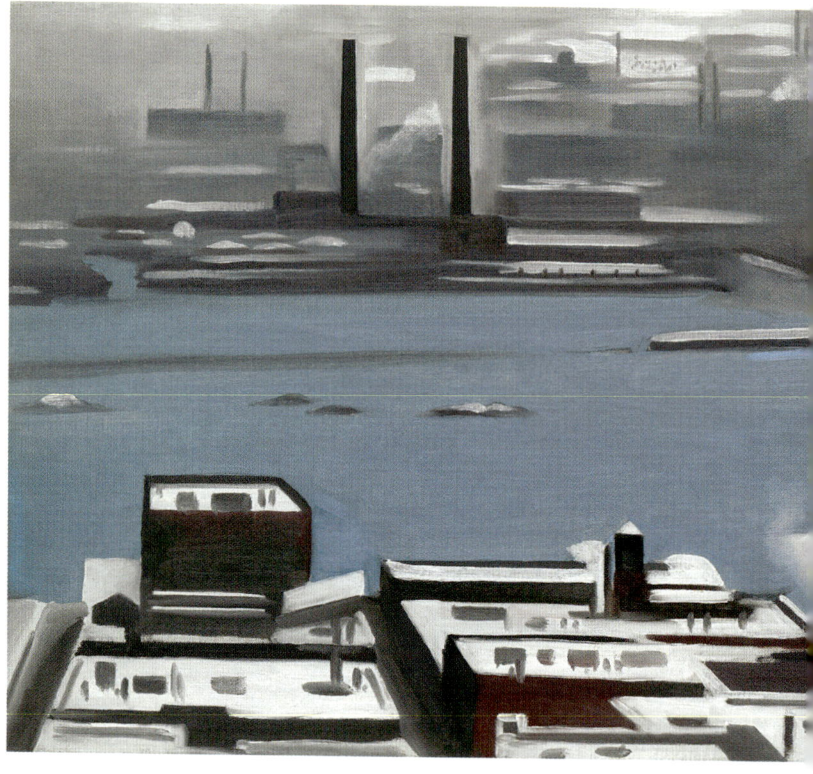

of (sometimes anonymous) cities form the core of the interests of painters and photographers such as Ralston Crawford (1906–1978), Morton Schamberg (1881–1918), Charles Demuth (1883–1935), Elsie Driggs (1898–1992), and many more. Charles Sheeler (1883–1965) was one of the most prolific and versatile artists of the movement; his paintings as well as his photographs represent key contributions to the visual definitions of U.S. "modern times"—to borrow the title of Charlie Chaplin's highly successful 1936 film.

Sheeler's *Skyscrapers* of 1922 (FIG. 2.12), as well as the work by Georgia O'Keeffe (who was also associated with the Precisionist movement) known as *East River from the Shelton Hotel*, 1928 (FIG. 2.13), depicts a specific place in the Manhattan cityscape. A year before painting his scene of the city's recently built tall buildings, Sheeler had collaborated with Paul Strand on a ten-minute documentary with shots of the streets, buildings, and harbor of Manhattan, as well as panoramic views of Manhattan from afar. This film, *Manhatta* (the original indigenous name

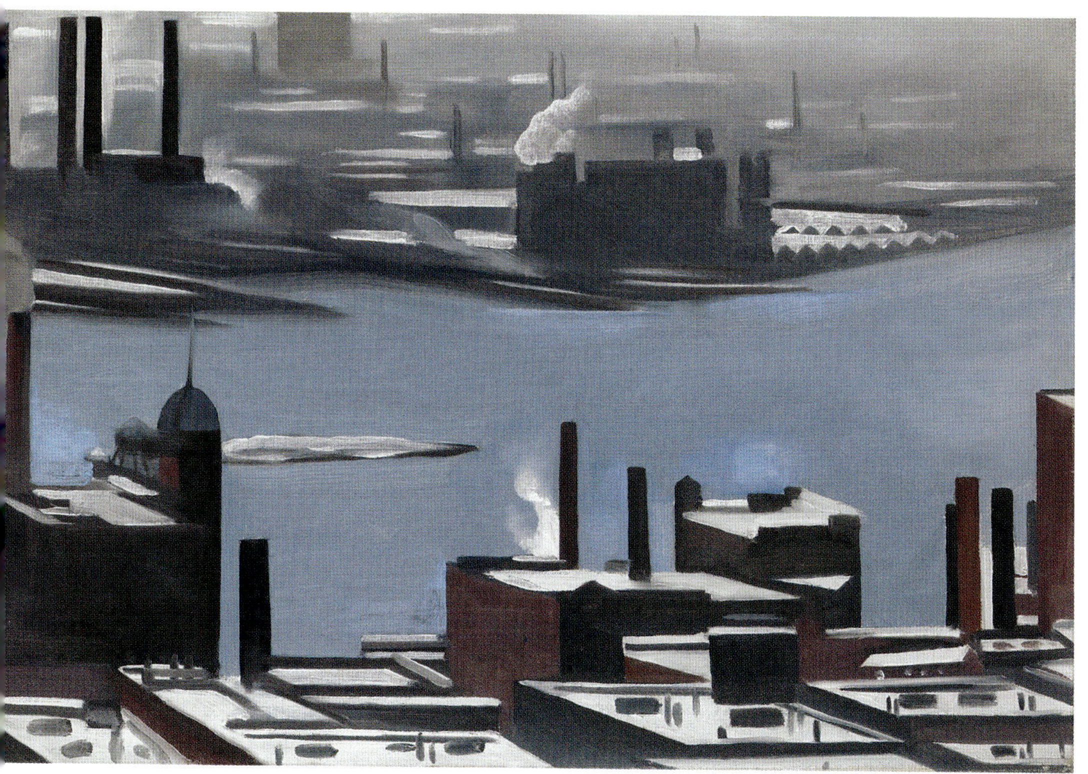

of the island), contains the kernel of what Sheeler decided to paint in *Skyscrapers*. When viewing the film it is clear that he was attracted to a shot of the back of buildings on Park Row, in the financial district of Manhattan. He isolated one of the frames of the film, brought the buildings up closer to the picture plane, and thus to the viewer, and created a hard-edge, highly compartmentalized depiction of the buildings themselves, the window, and the shadows cast on the lower portions of the structures. It is a highly structured, cube-dependent image that also suggests the meticulousness of the buildings and the consequent remoteness of the architecture's aura. This is a landscape created for labor by the use of steel, cement, and glass.

Georgia O'Keeffe's somewhat later work is horizontal as opposed to the strict verticality of the Sheeler, and this approach in itself creates a more relaxed atmosphere. This is a riverscape in winter. Snow covers the tops of the low-lying buildings; the view across the river from Manhattan's dockside factories to the industrial district of Long Island City in the borough of Queens is bleak and impersonal, with no human activity for relief. The bird's-eye vantage point creates a considerable distance between the cityscape and the artist working on the thirtieth floor of her apartment in the Shelton Hotel on Lexington Avenue and 49th Street (then the world's largest such structure), where O'Keeffe lived with Alfred Stieglitz on and off from 1925 for some dozen years.

One year after painting the *East River* O'Keeffe made her first trip to New Mexico, a journey that was ultimately to change her life. My description above of the lure of the sites throughout the state, but particularly those of the northern sector—including Santa Fe, Taos, and Abiquiú, the town outside of which the artist settled for the rest of her life in 1949—applies equally to O'Keeffe, whose most famous paintings invariably feature references to the mystically imbued starkness of the New Mexican high desert. One cannot help but think that the *East River* cityscape embodied some of the frustration with mechanized, impersonal modern society that ultimately led her to seek a place for quietude and meditation—a function that New Mexico served for so many other artists, including, as we have seen, Marsden Hartley and Rebecca Salisbury James.

Although New York was considered the quintessentially modern metropolis, no U.S. city was immune from an enchantment with the new in one form or another. A more detailed survey of the imagery of American cities would reveal analogous images of the mechanization of life and the romance of mega buildings in places like Chicago (which virtually witnessed the birth of the first skyscrapers after the Great Fire of 1871), or in the development of Los Angeles as the entertainment capital of the Western world (an advertising slogan that gained currency in the 1930s).

In 1930 and 1931, Missouri-born painter Thomas Hart Benton (1889–1975) created a series of murals for The New School for Social Research in New York, an alternative educational institution of higher learning founded by a group of professors from Columbia University who were disenchanted with what they saw as the restrictive teaching methods there. Bringing a new liberalism to university instruction in its downtown signature building on West 12th Street, designed in 1930 by Viennese architect Joseph Urban (1872–1933), The New

School became one of the most progressive institutions in the country, especially after it began to arrange asylum for many European intellectuals threatened with persecution or death in Nazi-controlled countries in Northern and Central Europe.

Art was a cornerstone of the philosophical direction of The New School; its president during the early years, Alvin Johnson (1874–1971), encouraged the development of the arts as part of the curriculum, and invited well-known artists from at home and abroad to decorate the rooms of the building. These included the Ecuadorean painter Camilo Egas (1889–1962), Mexican artist José Clemente Orozco, and Benton, who contributed a series of murals entitled "America Today."[37] Now in the Metropolitan Museum of Art, New York, these murals portray scenes of many aspects of the nation in the early 1930s, from images of agriculture in the south to the modernization of factory culture in virtually all parts of the United States. The panel known as *Instruments of Power* (FIG. 2.14) shows, rather than a specific metropolis, the elements by which a city expands: a speeding train to carry goods and passengers from one urban center to another, a plane and a dirigible, then a viable form of transport, a power station, and a series of quasi-abstracted references to manufacturing in the wheeled instruments in the foreground. Divided into sectors to fit the walls of the original room for

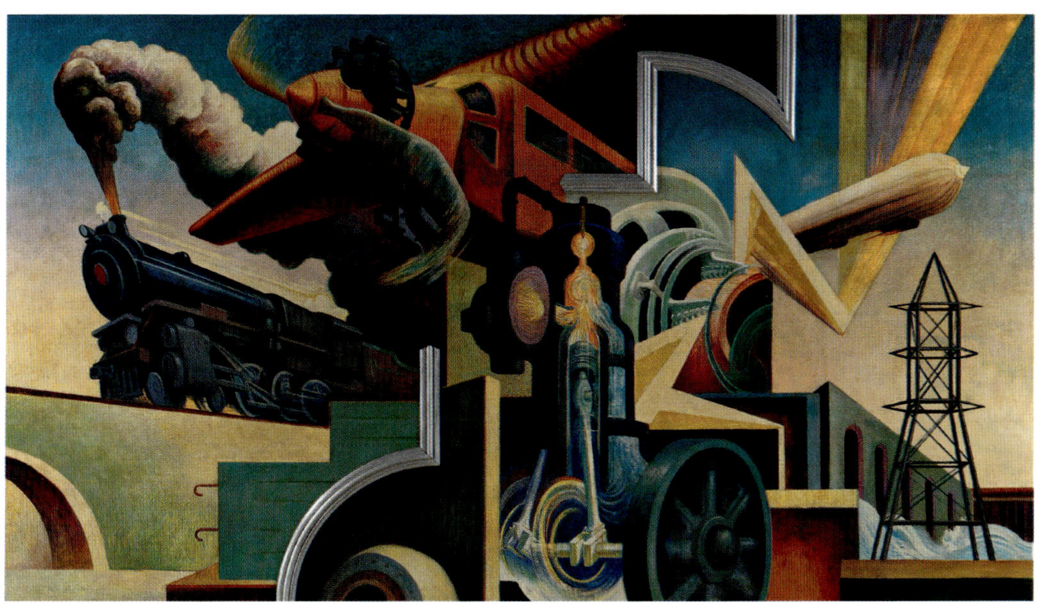

which it was intended, this picture takes on the guise of a mod-
ernistically segmented image, which in the end was somewhat
ironic given the taste of its artist. Benton was far more identified
with the conservative and representational Regionalist form of
painting that specialized in glorifications of the American rural
landscape than with the Precisionist-oriented results of his New
School commission.

South of the U.S. Border

Mexican painting of the 1920s is most associated with muralism
(discussed in Chapter 4) and imagery derived from the lives
of mostly rural inhabitants of the country. The so-called Tres
Grandes (three Great Ones)—Rivera, Orozco, and Siqueiros—
as well as many other artists often associated with their vision
of a timeless past, embodied the state through the promotion of
landscape and scenes of village life and the indigenous populations. Another equally powerful branch of the Mexican visionary imagination evolved during the years immediately after the
revolution. Paintings, graphic arts, and photography promoted,
in many cases, a consciousness of Mexico as a youthful country embarking on a new phase of modernization. Imagery of
modern buildings, power plants, cement factories, railroads, and
motorized transportation dominated a sector of the avant-garde
art world of Mexico City. Artists associated with a local variety
of Futurist aesthetic called *Estridentismo* (Stridentism) created
visual, musical, and literary works that reflected this interest in
progress and modernization. The urban scene was the backdrop
for their imagination and Rufino Tamayo (1899–1991) was one
of the artists who—particularly in his early works of the mid- to
late 1920s (done in Mexico City and, after 1926, in New York,
where he lived on and off until 1949)—expressed a spirit of
mechanization and industrialization in pictures of urban spaces
and factories.

Tamayo's *Rooftops* (FIG. 2.15) is one of several works he did in
1925 and 1926 that celebrate urban imagery. The painting shows
the recently constructed Indianilla power plant in the Mexican
capital, seen through a maze of electrical wires, smokestacks,
and a water tank. The rising steam is divided into facets and in
this way it is yet one more semi-sculptural element in this urban

scape of loosely constructed geometric forms. The composition is a study in segmented spaces in a way not unlike Joseph Stella's *Brooklyn Bridge* or Torres-García's Manhattan street, with its many markers of commercial activity.[38]

In some modernist images of the growth and industrialization of nations, forms of transport constitute the principal subjects. This is true in several key works by Tarsila do Amaral done in the first half of the 1920s. The railroads of Brazil have a long, complex, and fragmented history. Instituted in the mid-nineteenth century, train travel and train commerce were mainly concentrated along the Atlantic coast and in most cases

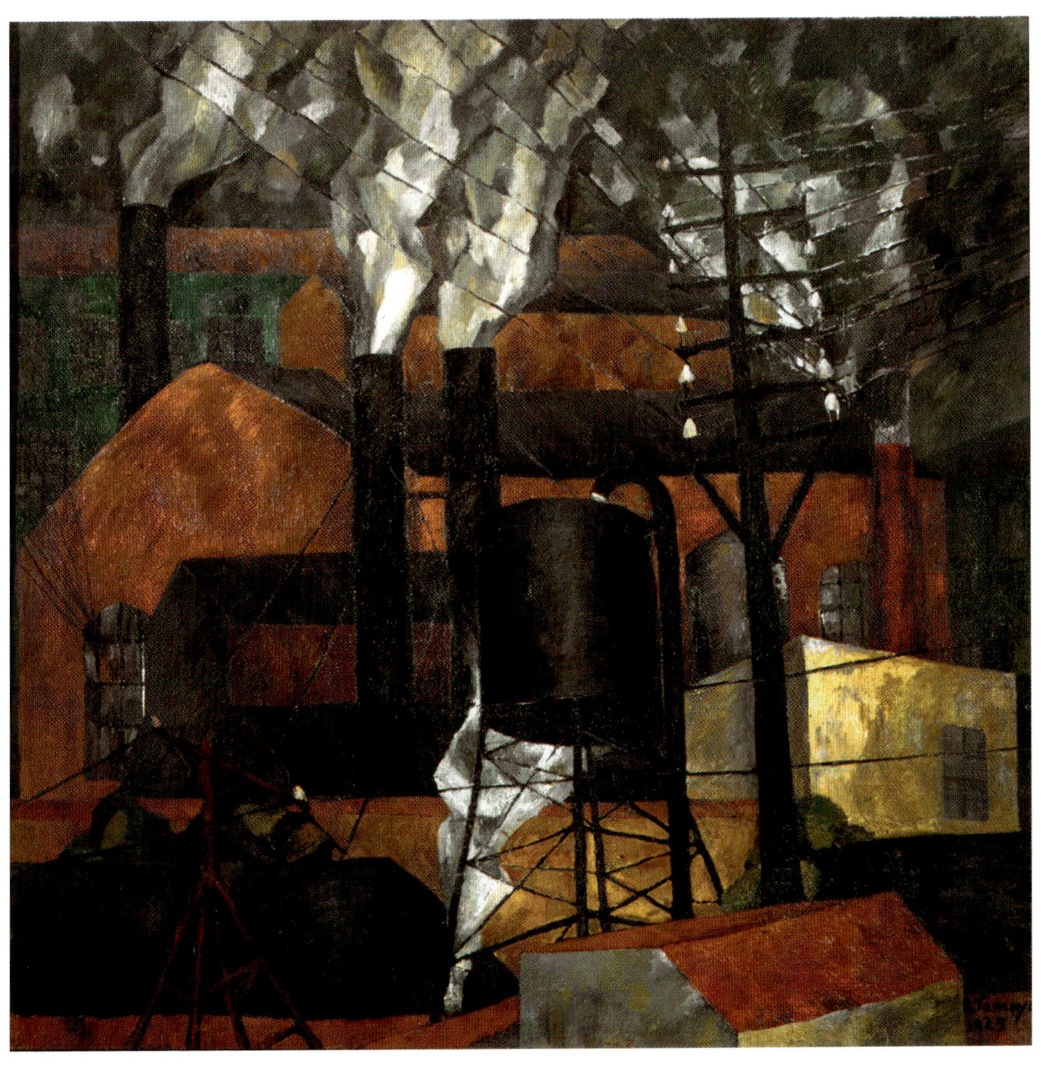

did not penetrate into the deep hinterlands of this sixth largest of the world's nations. Nonetheless, in the early twentieth century, numerous (often British-controlled) private companies ran many rail lines connecting parts of the country that had previously been isolated from urban centers. Tarsila's 1924 *Central Railroad of Brazil* (FIG. 2.16) is one of these examples.[39]

This painting demonstrates the stylistic technique associated with the artist from around 1923 to 1927, with its

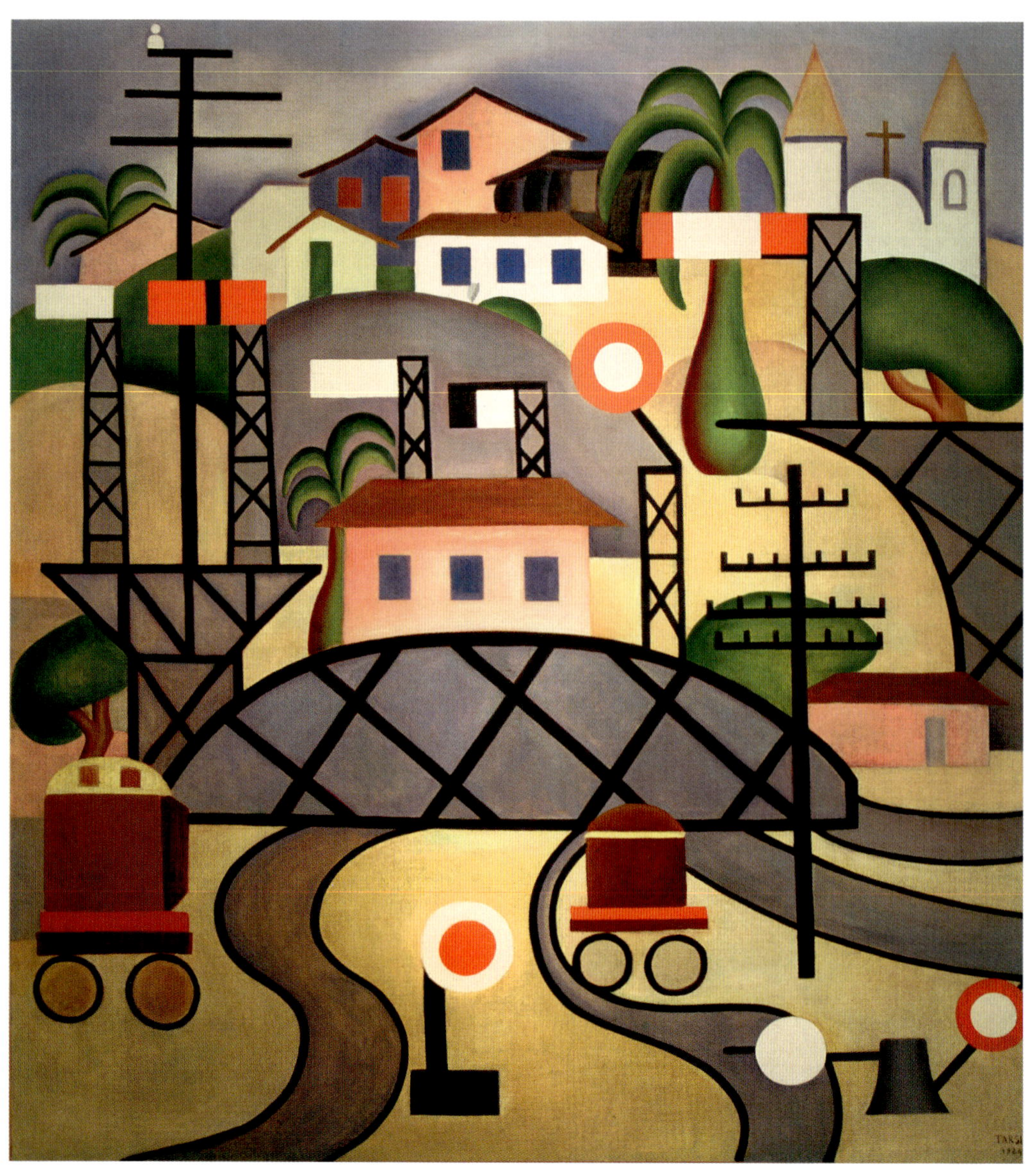

characteristic rounded forms, flat passages of color (reminiscent of the hues of traditional Brazilian architecture), and the geometric proportions of its components. We observe a suburban town dominated by signs of railroad transportation: a railway bridge in the foreground, railroad crossing signs in the lower portion of the composition, stylized railroad cars, and telegraph and electric poles throughout. The traditional small houses and the Baroque church at the upper right seem incongruous within the realm of these new signs of progress and travel. With this painting Tarsila creates a bridge between past and present, indicating a linking of not only places but also temporalities. The vast country is slowly becoming unified, but at the same time old traditions and forms of life are being transformed. *Central Railroad of Brazil* (named for the company that operated throughout the states of Rio de Janeiro and Minas Gerais, and connected Rio with São Paulo[40]) is an indication of a fissure within the culture of a place that was, in the 1920s, characterized by the existence of "timeless" hamlets and villages and vast urban expansion of mega metropolises such as Rio and São Paulo. In the order and quietude of this schematic suburban-scape, the contradictions and refashioning of Brazil at a critical moment in its early modernist history are charted. This image offers us a virtual avant-garde roadmap of the conflicts inherent in a rapidly transforming country, and a component of the hemisphere-wide reconfiguration of physical and psychic circumstances.[41]

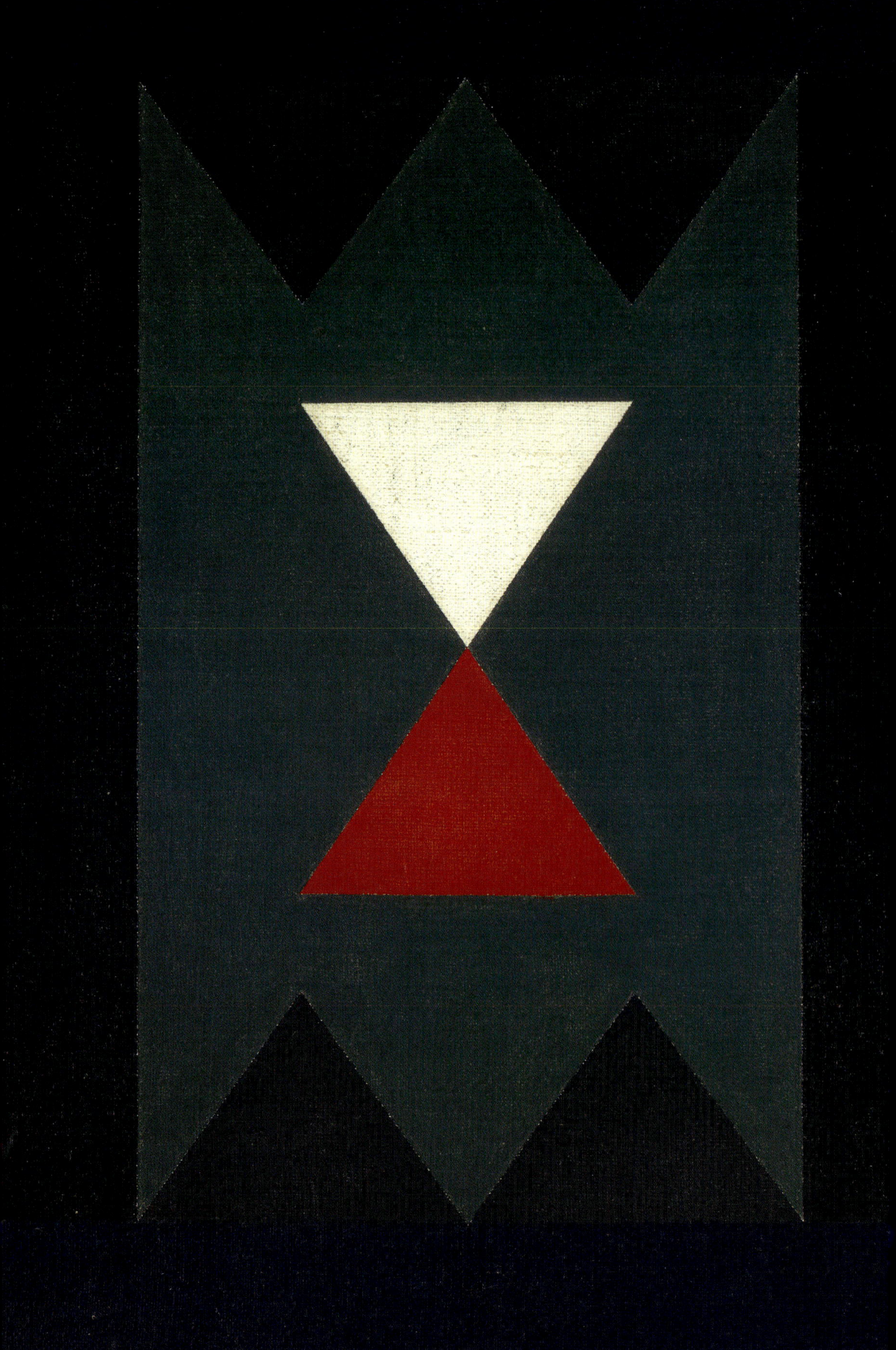

Chapter 3

Visualizing Blackness in the Americas

Throughout this book I discuss many artists of color within the framework of the stories told in each chapter. It is imperative, however, to dedicate considerable attention to the representation of people of African descent in the arts throughout the hemisphere between 1910 and 1960, and to underscore the achievements of the many black artists who were key players in the visual arts in this time period. While these subjects (the image of the black in art, and art by people of color) may appear at first to be interrelated, they are, in fact, separate entities and I have taken as much care as possible to differentiate, where necessary, the varying narratives.

Throughout the history of art in the Americas in the era prior to the one we are dealing with here, black artists held distinguished positions within the aesthetic histories of their respective countries. Afro-Brazilian Rio de Janeiro-based sculptor and architect Valentim da Fonseca e Silva (called Mestre Valentim [c.1745–1813]) and his contemporary, the sculptor and architect Antônio Francisco Lisboa (c.1738–1814), popularly known as O Aleijadinho ("The Little Cripple"), who worked in the mineral-rich area of Minas Gerais, both created some of the most characteristic examples of Brazilian Baroque art. The eminent Puerto Rican portraitist and religious painter José Campeche (1751–1809) was the son of a free man of color and a Spanish-born mother.[1] In the United States, the African-American landscapist Robert S. Duncanson (1821–1872) was influenced by pioneering American landscape painter Thomas Cole (1801–1848), and Philadelphia-trained Henry Ossawa Tanner

Rubem Valentim
Composition, 1960.
See fig. 3.20.

(1859–1937) became as famous in France, where he spent the mature years of his career, as he was in the United States. The sculptor Edmonia Lewis (1844–1907) was of African, Haitian, and Native American descent. Her mature career developed in Rome after initial training in Boston. Among the most successful neoclassical artists of her day, she commanded high prices for her likenesses of figures from ancient and modern history, many of them connected to stories of the struggle for black liberation.

There are dozens of other examples of distinguished artists of African heritage who played key roles throughout the nineteenth and early twentieth centuries. In this chapter I will attempt to suggest the accomplishments of a small representative example of their number. We begin, however, with an assessment of some of the meanings and the problems associated with images of blackness, by both Caucasian artists and those of African descent, as barometers of modernity, beginning in the 1920s.

Blackness in the Modernist Imagination
In around 1916, Brazilian painter Anita Malfatti (1889–1964) created *Tropical* (FIG. 3.1), one of her best-known works and an image that came to signify, along with other representations of people of color by artists associated with the São Paulo modernists, the beginnings of a visual revolution in Brazilian art. While painters of nineteenth-century Brazil (where abolition came only in 1888) had often depicted people of color, they usually did so in genre scenes that tended to emphasize a stereotypical quaintness or picturesque quality to their lives (which was also true in pictorial traditions throughout the hemisphere, at least in those nations where blacks formed substantial proportions of the population). In the worst of scenarios, blacks were shown in caricatures that exaggerated their physiognomic features and emphasized their so-called personal and social characteristics. While such racist images had by no means come to an end in the late 1910s and 20s, people of color were, by this time, being depicted in ways that tended to integrate them within the larger framework of visual imagery and artistic iconography of modern times.

Malfatti's subject has dark skin, although she is probably a person of mixed race.[2] She emerges from a background composed

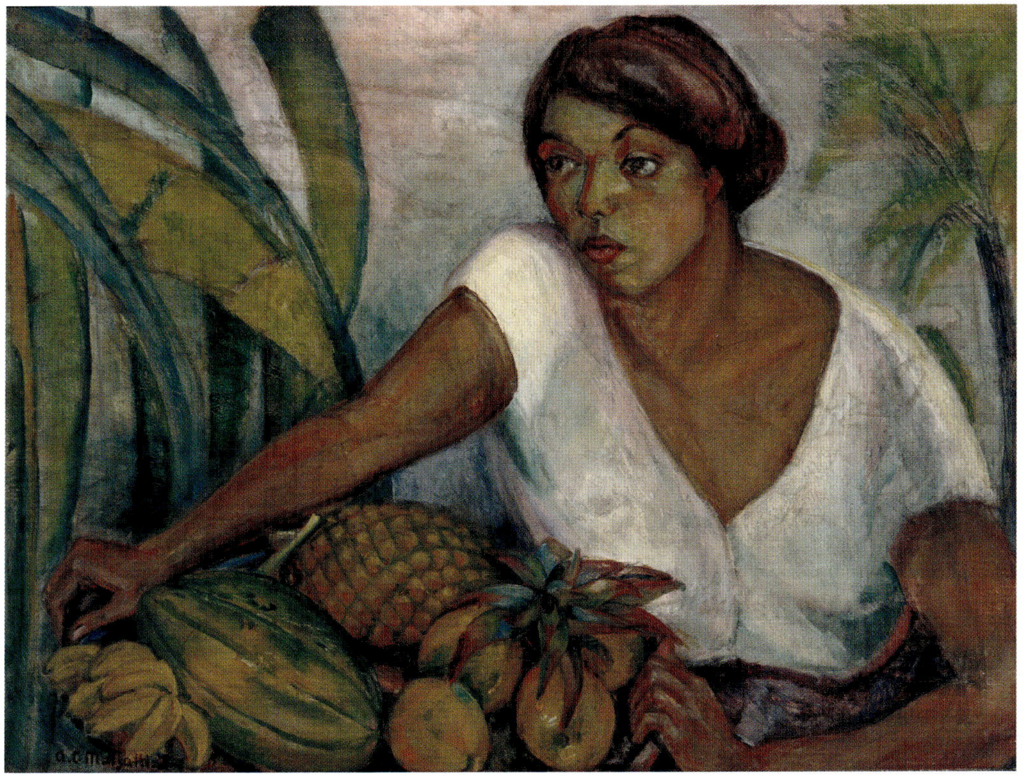

of a palm tree at the right and banana plants at the left, the cli-chéd markers of "tropicality." She proffers to the viewer a basket of locally grown fruits, as if to extend to us the bounty of nature as symbolic of the products of the Brazilian earth. Curiously, however, she avoids the eye of the beholder, turning her face, with its sober expression, to her right. The bright colors and the expressive application of paint look forward to Malfatti's work of the 1920s, in which she achieved her closest proximity to international Expressionism. Malfatti studied with the German Expressionists in Berlin in 1912 and with the experimental painter Homer Boss (1882–1956) at New York's Art Students League in 1915.[3]

Tropical was similar to many of the works in Malfatti's substantial representation in the landmark exhibition associated with the Week of Modern Art of 1922, which is generally thought to have marked the beginning of a wholesale re-evaluation of modern painting, sculpture, and architecture in Brazil.[4] The question of what constitutes the "modernity" in this picture, however, is

Fig. 3.1
Anita Malfatti
Tropical, 1916, oil on canvas, 30⁵⁄₁₆ x 40⁷⁄₈ in. (77 x 102 cm). Pinacoteca do Estado de São Paulo. Donated by the artist in fulfillment of the Art Grant Law, 1929.

often glossed over or not mentioned, with the exception of the novelty of the artist's pictorial approach to color and facture. The black body as representative of everyday life is, I believe, the ostensible aspect of the "newness" of this picture. Brazil's population is substantially mixed race and black, and artists of the modernist generation (including Tarsila do Amaral) employed black subjects as indicators of their dedication to the representation (although in often highly stylized forms) of contemporaneity. Yet this is, in effect, highly problematic, and the fact that white artists throughout the Americas consistently appropriated images of people of color belies a continuing dialogue of arguably latent racism toward blackness. Looking at other prominent examples of this phenomenon drawn from art traditions in several countries at this time might shed more light on this assertion.

Tarsila do Amaral's *A Negra* (The Black Woman) (FIG. 3.2) is well known to anyone interested in the art history of early twentieth-century Brazil, as it represents a jumping-off point for Tarsila's radically new signature style, fashioned by her absorption of the lessons of Cubo-Futurism combined with her particular blend of local references to Brazilian types and subjects. Although it may have been based on the artist's familiarity with Candomblé statuary of Afro-Brazilian deities, this painting stands as a barometer of the directions in which Tarsila do Amaral's art would go within the following ten years.[5] This is a monumental, indeed sculptural, rendition of a black female body whose anatomical features are exaggerated to an extreme degree. Her torso is truncated, her legs cross at an impossible angle, and her facial features are amplified in a way that recalls North American performers of the most nefarious varieties of minstrelsy in the nineteenth and early twentieth centuries. The stylized banana leaves in the background function as a stage set against which the black woman sits, thrusting her forward toward the viewer. Tarsila employed subjects of color in many of her paintings during the 1920s and beyond, especially in her townscapes, in which she inserts equally stylized black bodies as they go about their business on city streets.

A Negra is one of the most well-known emblems of early modernist painting in Brazil, and it is rightly hailed as a landmark in the development of a reconceptualized form of visual expression that marked the way forward in the art history of that country. This image has rarely been critiqued, however, for its obviously troubling representation of the monumental black woman. While the artist may not have intended this picture to be viewed as a caricature, like all works of art it assumes another life and is subject to other criteria of analysis and criticism with the passing of time. In this case, as we understand more accurately the possibly unintentional but nonetheless still pernicious ways of depicting blackness on the part of an elite Euro–Brazilian artist, its negative ramifications are inevitably brought into sharper focus.

Throughout much of his career the Lithuanian-born, German-trained Brazilian artist Lasar Segall (1891–1957) depicted his impressions of Mangue, the district of Rio de Janeiro well known in the first half of the twentieth century as the center of prostitution. Segall's paintings and prints were not the only works to show the female inhabitants of the neighborhood (named for a nearby mangrove swamp). Other painters and writers were fascinated by the activities of Mangue, and numerous works of art and literature resulted from the efforts of such painters as Emiliano Di Cavalcanti (1897–1976), and writers like Mário de Andrade and Jorge de Lima (1893–1953).[6] Among his many depictions of the black sex workers of Mangue is the 1928 engraving and drypoint print *Duas mulheres do Mangue com persiana* (Two Woman of the Mangue with Blinds) (FIG. 3.3). The woman closest to the viewer is seated and wearing a transparent shift or elongated blouse that allows us to see her breasts. Like the painting by Tarsila do Amaral discussed above, she has exaggerated facial features that render her physiognomy more masklike than real. Her companion faces away from us as she peers out to the street (in anticipation of

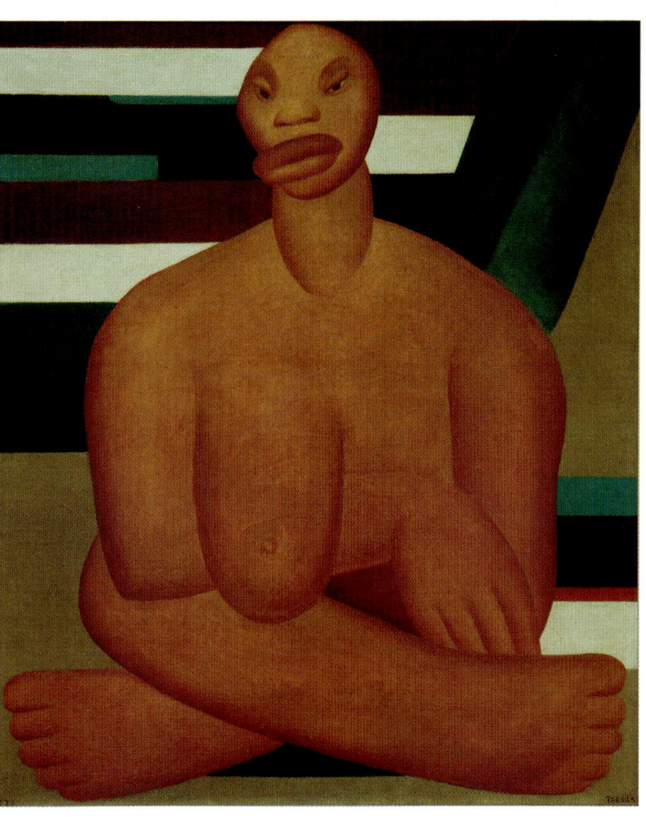

Fig. 3.2
Tarsila do Amaral
A Negra (The Black Woman), 1923, oil on canvas, 39⅜ x 32 in. (100 x 81.3 cm). Museu de Arte Contemporânea da Universidade de São Paulo.

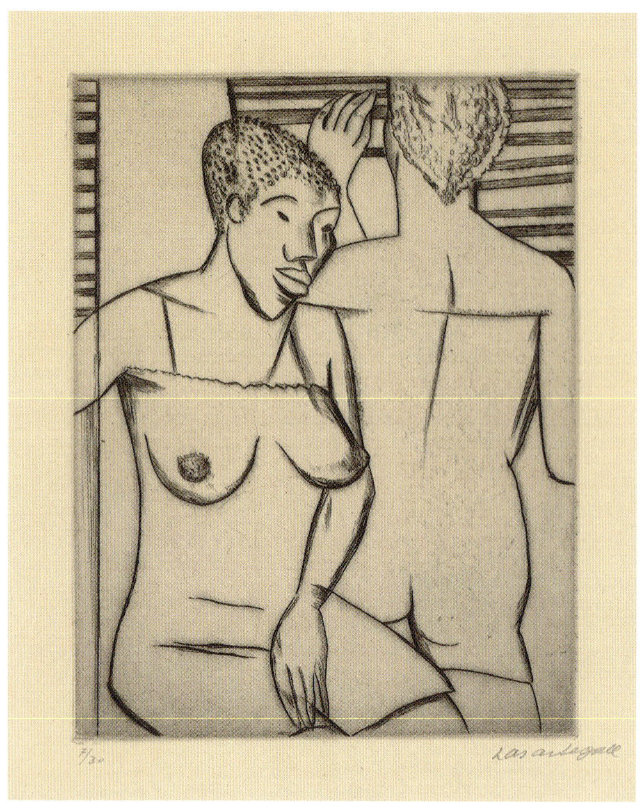

Fig. 3.3
Lasar Segall
Duas mulheres do Mangue com persiana (Two Women of the Mangue with Blinds), 1928, engraving and drypoint, plate 9⅜ x 7 in. (23.7 x 17.8 cm); sheet 22¼ x 15⅛ in. (56.5 x 38.3 cm). Museum of Modern Art, New York. Inter-American Fund (1388.1968).

the arrival of a client?) through a closed blind.

Such depictions of scenes from the lives of prostitutes are, of course, common within the transnational iconography of Expressionism, and their most enthusiastic practitioners were the German and Austrian Expressionists with whom Segall was trained in Berlin and Dresden.[7] All such images demean their subjects, commodifying their bodies and illustrating them as pawns in base commercial transactions. While Segall depicted Caucasian prostitutes from time to time, the black residents of Mangue were of greater interest to him as representative of the Otherness of an already a priori activity outside the realm of conventional respectability—and all the more tantalizingly so, given their status, both racially and socially. The black body becomes, in such prints and paintings by the white European immigrant to a highly racially varied society, a vehicle for his expression of displacement in the midst of diversity, and an instrument of his voyeuristic attraction to the clichéd notion of the potent sexual allure of blackness.

Another set of questions is presented by a work that represents a milestone in the development of modern art in the Caribbean. *Nude* (1941) by Dominican artist Celeste Woss y Gil (1891–1985) (FIG. 3.4) depicts a mulatta, a mixed-race and dark-skinned woman of primarily African descent, posing in a voluptuous attitude of a studio model.

Woss y Gil was the product of academic instruction in Santiago de Cuba and New York's Art Students League (where she studied between 1922 and 1924). This is her best-known depiction of a person of color. It is also a product of a vibrant period in the visual arts when Santo Domingo became a center for the immigration of Spanish painters fleeing the civil war in their country (1936–39). Woss y Gil had long been instrumental in modernizing Dominican art, and her representations of the female nude were groundbreaking in the conservative context of painting in that country.[8] The date of this work may seem to some to indicate a lack of synchronicity with the conventional view of the expected course of artistic developments, yet within the conservative context of Dominican painting, a picture of a black female nude—and one done by a woman artist—was revolutionary for the milieu in which it was created. This fact also serves to underscore the multiplicity of parallel and intersecting time lines that mark the advance of a modern spirit in art in the Americas, each center having its own pace and its own priorities.

Woss y Gil's nude model is not the product of a desirous male gaze, yet neither is it the product of a black artist observing individuals of their own race. The artist was a representative of the elites of the nation (her father, Alejandro Woss y Gil, had been president of the Dominican Republic between 1885 and 1887 and again in 1903) and in this and other related paintings, Woss y Gil evokes a subject—the mulatta—that had been a theme of Caribbean art and literature since the nineteenth century. Women of mixed race had often been depicted in paintings by artists such as the Hispano-Cuban painter Víctor Patricio Landaluze (1830–1889), while novels such as *Cecilia Valdés* (first published in Havana in 1839) by Cirilio Villaverde (1812–1894) explored and sometimes caricatured the sexual allure of women of color.[9] Therefore, we have in Woss y Gil's

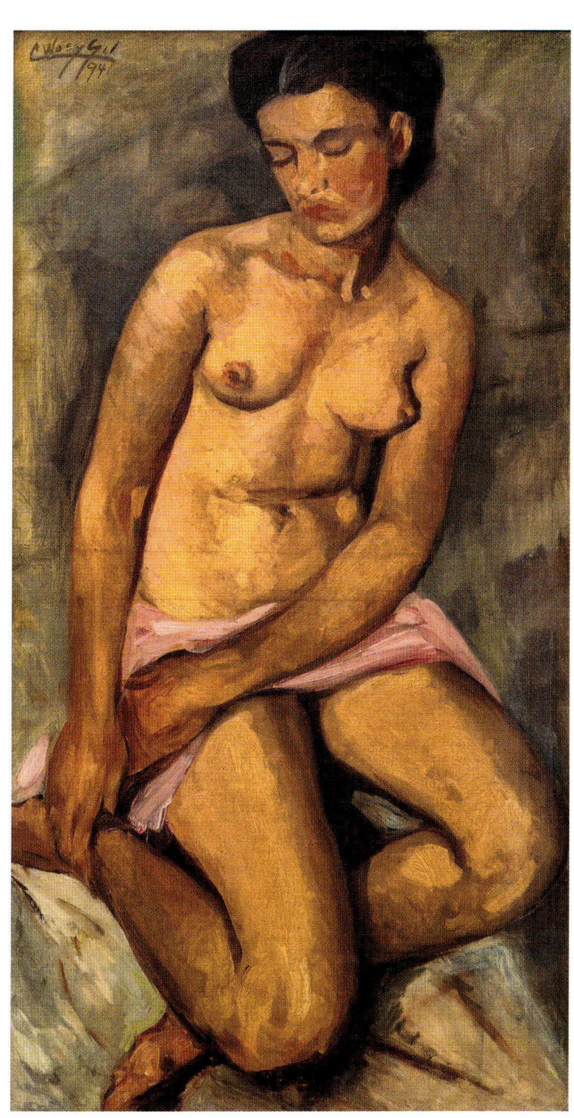

Fig. 3.4
Celeste Woss y Gil
Desnudo (Nude), 1941, oil on canvas, 26 x 33 in. (66 x 83.8 cm). Museo de Arte Moderno, Santo Domingo (Dominican Republic).

painting a modernized depiction of the black body seemingly without the voyeuristic baggage of such images painted by men. On the other hand, however, there is still the lingering exoticization and manipulation of the allure of blackness to appeal to the predominantly white, upper-class audience who would have constituted the consumers of this form of art.

Blackness, Dance, Music, and Ritual

The history of modern art in the Río de la Plata region (Buenos Aires and Montevideo) is often connected to the rise of geometric abstraction, beginning with Joaquín Torres-García and that of the members of his Workshop, and continuing on to the achievements of artists associated with more severe forms of abstract painting and sculpture, such as the members of the group known as Madí (See Chapter 7). Nonetheless, a key player in this complex story is that of Pedro Figari (1861–1938), a protean artist mainly known for his figure compositions of scenes in the rural and urban sites of his native Uruguay.[10] Many of his small paintings—often on cardboard—depict the life of the gauchos, the cowboys of the vast pampas, or plains, of Uruguay, Argentina, and Brazil, whose customs and lifestyle had almost completely ceased to exist when Figari's artistic career began in earnest in the early 1920s (he had played roles in Uruguayan politics and practiced as an attorney before then). Figari's style was an eclectic and highly original mixture of modernist visualities; his color-saturated paintings incorporate elements of Art Deco, Postimpressionism, Fauvism, and Expressionism, all in the service of his unique and often nostalgic vision of his nation.

The black population of Uruguay, which since the nineteenth century had been particularly extensive in Montevideo, was another favorite subject. Africans began arriving in Uruguay from the port of Buenos Aires as slaves in the eighteenth century, and by 1800 the country's population was 25 percent Afro-Uruguayan.[11] *Negro Dance* (FIG. 3.5) is undated (like most of Figari's paintings) but could plausibly be ascribed to the late 1920s or early 30s. The subject, a festival or simply a dance party in an outdoor urban setting, is an often-repeated theme throughout his work. The composition is divided into three parts. The main section depicts an isocephalically situated group of some 22 individuals, all dressed in fancy, party-colored clothing. They are dancing to the sound of drums being played by several men on a raised balcony at the upper right, while a woman in a window at upper left observes the scene. To suggest a special event, a large textile has been hung like a tapestry on the wall behind the dancers at the left. In some of Figari's compositions of black dancers (many of whom are shown performing the *candombe*, a dance and drum ritual mainly practiced in Uruguay, having originated in West Africa) the cloth adorning the space is recognizably African and reminiscent of kente cloth manufactured in the Akan ethnic communities of southern Ghana and the Ivory Coast, characterized by tightly woven and brilliantly colored geometric patterns. The faces of Figari's dancers are masklike and their features are exaggerated, as with the smiling face of the woman at the window. Figari's depictions of blacks have usually been understood as images of nostalgia for the popular traditions of the capital's past, yet the distinct Otherness of these people of color in a country that is now considered to be the whitest in South America (it had a negligible indigenous population and the

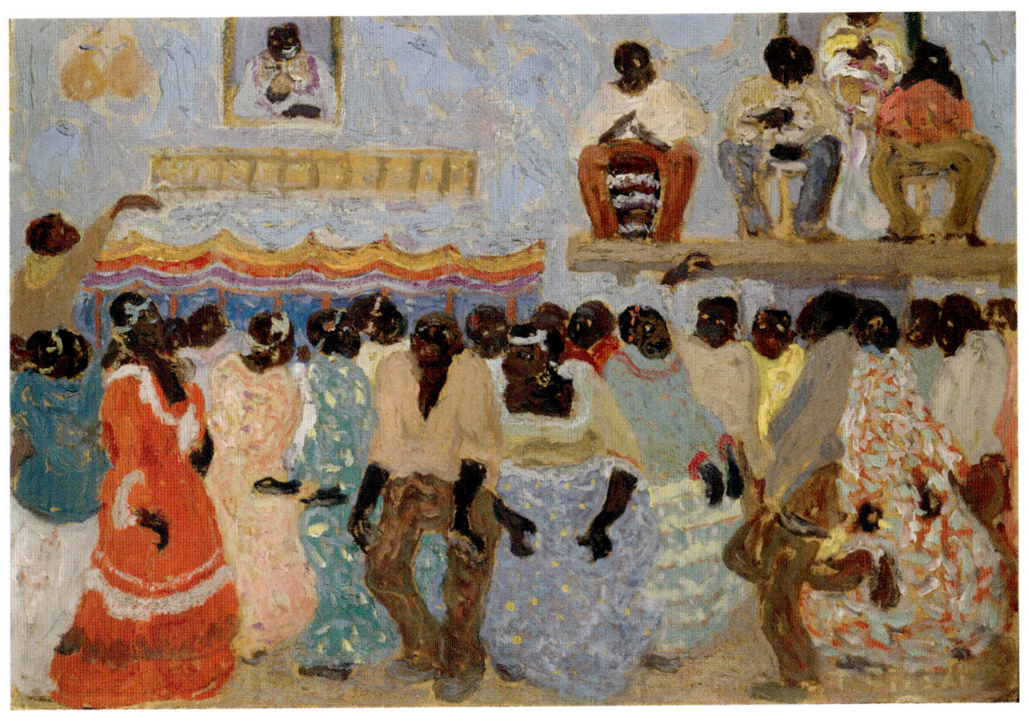

majority of its inhabitants were descended from immigrants from southern and eastern Europe) is hardly separable from sentiments associated with stereotypes surrounding the life and mores of blacks, including their interest in dance and music.

The history of modernity in art on both sides of the Atlantic could be written, in part, from the wide variety of references to and depictions of dance. There were, of course, "modern" popular dances such as the Charleston, which was, in itself, a mark of up-to-dateness. In many cases dance is associated with ethnicity, and ethnicity is associated with exoticism. The performance of ethnicity for audiences, whether in visual representations (paintings, photographs) or in real time in public spaces associated with cabarets, dance halls, or night clubs, also had associations of both "the modern" and "the primitive." Thus such dancer-performers as the African Americans Ada Smith (known as "Bricktop" for her red hair) and Josephine Baker—both of whom realized immense success in Paris, the destination city for so many African-American performers, artists, and intellectuals for its alleged lack of racial prejudice—represented for at least two generations of audiences in the United States and Europe both the glamorously exotic and the ultra-modern.[12]

A further look at (almost but not exclusively white) Latin American and Caribbean visual artists who employed themes of dance in compositions that, at the same time, evinced a sense of modernity in their rejection of any lingering strains of conservative academicism, will reveal the image of the black body as central to this performative sensibility—a sensibility that demonstrates the voyeuristic allure of the dance traditions themselves, and what they evoke as components of national identity. At the same time, however, the insistence upon the black body in movement underscores the trope of primitivism as it is evidenced in rhythmic syncopation.

Merengue by Dominican modernist Jaime Colson (1901–1975) (FIG. 3.6) was painted in 1937. In a small exterior space exposed to the open air, nine people participate in a dance party. They sway to the rhythms of an accordion, drum, and a güiro, a Caribbean instrument made from a gourd and played with a comblike pick or the musician's fingernails. The dance for which the picture is named probably originated with West African

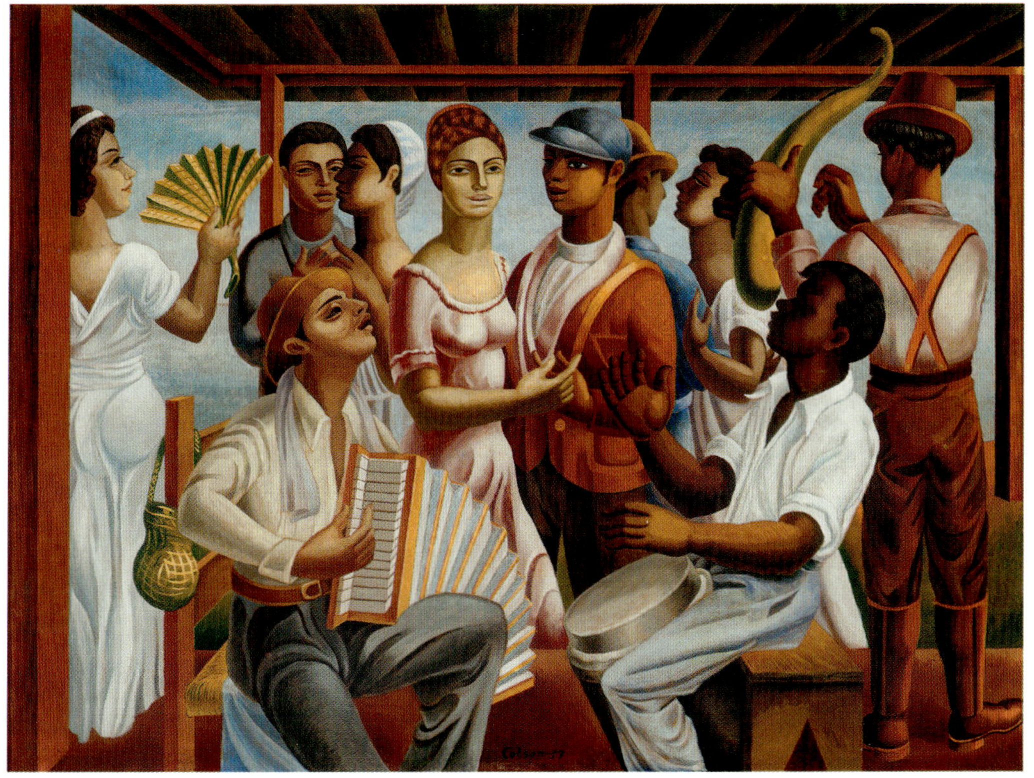

slaves working in the sugarcane fields of the eastern sector of Hispaniola, today known as the Dominican Republic. In this painting the couples dance close to each other to rapid music. Colson, an artist who spent several decades in Paris and assimilated a variety of modernist modes from Cubism to Surrealism, here (in a picture whose rounded forms present a faint echo of the art of Fernand Léger) translates his visual resources into a distinctly local idiom and, in his depiction of this group, offers the viewer a virtual encyclopedia of the variations on blackness in Dominican society.[13]

Victor Manuel García (1897–1969) was one of the most well-known members of the group of painters that emerged in Havana in the late 1920s. Known as the "Generation of '27" (for the landmark show of that year, *Exposición de Arte Nuevo,* in which Victor Manuel García and his artistic contemporaries participated), artists such as Eduardo Abela (1889–1965), Amelia Peláez (1896–1968), Antonio Gattorno (1904–1980), and others demonstrated their opposition to the lessons and the standard

Fig. 3.6
Jaime Colson
Merengue, 1937, tempera on board, 20½ x 26¾ in. (52 x 68 cm). Museo Juan José Bellapart, Santo Domingo (Dominican Republic).

subjects of the art to which most of them had been exposed in the Cuban capital's Academia de San Alejandro, one of the oldest academies in the hemisphere.[14] These artists represented the first of two Vanguard Generations (the second included Afro-Cuban artist Wifredo Lam [1902–1982], whose work we will examine shortly) that revolutionized Cuban painting and gained widespread recognition. The successful 1944 exhibition at New York's Museum of Modern Art entitled *Modern Cuban Painters* accounted, to a great extent, for their initial fame in the U.S. market of museums and collectors.[15]

Carnaval (Carnival) (FIG. 3.7) is undated but was likely painted in the 1940s. It depicts one of the quintessential moments in popular Caribbean culture when dance, song, and ritual performance meld into a week's worth of celebration prior to the start of the Lenten season. A pan-Caribbean phenomenon, Carnival has a particularly long and complex history in Cuba, where it was a product of colonial festivities, enhanced with the participation of enslaved persons or freed slaves who were permitted

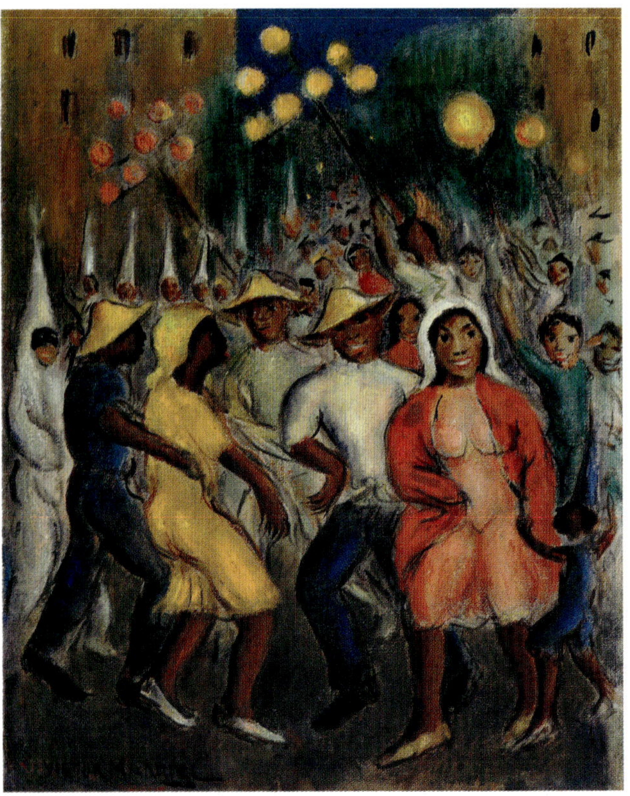

to participate in this as well as the post-Christmas celebrations of the Feast of the Epiphany, or Three Kings Day (January 6). Victor Manuel (as he is always called in Cuba) shows us a crowded street scene with men and women in both modern garb and traditional dress (including a group at the left wearing costumes resembling the conical-hatted *penitentes*, or penitent figures of the Spanish Inquisition). All participants are dark-skinned and all are involved in some form of dance. Carnival is not necessary an all-black ceremony/performance, yet Victor Manuel has chosen to paint black bodies, making them the embodiments of the musical and rhythmic components of the event. This sets up a dichotomy and a separation between the subjects and the artist (and, to a certain extent, the viewer—supposing that the audience for Vanguard painting in 1940s Cuba would be the white elite collectors and museum- or gallery-goers) based on racial terms.

At the heart of many of the remarks in this chapter is the question of the representation of people of color by Caucasians and other non-blacks, as opposed to the depiction of blacks by black artists. Perhaps such a binary is not present in any programmatically described fashion, and the objectification and even caricature of the black body that often exists in white artists' representations of blackness (which is perhaps more pronounced in art of earlier time periods, such as the nineteenth and the early twentieth century in the United States, Europe, and, to a lesser degree, Latin America) is present even in depictions of blacks by black artists, as has been eloquently pointed out by Richard Powell and other chroniclers of African-American arts.[16] Nonetheless it is imperative, I think, that we examine the differences and contrast images of similar subjects by artists on both sides of the racial divide. The theme that I have developed here, of representations of modern dance (and modern dancing—a different subject altogether), might be used in this instance as a "control" in an experiment aimed at analyzing the varieties of approach.

Archibald Motley (1891–1981) was a crucial figure in the Harlem Renaissance, a widespread cultural phenomenon that occurred throughout the United States in the 1920s and 30s. This was a loosely cohesive movement in the arts—literary, musical, and visual—that marked a culmination of black creativity, a direct engagement with transnational forms of modernity, and a point of departure for the careers of dozens of distinguished painters, photographers, writers, composers, and others who continued working on themes related to all forms of black life and experience, not only in New York but also in cities like Chicago (where Motley was born), Washington, Boston, and Baltimore.[17] Motley, whose career has been the subject of assiduous research and exhibitions in recent years, often employed the theme of dance as a vehicle to express not only lively movement but also the integration of people of color within the world of thoroughly modern cultural associations.[18]

Motley painted *Blues* in 1929 (FIG. 3.8). Couples are seated at small cabaret tables; others are dancing at the left-hand portion of the composition, which is also punctuated by the presence of the band's instruments—a trombone, a clarinet, and a horn. The color scheme is muted, to reflect the darkness of an after-hours *boîte*. Motley's picture was painted in Paris, where he had gone the year of its creation on a grant from the Guggenheim Foundation. Powell, who posits that the setting of the painting is the well-known Parisian cabaret Le Bal Nègre, has analyzed this composition. He states that

Motley (with his fractured approach to pictorial elements and humanity) accurately reflected the racial and cultural rainbow— European, African, Caribbean and North American—that characterized Jazz Age Paris at that time. Motley's multiplicity of composition elements in Blues … were not unlike the 'riffs' and 'stop time' of musical relative Louis Armstrong ….[19]

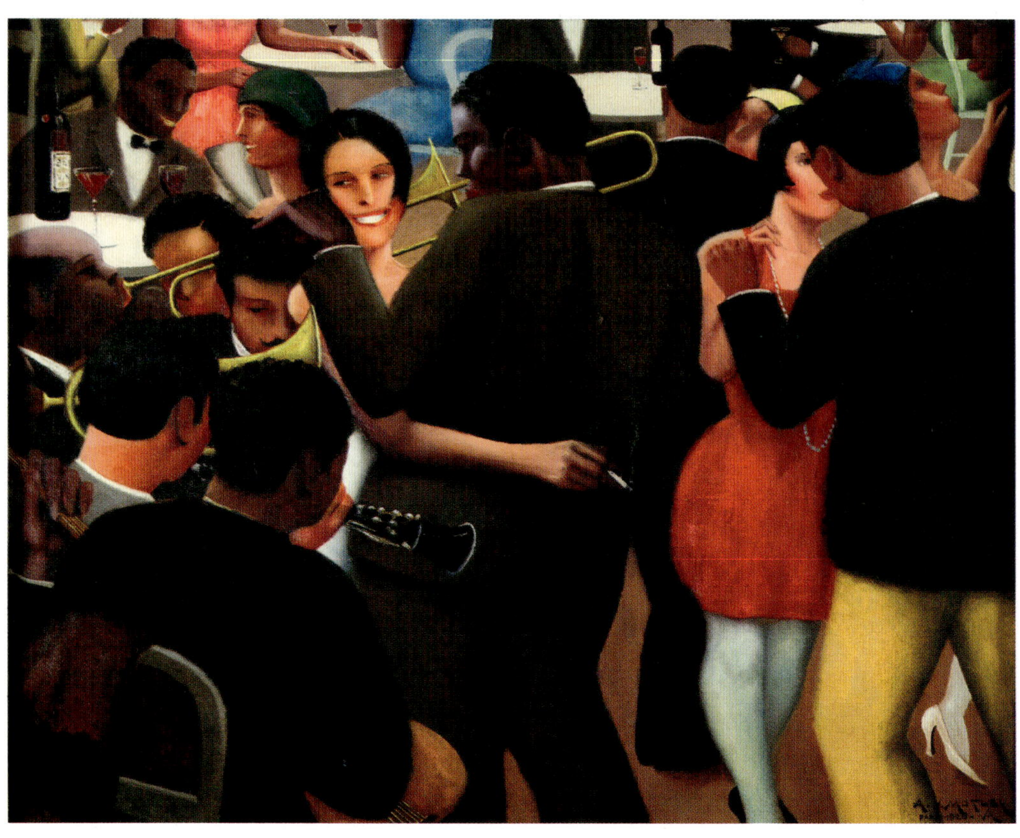

At the same time that Motley integrated the various participants within the "performance" of a modern social and musical experience—jazz and its danceable rhythms—he succeeded in de-exoticizing the presence of the black body within the space of a field of vision that was, in the hands of artists we have examined above, the venue for curiosity and even caricature. In Motley's imagining of blackness, dance is an integral part of a normal flow of emotional and physical movement in which participants of all racial hues could, and naturally would, participate.

Black Faces, Black Bodies

At the time that Edna Manley (1900–1987) created her mahogany sculpture entitled *Negro Aroused* (FIG. 3.9) in 1935, when Jamaica was a colony in the British Empire, she could hardly have known that this work, later reproduced in 1938 on a monumental scale in bronze, would become an emblem of Jamaican nationhood and a symbol of the strength of blackness on the island.

The work is composed of plain and imposing lines. It is virtually a relief; there is little depth and its curvilinear nature belies its family resemblance to Art Deco's sleek, sensuous forms. This male figure is depicted in half-length, his neck craning to see the sky. His arms are elongated and his large hands are clasped together, rooted in the base of the sculpture, which serves as a metaphor for the fertile earth of the country. Together with other of Manley's well-known representations of the male and female black body from the 1930s and beyond, *Negro Aroused* and Manley's art as a whole set a standard for the following generations of artists, painters, and sculptors alike, who would represent the first waves of modern artists in Jamaica.

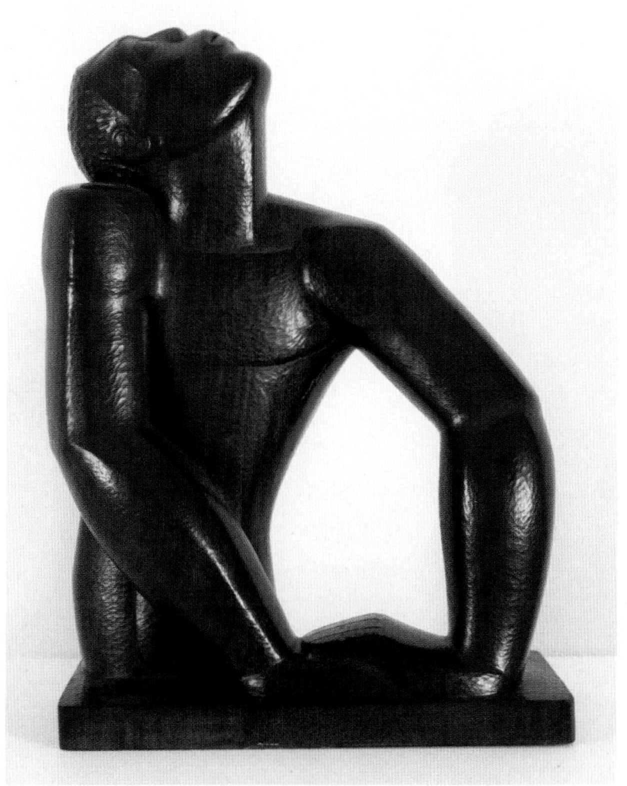

The subject matter of blackness and the expressions of the supremacy of the worker and the potential of the descendants of generations of enslaved Africans who had been nominally emancipated by the British colonial government in 1838 (although kept in check in many other less obvious but equally insidious ways since then) was apposite to the circumstances of the island in the 1930s. Although Jamaica did not achieve full independence until 1962, the 1930s was a period that proved to be crucial for the gradual march toward liberation. The emancipation campaigns of Marcus Garvey (1887–1940) were integral parts of this movement. This Jamaican native accomplished perhaps more than anyone else in raising the awareness of the working populations of the country, as he had done with considerable success in the United States and elsewhere where black populations continued to feel oppression and the effects of segregation on a daily basis. His "Back to Africa" project was a crucial tool for raising consciousness among black populations on both sides of the Atlantic.

The year of Manley's creation of *Negro Aroused* was a critical one on the road to independence. Throughout the English-speaking Caribbean, labor unrest in the form of strikes and riots broke out in many places due, mostly, to economic privation resulting from the global Depression. Marcus Garvey left Jamaica for Britain in 1935, continuing his activism for black agency and self-determination in the Caribbean from a base of operations across the sea. Manley's sculpture soon entered the collective consciousness of Jamaica's black and mixed-race populations not only as emblematic of the social and political desires of the vast majority of islanders of African origin, but also as the embodiment of the enthusiasm with which they embraced the anti-colonialist struggle. Stylistically, we may consider what Jamaican art historian Veerle Poupeye has described as the work's "silhouette quality." She further makes a connection to the formal and emotional content of the paintings and murals of Harlem Renaissance artist Aaron Douglas (1899–1979) and his Art Deco approach to design to suggest direct links with the artistic movements taking place among black artists in the United States in the 1930s.[20]

Manley was born in Bournemouth, England, the daughter of a Jamaican mother and a British father. She was trained at Saint

Martin's School of Art in London and moved to Jamaica with her husband, Norman Manley (1893–1969, also her cousin), in 1922. Norman Manley was the founder of the Jamaican People's National Party (and he served as the first Premier of Jamaica, from 1959 to 1962). His political consciousness and support of the black working classes found visual manifestations in the works of his wife. Her artistic efforts established a new path for Jamaican art and, in effect, influenced the directions of the teaching and practice of painting and sculpture in other parts of the Anglophone Caribbean.[21] Manley was as important a teacher as she was an artist; her pedagogical career had begun in 1940 when she began giving classes at the Jamaica Institute. Throughout the rest of her life her courses in drawing, painting, and sculpture, as well as those of the artists who joined her effort in Kingston, at the Jamaica School of Art and Crafts—later renamed the Edna Manley College of the Visual and Performing Arts—were crucial for the growth of a wide variety of modern art styles.

One of the constants of Jamaican subject matter in the arts in the period under consideration here is the role played by the black body within the social and political circumstances of the island's history and everyday life. Jamaica presents an interesting case within the development of the visual arts in the 1930s and 40s. Even though it was "relatively isolated from artistic developments in the neighboring islands until the fifties,"[22] there are a number of other sculptors of note (such as Alvin Marriott, 1902–1992) and the rise of the first generation of what have been called the Intuitives, self-trained artists whose dreamlike, highly personalized compositions garnered widespread acclaim.[23]

Other sites in the Caribbean also witnessed advances in sculpture by black artists who depicted people of color. If in *Negro Aroused* we sense reminiscences of African wood-carving (Edna Manley amassed a collection of African sculpture that became well known in Kingston), the same may be said of artists of all races in a pan-Caribbean framework who participated in the transnational fascination for African art.[24]

Teodoro Ramos Blanco (1902–1972) was a product of the Havana Academia de San Alejandro as well as numerous study trips abroad. He was one of the relatively few Afro-Caribbean artists (along with Wifredo Lam, discussed below) to gain

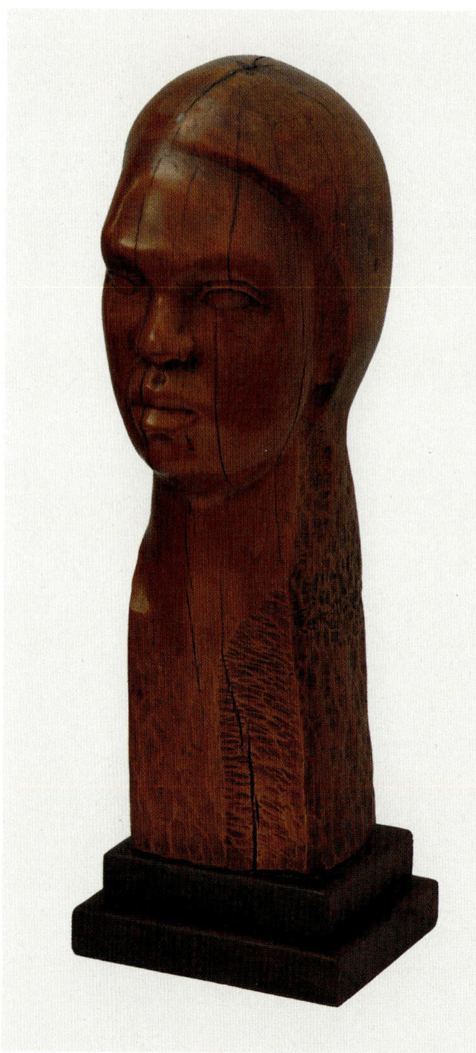

international fame in the first half of the twentieth century. His *Cabeza de negra* (Head of a Black Woman) (FIG. 3.10), made of mastic wood (called *jocuma* in Cuba) and carved only two years after Manley's *Negro Aroused*, evidences an interest in African art, which had impressed him during his trips to Paris. While Ramos Blanco's sculpture did not gain national-symbol status in Cuba, this and related heads and full-length figures of black bodies all express a sense of nobility and serenity that characterizes his conception of the Afro-Cuban form.

Portraiture by black artists at this time (the 1930s) often employs a realistic style and a sympathetic approach to the subject. Two examples from the repertory of portraits of African-American artists may serve to suggest the trends of the moment. Charles Wilbert White (1918–1979) is best known for his social realist murals at Hampton University in Virginia (1943), as well as for his teaching at the Otis College of Art and Design in his adopted city of Los Angeles, where he mentored, among others, Kerry James Marshall (b. 1955), celebrated for his monumental paintings representing his highly personal interpretations of African-American life in the contemporary United States.[25] However, White's portraits from the early phase of his development are representative examples of a manner of sober, refined depictions of African Americans. The 1936 *Untitled (Seated African–American Man)* (FIG. 3.11) is a study in muted color harmonies. The cigarette-smoking young model is shown in half-length wearing a multicolored shirt seen through his open brown jacket. He looks out to his left in a pensive manner. The background is articulated with shades of gray, dark green, and deep brown, pushing the figure out from the murky darkness into our own space. White builds up the surface of the picture with broad strokes

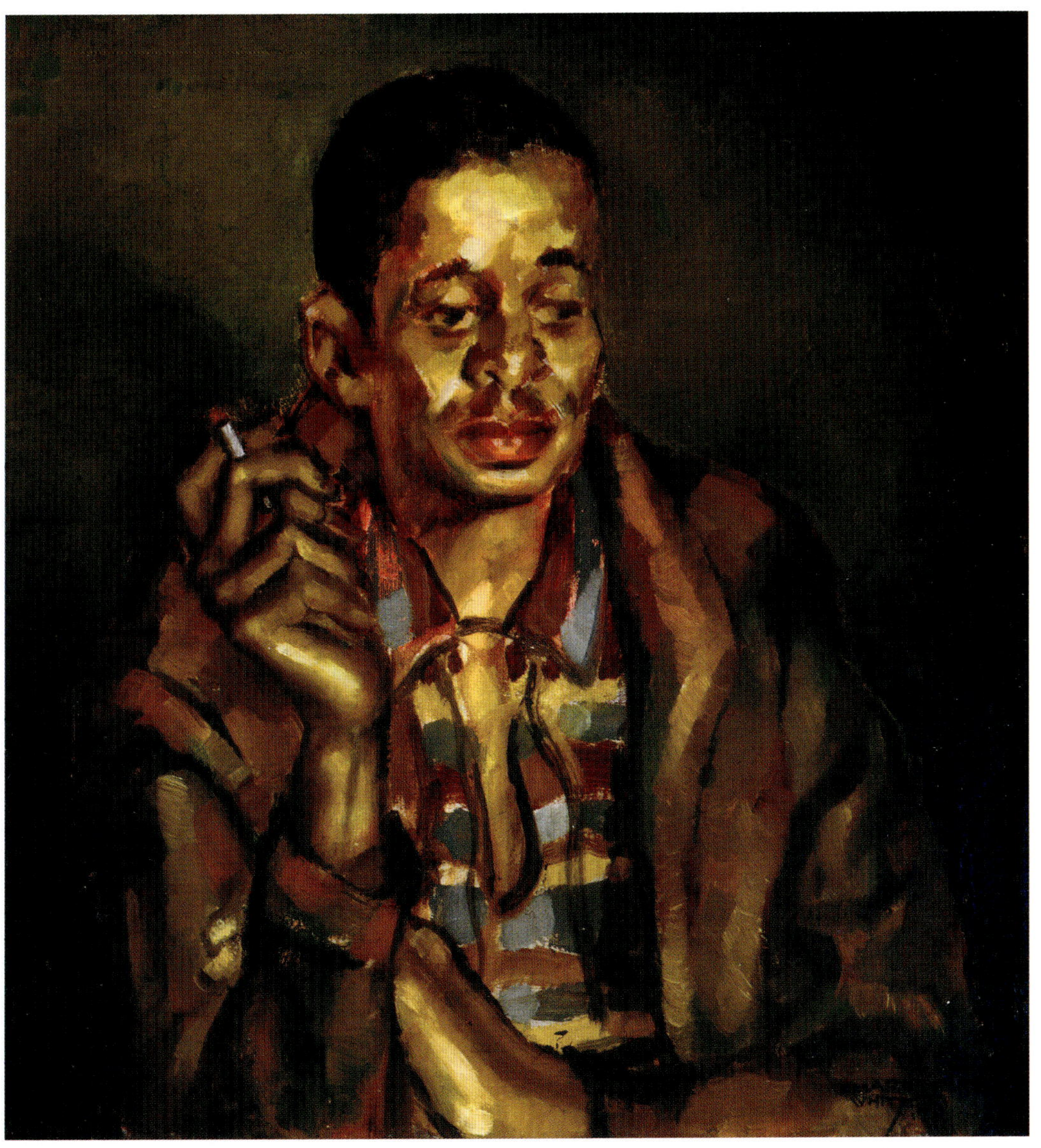

of paint. The definition of the pattern of the shirt as well as the faceting effect of the face remind us of the early impact of Cubism on the artist's sensibility. There is an air of reverie, a meditative sensibility in this painting that inevitably leads us to think of the melancholy pervasive within the portrayal of this individual.

The sitter in Loïs Mailou Jones's *Dans un café à Paris (Leigh Whipper)* (FIG. 3.12) is well known. Whipper was a renowned

Fig. 3.11
Charles Wilbert White
Untitled (Seated African-American Man), 1936, oil on canvas, 22 x 20 in. (55.9 x 50.8 cm). Courtesy of Michael Rosenfeld Gallery LLC, New York.

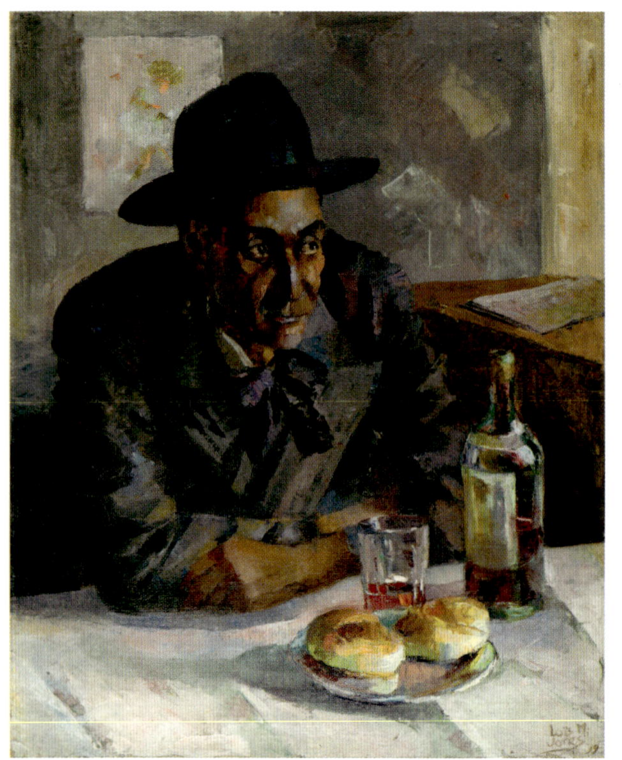

black actor on Broadway and in Hollywood who, in 1939, the year he was painted by Jones, was acclaimed for his performance in the film adaptation of John Steinbeck's novel *Of Mice and Men*. His success represented an important step in breaking down one of the many color barriers that threatened and intimidated blacks in the American entertainment industry.

Jones (1905–1998) was a major figure in the Harlem Renaissance as a painter and teacher for some 40 years at Howard University in Washington, D.C. When she painted Whipper, the Boston-trained artist had recently returned from a year's study trip to Paris, where she attended the Académie Julian, an institution that had traditionally admitted scores of foreign students since its founding in the nineteenth century. The Whipper portrait, in which the sitter wears a large black hat and extravagant cravat, attests to Jones's absorption of academic modes of representation of the human figure, combined with structural components derived from Cubism as well as nineteenth-century Realism and Impressionism. This café scene, with its foreground still life of a plate with bread, a wine bottle, and a glass, brings to mind similar renditions of single or multiple figures in a bistro setting by Édouard Manet (1832–1883) or Edgar Degas (1834–1917). Jones maintained significant relationships with other artists of African descent in the United States, France, and the Caribbean. Haiti was a country to which she was particularly attracted. She taught at the Centre d'Art (the country's principal art school and gallery) in the 1950s, and many of her later paintings and drawings are drawn from remembrances of her extensive experiences both there and at the Foyer des Arts Plastiques in Port-au-Prince, an artist's group that championed internationalist modern forms of art.[26]

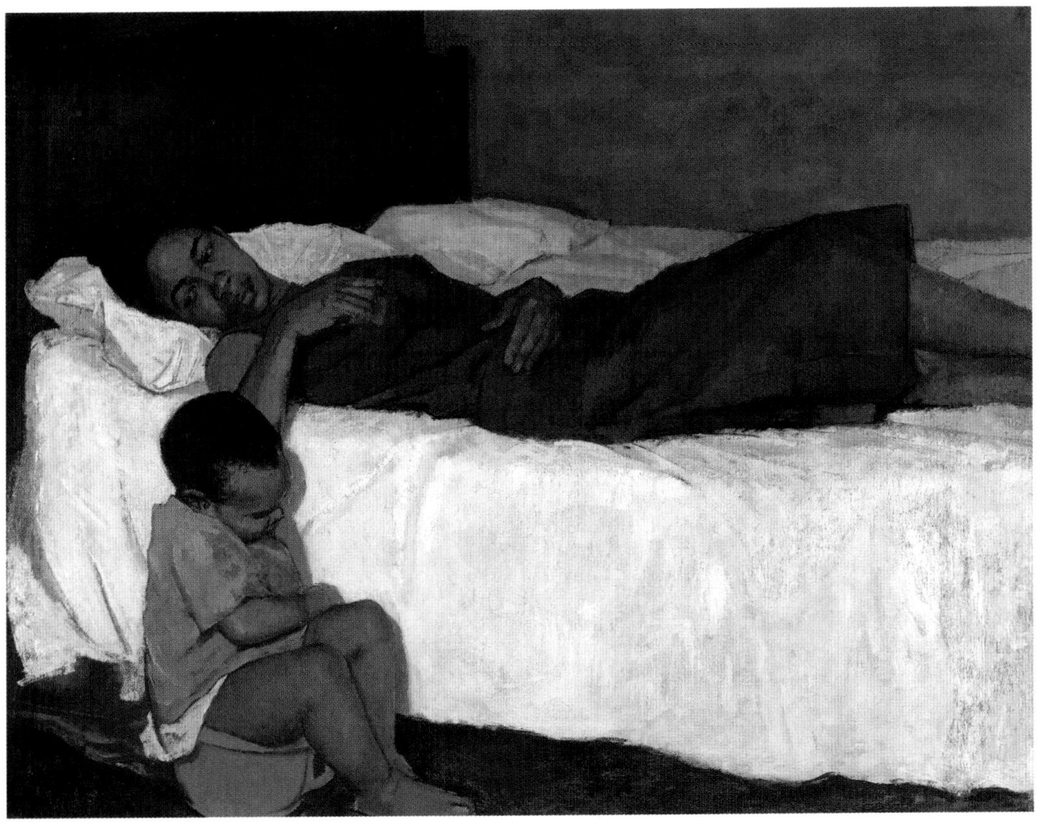

As a final image in this section I return to Jamaica and the traditions of representing the black body that had been established in Edna Manley's classrooms and in those of her students from the 1930s onward. The 1958–59 painting *Mother and Child* by Barrington Watson (1931–2016) (FIG. 3.13) is a poignant image that represents a daily activity in the life of a young woman—toilet-training her child. The mother, wearing a simple green dress, reclines on a bed covered by a white sheet. She looks both lovingly and exhaustedly at a small boy sitting on a commode—an unusual subject, but one that evidences the artist's interest in confronting all the elements of human experience, including bodily functions. The mundane, even anecdotal, aspect infusing this picture removes it decisively from the realm of the sentimental and places it squarely within the practice of subtly ennobling the quotidian affairs of black Jamaicans. Watson's narrative thus emerges from the mode of genre painting to enter the realm of social engagement.

Fig. 3.13
Barrington Watson
Mother and Child, 1958-59, oil on canvas, 39⅜ x 50 in. (100.3 x 106.1 cm). National Gallery of Jamaica, Kingston. Gift of Valerie Facey and the Boswell Facey Trust.

Labor and Struggle

Albert Huie (1920–2010) painted *Crop Time* (FIG. 3.14) in 1955 Jamaica, during an era of continuing political and social crisis for the country. British rule would last for only seven more years. Labor strikes were common and the nation was experiencing a period of transition that also included the stark contrasts of the urban/rural divide. Huie's painting defines this consequential period within the context of two forms of labor, manual and industrialized. This picture is an evocation of a double landscape. The lower two thirds of the image are taken up with a view of sugar harvesting. Dozens of men and women are involved in all the manual activities implied in the cutting, bundling, and transport of the sugarcane. The men wear hats and white clothes as they undertake the often-dangerous work. The women wear head wraps and plain dresses as they hover at the lower left

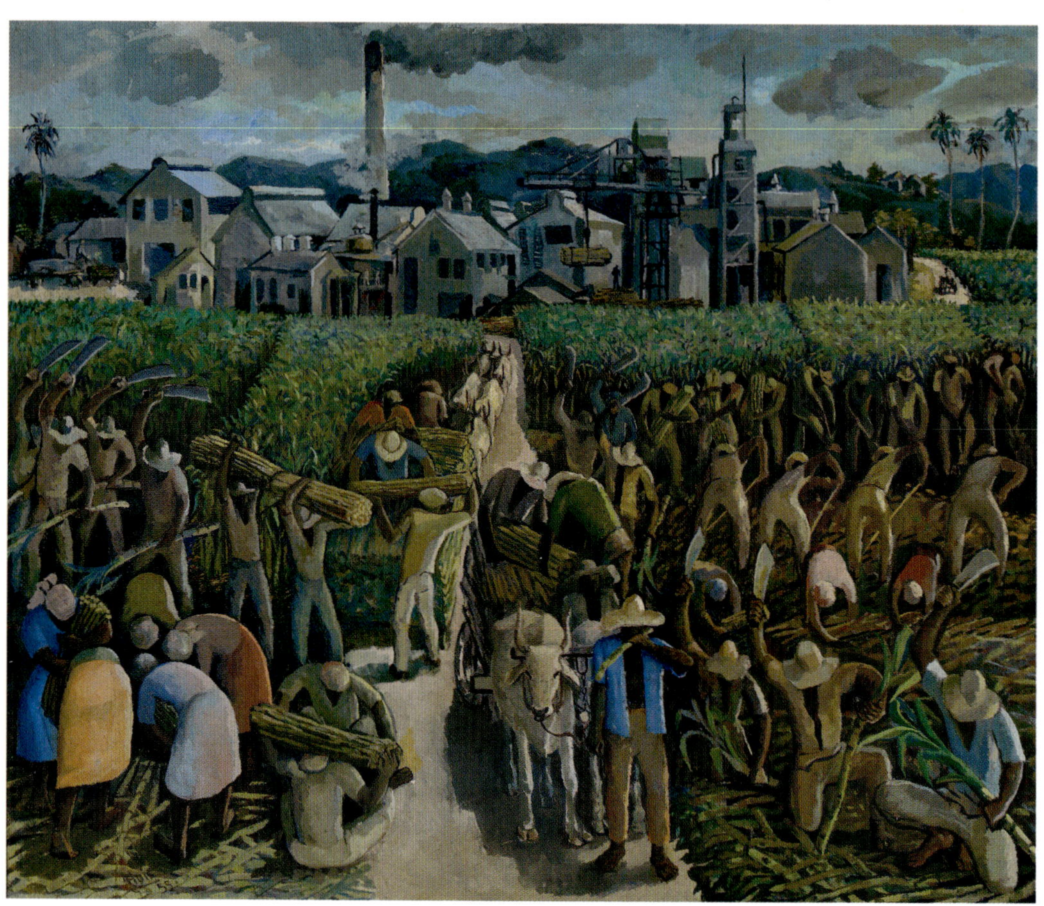

of the painting, preparing the cane or gleaning the remaining bits from the ground. A path between the foreground and the background connects the two registers of the painting, forming the road taken by the ox-drawn carts from the fields to the processing plant in the background. The lower to middle half of the work represents a veritable sea of black bodies engaged in their exhausting labors, just as they had for centuries all over the Caribbean. The plant is a modern structure with numerous buildings, a smokestack, and an elevator.

Jamaican art historians David Boxer and Veerle Poupeye believe that this work represents a modern agrarian industry, in turn reflecting the hopes of the nation for the future.[27] I would argue that the opposite is true. Huie emphasizes the dehumanizing nature of manual labor. We see none of the faces of the workers; either they are covered by their hats, or their bodies are turned away from the observer. The sheer number of laborers also speaks to the anonymity of the work they are doing. There is nothing picturesque about this scene and most of the area of the picture frame is concerned with antiquated modes of sugar production. In fact, Huie's painting evinces the opposite sensibility from the long tradition of Caribbean sugar-harvest pictures (mostly by European artists such as British painter George Robertson [1724–1788]), which created idealizing depictions of slave labor on the plantations, attempting to communicate a pastoral or even utopian sensibility, suggesting that the harvest was accomplished by happy laborers not taxed by the back-breaking work in which they engaged. Huie appropriates the pan-Caribbean eighteenth- and nineteenth-century sugar plantation genre, subverting it by stressing the living heritage of enslavement in the field workers' black bodies, laboring at the expense of their own welfare in order to create an internationally traded commodity.

In this picture Huie contrasts the old with the new, by showing the modern, looming structure in the background. In observing this factory (which reminds us of images of industrialized landscapes by the North American Precisionists discussed in Chapter 2) we wonder when the Jamaican sugar industry will become more fully mechanized, and when the many workers here will be made redundant. In my reading of this image, it assumes an aura of transition and anxiety—showing a country

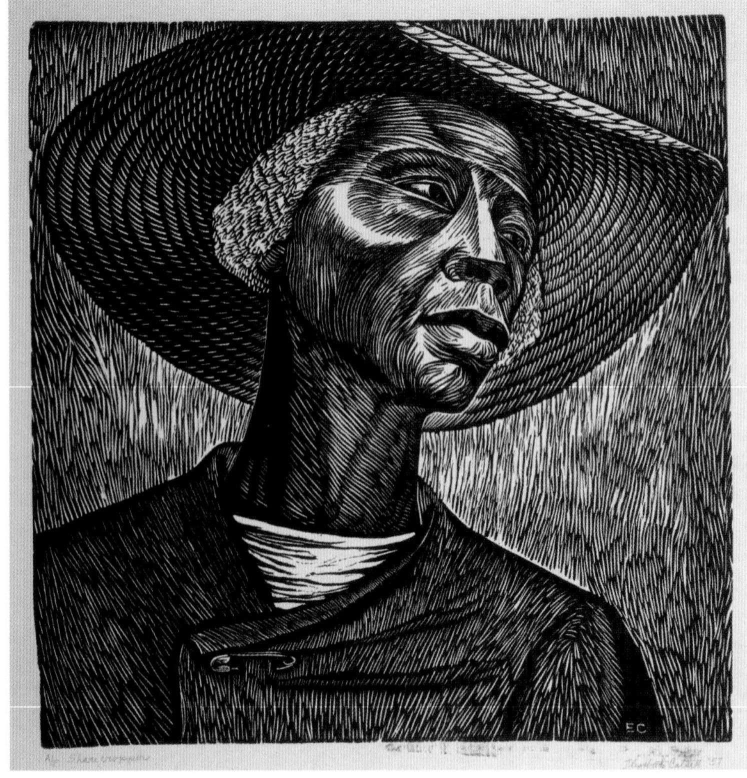

on the cusp of an upcoming change in its social and political order, and the threat (or promise) of greater industrialization. Thus it becomes a disturbing and unsettling image, far from the pacific and tranquil representation of labor and landscape that it has appeared to others.

Field work and the heritage of the pernicious cycle of indentured servitude that was firmly in place during the Jim Crow years in the Southern United States is suggested by the 1952 linocut entitled *Sharecropper* (FIG. 3.15) by Elizabeth Catlett (1915–2012), an outstanding representative of African-American arts of resistance to the social injustice against black citizens, and a notable member of the Mexican printmakers' collective known as the Taller de Gráfica Popular (People's Graphic Workshop, discussed at length in Chapter 5).

The Taller flourished from 1937, the date of its founding in Mexico City, throughout the 1950s and beyond. This artists' cooperative produced posters, single-sheet prints in a variety of media, and albums that, for the most part, addressed social causes in Mexico and elsewhere, from a progressive perspective. Catlett's image is a moving depiction of a woman in late middle age; her face is lined by wrinkles from the sun, and her gray hair is covered by a field worker's hat that is partly cut off due to the direct, close-up view of the image. She turns her face to her left, thus avoiding direct confrontation with us. This sharecropper, a farmer who worked the land owned by an absent landlord for often excessively low wages (a phenomenon that had defined pervasive rural practices, especially in the southern United States, since the later nineteenth century), has continued the agricultural practices common to the techniques of harvesting cotton, the principal crop in the South prior to the Civil War.[28] Her social plight is not very far elevated from that of her ancestors raised under slavery.

This well-known print, defined by the weblike structure of short strokes of the knife as it pierces the linoleum surface of the matrix, evokes a curious psychological state between resignation and indignation. It also provides us with a link to the artist's own biography. Catlett was born and grew up in Washington, D.C., a nominally liberal city, but one where social prejudice in the years of her youth was as pervasive as it had been for decades. Both of her grandparents had been enslaved and Catlett understood at first hand the trauma of bondage from the lessons learned from them.[29] She studied with Loïs Mailou Jones at Howard, the most prominent of the historically black universities, in Washington, D.C., and, after her career began to thrive, won a fellowship to travel to Mexico in 1946 in the company of her then-husband, Charles Wilbert White. This was a momentous choice on the part of Catlett, who was one of the principal heirs to the achievements of the Harlem Renaissance. As her biographer Melanie Anne Herzog has stated:

Catlett's decision to make her home in Mexico was in part a response to the U.S. Government's increasingly vicious attacks on progressive artists, intellectuals and activists following the end of World War II …. In Mexico she also found relief from the daily occurrences of racism that she had experienced in the United States.[30]

Shortly after arriving in Mexico City, Catlett (who was also interested in muralism and came to know Diego Rivera, Frida

Kahlo [1907–1954], and many other members of the Mexican School in the first months of what would prove to be a lifelong residency in the country) began working with members of the Taller and made dozens of socially engaged prints with them throughout her career. Catlett became a Mexican citizen and was long denied re-entry into the United States for her Leftist views. Between 1946 and 1947 she produced a series of 15 linoleum prints called "The Negro Woman" that brought to life in dramatic images a series of renowned black female protagonists of past struggles for freedom and justice. They include three enslaved women—the poet Phillis Wheatley (1753–1784), the abolitionist Sojourner Truth (1797–1883), and Harriet Tubman (1820–1913), who helped organize the Underground Railroad.[31] Catlett's later career was also dedicated to making wood sculpture, a medium in which she created a large body of work that invariably reflected her interest in the bodies of people of color, as well as the monumentality of pre-Columbian statuary.

Of all images of the black body at work there are few as moving as those in "The Migration Series," 60 modest-size paintings done in casein on board by Jacob Lawrence (1917–2000) between 1940 and 1941. This series, half of which is housed in New York's Museum of Modern Art and the other half in the Phillips Collection in Washington, D.C., concerns the Great Migration of African Americans from the rural South of the United States to the cities and towns of the North, Midwest, and West that occurred from the years of World War II to the end of the 1960s.[32] Panel number 57 of the series is *The Female Workers Were the Last to Arrive North* (FIG. 3.16). A woman clad in a simple white shift faces downward, holding a large stick with which she moves a bundle of clothing in a washing tub. Her body is summarily defined and her head is a mere triangle of dark color relieved by the white of her head wrap. The other details of this composition are equally abstracted; the clothing is defined by fluid masses of form and the background by panels of color (reminiscent of the geometric patterns of African textiles) that severely reduce the space inhabited by the woman. The suggestion here is of abject poverty and unending toil. Women who migrated (often alone) to northern cities could find only the most menial of positions and would sometimes be reduced to hiring themselves out as day laborers in the homes of

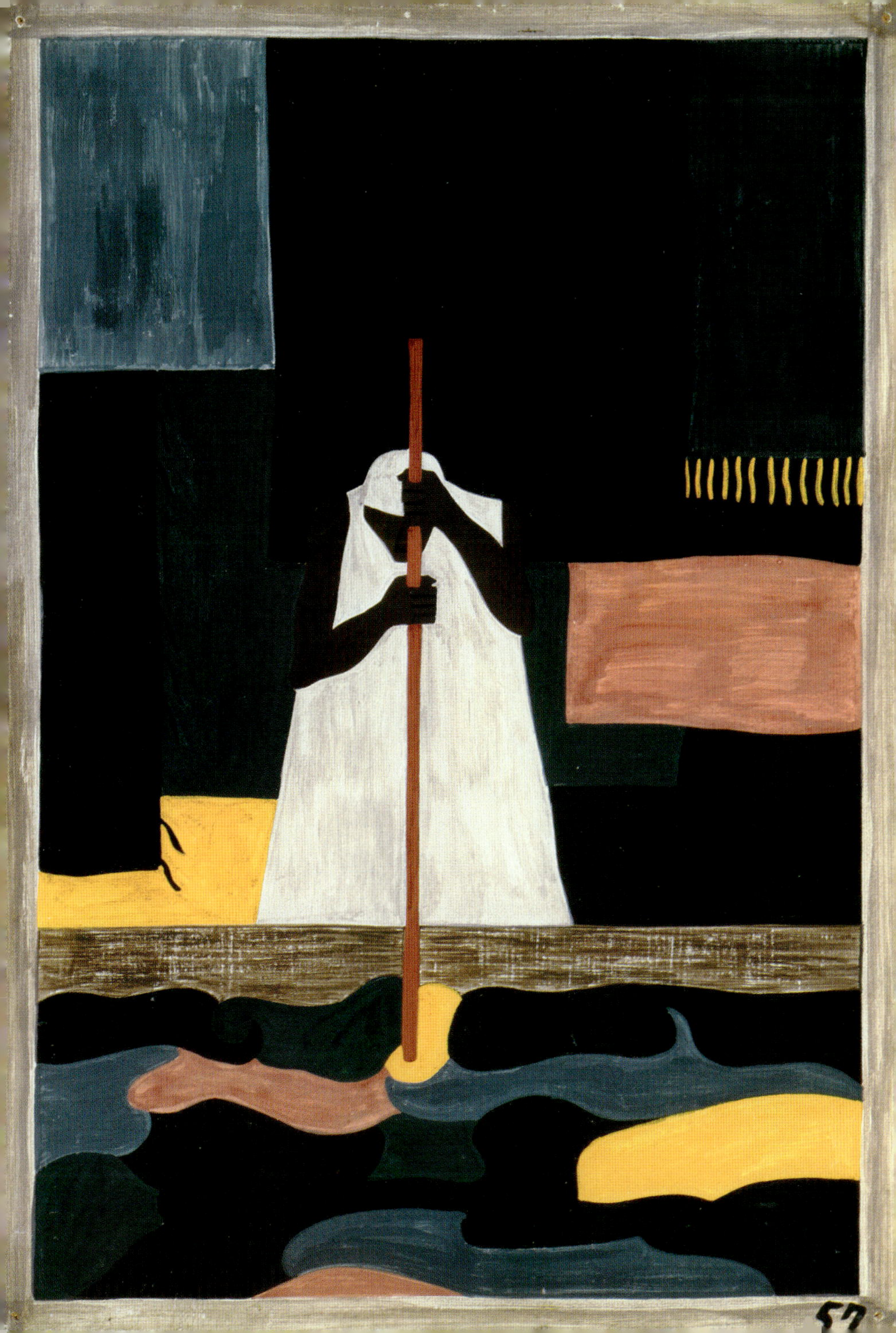

white families. Gathering in places that became known as "slave markets," often-destitute females would earn meager wages to sustain themselves on a daily basis as domestic workers.[33]

"The Migration Series" is one of many works done by Lawrence in multiple images. This quintessential recorder of African-American everyday life, as well as its moments of historical triumph, executed well-known series of paintings and prints of such figures as Toussaint L'Ouverture (1743–1803), leader of the Haitian Revolution, and Harriet Tubman and Frederick Douglas (c.1818–1895), both architects of movements of black self-determination and forerunners of the Black Liberation projects of the later twentieth century. Lawrence's series of black heroes parallels that by Elizabeth Catlett on the most outstanding female participants in the drama of African-American emancipation.[34]

Factory Workers (FIG. 3.17) by Romare Bearden (1911–1988) is an example of this artist's early figurative painting, pre-dating

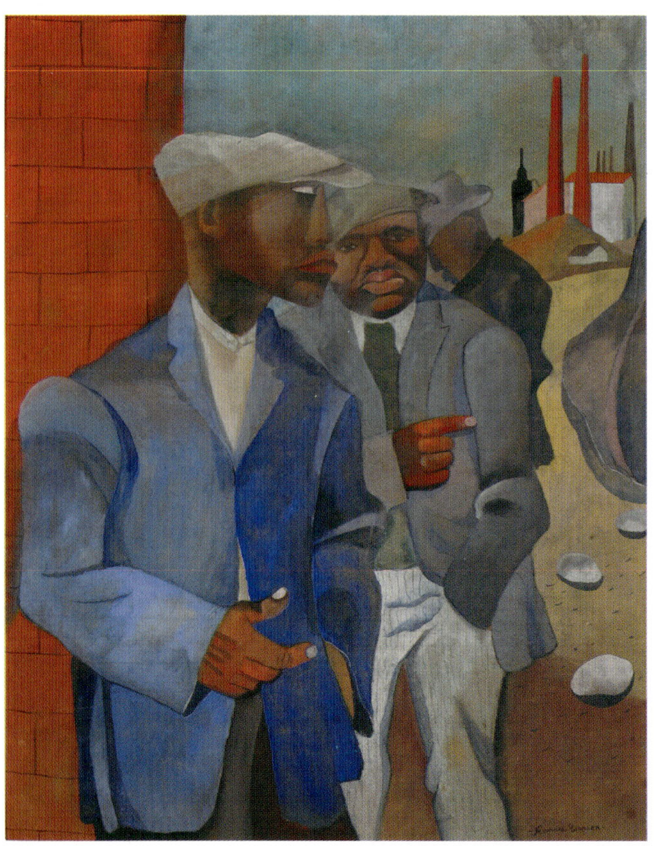

his most characteristic semi-abstract collage work from the 1960s onward. Created in 1942 in oil and casein on paper, this scene represents an episode of urban labor, or rather, unemployment—a situation that so often faced African-American men when they attempted to find work in a white-dominated environ-ment. Here, a group of three individuals stand outside a factory, defined by a brick wall at the left and industrial build-ings with smokestacks at the right. The expressions of the two men in the foreground are dejected, while the figure in the background hunches over, looking at the ground. The mood is set by the use of contrasting shades of muted brown, red, blue, and gray, and it displays a flat perspective as well as a series of intersecting forms, reflecting Bearden's admiration for Cubism. Its subject matter—factory workers (or would-be employees)—relates it to the themes developed by the Mexican muralists in the United States (especially Orozco and Rivera), much admired at the time by the artist.

We know the precise context of this image because it was used as the frontispiece for an essay in the June 1942 issue of *Fortune* magazine, examining the high cost to the United States of racial discrimination during World War II. Through images by leading African-American artists Bearden and Charles H. Alston (1907–1977, with whom Bearden shared a studio in Harlem), the anonymously written essay examined the detrimental effects of the denial of employment in factories and other sources of labor that served the war effort throughout the United States. In June 1941, President Franklin D. Roosevelt had signed an executive order prohibiting discrimination in defense industries.[35] Bearden's painting was done while he was serving a three-year stint in the army during the war. While the work was a commission for a mainstream magazine whose readership was predominantly white, it is evident that Bearden's depiction of black men who would soon be near the stage of destitution served as a powerful acknowledgment of, and protest against, the social realities facing African Americans in the labor force.

The "color line" and its attendant segregation and discrimination did not, of course, end with the war. Its consequences accounted for the rise of black empowerment movements in the 1960s and, ultimately, the Civil Rights Act signed into law by Lyndon B. Johnson in 1964, forbidding discrimination on the basis of race within a broad spectrum of U.S. society. In the end, the act did little to put an end to bigotry and intolerance and thus Bearden's image of protest and resistance had a lengthy afterlife within American society. It also served as a harbinger of Bearden's continued engagement with the situation of African Americans—an engagement that preoccupied him and his art as he gradually abandoned overt social realism, his art taking on greater experimental proportions throughout the rest of his career.[36]

Black Abstractions

Wifredo Lam is arguably the most well-known Cuban artist of the twentieth century. A product of a family of African, Chinese, and Spanish descent, he represents, in the mind of many, the directions of Cuban modernism within an international context. A product of the Academia de San Alejandro in Havana, Lam received his most enduring educational experiences during a long sojourn in Europe (1923–41), which included a lengthy stay in Spain (where he fought in the Spanish Civil War with the Republican forces) as well as a 1938–41 residence in Paris, where his relationships with Picasso, Joan Miró, and other leaders of the interwar artistic scene in the French capital shaped his artistic sensibility in an indelible way.[37] Lam developed a form of painting that synthesized both Cubism and Surrealism. Nonetheless, his most characteristic contribution came about with the insertion of a new visual language into his artistic sensibility—a syntax that he was only able to assimilate back in the country of his birth.

Lam's re-encounter with his native Cuba was an obligatory return to his homeland due to the menace of World War II. He left from the port of Marseilles in the summer of 1941 with a group of like-minded artists and writers, among them André Breton and the anthropologist Claude Lévi-Strauss (1908–2009). After a lengthy trip that included an unexpected incarceration in Vichy-controlled Martinique, Lam reached Havana, where his career took on a new cast. The artist's reconnection with the island and its black culture marked a turning point in his art. He had never been a practitioner of any of the Afro-Cuban religions that abound in the country, yet he was inevitably touched by both the religious rituals and the iconography of such forms of worship as Santería, Palo Monte, and Abakuá, all of which have their origins in West African forms of faith imported into Cuba by slaves. During World War II, Lam created a series of highly original paintings (as well as prints and, eventually, sculptures) in his Havana studio that, while not illustrating Afro-Cuban religions per se, evokes their *orishas* (spirits)—both benign and malevolent—while evincing a continued engagement with forms of the international avant-garde.

Lam never created a totally abstract work. Yet in the majority of his mature paintings and drawings, shapes seem to change and

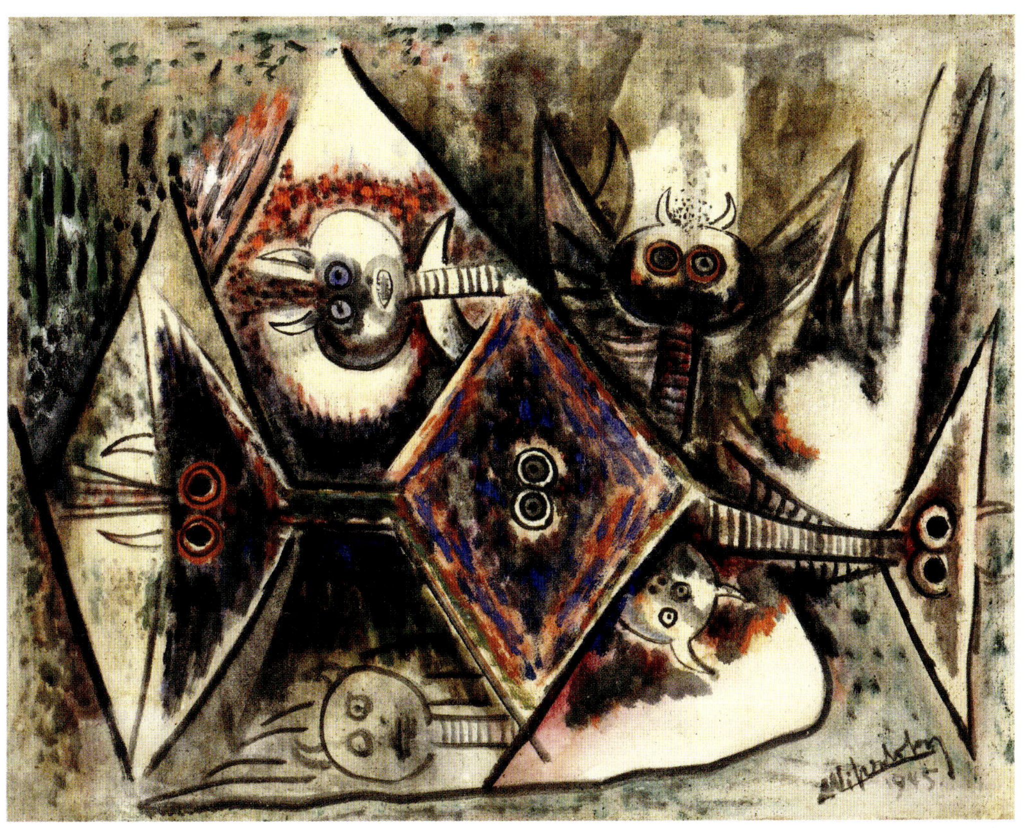

transform themselves from one element to another, moving from representational images to poetically ambiguous suggestions of spiritual force. Such is the case in the 1945 *Devils* (FIG. 3.18), an oil on canvas painted in the characteristic jewel-like colors that Lam employed at this time. Several horned creatures, recalling but not illustrating the attributes of the many *orishas* of the forest world that they inhabit, are linked together in a central core that floats through an atmosphere of rich red, green, and yellow colors. Form and meaning float in our imagination. Lam creates a hazy atmosphere of indistinct yet nonetheless palpable otherworldliness in this compelling composition.

The direct impact of Lam's work was negligible within Cuba (he ceased being a full-time resident of Havana after World War II to return to travels throughout Europe), but it continues to have significant resonance throughout the Caribbean to this day. Among the Cuban artists who continued to internalize the spirit of Lam's work was Guido Llinás (1923–2005), one of the leaders of a generation of Havana-based gestural abstract artists who began to show their work in the early 1950s. The exhibition of the group called Los Once (The Eleven) marked the first appearance of an organized abstract movement within an artistic atmosphere of painting and sculpture that had been reliant on figuration. Llinás and the sculptor Agustín Cárdenas (1927–2001) were the only Afro-Cuban members of this group.[38] These artists, especially Llinás, had looked carefully at the work displayed in a major Lam retrospective held in Havana in 1946. The references to Afro-Cuban symbolism as well as the visual language of African art that had entered Lam's own vocabulary through his examination of ethnographic collections in Paris in the late 1930s also stimulated Llinás's imagination, and he conceived a form of gestural painting that would characterize his art until his death. While there are no direct allusions to any works by Lam, his art served as the stimulus for Llinás's series of "Pinturas Negras" (Black Paintings), created during the years he spent in Paris, beginning in 1957. Prior to traveling to France, he had spent time in New York and Washington (1953) and participated in an exhibition in Manhattan's Galería Sudamericana in 1955. The effects of his examination of the work of the New York School of Abstract Expressionists and, later, the impression made on him by French abstract painters such as Pierre Soulages (b. 1919), are evident in most of his paintings.

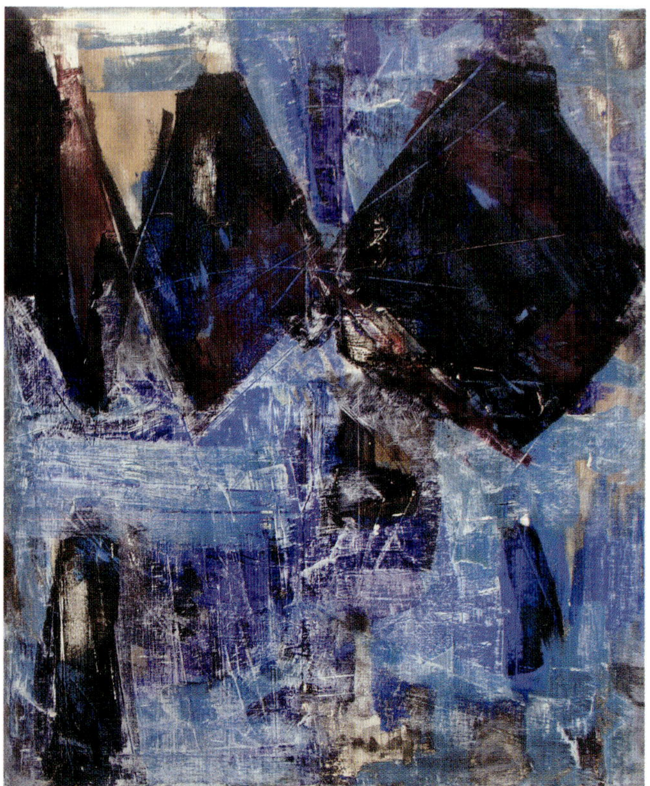

Llinás's 1958 *Sin título* (Untitled) (FIG. 3.19) could easily be understood as the synthesis of a variety of sources. Several masses of black diamond-shapes penetrate a background of slashing brushstrokes containing a variety of shades of blue. The composition is not unrelated to the type of semi-figurative work done by Lam in the 1940s, as we have seen above—an example of the older artist's painting that Llinás would undoubtedly have admired in Lam's 1946 Havana exhibition. Llinás later expressed his admiration for Lam by dedicating a major 1980 canvas called *Homage to Wifredo Lam* to his spiritual mentor. In addition, examples of traditional African arts available to Llinás in the Paris museums were crucial for the development of his "Pinturas Negras" series. The artist stated:

I brought nothing, not even a drawing [with me to Paris]. So I started to use the Cuban signs, which integrated little by little until they disappeared in the painting. Later on I saw in the Museum of African and Oceanic Arts the Bambara drawings from Mali ... and I began to use some of them.[39]

French critic Severo Sarduy poetically evoked Llinás's later work by again referring to the covert presence of Cuban religious subject matter in his art: "Black Signature that in its night of ink, in the intensity of the stroke, evokes ceaselessly other insular signatures: those geometrical emblems ... through which the Orishas give testimony of their descent ...."[40]

The interest in geometric form on the part of Brazilian artists in the 1950s and beyond is examined in Chapter 7. The Concretists and Neo-Concretists who formed the core of the most well-known groups of artists representing the Rio de Janeiro–São Paulo axis at the time, were composed, for the most part, of middle- and upper-middle-class white artists. Brazil, however, produced many other varieties of, and solutions to, the artistic questions brought about by race and social circumstances, and the existence of a "Black Brazilian Art" has been extensively examined by both local and foreign scholars.[41]

The case of Afro-Brazilian painter, sculptor, and printmaker Rubem Valentim (1922–1991) is of particular relevance to this chapter. Valentim created religious forms based on the iconography of one or more of Brazil's several syncretistic faiths that blend African and Christian imagery and practices.[42] Valentim, from Salvador in the northeast state of Bahia (the heartland of Afro-Brazilian spiritual practices), was thoroughly knowledgeable about contemporary experiments in form, and yet, at the same time, deeply engaged with the religions of Candomblé and Umbanda, both related to the Santería practiced in parts of the Caribbean and to Haitian Vodou. A self-taught painter, Valentim was also an accomplished sculptor. In the late 1940s he was aligned with a group of modern artists in Salvador who, through copying European art, attempted to raise the level of academic painting that was taught at local schools. At the same time, he participated, along with his father, in the rites of Candomblé, whose art, as in the 1960 *Composição* (Composition) (FIG. 3.20), embraced the inherent geometric proportions of sacred forms of expression, with which Valentim was intensely familiar from his geographical and spiritual environs in the state of Bahia. A strictly geometric image, this painting has as its main features two triangles—one white, the other red—that

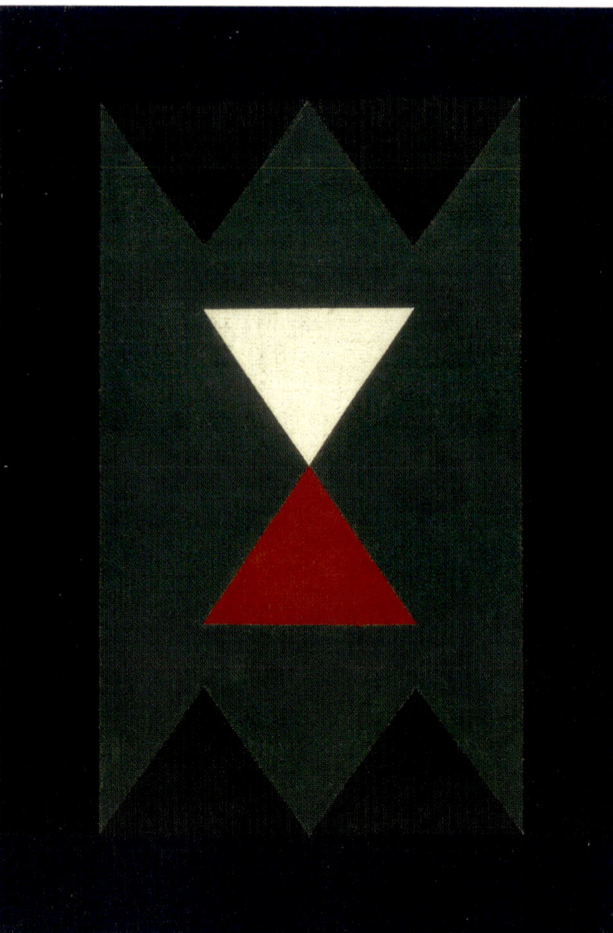

meet in the center of the composition. They are placed within an elongated field of dark green, punctuated by black triangles that disrupt the space in the upper and lower portions. This painting, whose shapes are all set against a deep black background, may be read as a banner or a flag and thus it takes on the aura of a sacred object.

Yet Valentim's artworks were not conceived as religious objects in themselves. His paintings, such as this example in which the colors are associated with specific deities or *orishas* of Candomblé, are, nonetheless, informed by and in harmony with the then-current practices of Vanguard secular artists, evidencing the breadth and richness of Brazil's visual and cultural landscape. Valentim's affinities were with both the so-called mainstream metropolitan art world and the visual traditions of Brazil's northeast, which embraced many elements of black visuality. He participated twice in the Venice Biennale (1964 and 1966) as well as the First World Festival of Black Arts in Dakar, Senegal, in 1966. His work indicates the syncretism of both aesthetic and spiritual dimensions. It appropriates, fuses, and adapts the visual language of Brazilian Concrete art, raising it to a level of black spirituality that reflects the aura of a specific locale within the spectrum of Brazilian life. To this end it may be helpful to offer a lengthy quotation from one of the artist's own statements, made in 1976, about the qualities he considered most important in his art:

My plastic, visual and sign-permeated language is linked to the profound mythical values of Afro-Brazilian culture (mestizo, animistic and fetishistic). With the weight of Bahia upon me—a living culture, with black blood in its veins—atavism [but] with eyes open to what happens in the world—contemporaneity; in creating its signs-symbols I try to transform that enchanted, magical and probably mystical world that flows constantly through me into a visual language. The substrate derives from the land itself, as I am so linked to the cultural complex of Bahia: a city that is a product of a great collective synthesis that interprets its fusion of European, African and Amerindian cultural elements. With these places and persons as my point of departure I seek a poetic, contemporary and universal language to express myself in terms of art. The difficult path toward the creation of an authentic Brazilian [artistic] language develops out of the cultural reality of the country ... but without ignoring or denying everything that it represents in the world—which would be impossible with the means of communication at our disposal ... [I seek to create a] sensorial artistic language, The Feel of Brazil.[43]

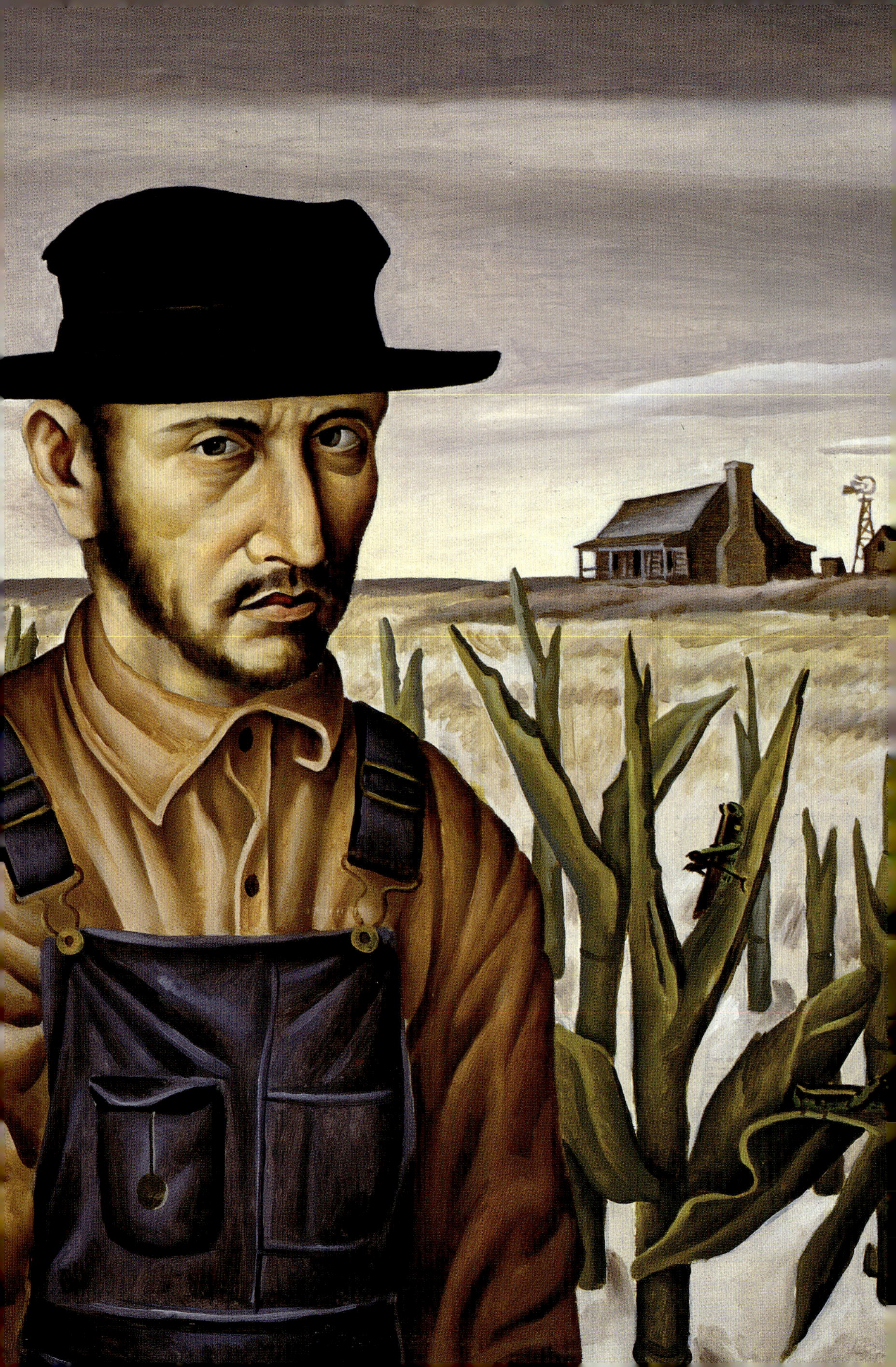

Chapter 4

Cross-Border Dialogues

This chapter and the subsequent one will concentrate on images that attest to the importance of socially engaged art within the hemispheric aesthetic and political consciousness at a time of universal trauma, which followed in the wake of warfare and other devastating events.

I will concentrate here specifically on public art, which may be defined as those forms of visual expression created for didactic or emblematic purposes—that is to say, works that communicate specific ideas or political attitudes to a large number of viewers at the same time. The majority of works considered are mural paintings or other large-scale images in public places, done on both sides of the Mexico–U.S. border. Yet I begin with a photograph, as photography had become in this period, as in previous eras of collective turbulence, a quintessential medium of mass communication via its dissemination in magazines and newspapers. The graphic arts offered an equally potent vehicle for shared public knowledge and expressed socially oriented opinions in the 1930s and 40s. This category included posters, which were often made in large editions by organizations founded during this time period, including the Graphic Arts Division of the Works Progress Administration (WPA), a New Deal initiative in the United States, discussed below. Posters were also produced by, among many other artists' groups, the Taller de Gráfica Popular, the workshop of politically engaged Leftist artists working in Mexico City (see Chapter 5), and artists working within the Puerto Rican graphics movement that emerged in the 1940s.

Jerry Bywaters
Sharecropper, 1937
(detail). See fig. 4.5.

Revolutionary Art: Between Exaltation and Despair

As World War I raged in Europe (with troops from many American nations participating), the Mexican Revolution (1910–20) marked the most salient large-scale conflict on American soil. After ten years of successive uprisings and civil wars, the end of the revolution witnessed a reconfiguration of Mexican society in ways that affected virtually every aspect of the social, political, and cultural fabric of that country. A desire to express national sentiments, histories, social goals, and partisan aspirations resulted in an emphasis on subject matter (in every artistic genre) that referred to both past and present visual emblems, sometimes reinforcing national myths, and creating a sense of time, place, and purpose. Our first image, a photograph called *Mexican Revolution. Guitar, Corn and Ammunition Belt* (FIG. 4.1) of 1927 by Italian-born, American-trained photographer Tina Modotti (1896–1942) (discussed in detail below), encapsulates tropes that immediately identify the subject as Mexican.

Public art, and muralism in particular, had a special position in the development of visual communication in modern Mexico, and 1922 marked its earliest beginnings as a cohesive movement. Throughout the 1920s, Diego Rivera, José Clemente Orozco, David Alfaro Siqueiros, Ramón Alva de la Canal (1892–1985), Fermín Revueltas (1901–1935), and others participated in the decoration of the Escuela Nacional Preparatoria, or ENP (National Preparatory School), in downtown Mexico City. Murals embodied the egalitarian and politically charged nature of their messages. The artists worked collectively alongside the carpenters who made the scaffolding, as well as the assistants who ground the colors and prepared the section of wet plaster that would cover parts of the wall so that the painter(s) could do their work one day at a time (at least in the case of true fresco, which

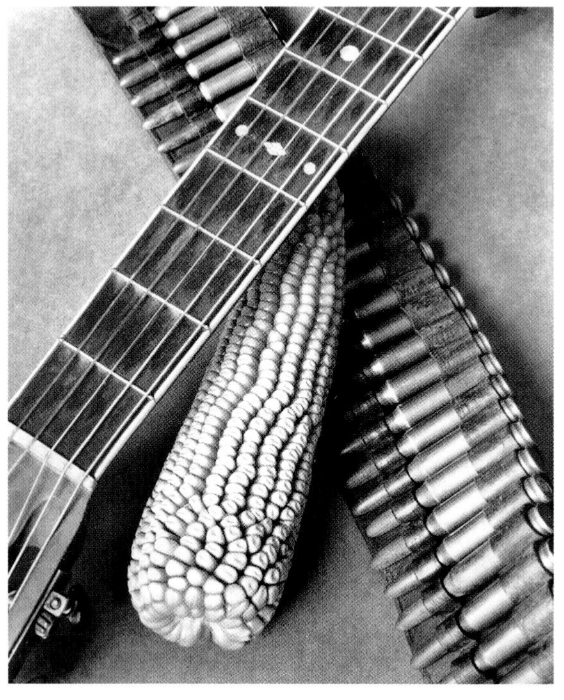

Fig. 4.1
Tina Modotti
*Mexican Revolution.
Guitar, Corn and
Ammunition Belt,*
1927, black and white
photograph.

was used in the majority of cases). Artists formed unions that fostered this collectivity and lobbied against censorship and for social justice.

The most well known of these organizations was the Leftist-leaning Liga de Escritores y Artistas Revolucionarios (League of Revolutionary Writers and Artists, or LEAR), which constituted a physical meeting and exhibition space. This was an artists and writers' cooperative and an organization for social action, in existence from 1934 to 1938. The LEAR supplanted an earlier organization called the Sindicato de Trabajadores Técnicos, Pintores y Escultores (Syndicate of Technical Workers, Painters, and Sculptors), a branch of a similar organization that existed in the Soviet Union.

From a historical vantage point, muralism also held particular pride of place in Mexican art history. In pre-Hispanic times public and private buildings were often covered inside and out with both figurative scenes and abstract patterns. The colonial era witnessed yet another resurgence of interest in large-scale painting, whether on the domes and ceilings of churches, convents, and monasteries from the sixteenth century to the nineteenth, or in the form of mammoth canvases of religious subjects that covered the walls of churches, creating an effect of overall mural decoration. While twentieth-century mural artists may not have been consciously imitating any of these precedents, they were keenly aware of the role that monumental painting had played in their country, judging by the interest on the parts of artists and writers in the pre-Columbian and Spanish colonial-era examples of muralism.[1] In addition, many of the Mexican muralists took direct inspiration from European models of the Middle Ages and the Renaissance that some of them, particularly Rivera, had studied in situ. Muralism in Mexico was seen as part of an aesthetic continuum whose roots stretched far back into the past, even before the beginning of what could be called the consciousness of Mexican identity (*mexicanidad*), which (in its twentieth-century articulation) was intimately linked to the concept of *mestizaje*, or the power of the blending of races.[2]

The modern Mexican mural movement, which had had an aborted start prior to and in the very early years of the revolution, continued to be a viable entity into the 1950s. It had consequences throughout the hemisphere. A generation of artists in the United States during the 1930s was especially affected by the example of their Mexican contemporaries, resulting in thousands of socially engaged realist (and some abstract) murals in public buildings such as post offices, hospitals, and schools. The mural movement, partly inspired by the Mexicans, also flourished (although on a smaller scale) throughout Latin America. Figurative art with a particularly marked dedication to subjects related to social injustice and distinctions of class and race, flourished in the 1930s and 40s throughout the regions discussed here. Argentina, Uruguay, Cuba, and Brazil all had significant if limited mural movements, although they differed markedly from the Mexican example.

Art responded to many well-known as well as many almost-forgotten circumstances. Among the most catastrophic and widest-reaching occurrences was the New York Stock Market Crash on October 29, 1929. The failure of the financial system on that Black Tuesday soon had consequences worldwide. These effects were acutely felt throughout the Americas, and artists were compelled to react; the pictorial results of the privations caused by the Depression could be seen in every manifestation of the visual arts for at least two decades after the disaster occurred. Concurrent with the Depression were numerous natural or climatic disasters. In the United States the 1930s witnessed the Dust Bowl—the effect of indiscriminate planting of wheat without rotation throughout the states that formed the central core of the country. Crops failed, the depleted land dried up, and millions were forced to abandon their homes from as far north as North Dakota and as far south as Texas, fleeing for such places as California or the east coast. There was no more poignant codification of the effects of this early manifestation of what we know today as climate change than John Steinbeck's 1939 novel *The Grapes of Wrath*, which achieved worldwide fame through its 1940 film adaptation.

Modotti's *Mexican Revolution. Guitar, Corn and Ammunition Belt* is an emblem of the ten-year war that Mexico experienced from 1910 to 1920. Large-scale agrarian reforms and redistributions were undertaken; the Catholic Church was suppressed and its lands and religious buildings nationalized. Nationwide literacy campaigns were undertaken, as were plans for introducing the teaching of art to sectors of society that had not experienced instruction in painting or drawing in the past. The latter two reforms were initiatives of the post-revolutionary Secretaría de Educación Pública (Ministry of Public Education), or SEP. The arts became, in fact, critical tools in the attempts to refashion society. The first Secretary of Public Education, José Vasconcelos, a politician and philosopher, was conscious of the power of visual images and he invited a group of mural painters to start a campaign of decoration of public and semi-public buildings—such as schools—that resulted in the Mexican mural movement (sometimes referred to as the Mexican mural renaissance). While muralism became the most public of the arts of the revolution and post-revolutionary eras, it was by no means the only visual tool in the broad and multifaceted campaign to express engagement with issues of public interest and political concern. Photography held a virtually equal rank within the hierarchy of forms of art that suggested an awareness of the concerns of the populace at large.

Tina Modotti was one of a group of highly influential women photographers to work in Mexico beginning in the 1920s and her art represents one of the highest points of accomplishment in a medium that had served an important function for disseminating information and fulfilling propaganda purposes since the early days of the twentieth century. Photography in Mexico matured as a modern form of visual expression during the years of the revolution when such artists as Agustín Casasola (1874–1928) and the many members of his studio, as well as the German-born photographers Hugo Brehme (1882–1954) and Wilhelm (Guillermo) Kahlo (1871–1941, father of Frida Kahlo), created indelible images of the war's heroes and its battles or, in the case of Kahlo, pictures of the land and cityscapes of the country in the 1910s and 20s.

The women photographers of Modotti's generation as well as some of the younger figures within this pantheon (Lola Álvarez Bravo [1903–1993], Kati Horna [1912–2000], Mariana Yampolsky [1925–2002], and others) often demonstrated a political awareness and, like Modotti, a strong commitment to Leftist causes that became very popular in Mexican (and North American) politics in the 1920s and 30s. Lola Álvarez Bravo is well known for her many portraits of artists and intellectuals, yet her more experimental photographic production marks her as one of Modotti's most distinguished contemporaries and one of the principal stars in the extended firmament of women photographers in Mexico. *El sueño de los pobres* (Dream of the Poor), a gelatin silver print of a photomontage from 1935 (FIG. 4.2), depicts a bedraggled child, dressed in rags, asleep upon a rude bed of discarded cloth. Unbeknownst to him a huge "money machine" comprised of a fantastical concatenation of immense coins and metal wheels appears to bear down upon his figure. Such a dramatic imagining carries more visual and psychological weight than most photojournalistic images, and marks the artist as one of the most artistically advanced and politically savvy members of her cohort.[3]

Returning to Modotti's composition, this vertically oriented photograph is related to several similar images taken by her during the late 1920s that depict corn, ammunition belts (or bandoliers), and guitars (and, in one instance, a sickle), and is elegantly composed with the three elements overlaying one another. The bandolier (referring to the armed conflict of the revolution and continuing sectarian violence in Mexico during the 1920s) provides the ground for the scene over which is placed the corn (the staple of the Mexican diet) and finally the neck of

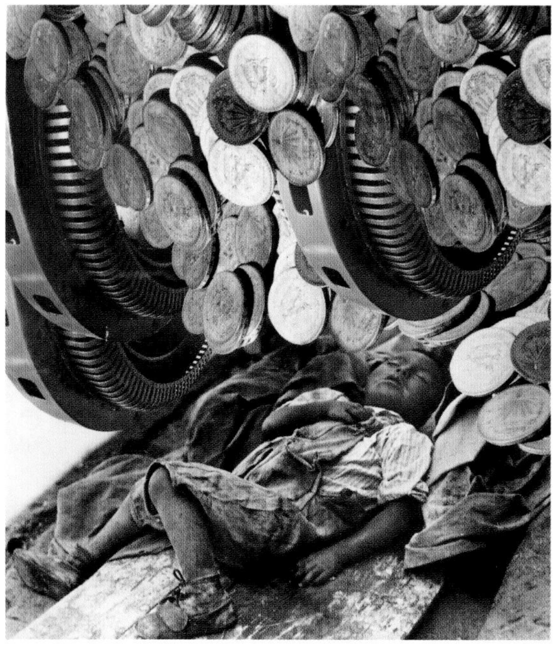

the guitar, the musical instrument that is most associated with popular music in the country. This photograph may, in fact, be understood as an allegory not only of revolution but also of physical sustenance. It is a metaphor for three of the five senses: hearing (guitar), taste (corn), and touch (ammunition belt). The prime element in this work is the guitar that constitutes the uppermost object in the scene. This is especially appropriate given the original context of the photograph, initially published shortly after its creation in the journal *Mexican Folkways*, whose editor Anita Brenner (1905–1974, a Mexican-born American writer) was influential in disseminating information about

Mexican culture, history, and politics to English-speaking audiences—mainly in the United States, as well as to an elite public in Mexico, where the journal was printed.[4] The photograph appeared in a text by Modotti herself in the October–December 1927 issue of the magazine, opposite the lyrics to a popular song, or *corrido*, that lauded the efficiency of the "30-30" Winchester rifle, a favorite weapon used during the revolution. The song would have been played on the guitar and the ammunition in the photograph was the principal source of the gun's deadly trajectory. Modotti continued to use these motifs, including them among other revolutionary emblems and texts, such as passages from the Articles of the Mexican Constitution.[5]

Modotti's work shares many points of stylistic and thematic content with her U.S. contemporaries and colleagues Edward Weston (1886–1958), with whom she had originally traveled to Mexico, and Paul Strand. Modotti joined the Mexican Communist Party (PCM) the same year that she took this photograph. She created many similar images for the Party's newspaper *El Machete*, and some of her best-known pictures contain obvious references to the iconography of Soviet Marxist–Leninist ideology.

In Mexico many artists became members of the PCM, and throughout the period under consideration here, vestiges of Communist visual culture lingered well into the mid years of the century. Virtually all of the most famous muralists and members of the Mexican School of painting, as well as some of the principal printmakers, were Party members. Although some, like Diego Rivera, were eventually expelled, the ideals of Communism were powerful factors in the fashioning of the politics and aesthetics of the artistic elite of Mexico. This situation changed somewhat (as it did in the United States, where there were many artists who sympathized with Communism although relatively few actually belonged to the Party) in the late 1930s when the abuses of Joseph Stalin became more apparent and the Hitler–Stalin nonaggression pact made clear the paths of the future of orthodox Communist sympathies.[6] Nonetheless, subject matter related to a broader framework of the ideals of socialism persisted in the arts in the United States and, especially, Mexico into the World War II years and beyond.

Tina Modotti was a charismatic personality. In California in the later 1910s she had served as a popular model for portrait photographers, and in 1919 she began her brief career as an actor in silent movies.[7] Her involvement with the Mexican community in Los Angeles during her show-business career, and her romantic as well as professional liaison with Weston (who was already interested in pre-Hispanic art and architecture prior to crossing the border), were among the factors that drew her to Mexico. In 1923 she and Weston set up a portrait studio in the capital and quickly inserted themselves into the artistic and literary avant-garde of the early post-revolutionary era. Among Modotti's friends were Rivera and Frida Kahlo, and it is likely that Modotti reintroduced the two (Kahlo had first encountered Rivera when she was still a student and he was working on a mural at the National Preparatory School). Rivera went on to include the figure of Modotti in a number of his works—specifically several fresco panels in his most ambitious project, and the murals for the SEP in the historic center of Mexico City.

The mural known as *The Distribution of Arms* (FIG. 4.3) is one of the best-known details from an immensely ambitious cycle on which Rivera worked throughout the 1920s, starting in 1923. Although he had begun collaborating with other artists on this project, which encompassed three floors of the newly built SEP headquarters (a structure that incorporated portions of a colonial monastery plus modern additions in the then-popular neocolonial style), he effectively accomplished this massive project single-handedly. As the art historian James Oles has stated,

In his frescos in the SEP Rivera sought to unite Mexico's cultural, ethnic and geographic diversity in a single coherent program covering three floors. The bright colors, crisply outlined figures, exhaustive details, and pleasantly rounded forms would typify his murals for the next three decades.[8]

In other sections of the building, scenes of everyday life in the countryside, images of teachers instructing indigenous children, and representations of popular festivals and dances comprise the bulk of the subject matter. The last series of paintings (done in true fresco—watercolor on wet plaster) presents a more militant and politically engaged view of the present time.

A clear reference to the worldwide class struggle, "the revolution," evoked here is more of a generalized concept of battle against oppression (social, political, and cultural) than a remembrance of the previous decade of the Mexican Revolution. Yet the image also deals directly with Mexican politics of the late 1920s. Rivera includes figures from the various factions within the Leftist panorama of the nation's ideology. In general, however, this fresco (painted one year after the artist returned from a trip to Moscow to celebrate the tenth anniversary of the Russian Revolution) may be read today as a display of Communist iconography. It is present in the form of the red stars on the workers' overalls, the hammer and sickle on the red flag at the upper left, and the sickle on the banner in the rear right of the scene, which calls for "land and liberty," thereby evidencing the artist's affinities for the ideology of the Left. Rivera personalizes this allegory of confrontation with the inclusion of a number of easily recognizable figures, including his fellow muralist (and sometime antagonist) Siqueiros at the extreme left, Kahlo in the center, and Tina Modotti at the extreme right. The composition is crowded, yet it is perfectly legible, with its successive groups of participants leading the eye from the first frieze of individuals to the crowd scenes in the back. Rivera was always fascinated by technology

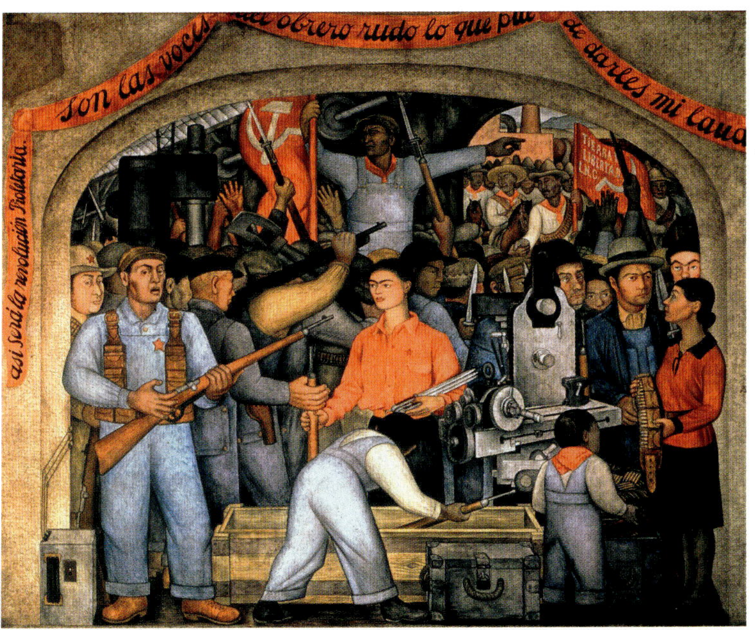

Fig. 4.3
Diego Rivera
The Distribution of Arms, 1928, fresco. Court of Fiestas of Secretaría de Educación Pública, Mexico City.

and science, and his concentration on the details of the weapons, ammunition, compressors, and other types of machines testifies to his interest in the specific tools of progress and modernity. The "modernity" of this scene is offset by the artist's use of a banderole with an inscription resting just outside the fictive frame that sets this section of the fresco apart from those on either side. Such techniques as this are derived from Mexican folk motifs and can be seen in paintings by untutored artists from the nineteenth century and earlier, providing an explanation of the action within a picture so that the viewer would more easily understand the meaning of the image.[9]

Rivera, like most of his fellow Mexican artists of the time, embraced anti-capitalist sentiments (when it was most advantageous for him to do so). Official relationships between Mexico and the increasingly conservative United States were becoming strained as the 1930s progressed, ultimately leading to the historic and highly controversial nationalization of the Mexican oil industry (which had previously been, to a large extent, in the control of the United States) in 1936, during the presidency of Lázaro Cárdenas (1934–1940). This was a manifestation of Mexican nationalism as well as an indication of a turn to a right-of-center self-sufficiency. Politics during the 1930s was considerably less liberal than in the previous decade, and large-scale mural projects of this kind, with their Leftist messages, declined in number (although they did not disappear altogether) as Mexico felt the effects of the financial disaster of 1929 and the rhetoric of revolution diminished in popularity and viability.

The start of the 1930s found Rivera and Kahlo (who had married in 1928) traveling for the first time to the United States. Already familiar in Mexico with members of prominent U.S. families in the realms of politics, culture, and big business, Rivera was invited to do a series of murals in San Francisco and its environs. In 1931 he was given a highly successful one-artist exhibition at New York's Museum of Modern Art, an effort spearheaded by the Rockefeller family, and in January 1932 he traveled to Detroit. The "motor city" was then one of the most prosperous cities in the country. Home to the Ford Motor Company, it stood as a symbol of power, and the possibilities of advancement and economic strength, despite the gradually growing misery experienced throughout the country by the spiraling effects of the economic downturn. Nonetheless, the veneer of prosperity and tranquility was easily penetrated when a curious and socially committed individual like Rivera looked for cracks in the proverbial armor. Prior to his arrival in Detroit there had been violent riots protesting strict working rules at the River Rouge automobile manufacturing plant in nearby Dearborn. Large sectors of the immigrant populations, especially the hundreds of Mexican workers in Detroit, were living in dire poverty (Rivera attempted to relieve the misery of some by financing their return to Mexico via train). Nonetheless, Rivera acceded to the invitation to paint the central courtyard of the newly built Detroit Institute of Arts. The prime mover behind this commission was Edsel Ford (1893–1943), who financed the bulk of the project.[10]

The issue of Rivera's seemingly close relationship with major representatives of industrial capitalism such as the Fords and Rockefellers has always existed as a question mark within the many commentaries on the artist's life and work. Rivera was both ambitious and practical. He accepted many invitations for portraits, mural series, and other types of works financed by big business and its tycoons. It was good for his career and, in the end, spread his fame (and the knowledge of the communicative power of muralism) to places outside the borders of Mexico. Nonetheless, Rivera often encountered resistance to his particular brand of expression and his often overt references to Leftist philosophy.[11] The most famous example of this occurred in 1933, when a mural he had begun for the new RCA building in New York's Rockefeller Center complex was destroyed because of its inclusion of the head of Lenin.

The Detroit Industry murals are the most complex series of paintings Rivera executed in the United States. They cover all four walls of the courtyard. The North Wall (FIG. 4.4) seen here is divided into seven sections. The main portion displays, like its opposite image on the south wall, an allegory of the automotive industry. Massive human movement within the setting of towering (and depersonalizing) machines is the main subject of this and the facing panel. The complexity of activity—the making of a motorcar—does not focus on a single individual, and indeed, all of the participants are anonymous; there are few workers who face the viewer. Rivera divides the scene according to individual sections to lend order to the surging activity. This segmentation regulates and subdivides the field of vision, an approach that harks back to his experiments with Cubism between 1914 and 1917. The "Cubist grid" provided a path that allowed the artist to create such a seemingly chaotic scene in a legible way.

Rivera's attitudes toward mechanization were ambivalent. Although we are presented with a quasi-cinematic view of dozens of men working in the service of industry amidst a landscape of overpowering apparatuses, it is not impossible that he was, at the same time, in awe of the power of mechanization. His early biographer Bertram Wolfe (1896–1977, a founding member of the American Communist Party) wrote that

Painting … must absorb the machine if it was to find the style for this age, assimilate it as easily and naturally as still-life objects, landscapes, dwellings … and make it live again on walls as vividly and movingly as ever art had in historical scenes, old legends, and religious parables.[12]

In this attitude to the machine and contemporary life we see parallels to many other artists on both sides of the Atlantic who, in the 1920s, had made industrialization and its tools one of their principal themes.

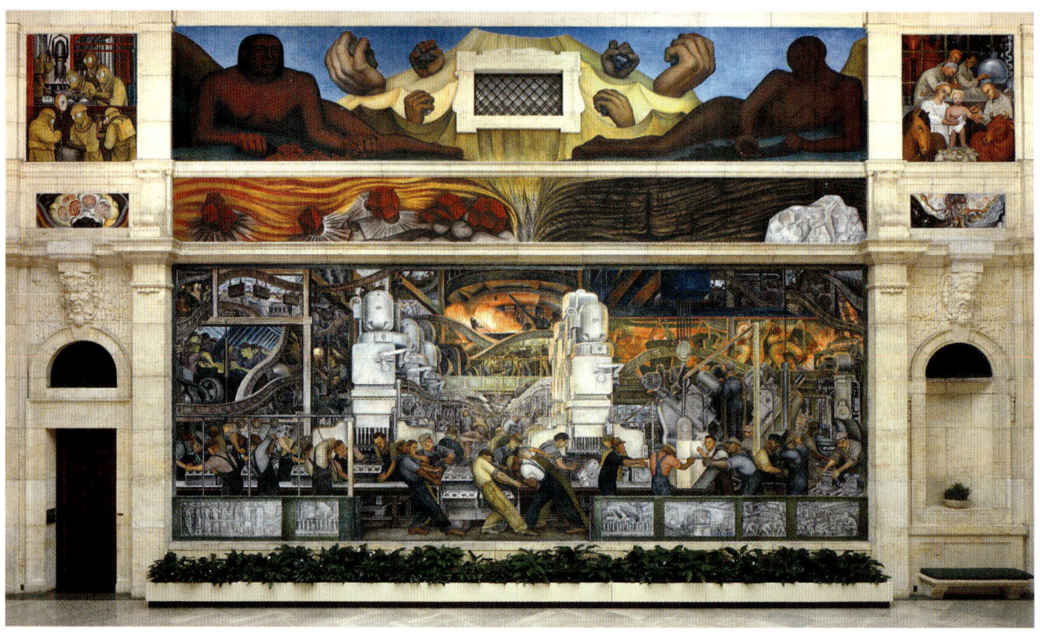

136

The upper segments of the Detroit Industry murals include allegories of the continents (here, Asia and Africa in the forms of two dark-skinned female figures who recline on a volcanic landscape with large hands holding rocks enigmatically emerging from the mountain). Below them is a sectional view of the earth. This detail suggests that the artist had cut through the depths of the planet and revealed its inner crevices and variegated forms of rock. In the middle of this register there are stalks of blooming wheat, symbolizing the fertility of the earth (a subject about which Rivera had done an entire series of murals at the Agricultural School of Chapingo near Mexico City in 1926). At the upper left and right Rivera painted scenes of modern-day science and medical technology. At the left poison gases are manufactured, a testimony to the most savage techniques of warfare. Most outstanding is the section at the upper right where a doctor and nurse administer a vaccination to a child. A cow, horse, and sheep populate the lower portion of the scene, and at the upper area scientists are engaged in study. This scene is one of several that aroused the ire of a sector of the local Detroit populace, who asserted that Rivera was secularizing a reference to the Holy Family (complete with farm animals in the stable and the three Magi in the form of the scientists) in an inappropriate way. For this and other such controversial details, the cycle was under threat of destruction for months during and after its completion. Nonetheless, the museum's director, the noted art historian Wilhelm Valentiner (1880–1958), prevailed and the frescos stand today as one of the outstanding examples of muralism in 1930s North America.

Public Arts on Both Sides of the Border

While working on his murals in the United States and Mexico, Rivera employed numerous assistants drawn from the ranks of local artists, including Ben Shahn (1898–1969), who worked on the Rockefeller Center mural project in New York. Emmy Lou Packard (1914–1998) was the full-time assistant to Rivera on his last U.S. mural project entitled *Pan American Unity* (still extant at San Francisco City College) and painted for the Golden Gate International Exposition of 1940. Packard went on to have a significant career of her own as a muralist and printmaker of subjects related to local labor. She also served as an advisor and promoter of the nascent Chicano mural movement in San Francisco. Rivera and the many other Mexican artists who worked in the United States until World War II (and beyond) had an enormous effect on the development of figurative art there. While the United States did not have the historical connection to a tradition of mural decoration that Mexico did, this mode of expression, with its depictions of labor and the everyday life of believable individuals (as well as more lofty themes of history and heroic deeds), had a considerable legacy. The U.S. mural movement was prompted by the success of the Mexicans—not only those working in the United States, but also those in Mexico itself—as observed by many American visitors who made the trip south of the U.S. border.[13]

The mural movement in the United States in the Depression years was backed by the personal enthusiasm of President Franklin D. Roosevelt, who had heeded the advice of his friend the painter George Biddle (1885–1973) to create opportunities for out-of-work artists and formulated the WPA's Federal Art Project (FAP) in 1935. Literally thousands of artists, both members and non-members of the WPA, created murals, paintings, and prints on themes related to the social situation of the country, local, regional, and national history, and allegorical subjects meant to bolster the spirits of the public who would interact with these images in their daily lives, either as viewers of public art or as owners of the many inexpensive print series that were done at the time.[14] Photographers were also employed by a parallel project that grew out of the vicissitudes of the Great Depression. The Farm Security Administration (FSA), discussed in the following chapter, created a platform for the documentation of the privations witnessed and suffered by rural citizens in all of the states, as well as in the U.S. territory of Puerto Rico.

Artists in the United States at this time were keenly aware of, and sensitive to, the unique circumstances of place. The historical conditions and the fabric of society where they lived created many regionalisms (which may be gathered together under the umbrella term American Scene Painting) within the overall picture of figurative art of the time, especially during the 1920s and 30s. In the case of Texas, for example (one of the country's largest states and one of only three that had once been independent nations),[15] artists in such centers as San Antonio,

Dallas, Houston, and Galveston produced art that reflected the industries as well as the calamities of the time, such as the large-scale droughts that occurred across the plains.

The 1937 canvas *Sharecropper* (FIG. 4.5), by Gerald (Jerry) Bywaters (1906–1989), is reminiscent of his social realist murals. The scene describes several phenomena of the time. Sharecropping, whereby a landowner would accept the products of the agricultural efforts of his tenant, had been a long-standing system in place in the southern United States since the nineteenth century. Poor farmers, both white and black (as in Elizabeth Catlett's *Sharecropper* print discussed in Chapter 3), often suffered from the indignities of economic inequality, especially at times of natural disasters such as droughts, when crops failed and land was often repossessed. This painting (in which Bywaters used himself as a model for the forlorn man in the foreground) captures the depressive quality of a moment of despair. Grasshoppers devour the corn crop at the right and the simple farmhouse, barn, and windmills are far behind the sharecropper, indicating perhaps an imminent eviction.

Bywaters was one of the most prominent Texas regionalists and had a direct connection to modern Mexican art, which he had come to know by reading the magazine *Mexican Folkways*. In 1928 he traveled to Mexico City and sought out Rivera, who was then working on the SEP murals. Bywaters became friendly with most of the well-known artists in the Mexican capital. Deeply inspired by this experience, and by his new friendships with Tina Modotti and other members of the late 1920s art circles, Bywaters returned to Texas and started his own career as a muralist for numerous public buildings, such as the Old City Hall of Dallas, the Parcel Post Building in Houston, and the Paris (Texas) Public Library, all of which evidenced the strong attraction for him of Mexican monumental art. Bywaters was, in addition, a distinguished art historian,

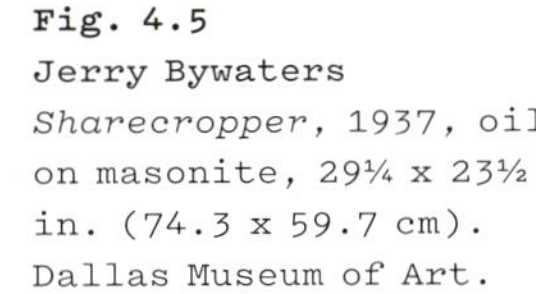

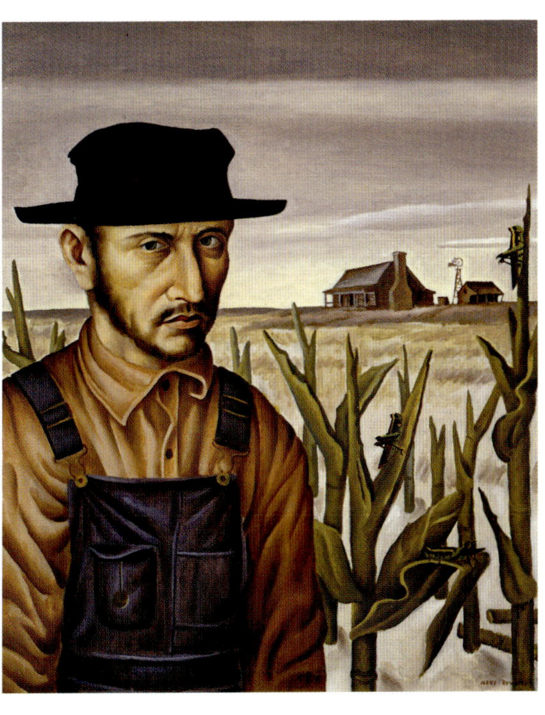

museum director, and arts administrator. He also contributed to the fame of Rivera and other Mexican artists of the mural and parallel movements by writing about their work in 1927 in the influential *Southwest Review*.[16]

The attraction of Mexico as a place for participating in the cradle of the muralist movement was inescapable for many artists from all parts of the United States. Jerry Bywaters was only one of many mostly very young American artists to travel to Mexico and work with Rivera and his contemporaries on individual projects or group efforts as muralists in teams to create complex series of frescos in public buildings such as schools or markets. Between 1933 and 1934 Philip Guston (1913–1980, then known as Philip Goldstein) traveled with his friend Ruben Kadish (1913–1992) from California to Morelia, capital of the state of Michoacán, where they painted a mural in a colonial-era building that now houses the Museo Michoacano. This mural incorporates many Surrealist elements in its overall anti-Fascist theme.[17]

A number of less well-remembered U.S. muralists working on both sides of the border were women. Marion Greenwood (1909–1970) was a Brooklyn-born artist who had studied in Paris and at New York's Art Students League before going to Mexico in 1932 to work with Rivera. He was not in the capital at the time, but Greenwood made the acquaintance of Paul (Pablo) O'Higgins (1904–1983), a native of Utah who had become one of the major players in the history of muralism in Mexico. O'Higgins was one of the most ardently politically engaged of his contemporaries, and virtually all of his work contains strong references to democratic ideals and the fight against oppression of the disenfranchised sectors of society. Greenwood and her sister Grace Greenwood (1905–1979) worked on murals in Morelia (after the earliest attempt in fresco painting by Marion at the Hotel Taxqueño in Taxco, where another American artist, Howard Cook [1901–1980], also completed a mural). The sisters' most important commission was for a large staircase mural at the Abelardo Rodríguez Market (built 1935–36) in Mexico City, part of an ambitious project directed by Rivera to decorate the upper and lower floors of a newly built commercial center close to the main square (*zócalo*). The Greenwoods' subject was a complex series of evocations of rural labor and its hardships as the countryside was industrialized, juxtaposed with the representation of market commerce in an urban setting.[18]

Upon her return to the United States, Marion Greenwood continued her career as a muralist, and an art teacher at Columbia University in the late 1930s. She became a member of the Federal Art Project of the WPA and continued to work in the mode that she had developed in conjunction with Diego Rivera's manner of monumental realism. Greenwood's 1940 fresco in the Red Hook Housing Project (FIG. 4.6) in Brooklyn, New York (the largest such public housing project in the borough, with over 6,000 residents), bears the title *Blueprint for Living*. It was created for the lobby of the community center of the project but has since been painted over. Its theme, as one may intuit from the peaceful gathering of young people in this photograph showing the artist on the scaffold before a section of the fresco (taken as part of the WPA art project by an unknown photographer), refers to peace and harmony as well as cooperative work and play among citizens of the city (and, by extension, the residents of the Red Hook houses).

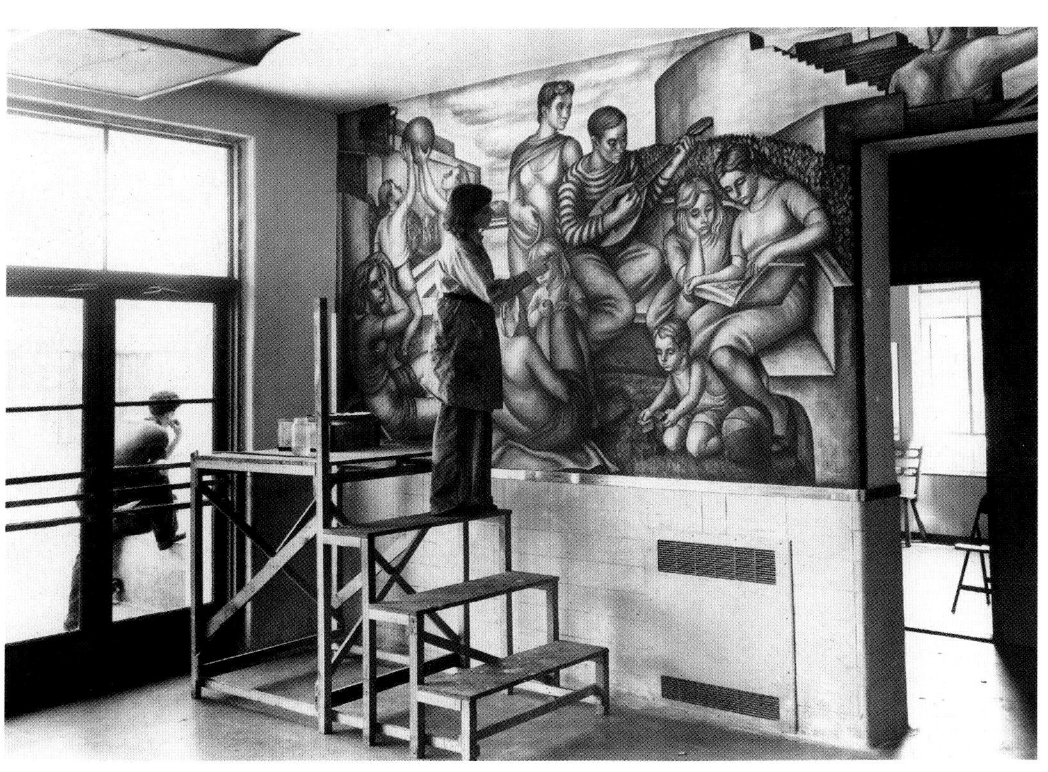

Lucienne Bloch (1909–1999) is best known today for the many photographs she took of Diego Rivera and, especially, Frida Kahlo in the United States and Mexico. In addition, this professional photographer (whose work appeared for several decades in *Life* magazine) was able to take the only surviving pictures of Rivera's condemned Rockefeller Center mural shortly before its destruction. Nonetheless, Bloch (born in Switzerland, the daughter of the opera and symphonic composer Ernest Bloch [1880–1959]) had a successful career as a muralist, employing the training that she learned as Rivera's assistant in New York and Detroit, as well as the technical expertise she gained from her husband, Stephen Dimitroff (1910–1996), who worked as Rivera's plasterer for the Rockefeller Center project. Both Bloch and Dimitroff worked throughout the United States for over four decades, creating murals in public buildings that carried the 1930s WPA mode of fresco painting into more modern idioms.

Bloch's own work in the 1930s was supported by the WPA/FAP. Her New York murals included frescos in Madison House, a social welfare residence on Madison Street in Manhattan's Lower East Side, and an allegory of music for the music room of New York's George Washington High School in Upper

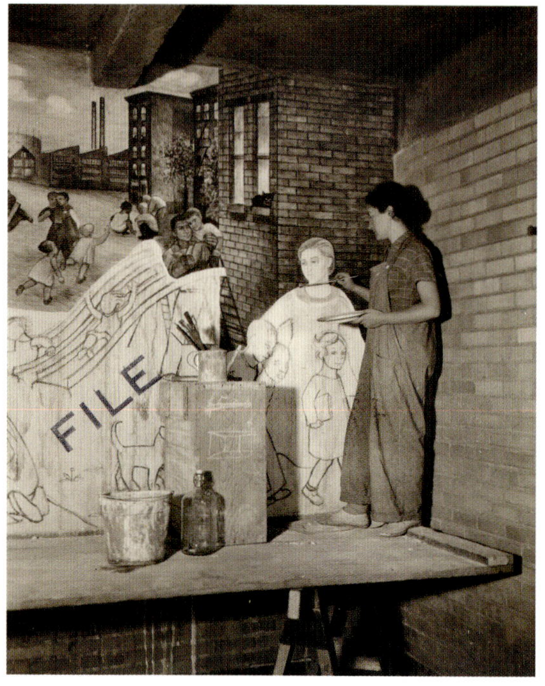

Manhattan. In 1935 she designed a mural for the House of Detention for Women on Greenwich Avenue in New York City, a building erected in 1929 and demolished in 1974. The subject was the *Cycle of a Woman's Life* (FIG. 4.7) and it featured a panoramic street view of mothers and children of mixed race playing and conversing on a city street in the Greenwich Village neighborhood where the prison was located. The sentiments in this mural (only one panel of which was finished due to the difficulties the artist encountered with dampness on the walls[19]) are analogous to those of Greenwood's Red Hook Housing Project fresco discussed above, and add a level of tranquility and uplifting feeling befitting the location of the work, in a place where women were deprived of the presence of their loved ones. This emotional quality is a translation into personal terms of the strong partisan sentiments expressed in the politically engaged murals of her mentor.

Muralism, Teaching, and Learning

There are close links between the muralist movements in both countries and pedagogy. As we have seen above, the first major project of the so-called mural renaissance was produced in Mexico City at the elite ENP (National Preparatory School) as early as 1922. We have examined Rivera's project for the Ministry of Public Education and mentioned his work at the National School of Agriculture in Chapingo.[20] The revolutionary public schools (*escuelas revolucionarias*) in the cities throughout Mexico became hallmarks of the literacy and pedagogical projects of the post-1920 federal governments, and they also became venues for mural decoration.[21] The act of teaching became a common theme in many mural cycles. When the Mexican muralists traveled to the United States, it was often at the invitation of educational institutions. Rivera painted a well-known mural for the San Francisco Art Institute in 1931,[22] for example, and Siqueiros's work as a teacher at the Experimental Workshop in New York had considerable influence on younger artists. However, the muralist who dedicated the bulk of his fresco-making efforts to institutes of higher learning was Orozco.

José Clemente Orozco painted the largest number of murals in the ENP between 1922 and 1926. In 1930 he was invited to Pomona College (Claremont, California) to execute a mural on the theme of *Prometheus Bringing Fire to the Earth*, an allegory of enlightenment and sustenance. In the same year he did a famous series of frescos on the theme of universal brotherhood and the worldwide struggle for peace for The New School in New York. Yet by far his most outstanding achievement in the realm of muralism in a U.S. setting was the project carried out between 1932 and 1934 at the Baker Library, Dartmouth College, in Hanover, New Hampshire (FIG. 4.8). While Rivera's frescos embodied a narrative character to create his didactic stories of themes from the vast panorama of Mexico's history (using his characteristic linear style of drawing ultimately derived from his careful study of Early and High Renaissance muralism in Italy between 1920 and 1921), Orozco's manner was radically different. His works in all media evidenced a high degree of expressionism. Anxiety and trauma often characterize the subjects in his murals and this mood is enhanced by the dramatic colors and strong lines that produce often shocking effects, as seen in the Dartmouth murals. Orozco began his career as a newspaper caricaturist (deriving inspiration from the work of José Guadalupe Posada, discussed in Chapter 1). The spirit of his art is comparable to the dramatic renderings of German and Austrian Expressionist contemporaries such as Max Beckmann (1884–1950) or Oskar Kokoschka (1886–1980), although it is uncertain if Orozco knew those painters' works. Even if he did not, Orozco's contribution must certainly be assessed within an international panorama of art that openly reflects the stresses of the era in which it was produced.

Orozco's Dartmouth murals are collectively entitled "The Epic of American Civilization." They were painted between 1932 and 1934. Commissioned with the support of the faculty and

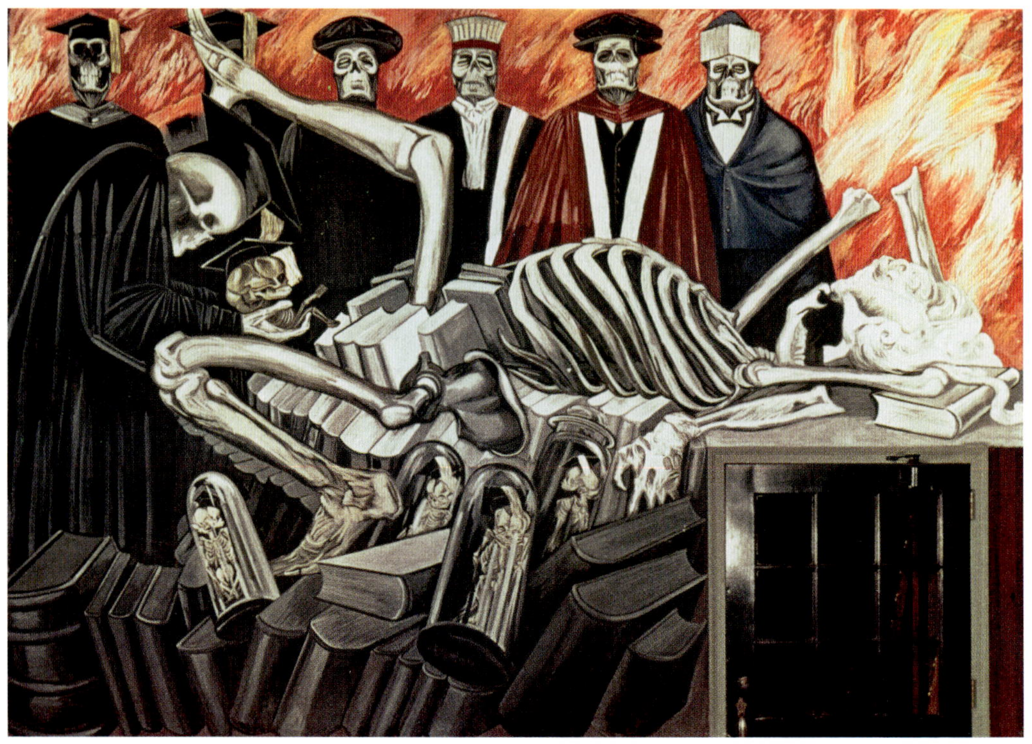

President Ernest Hopkins (although not without vigorous criticism from some students and alumni) of the prestigious college in rural New England, the paintings retain their shock value to this day, and when seen in person, represent dramatic contrasts with the bucolic surroundings of the institution.[23] There are 24 individual panels, mostly separated by the architectural features of the underground room where they are situated. The overall program consists of a mythological and historical narrative of the Americas, from the arrival in Mexico of the god Quetzalcoatl, to the coming of the Spaniards with Hernán Cortés, through to the rise of modern industry throughout the hemisphere, with its positive and negative aspects.

Education itself plays a major role in these paintings. One of the panels reveals a blond-haired North American teacher protecting and guiding her diminutive students. A far more strident and even shocking section illustrated here depicts a series of ghostly skeletons, clad in academic robes and mortarboard hats, standing as sentinels before the flayed body of a woman whose head rests upon a table (which is actually the top of one of the doors in the room). She is shown giving birth to a large, old, and dusty book as bell jars filled with desiccated fetuses rest on the tops of other volumes that form the lower portion of the picture. This grisly scene, called by the artist *Gods of the Modern World*, represents a scathing indictment of the uselessness of modern education, which Orozco saw as riddled with emphasis on unusable facts imparted by pompous, self-important academics out of touch with the real world of struggle and socio-economic misery.[24] The color scheme of mainly reds, grays, and blacks enhances the dramatic value of this ghastly tableau.

Siqueiros was the most politically active of the three muralists mentioned above. During certain periods of his life (for example, at the time of the Spanish Civil War) he gave up painting altogether for political activism. He was exiled from Mexico in the early 1930s for his Leftist activities and was later implicated in the assassination of the exiled Russian revolutionary Leon Trotsky (1879–1940) in Mexico City in 1940. Like Rivera and Orozco, Siqueiros had worked on the murals of the ENP in the early 1920s, and for his earliest mural in the United States (where he first arrived in Los Angeles in 1932, having been banished from Mexico) he also executed a painting for a school.

The Chouinard Art Institute was founded in 1921 in downtown Los Angeles (it exists today as CalArts). On its facade, Siqueiros, in collaboration with students at the institute, painted a mural known as *Street Meeting*, showing a gathering of laborers of various races. This outdoor mural (on cement) was long thought to have elicited protest for its socialist content related to labor and the gathering of workers from across ethnicities. Nonetheless, the art historian Olivier Debroise points out that *Street Meeting* was actually well received in the press (both Anglo and Mexican) at the time, and that its destruction was gradual, a result of rain and other elements. Due to the fragility of the colors, which had been hastily applied to the cement surface, the image began to fade within a year of its creation.[25]

Four years after his works of public art in Los Angeles (which also included a recently restored mural called *Tropical America* for the Italian Hall on Olvera Street that set a precedent for a later development of muralism by artists of Mexican heritage in that city), Siqueiros went to New York to attend the American Artists' Congress, "a broad affiliation of artists opposed to war and fascism," according to James Oles.[26] His stay in Manhattan did not produce any murals, yet it was notable for the establishment of his own school, the Experimental Workshop, on West 14th Street. From this institution Siqueiros was able to further his investigations into nontraditional art materials (he used industrial paints and found objects in his paintings, as we will see below). The Experimental Workshop also provided a platform for socially engaged artists to create such things as props and costumes for use in political demonstrations and parades. In Siqueiros's own paintings done during his years in New York (and beyond), serendipitous shapes suggested by paint dripped onto canvases or plywood supports laid upon the floor were a critical part of the artistic testing that took place in the school, whose pupils included several fellow Mexican artists, including Antonio Pujol (1913–1995), as well as American painters Sanford McCoy (1909–1963) and his half brother Jackson Pollock (1912–1956).[27]

The relationship between Siqueiros and academic institutions came to a culminating point between 1950 and 1952 when he participated in the adornment of the new buildings of the National Autonomous University of Mexico (UNAM), created in the then nearly empty district of Mexico City known as the Pedregal (a vast lava field that covered the ruins of the pre-Hispanic site of Cuicuilco). The creation of the immense campus under the presidency of Miguel Alemán (1946–52) was a major statement of the country's modernity and prowess in both economic and intellectual fields of endeavor. The university had long occupied many colonial buildings in downtown Mexico City but the coming together of all of the facilities in one venue, with buildings designed by some 150 architects and engineers, also marked a milestone for the country's art.[28] Muralism, a form of public expression that had played such a key role in Mexico since the early 1920s, was still a viable force in the art world, if judged by the efforts of Siqueiros, Juan O'Gorman (1905–1982), José Chávez Morado (1909–2002), and others, despite the fact that younger artists were fast moving away from figurative forms of painting to experiments in abstraction.

The physical situation of the Ciudad Universitaria (University City, or CU), the main campus of the UNAM, was meant to evoke other venues of historical importance in Mexico. As the art historian Mary Coffey has stated:

its central axis and stepped structure refer to the Calzada de los Muertos (Way of the Dead) at Teotihuacán, while the asymmetrical organization of the buildings along a central plaza draw upon the Zapotec city plan at Monte Albán.[29]

Siqueiros, along with fellow artist and architect Juan O'Gorman, was given pride of place in the CU decorative program, although, as we will see, their approaches were vastly different. Siqueiros created a monumental mural sculpture in painted plaster for the northern and southern facades of the rector's tower (FIG. 4.9). Entitled *The People to the University, The University to the People,* this work is an allegory of both the humanities and the sciences. Five male bodies project outward into space, their three-dimensional torsos sculpted in relief and painted in shades of blue, tan, and orange. Their heads and elongated arms stand out most forcefully, while the lower parts of their bodies are dramatically truncated. They hold books, a compass, and, in the center, an architectural model for the viewer to contemplate. At the upper right corner small figures carry flags and march as in a student

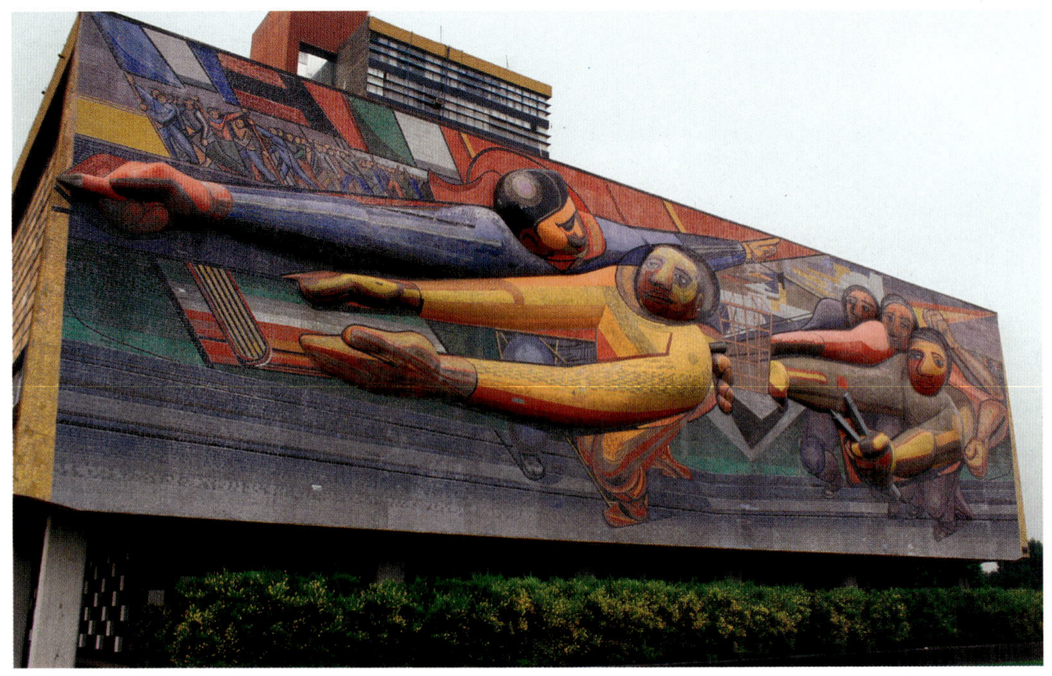

demonstration. The background is faceted into irregular, vaguely geometric shapes, a nod perhaps on the part of the artist in the direction of nonobjective art. This mural is, in fact, considerably more legible and concretely representational than passages in many of Siqueiros's earlier works in which, stimulated by his interest in film and photomontage, he compressed and summarized figures in a way that created dynamic effects but sometimes visually perplexing results for the audience.[30]

Siqueiros was insistent on the "readability" of this work and strongly criticized that of O'Gorman, who, with his 4,000-square-meter mosaic mural on the four sides of the CU's library (FIG. 4.10), executed one of the largest such projects to date. The two principal facades display symbolic images from the pre-Hispanic era and the colonial period (seen here, with such emblems derived from Ptolemaic and Copernican cosmologies as the zodiac, sun, and moon). The viewer also observes juxtapositions of an Aztec temple and a Christian church and myriad symbols attesting to the Spanish conquest and the suffering of the vanquished indigenous peoples. The effect is dizzying and provides the viewer not so much with a coherent visual program as with a comprehensive inventory of signs referring to a vast array of moments in both Mexican and world history. Siqueiros found it to be excessively decorative and accused the artist of creating a folkloric patchwork.[31] The O'Gorman mural did, in fact, become a major tourist attraction and has been reproduced via millions of postcards, maps, brochures, and Instagram images since it was finished in 1952. Yet it represents an alternative mode to the many forms of muralist expression that characterize the UNAM's campus, a site that constitutes a virtual encyclopedia of approaches to the possibilities inherent in the late phases of this hemisphere-wide, but quintessentially Mexican, form of public art.

At precisely the same time that Siqueiros was planning his monumental projects for UNAM, the African-American artist Hale Woodruff (1900–1980) was engaged in creating a series of six large-scale murals for the historically black Atlanta University (now Clark Atlanta University), where he had previously served as Chair of the Art Department (by 1950 Woodruff had been named Professor of Art at New York University, where he taught until his retirement in 1968).[32] The paintings are in situ in the

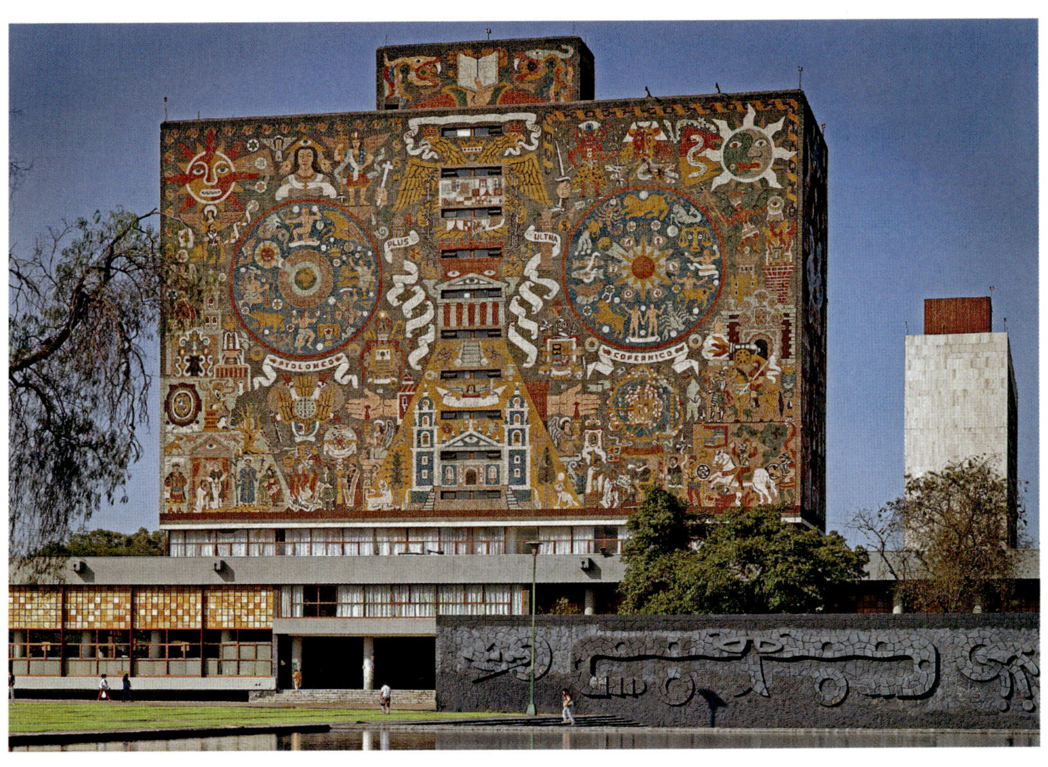

atrium of the University's Trevor Arnett Hall and Art Gallery. The overall title of this 1950–51 series is "The Art of the Negro" and it is a multipart allegory for the achievements of Africans and African Americans in the visual, musical, and literary arts, and a variety of other cultural activities.

Artists (Study) (FIG. 4.11) is a preliminary painting for one of these murals. These paintings chart the pre-European civilizations of Africa, the contact with Western imperialist powers and the beginnings of enslavement, and the relationship between African cultures and other non-Western civilizations, among other themes. The final version is somewhat different in its disposition of figures, but what we see in this initial oil on canvas adheres fairly closely to the final composition. It is a bipartite configuration with an upper register including the figure of Shango, one of the principal deities of the Yoruba pantheon, who reigns as the god of thunder. Shango is flanked on the right by Buddha, representing Asia, and on the left by an allegorical image of Europe in the person of a nude white female. Below, as in a traditional Christian Renaissance or Baroque altarpiece, is a gathering of 17 African-American artists of note, including Joshua Johnson (1763–1832), the first

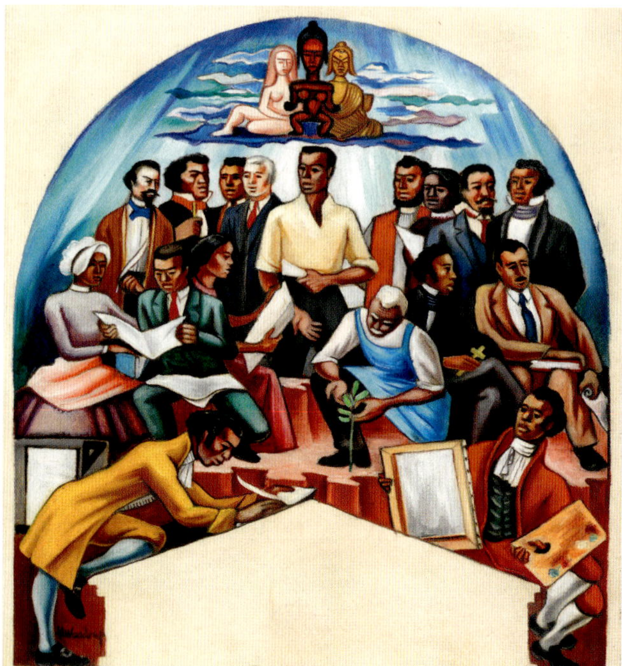

black colonial portraitist, Henry Ossawa Tanner, and Woodruff's contemporary Jacob Lawrence.

The juxtaposition of images referring to both African and African-American cultures in the Woodruff murals attests to the pervasive influence of the 1925 text entitled *The New Negro*, an anthology of essays, fiction, and poetry by Howard University professor Alain Locke (1885–1954), whose work laid the basis for an admiration and appreciation of the links between African and American cultures.[33] The term itself ("new Negro") was widely used throughout the later 1920s and 30s to indicate cultural resistance to the white-imposed status quo. The paintings are also appropriate to consider within the pedagogical context for which they were executed. Atlanta University was, and continues to be, a highly regarded center of advanced learning that, at its core, instills the values of African-American achievement within the larger context of higher education. About the paintings (and evidently referring specifically to this composition), Woodruff stated:

It portrays what I call the Art of the Negro. This has to do with a kind of interpretive treatment of African art ... I look at the African artist certainly as one of my ancestors regardless of how we feel about each other today. I've always had a high regard and respect for the African artist and his art. So this mural ... is for me, a kind of token of my esteem for African Art.[34]

Stylistically the links between Woodruff's murals and those of Diego Rivera are sometimes striking. In the study examined here, the upper register with allegories of three continents brings to mind Rivera's murals in the Detroit Institute of Arts. Woodruff's enthusiasm for Rivera and Mexican muralism—an affinity he shared with many African-American artists who found their way to Mexico in the 1920s and 30s, seeking both inspiration and greater freedom of creativity away from the racist atmosphere of the United States—dates from his own trip to Mexico in 1936 to learn the fresco technique from Rivera. Woodruff's murals therefore represent a latter-day continuation of the interchange between U.S. and Mexican artists, both technically and in terms of their shared dedication to subject matter derived from social concerns.[35]

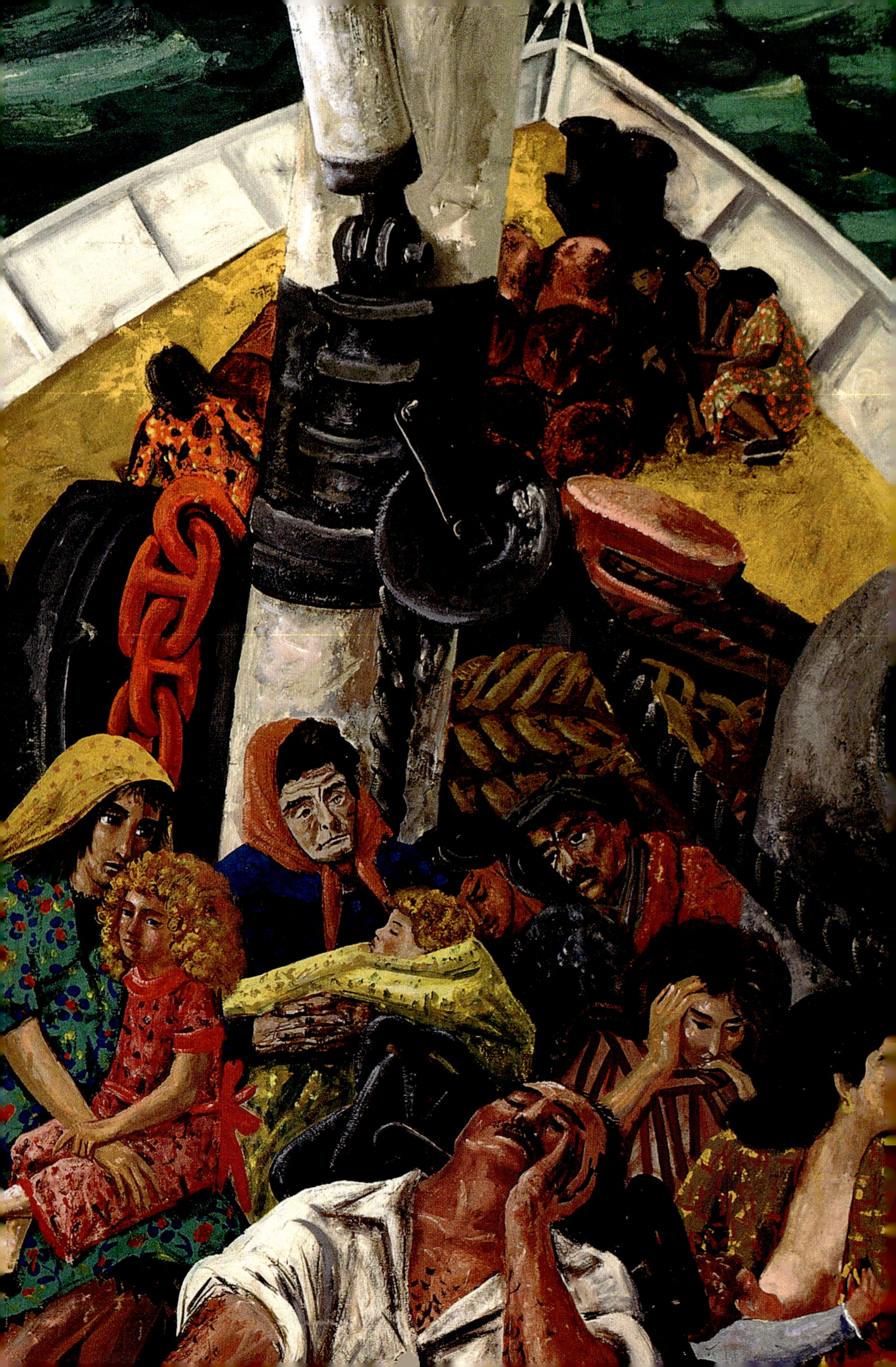

Chapter 5

Labor, Anxiety, and a New Social Order

This chapter, like the previous section, examines artistic responses to societal disruptions, global economic depression and the trauma of World War II, across a broad spectrum of paintings, prints, and photographs. These phenomena created an atmosphere of profound tension and stress that was manifest in thousands of images of displaced persons, the ravages of poverty and homelessness, and the violence of racial and ethnic prejudice. The ultimately existential anxiety of worldwide annihilation followed from the dramatic start of the nuclear age with the 1945 bombings of Japan by the United States. The collective anxiety of this time is perfectly encapsulated in David Alfaro Siqueiros's 1936 *Niña madre* (Girl Mother), the first work analyzed below (FIG. 5.1).

Ecological disasters continued to set the stage for human suffering. I alluded previously to the Dust Bowl in the United States in the 1930s. Major droughts in the Brazilian northeast occurred simultaneously. History always repeats itself and, as this volume is being written, the entire eastern sector of Brazil has been suffering from a calamitous drought since 2013 that has had a particularly negative effect on the coffee crop in a country that was made immensely wealthy from the cultivation of that commodity in the first decades of the century.

Among other environmental catastrophes of the period should be counted the San Zenón Cyclone of 1930, which virtually destroyed the infrastructure of the capital of the Dominican Republic and served indirectly as the catalyst for the rise to power of long-standing dictator Rafael Trujillo, president (between

Antonio Berni
Los Emigrantes
(The Emigrants),
1956 (detail).
See fig. 5.16.

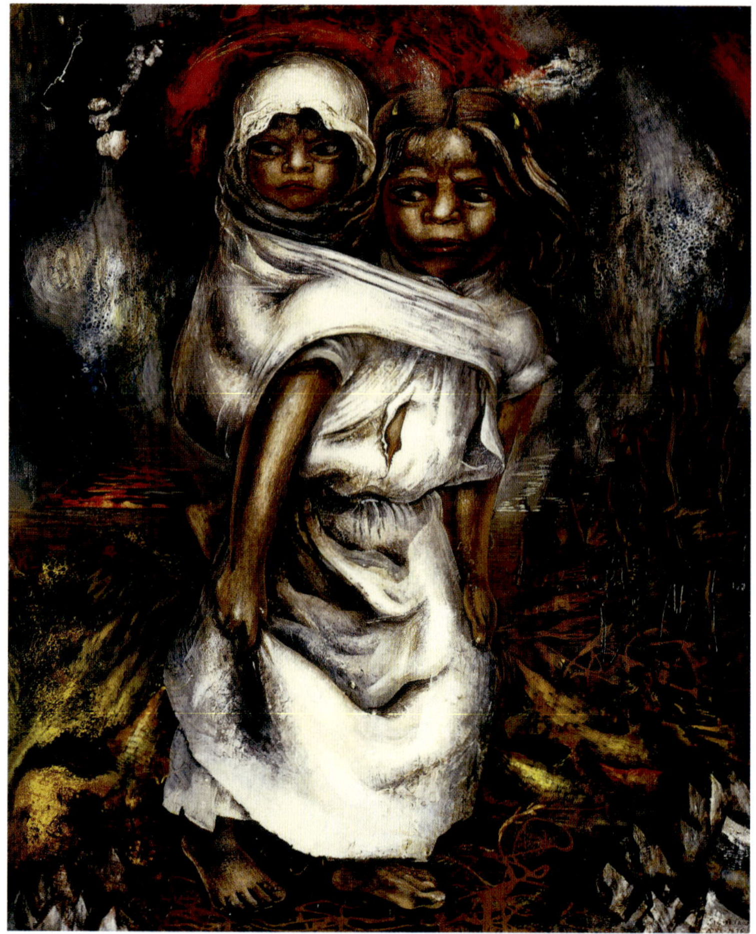

1930 and 1961) of this nation searching for a "strongman" (or *caudillo*, to use a politically loaded Spanish term for the type of despot who has had a long history in the region). The rise of dictators and presidents who assumed unusually autocratic powers throughout the Americas in the period under consideration here also accounted for the reactions of many artists in the visual and literary arts, either directly or by implication. Notable examples include the presidencies of Juan Vicente Gómez (1908–1935) and Marcos Pérez Jiménez in Venezuela (1952–58), Juan Perón in Argentina (1946–55), and Gerardo Machado and Fulgencio Batista (1940–44 and 1952–59) in Cuba, whose abuses of power set the stage for the Cuban Revolution of 1959, after which Fidel Castro (1926–2016) assumed virtually total control of politics and society in that island nation.

A continued effort on the part of the United States to project its political, military, and economic hegemony throughout the hemisphere either directly or indirectly was a hallmark of the earlier phases of our study. Such interventions were especially common in the Caribbean and Central America. Military and naval presences expanded the sphere of influence of U.S. imperialism for lengthy periods of time in Nicaragua (1912–33), Haiti (1915–34), the Dominican Republic (1916–24), and Honduras (1911). Cuba and Puerto Rico, as well as the Panama Canal Zone, had already been under U.S. domination, directly or indirectly, since the end of the 1890s. Throughout the 1920s and into the mid-twentieth century (and beyond, to the present), U.S.–Latin American political relations continued to be fraught, with periodic rapprochements contrasting with episodes of virulent resistance to what was often termed Yankee Imperialism being more the rule than the exception.

Cities like São Paulo, Buenos Aires, and New York felt the profound effects of successive waves of immigration from southern and eastern Europe (and, in the case of Brazil, Japan) during the first years of the twentieth century. Yet another, even more massive, wave of forced immigration and exile occurred in the 1930s and 40s as a result of thousands of refugees coming to the Americas from Spain at the time of the Spanish Civil War and, concurrently, fleeing from the rise of Nazism and the terrors of the war in Germany, and central and eastern Europe. Many foreign artists came to the centers of artistic creativity in the Americas. The theme of exile and migration itself becomes one of major preoccupation to many artists well into the 1950s and beyond, as we will see in the case of Argentinean painter Antonio Berni (1905–1981).

American Scene painters of the 1930s and 40s flourished in the United States. Among the most famous of this loosely defined group were Grant Wood (1891–1942), John Steuart Curry (1897–1946), and Thomas Hart Benton, all of whom came from states in the Middle West. Their contemporaries in the Andean countries of Ecuador, Peru, and Bolivia were equally adept at suggesting the lives of the oppressed working classes in both urban and rural settings. Ecuadorean artist Eduardo Kingman Riofrío (1913–1997), whose art is examined below, is a particularly fine example of Andean *Indigenismo* (Indigenism), a form of painting, sculpture, and printmaking that examined the social circumstances of individuals who lived at the margins of societies that were hierarchically divided, between levels of extreme poverty of peoples of native heritage and the lavish wealth of the white elites.

Anxiety

The previous chapter included a brief analysis of the late monumental outdoor sculptural murals by David Alfaro Siqueiros for the University City complex in the Mexican capital. Here I return to Siqueiros as a major protagonist in the visual embodiment of anxiety, which was a pervasive theme in the figurative art of the 1930s and beyond throughout the western hemisphere. In his painting on panel entitled *Niña madre* (Girl Mother), a young girl, no older than 13 or 14, shoeless and clothed in a tattered white dress, carries a baby on her back in her *rebozo* (a shawl traditionally worn by Mexican women).[1] The faces of both mother and child betray tension and worry. They trudge through a fissured landscape that appears to be enveloped in smoke and dust. The countryside is burning; flames are visible in the background and the sky above the hapless pair creates a halo of red that frames their heads.[2]

Among Siqueiros's most astonishing achievements in the realm of trenchant suggestions of human suffering is his 1937 *Echo of a Scream* (FIG. 5.2), based on a terrifying photo of a suffering child he had seen in a newspaper, an episode of the 1937–45 Sino-Japanese War. This image depicting a crying child posed within a ravaged landscape, against an oversized depiction of its own head arrested in an eternal exclamation of torment, captures the essential qualities of physical and psychic anguish.

Girl Mother and *Echo of a Scream* were both painted with Duco, a commercial name for a type of lacquer made in the United States by the DuPont company, beginning in the 1920s, for use in the automotive industry. Siqueiros was noted for his employment of nontraditional media, which, at this period in his career, he often applied to the canvas or panel in energetic strokes that heightened the impression of randomness, even though he probably never meant any of his compositions or painterly techniques to be conceived of as unplanned. In *Girl Mother* Siqueiros

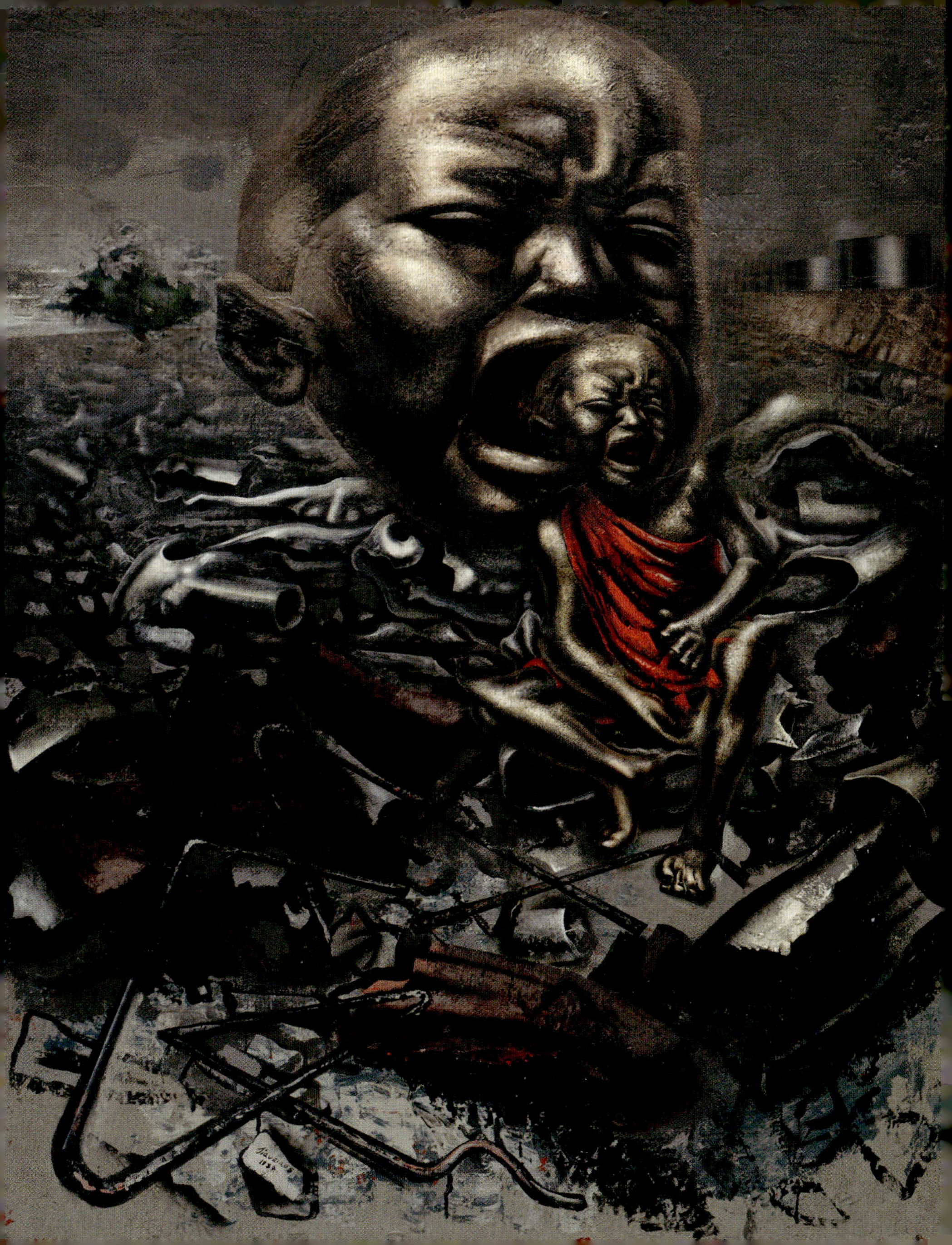

combined his interest in innovative techniques and unorthodox materials. The use of the viscous commercial color substance creates a web of calligraphic forms and quasi-sculptural protuberances of thick, dry paint on the picture's surface that may be observed only when seeing the work in person.[3] Siqueiros was certainly well aware of these visual serendipities when applying the Duco to the surface as it appears thoroughly deliberate and acts in concert with the overall sense of tension throughout the pictorial elements. It was precisely these materials and practices that he taught in his classes at the Experimental Workshop that opened on New York's West 14th Street in April 1936.[4] The young Jackson Pollock was one of the heirs of the techniques taught there.

Pollock's lithograph with airbrush additions called *Landscape with a Steer* (FIG. 5.3) is a compelling image, both a multiple and a single, unique work. Pollock began creating prints in 1932 at the Art Students League in New York, and there is at least one version of this same composition without the colors added with the airbrush.[5] Pollock, who of course would go on to become one

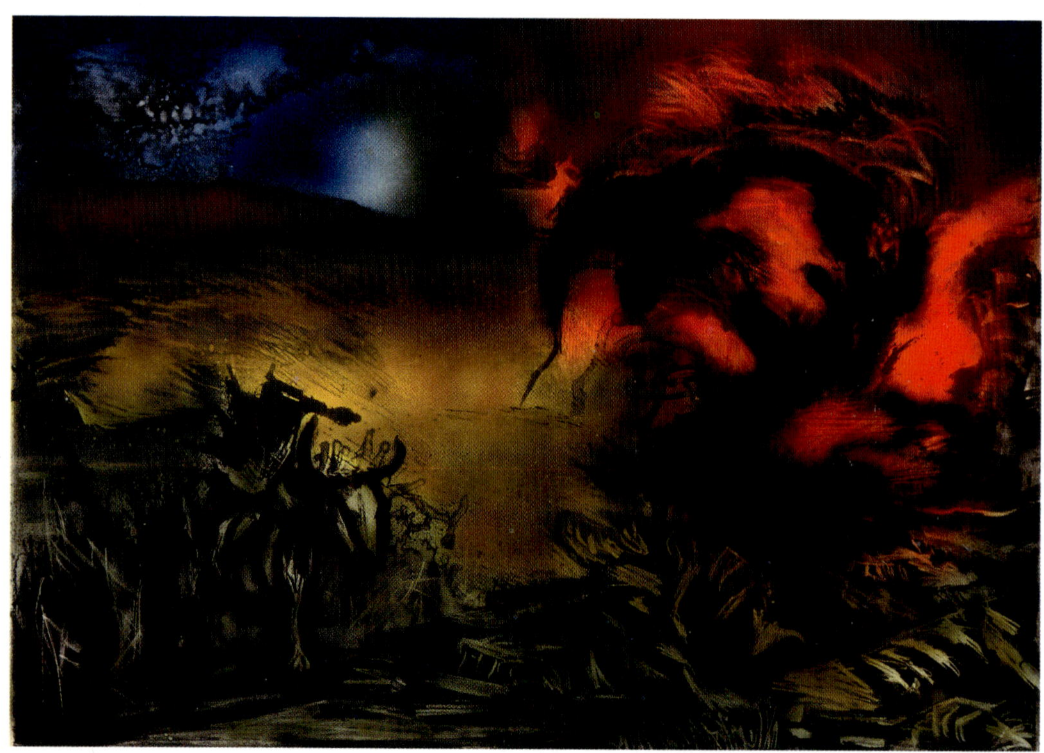

of the most well-recognized members of the New York School of Abstract Expressionists, began to experiment with airbrushing and other unconventional painting techniques, such as the potential of random application of paint on a support, at the Experimental Workshop. While the question of precisely where Pollock may have painted his landscape print is not certain, what is indisputable is its position within the genealogy of works of art of this era that refer to the tortured images of Siqueiros and create within themselves a mood of darkness, or even despair.

In *Landscape with a Steer* the slashing, virtually out-of-control lines that define mountains, sky, and ground obscure the details of geography. The colors (blue, red, and golden yellow) function as they do in Siqueiros's *Girl Mother*, creating an ambiguous mood that ranges from intimations of hellish scenery to a possible note of hope in the blue sky of the far distant upper-left portion of the work. Thus, while not specifically narrative in nature, Pollock's image evokes analogous sentiments of the times— intimations of angst and bleak despair. Pollock, of course, took the lessons he learned from the Mexicans, especially Siqueiros, to new limits. While Siqueiros was open to experimental forms and effects, created in his paintings by the use of industrial and other nontraditional media, he did not, as suggested, employ them as pictorial ends in themselves.[6] Pollock would take such "painterly accidents" in other directions with, for example, his drip paintings (begun approximately a decade after the lithograph in question here), in which he applied paint to a canvas placed on a floor with seemingly random gestures to create "all-over" patterns of nonobjective form. In *Landscape with a Steer*, however, Pollock clearly follows the pathway of storytelling that characterizes the work of all the artists considered in this chapter.

Lynchings

Thoroughly explicit, utterly shocking, and directly representative of one of the most heinous social realities in the United States during the 1930s is *American Justice* (FIG. 5.4) by Joe Jones (1909–1963). This work was painted in 1933 and is a reaction to the rise of lynchings in the American South during the Jim Crow era, which lasted from the end of Reconstruction after the U.S. Civil War all the way to the years of World War II.[7]

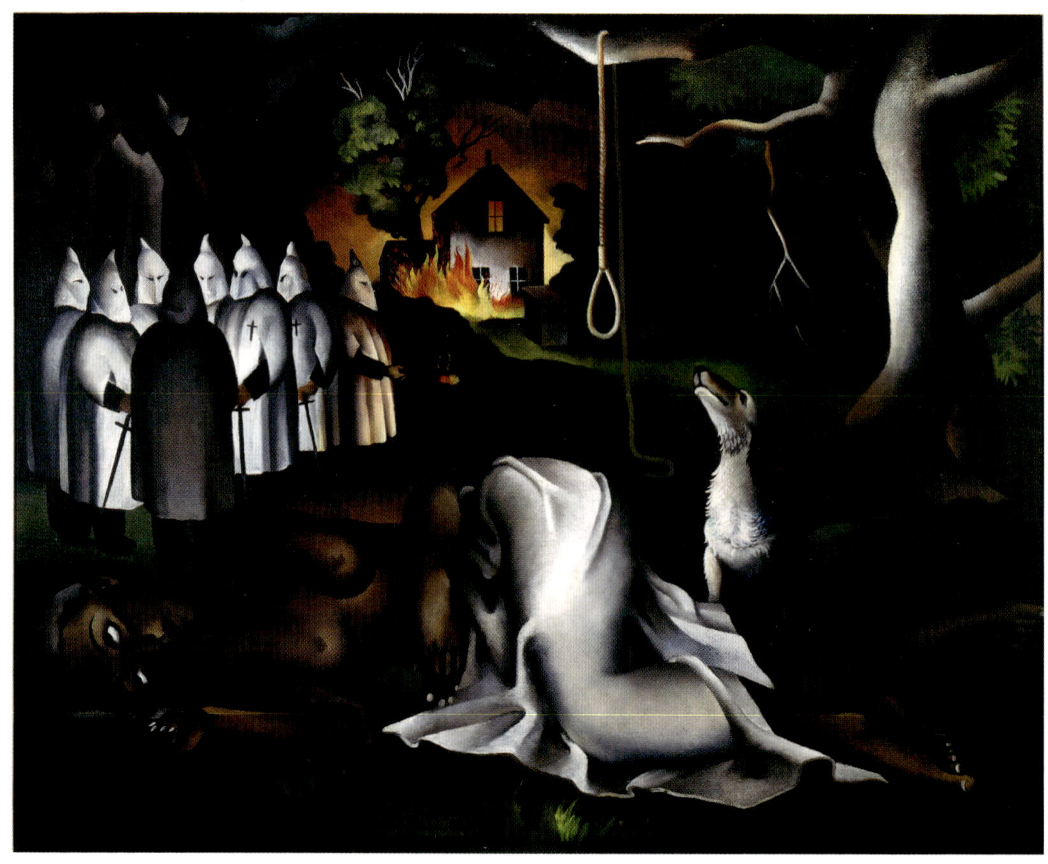

It witnessed the enactment in states below the Mason–Dixon line (the border dividing the northern states of Pennsylvania and Delaware from southern states of Maryland, Virginia, and West Virginia) of a wide variety of laws enforcing racial segregation and other regulations that highly disfavored the black population. Racial tensions were constantly in a state of volatility, and from as early as the 1880s (and as late as the 1960s) several thousand African-American men (and some women) were hanged from trees by uncontrollable mobs of self-described vigilantes. Many of the perceived offenses for which they were murdered included alleged molestation of, or even consensual relationships with, white women.

Jones was a painter and muralist from Saint Louis, Missouri. He became a member of the American Communist Party the year that he painted *American Justice*. Saint Louis had a long tradition of social equality movements even though Missouri

160

had been a slave state during the Civil War. Many of Jones's paintings, murals, and prints executed under the auspices of the Federal Art Project of the WPA refer to his ardent resistance to racial inequality, and *American Justice* is one of his most outstanding contributions to the iconography of ethnic prejudice and its horrible consequences. This is a dark image in every conceivable way. It is essentially a tableau separated into four sections. Jones's segmentation of space in this work is not unrelated to his admiration for two cycles of murals he had viewed only months or days before beginning work on this picture. In May 1933 he traveled to New York with the specific purpose of studying the murals by Orozco and Jones's fellow-Missourian Thomas Hart Benton at The New School and, several weeks later, those by Diego Rivera at the Detroit Institute of Arts. All of these pictorial cycles were of interest to him for their social content as well as the readability of their narratives, which, despite their complicated themes, remain pictorially coherent due to the artists' skill at spatial construction.

In *American Justice* the first focal point is the lower portion of the partially nude female lying dead in the foreground. A white sheet covers her thighs and upper legs. Her eyes are wide open in death. A dog, most likely her faithful companion, is howling in mourning. The creature looks up at the noose hanging from the tree that forms the right-hand portion of the quadripartite composition. The white fur of the dog's neck is eerily illuminated by the light of an unseen moon and the fire below the figures of the hooded Ku Klux Klan members at the left. There are eight men in this group; seven of them form a circle facing inward, while one man who holds a torch looks out into the middle ground. The Klan members hold swords. A cross is imprinted on the white robes of at least two of them. At the center background a house, presumably that of the victim of the monstrous crime, is engulfed in red and yellow flames that recall the conflagrations suggested in the works of both Siqueiros and Pollock discussed above.

I will analyze an example of a more well-known genre of lynching images in a moment, but we must first consider the meaning of this unusual picture within the range of such depictions of societal terror. The female figure in Jones's painting was described in a 1935 *Time* magazine article as a "vivid picture of a prostitute who had been lynched by hooded Ku-Kluxers."[8]

Yet, as art historian M. Melissa Wolfe points out, "there is no real evidence to suggest she is a prostitute, and the conclusion seems couched in the pervasive racist refusal to accord a black woman the same innocence and respectability as a white woman."[9] Wolfe also points to the empty noose and the possibility of this being a scene of gang rape as well as murder by the Klan members. In this picture Jones presents us with a haunting, terrifying glimpse of one of the darkest chapters in the 1930s American scene.

On the night of August 7, 1930, two African-American teenagers, Thomas Shipp and Abram Smith, were taken by a mob from the Grant County Jail in Marion, Indiana (a small city in the north central part of what had not been a slave state but one where, nevertheless, racial tensions had been acute since Reconstruction), and hanged from a tree near the courthouse. This event, precipitated by the charge of murder of a white man and the rape of a white woman (crimes unsolved to this day), became infamous through its visual testimony in what has been

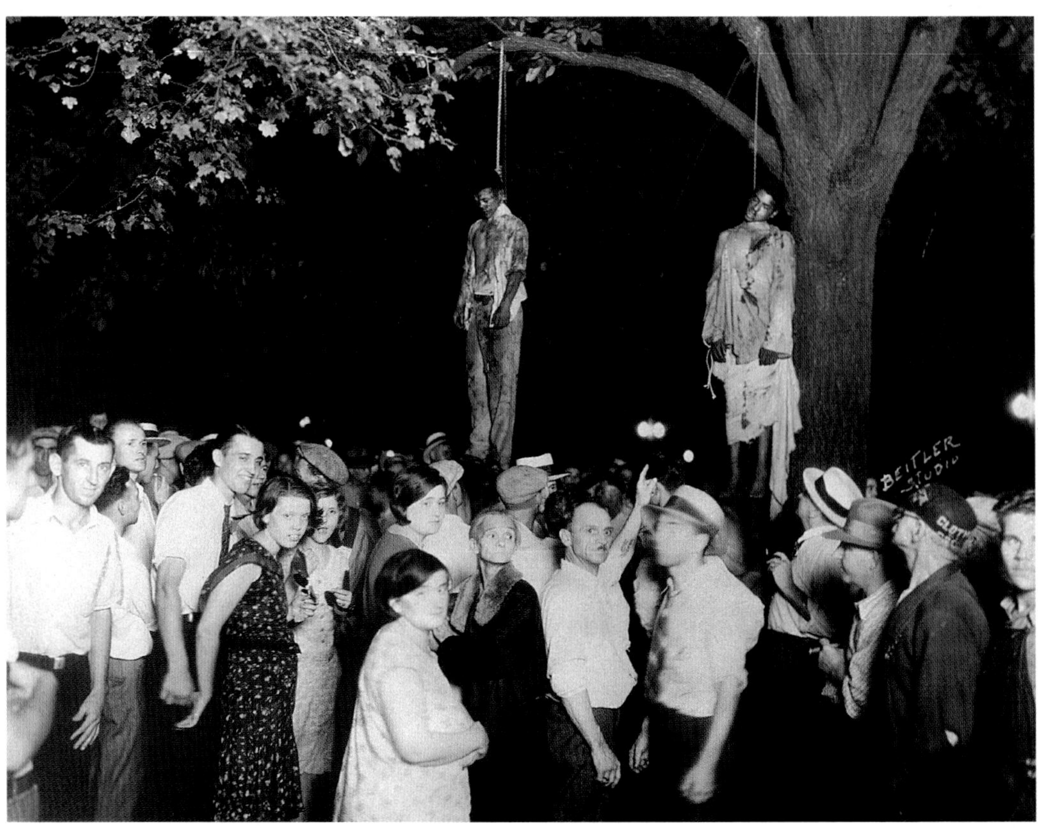

called the most famous lynching photograph in the history of this unsettling category of documentation. The image, called *Lynching in Marion, Indiana, 1930* (FIG. 5.5), was taken by a local photographer named Lawrence Beitler (1885–1961) and was reproduced by his studio, selling hundreds of copies as "souvenirs" of this grisly event.[10]

Both victims hang lifeless from the tree in the background. The foreground comprises the most shocking element of the photograph, and one that is seen in most lynching photography: the presence of witnesses. A crowd of dozens of middle-class white people, probably townsfolk and farmers curious about the crime, gather before the victims. A man in the center points to the lynched men as he faces the camera, as if to say, "I was there." This is a pictorial element that has been used in Western art since the Middle Ages, when painters included "witnesses"—at times, people in contemporary dress present at scenes of heavenly activities, or even self-portraits of the artist in a genre picture—to testify to the compellingly "real" nature of a scene, or to bridge the gap between the viewers' time and space and that contained within the picture frame.

Beitler's photograph is made even more shocking and disorienting by the presence of other witnesses who turn to the camera and smile, as if completely oblivious to the horrifying events taking place only steps from them.[11] The stark disparity between black and white participants, life and death, violence and pleasure is almost too much to bear when we observe this and hundreds of other such pictures that populate the history of photography, but which became more prevalent than ever in the 1930s—a period when the federal government attempted but failed to pass two distinct anti-lynching bills in Congress.[12]

These disturbing images of lynching done in the United States have a hemispheric precedent in a series of paintings and drawings by Francisco Goitia (1882–1960) of decapitated heads and, especially, representations of dead Mexican revolutionary soldiers hanging from trees. Goitia, from the central-northern Mexican state of Zacatecas, studied at the Academia de San Carlos in the Mexican capital where he worked with (among others) the great landscapist José María Velasco (1840–1912) and the symbolist painter Saturnino Herrán (see Chapter 1). Between 1904 and 1912 Goitia was in Spain and Italy, but he returned to Mexico where he affiliated himself with the revolutionary forces of the North under the direction of Francisco (Pancho) Villa. Goitia was a direct observer, an eyewitness to the atrocities committed during the war that accounted for upwards of three million deaths over the course of its ten years. Goitia perhaps most dramatically captured the intensity, horror, and unremitting violence of the Mexican Revolution, although many others (including José Clemente Orozco) capitalized on their first-hand observations of what Francisco de Goya had termed "The Disasters of War," the name of his famous series of prints of 1810–12.[13]

The sparseness and starkness of the imagery in Goitia's paintings and drawings have an especially intense impact on their viewers. In the circa 1914 *Paisaje de Zacatecas con ahorcados II* (Zacatecas Landscape with Hanged Men II) (FIG. 5.6), a parched

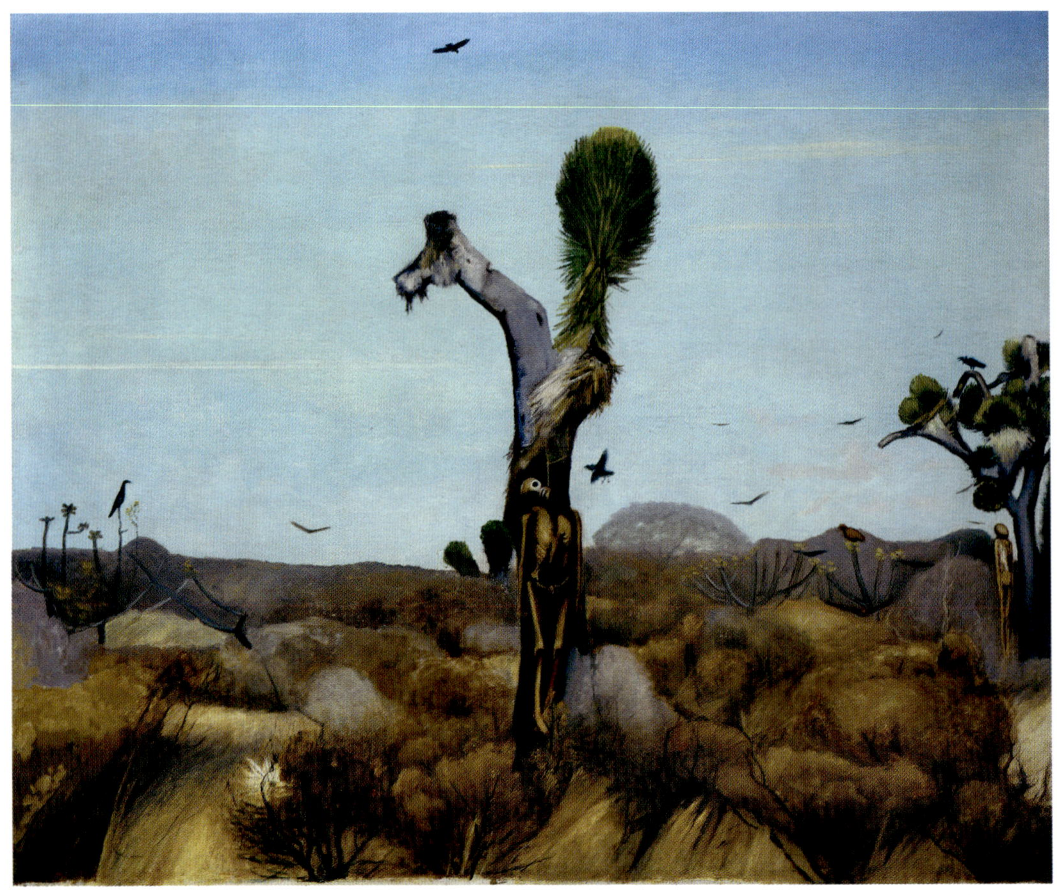

164

countryside punctuated by scrubby bushes and dead trees evokes an atmosphere of desolation and hopelessness—the terrible aftermath of a battle. From the tree that forms the central focus of the composition, as well as from the giant cactus at the right, hang the lifeless bodies of executed soldiers. They have been turned into skeletal remains thanks to the efforts of the vultures that relentlessly prowl the skies in search of further signs of carrion. Goitia evidences, in a way as shocking as the works of his U.S. counterparts 20 years later, the inhumanity and senselessness of violence. The circumstances of the creation of the works, though, are markedly different. Goitia defines a war crime, while Jones's painting and Beitler's photograph depict the consequences of racial discrimination and blind hatred, although each of these situations is equally repellant in its own perverse way.[14]

Clouds of War

The American artist Alice Neel (1900–1984) created *Nazis Murder Jews!* (FIG. 5.7) in 1936 as part of a series of socially engaged paintings of the first half of the 1930s in which she acknowledged the historical weight of the Mexican muralists as well as that of Goya.[15] It was directly inspired by the artist's growing concern for the Jewish populations of Europe as National Socialism spread its pernicious influence and toxic ideology throughout Germany, and ultimately much of Western, Central, and Eastern Europe.[16] Nonetheless this image may also be cogently situated within the larger pattern of depictions of human conflict and emotionally fraught situations. Neel was a witness to a demonstration

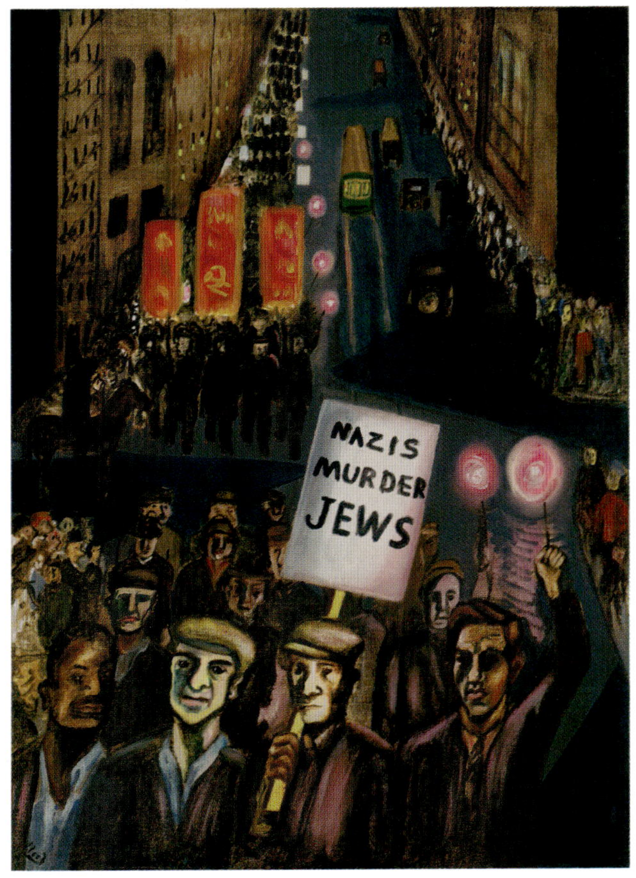

Fig. 5.7
Alice Neel
Nazis Murder Jews!,
1936, oil on canvas,
42 x 31 in. (106.7
x 78.7 cm). Private
collection.

in Manhattan organized by the Communist Party in which attention was called to the Nazi threat by the display of banners and placards such as the one carried by the middle figure in the group of four men that defines the lower portion of the composition. The marchers represent different races; the central two figures are light-skinned, while the flanking individuals are men of color. Dozens more figures follow this group and the crowd stretches into the far background of the composition. This painting of an urban protest takes place at night and the palette is therefore dark, reflecting the menace of the theme against which the men and women protest. The somber shades of Neel's palette are relieved only by the glowing red of the banners at center left, which bear the Communist hammer and sickle, and the sickly green representing the light from the bus in the background.

Neel's painting was first exhibited in New York at the American Contemporary Art Gallery in the year of its creation. The gallery, one of very few to exhibit living U.S. artists exclusively, had opened in 1932 on Madison Avenue (it is still in existence today in New York's Chelsea district). Neel was one of the many artistically forward-looking and politically progressive artists that ultimately formed the first group of regular exhibitors. The show in which *Nazis Murder Jews!* was seen was organized to honor the winners of a competition held by the American Artists' Congress (AAC), an organization that was founded in February 1936 as a platform for the creation of visual manifestations of the Communist Party's protest against the rise of despotism and dictatorship. Siqueiros attended the Congress, as we saw in Chapter 4. The AAC's concern was compelled not only by the rise of Hitler but also by the increasingly close relationship between the German Chancellor and his Italian counterpart Benito Mussolini, as well as the gathering menace of Spain's dictator Francisco Franco. Neel's painting was probably executed in the summer of 1936 (its first showing was in September of that year) and the Spanish Civil War had broken out on July 18. Writing in the *New York World-Telegram* the noted art critic Emily Genauer stated, "Alice Neel brandishes the torch which she and the members of the Artist's Union along with her hope will eventually lead to enlightenment and the destruction of Fascism."[17]

What May Come of 1945 (FIG. 5.8) by Mexican printmaker Leopoldo Méndez (1902–1969) may stand as a summation of many of the elements of fear, despair, and accusation that I have commented on in the works discussed above.[18] Méndez was one of the principal founders of one of the most outstanding graphic-artists organizations of the twentieth century. The Taller de Gráfica Popular (Popular Graphic Workshop or People's Graphic Workshop, usually called the TGP) began its work in 1937 in the wake of other organizations such as the LEAR (previously discussed) that had been created to serve as outlets for the activities, both artistic and political, of Left-leaning artists and writers. The Taller represented a critical link in a long and revered series of printmakers in Mexico who worked either on their own or in groups.[19] We opened this volume with a consideration of the art of José Guadalupe Posada and I noted then the significance of single-sheet or series of lithographs, zinc engravings, and other forms of easily transportable and collectible images as crucial to the establishment of a visual vocabulary of Mexico during the pre- and post-revolutionary eras. Méndez served a role in mid-century analogous to that of Posada in its opening years. The Taller was in existence as a cohesive group in one form or another until as recently as 2010, and it nurtured the imaginations of a wide variety of socially concerned artists, both Mexican-born and foreign.[20]

This print, made as World War II was ending, is an allegory of a society at a critical turning point. It is a complex composition that must be read from bottom to top and from the foreground to the deep recesses of the background. *What May Come* is also a self-portrait. Méndez lies atop a large book, spread open to reveal

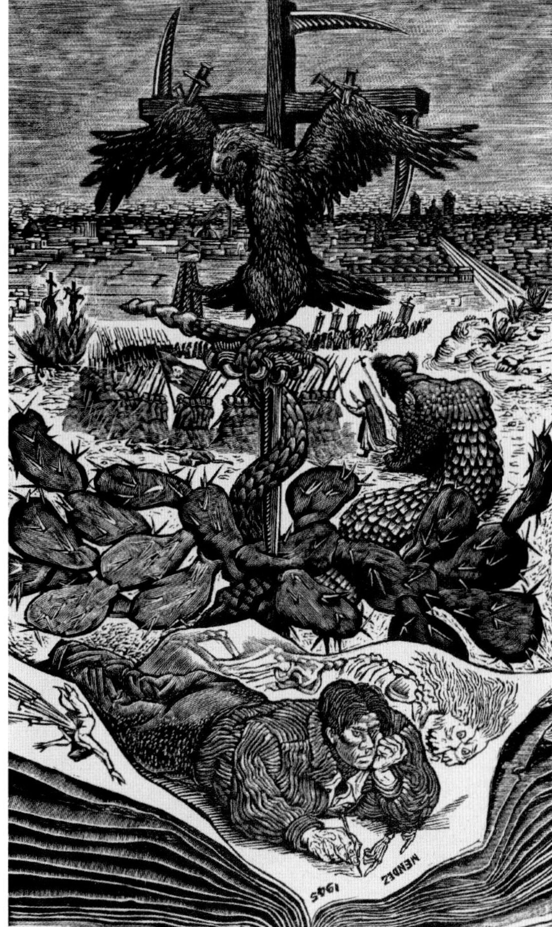

Fig. 5.8
Leopoldo Méndez
What May Come (Mexico, 1945), 1945, wood engraving, 11⅞ x 6⅝ in. (30.2 x 17 cm). The Art Institute of Chicago, Illinois.

a print of a monstrous skeleton—a direct reference to Posada and his *calaveras*, a logical and inevitable point of departure for most Mexican printmakers of the twentieth century, and an image that still evokes strong feelings in viewers and provokes intimations of both caricature and fear.

Méndez's left hand is raised to his face and supports his head as he contemplates his work; his right hand wields a lithographic tool. His surname and the print's date of creation are inscribed on the book. It rests on a desertlike landscape, reminiscent of what was formerly the volcanic wasteland of the outskirts of Mexico City (today a densely developed extension of the metropolis to accommodate the city's enormous population). A large cactus grows up behind the figure of Méndez, and rising from it is an ominous cruciform shape made of scythes that together form a swastika, the symbol of Nazism. Onto this cross is nailed an eagle, a clear reference to the creature that inhabits the creation myth of the Mexican capital, founded by the wandering indigenous people known as the Mexica. According to legend these indigenous peoples were to build their city on the spot where they observed an eagle consuming a serpent. The serpent in this print has become a gigantic monster that slithers away from the cross and away from the menace of the eagle. This pictorial element represents for Deborah Caplow, Méndez's biographer, an allusion to the threat of Fascism that had plagued Mexico during the war years, when a considerable swath of the population aligned themselves ideologically with Hitler, even though Mexico was by no means an Axis-sympathizing nation.[21]

In the middle ground a bishop holding a sword aloft follows faceless soldiers whose uniforms and helmets remind us of German stormtroopers, as if to bless the men with his weapon. At the middle left, heretics from the times of the Spanish Inquisition (which was active in Mexico well into the eighteenth century) burn at the stake. The background view is a panorama of the vast Mexican capital under a troubled gray sky. The title of the print refers to the hopes of the creator of this dramatic image that darkness will not once again settle over the city, the country, and the earth. Nonetheless there is an emotional ambiguity deeply imbedded in this work that portends a future perhaps even more unsettled than the recent past.

Eye Witness

Documentary photography, the capturing of specific events or persons in order to disseminate knowledge of them or their circumstances, has been in existence since at least the mid-nineteenth century. Only several decades after the art form's development in the 1830s, photographers sought to concretize the effects of war, famine, poverty, natural disasters, political events, and many other noteworthy happenings for the larger public. It is therefore fitting that within the category of art with which I am dealing here—namely, the interpretation and factual certification of moments of history or human struggle within the western hemisphere during the years 1910–60—we should examine at least some iconic examples of photographic "witnesses" to moments, both intimate and public, of anxiety or social disruption.

In 1932 Mexican photographer Manuel Álvarez Bravo (1902–2002) recorded a heartrending scene in the small city of Metepec, in the state of Mexico, some 50 kilometers to the west of the Mexican capital. In *Enterramiento en Metepec* (Burial at Metepec) (FIG. 5.9) some 70 figures, all women and very young

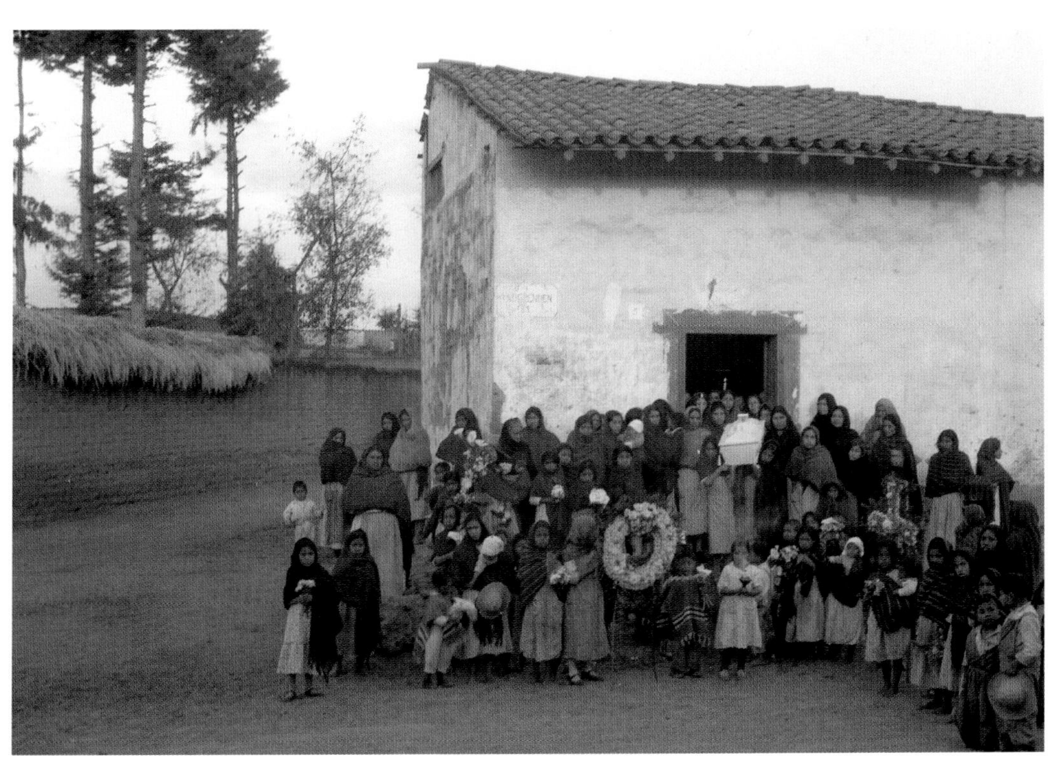

children, gather at a modest building, a chapel with one door and, seemingly, no windows. The crowd, some bearing candles and others holding flowers and a large funeral wreath, is spread out across the foreground, posing in commemoration of a sad event. From the church several women emerge, their heads and upper bodies—like those of all the other women in this elegiac moment—covered by long shawls or *rebozos*, similar to the garment we observed in Siqueiros's painting of the *Niña madre*. They carry a small white coffin, the miniature casket of a child who had died perhaps the day before. This is the central focus of the image, what philosopher Roland Barthes (1915–1980) would call the *punctum* or central feature of the picture to which the eye of the beholder is inevitably drawn.[22] The camera freezes the mournful commemoration forever. We do not know the identities of any of the subjects, but at its core this is a group portrait of death, and specifically child mortality, which, in the 1930s in Mexico and most of the nations throughout the hemisphere, was an alarming and nearly everyday reality. Neither rural nor urban centers were immune from the ravages of disease for which no remedy existed. Poor families naturally suffered the most. Dead children became the subjects of painters' and photographers' fascination and even morbid obsession. At times, photographs of deceased infants and children were taken and printed as postcards in order to convey the news of their passing to larger domestic circles than those in the immediate proximity to the grieving family.

Álvarez Bravo, Mexico's most well-known producer of photographic images in the early and middle years of the twentieth century, acknowledged his fascination with the iconography of death and associated it with the celebrations and commemorations of the dualities of life and death (a leitmotif throughout Mexican culture from pre-Hispanic times) that occur on November 1 and 2, the Days of the Dead (All Saints and All Souls Days).[23] Indeed, during the 1930s and early 1940s he produced a number of works that referred to mortality. The most famous of them is his 1942 image of a *Striking Worker Assassinated* (FIG. 5.10) in which we observe a young man, photographed from the waist up, lying in a pool of blood.

Álvarez Bravo's young worker captivates and shocks with its immediacy. The blood stains the young man's shirt. It pours

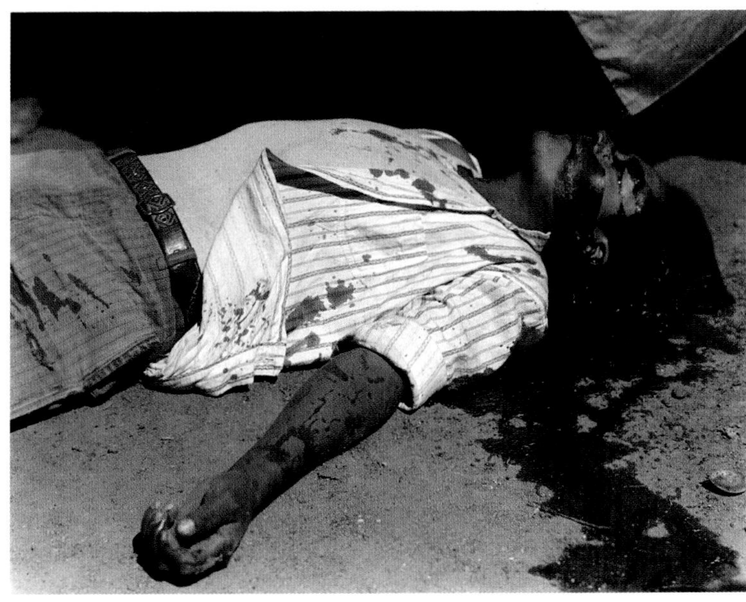

from his nose and ears as well as his head wounds. It is well known that at the time this photograph was taken, the artist was working in the Tehuantepec Peninsula in southern Mexico with Soviet filmmaker Sergei Eisenstein (1898–1948) when he witnessed a railroad workers' strike that turned violent, resulting in the murder recorded here. Knowing this fact adds another level of "eye witness" quality to the picture; indeed it has been utilized as an emblem of aggression and its deadly consequences by many commentators, and has produced numerous visual progeny.

The violence and anxiety inherent in Álvarez Bravo's famous photograph also characterized some of the many images created by the U.S. photographer Walker Evans (1903–1975) during a month's stay in Cuba in 1933. Evans is perhaps best known for his work in the area of photojournalism during the Depression. As a member of the corps of photographers employed by the FSA, Evans took many now-emblematic images of the destitution of the American heartland that had been affected by crop failure and other natural and economic disasters during that decade. His photographs of urban scenes, such as those taken surreptitiously in the New York City subway (1938–41), reveal the tensions and suspicions of the masses that travel in public transport. Yet his *Coal Dock Workers, Havana* (FIG. 5.11) is one of the key images in a series he executed in the spring of 1933

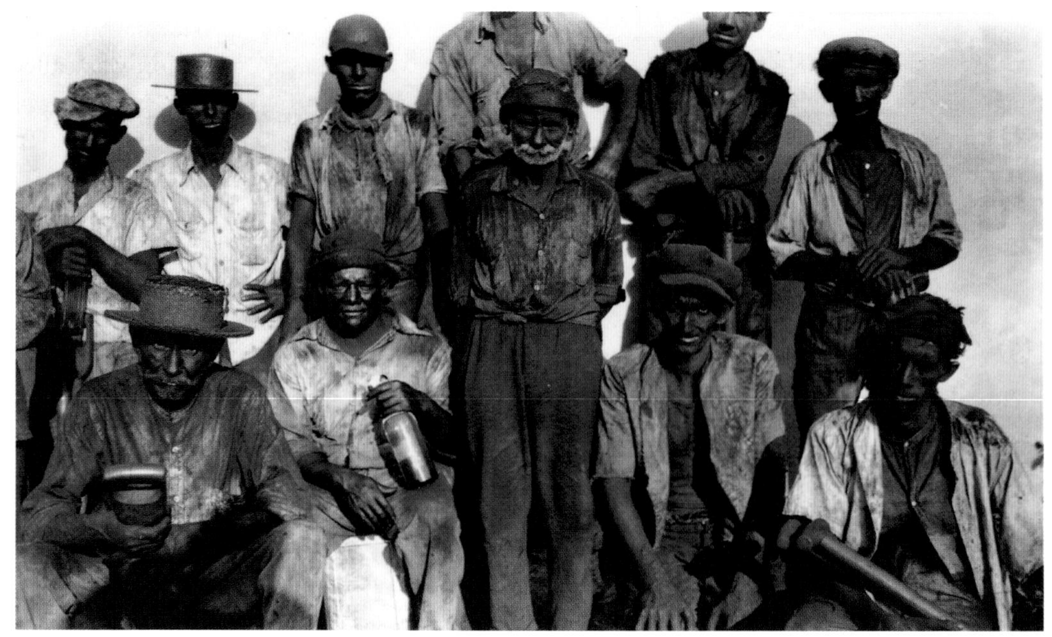

in the Cuban capital for a publication by the Leftist journalist Carleton Beals, entitled *The Crime of Cuba*.[24] This book is a strongly worded text, accompanied by the photographs of Evans, that serves as a denouncement of the corrupt dictatorship of Gerardo Machado. The United States had supported the dictatorship (as it had in so many other cases of abusive right-wing governments throughout the twentieth century), but it collapsed in the summer of the year the book was published.

In this photograph we see 12 men (one of whom, at the extreme left, is captured only in fragmentary form), posed against a blank wall, staring at the camera. Their blackened faces and dust-covered clothing attest to the long and intensely laborious hours they spend each day at their work. There is an exhausted resignation to this group, while at the same time they display a curiosity and eagerness to be included within their cohort. Some of them appear to engage with the photographer, while others have a bored or even defiant expression. Evans shot this scene as one of the wide variety of human subjects that he observed on the streets of the Cuban capital. This image of the dockworkers is linked with the long-standing tradition of representing "types" of professions or social classes that marked the history of Western art from the Renaissance onward.[25] He also took individual photos of a number of these men, including the oldest participant in the group—serving as portraits of a genre of laborers of a variety of racial backgrounds whose exhausting efforts contribute to the commercial viability of the city and, by extension, to the industrial machine of the dictator Machado.

American Gothic, Washington D.C. (FIG. 5.12) is a quintessential photograph of the American scene of the interwar years. Its intimations of racism and the underlying violence pervading the lives of African Americans do not approximate the overt aggression seen in the lynching photographs described above, but it is equally provocative in its own subversively unobtrusive way. Taken in 1942 by African-American photographer Gordon Parks (1912–2006), this image embodies themes of labor, racial tension, and the irony of African-American people living under the protection of the laws of the United States while often remaining the subject of discrimination and bigotry. Parks was a member of the FSA from 1942 until its final year, 1944. His long and distinguished career included a more than 20-year stint as a photojournalist for *Life* magazine, a publication usually associated with white middle-class life in the United States. Parks helped to upend the predilections of the publication with his series of photographs and texts regarding urban and rural poverty in the United States and abroad (especially among black populations), as well as his documentation, during the 1950s, 60s, and 70s, of the Civil Rights movement.[26]

This image represents Ella Watson, a maintenance worker at the FSA headquarters in Washington, D.C. Watson is a diminutive, bespectacled woman wearing a simple dress, with short-cropped hair. She stares directly at the viewer and is posed against an American flag. Parks recalls that

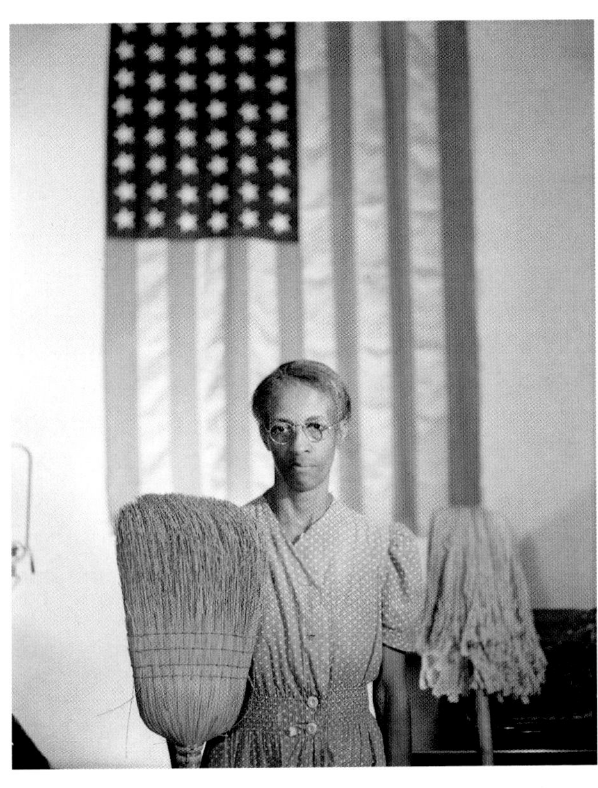

Fig. 5.12
Gordon Parks
American Gothic, Washington D.C., 1942, gelatin silver print. Image 13¼ x 9⅝ in. (33.5 x 24.4 cm); sheet 14 x 11⅛ in. (35.5 x 28.3 cm). Library of Congress Prints and Photographs Division, Washington, D.C.

she had been a charwoman there for many years. Yet she had been to high school, and deserved a much better job. I took her into a room where there was an American flag draped on the wall. I posed her against it—Grant Wood style—with a mop in one hand and a broom in the other.[27]

Ella Watson's stern countenance and thin body suggest a life of difficulty and hard work. Her features also indicate, according to the artist, the woman's survival of the endemic racism and prejudice that marked her everyday existence (as it had marked Parks's own experience in Washington).[28] This was the first of a series of photographs of Watson taken by Parks in 1942. In some of them she is seen reading the Bible to her children and grandchildren, or sitting in her modest apartment. Yet *American Gothic* is the most dramatic and thought-provoking component of the series because of its monumental simplicity and its implications of controlled yet corrosive anxiety spread out over the course of an entire life.

Labor and Exile

Depictions of labor became pervasive throughout the Americas during the period under consideration here. For the most part, nineteenth-century Romantic imagery of the noble worker was abandoned in favor of representations of the hardships of the life of the modern urban or rural worker. We may trace the representations of labor during our time period to the nineteenth-century Realist modes of artists such as Gustave Courbet (1819–1877) or Honoré Daumier (1808–1879). Nonetheless, while those artists tended to create images that embodied a non-geographically or temporally related concept of work, the artists dealt with in this section, as well as scores of others throughout the hemisphere, took the specific realities of their time, place, and local social conditions into account when creating their visualizations of toil.

The interwar period had immense economic repercussions for virtually every sector of life in the hemisphere, and the iconography of work became in itself a marker of artistic modernity. Facing the realities of failing crops in the central United States, the imminent collapse of the coffee market in Brazil, and the precarious state of the sugar industry in post-enslavement Caribbean (when the commodity suffered price drops during the Depression and many islands began to concentrate on banana and fruit exportation), work-related subject matter became ever more compelling for painters, photographers, and printmakers. The terms of labor—wages and working hours—were also in transition in this era, as were the regulations adopted by labor unions and other forms of worker cooperatives that were established at varying times from the later nineteenth century onward, acquiring, in some cases, renewed strength in the pre-1960 era. Labor unions in the United States began to be formed as early as the late eighteenth century, but were reconfigured and held pride of place within middle-class society in the pre– and post–World War II period. Between 1920 and 1940 the Mexican government, for example, promoted the creation of labor unions throughout the country as a means to strengthen its own position, encouraging the union members to affiliate themselves with the ruling Partido Revolucionario Institucional (PRI). The situation in many South American nations was markedly different. In Brazil, Argentina, Chile, and the Andean countries a variety of workers' federations served as quasi-Marxist organizations and promoted social justice, cooperative activity, and protest against government interference. Violent strikes (such as that of the Buenos Aires dockworkers alluded to in my discussion of Pío Collivadino's depiction of the city's port in Chapter 2) marked the second decade of the century, yet by the end of World War I the unions served as more of a stabilizing factor in the social fabric of their respective countries.

The theme of exile is inherently linked to that of labor. Prior to both world wars, massive exile from Europe and elsewhere to the Americas was stimulated by a search for economic stability as well as a need to escape (in the case of the 1930s onward) the threat of Fascism. There were internal exiles as well. We have seen how the Dust Bowl crisis in the central United States caused vast waves of migrants to flee to the east or, mainly, the west coast. Similar instances occurred in northeast Brazil in response to a shift in climatic conditions. Exile becomes a pervasive theme in American art, as encapsulated in the dramatic image of a loaded boat on a troubled sea by Argentinean artist Antonio Berni, discussed below.

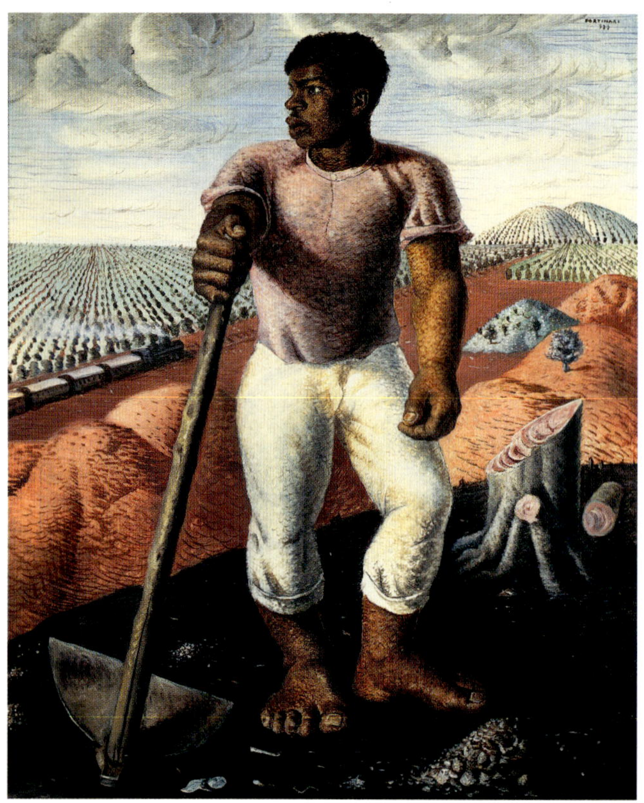

O Lavrador de café (Coffee Worker), 1939 (FIG. 5.13) by Cândido Portinari (1903–1962) is often referred to as an image of a "heroic" worker, yet I wish to suggest some ideas about this picture that might tend to subvert the optimism of writers on this Brazilian modernist. The art historian Jacqueline Barnitz, for example, states that Portinari "portrayed laborers as strong, stoic, heroic figures rather than as helpless victims … in [*Coffee Worker*] a young male laborer stands resolutely in the foreground, as if he owned the land he worked on."[29] In this canvas we see a youthful Afro-Brazilian man standing in a field that has been recently cleared, judging from the felled tree to the right. He looks off to the distance, his face portrayed in profile, a pose that tends to heighten the monumentality of his figure. He is simply dressed, with white workers' trousers rolled up to his calves and a pink short-sleeved shirt. His torso and thighs are muscular, attesting to a young life of hard labor. The man's unshod feet are unusually large, a feature that has the effect of seeming to literally plant him within the earth he tills. He holds a simple handmade hoe in his right hand.

There are three distinct planes to the picture. The foreground where the protagonist stands consists of dark, loamy earth, ready for planting. The middle ground is hilly and awaits leveling in order for a coffee crop to be planted. In the distance the coffee plants grow in regular rows that seemingly stretch for miles from left to right. The rich vegetation reminds us that in many parts of Brazil thousands of square kilometers of forest were cleared to make way for what became, by the late years of the nineteenth century, the premier crop and export product of the country. By the 1830s and 40s Brazil became immensely wealthy, in large

176

part due to the production and sales of coffee, which was grown on immense plantations (*fazendas*) worked by enslaved people whose liberty was not fully granted them until abolition occurred in Brazil in 1888. This prosperity and the cyclical "coffee booms" lasted until the 1920s. Portinari was intimately familiar with life on the plantations, having grown up (the son of Italian immigrants) in relative poverty on a *fazenda* adjacent to the town of Brodowski in the state of São Paulo.

By the time Portinari painted his *Coffee Worker*, however, conditions for laborers of the crop had changed and the role coffee played in the Brazilian economy—and in the national imaginary—had been altered. The Depression had reduced the demand for Brazilian coffee imports by nations in North America, Europe, and elsewhere (as it had for Caribbean sugar), and the outbreak of World War II and the difficulties of commodity exchange further undermined its significance as the staple of Brazil's economy, even though the most precipitous drop in production was not to happen until the 1950s. Brazil's urban centers gained in importance due to the rise of a multitude of industries. Many former coffee workers (the scions of slaves who had worked on the *fazendas* for centuries) migrated to Rio and São Paulo and other coastal cities, leaving the former plantations, in some cases, without sufficient workers to sustain harvesting and processing.

It is not difficult to think of Portinari as an optimistic painter, judging from his many representations of arguably placid rural scenes on canvas and in fresco (for the Hispanic Reading Room in the Library of Congress in Washington, D.C., in 1941, and the Ministry of Culture headquarters in Rio in 1942). The *Coffee Worker* is arguably related to this type of imagery. By the mid-1940s his imagination and subject matter turned more directly toward the harsh realities of life in his country's northeast in a series of paintings representing the death of children, interior migration to the cities, and degradation of the environment due to a series of droughts and storms. The painting under consideration here foreshadows this darker side of Portinari's vision of Brazil. The Afro-Brazilian worker is alone in the landscape; he appears fatigued rather than heroic. His expression is one of weariness rather than fortitude. He turns his head to his right in response to the whistle of the train that travels through the landscape, bisecting the middle and background of the composition. It rushes toward another place, certainly a city, carrying cargo for sale and people on the move. The train, a classic symbol of modernity and progress, leaves the laborer behind on his minuscule plot and he contemplates the ultimate fate of his rural existence in a land on the cusp of greater industrial development than ever before.

Coffee, cotton, cacao, and sugar were among the staple crops produced throughout Brazil, the Caribbean, and what is now the United States from the earliest moments of colonial exploitation. Enslaved Africans who had replaced the indigenous groups that comprised the first slaves for Europeans in the sixteenth century originally harvested these products. Their subjugated descendants remained in bondage in the British and French colonies until the early nineteenth century, in the United States until the end of the Civil War in 1865, in Puerto Rico until 1873, and in Brazil and Cuba until 1888. Thus Portinari's coffee worker and the *Los Cortadores del caña* (Sugarcane Cutters) in the linocut (FIG. 5.14) by Puerto Rican artist Rafael Tufiño (1922–2008) are undoubtedly, or in part, the descendants of slaves.

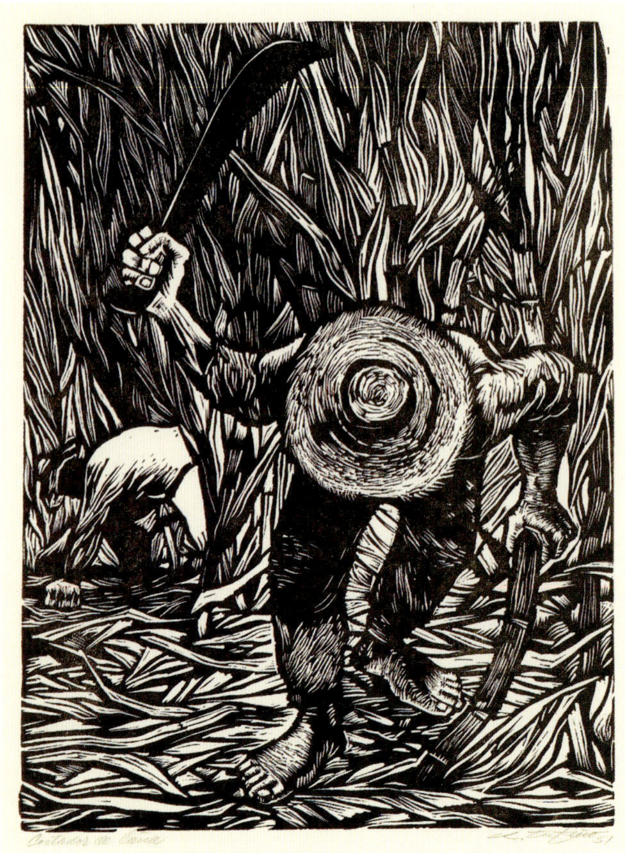

The backbreaking labor of work in the sugarcane fields is powerfully suggested by two figures in the Tufiño print, both working within a virtual cosmos of stalks, some of which have already fallen to the machete's lethal blows (which often accounted for mortal wounds to the workers themselves). Other stalks remain firmly in place behind the men bent over their work, gathering or cutting the plants that would yield the substance to be refined in the large factories (*ingenios azucareros*)

178

that dotted the Caribbean countryside before the decline of the industry and the transport of cane to refineries abroad, in places like Brooklyn, New York, which eventually became one of the most significant sugar refining capitals of the hemisphere.[30] The monochromy of this image adds to its starkness and drama. The main protagonist is anonymous, like his fellow cane worker. Only the top of his straw hat greets the gaze of the observer, serving as the fulcrum around which the composition revolves.[31] He grasps a stalk with his left hand as his right vigorously wields the instrument of the harvest. As in the case of Portinari's coffee worker, the laborer's feet are exaggerated in size, as is the length of the machete. Puerto Rican art historian Teresa Tió describes the "lines of the plate cuttings wav[ing] like flames that enfold the main figure."[32]

The expressive quality and implicit social commitment of this image relate it to the powerful and politically engaged work done by the members of Mexico's TGP (including Leopoldo Méndez), described above. This is no coincidence as Tufiño spent three years in Mexico (1946–49) studying at the Academy of San Carlos and working with TGP members at their workshop. The *Sugarcane Cutters* was among the first major works he did after his Mexican sojourn and it may be said to connect directly with not only the TGP aesthetic but also the expressive force of the work of José Guadalupe Posada, the doyen of early twentieth-century Mexican graphic arts.

Tufiño, of African and Spanish descent, was one of the key figures in the generation of Puerto Rican artists who came to maturity in the 1950s, at a crucial moment in this island's history. A colony of the United States since 1898 (it is officially called a Free Associated State), the economy had been decimated throughout the first half of the twentieth century, the Spanish language was banned in public schools, and an independence movement was growing exponentially, culminating in an act of violence on the part of a group of political activists in the U.S. House of Representatives in 1954, resulting in the wounding of five members of Congress.[33]

The artists of the time were politically active in their own way, and a populist form of visual expression was born in the early 1950s in the posters and print portfolios that emerged from the U.S. government-supported Division of Community

Education, a project for overall public improvement that was initiated in 1949. Indeed, easily reproduced and distributed posters and prints came to represent the principal medium of artistic expression in Puerto Rico at this time. Tufiño, along with fellow artists Lorenzo Homar (1913–2004), José Antonio Torres Martinó (1916–2011), and Félix Rodríguez Báez (1929–2013) (among others), founded the Centro de Arte Puertorriqueño (CAP), which opened in San Juan in 1950. It was at the Centro's headquarters that Tufiño created the *Sugarcane Cutters* as a component of a collective project by the CAP's members entitled "La Estampa puertorriqueña," a portfolio of scenes of rural and urban life of the working classes of the island.

Throughout the first half of the twentieth century in the Americas, native populations were the subjects of works of literature and art generally created by white or mixed-race artists and authors. In many cases there was a strong political undercurrent to the depictions, in words or images, of Native Americans. Mexican artists, writers, composers, and filmmakers employed the Indian as a main subject in the post-revolutionary era, following the example of urban intellectuals such as José Vasconcelos (discussed in the previous chapter), first Secretary of Public Education, originator of the first mural programs, and author of the influential treatise *The Cosmic Race*, which discussed the strength of ethnic hybridity in the modern nation. The Andean nations also experienced a pronounced movement of Indigenism. A concise definition of this cultural project has been provided by the art historian Michele Greet in her study of Andean art from 1920 to 1960. Greet states that

Indigenism is a Pan-Latin American intellectual trend that denounced the political and economic exploitation of Native American populations. While directed at Native Americans, Indigenism was the brainchild of the urban mestizo and creole elite who expressed their indignation at the plight of the indigenous masses through literary, artistic and social projects.[34]

The Andean nations of Ecuador, Peru, and Bolivia possess unique social circumstances as well as dramatically varied topographies, combining torrid lowlands with the precipitous heights of the Andes. Bolivia is the most mountainous of the three countries, although its eastern plains offer a hot and steamy atmosphere. It is also a nation where the indigenous populations have been especially active in social and political concerns, especially in recent decades, as attested to by the election to the presidency in December 2005 of Evo Morales (b.1959), of Aymara ethnicity and a staunch promoter of indigenous rights in his country, who has galvanized the indigenous populations to seek greater representation and collective responsibility.

Indigenist images in painting and graphic arts flourished from the second decade of the twentieth century. While at first both female and male artists (almost all of whom were from the privileged creole class) created romanticized (and often condescending) depictions of the Indian populations, the 1930s to the 50s witnessed the creation of many trenchantly poignant depictions of the poverty and hardship to which the native groups were constantly subject. Indigenism in Ecuador, Peru, and Bolivia marked the most advanced and modern style of painting and graphic arts in the pre-World War II period.[35] It also served as a strong marker of national identity and self-projection.

Among the most outstanding members of the Andean Indigenist circle was Ecuadorean artist Eduardo Kingman, who was one of the moving forces in the art world in Quito in the 1930s and 40s. While during the later decades of his life he painted a series of pictures that evoked his engagement with Expressionism (especially in his many images of tortured faces and outstretched, elongated arms and hands), his paintings from the earlier period represent the epitome of visual social protest and a deep awareness of the misery of a large sector of his countrymen.[36] *Los Guandos* (The Haulers) of 1941 (FIG. 5.15) takes place in the highlands of the country. The mountains are suggested at the upper right and left portions of the canvas, and a broken tree in the lower right suggests the roughness of the terrain. The sky above is dark and menacing, with white clouds set dramatically against a virtually black atmosphere.

Eleven men labor in the mountains, crossing the Ecuadorean Andes on foot while an overseer on horseback wields a whip to prod them, like cattle, along on their arduous journey to an unknown place. The overseer—whose back is to us, rendering him anonymous—wears a bright red poncho and yellow

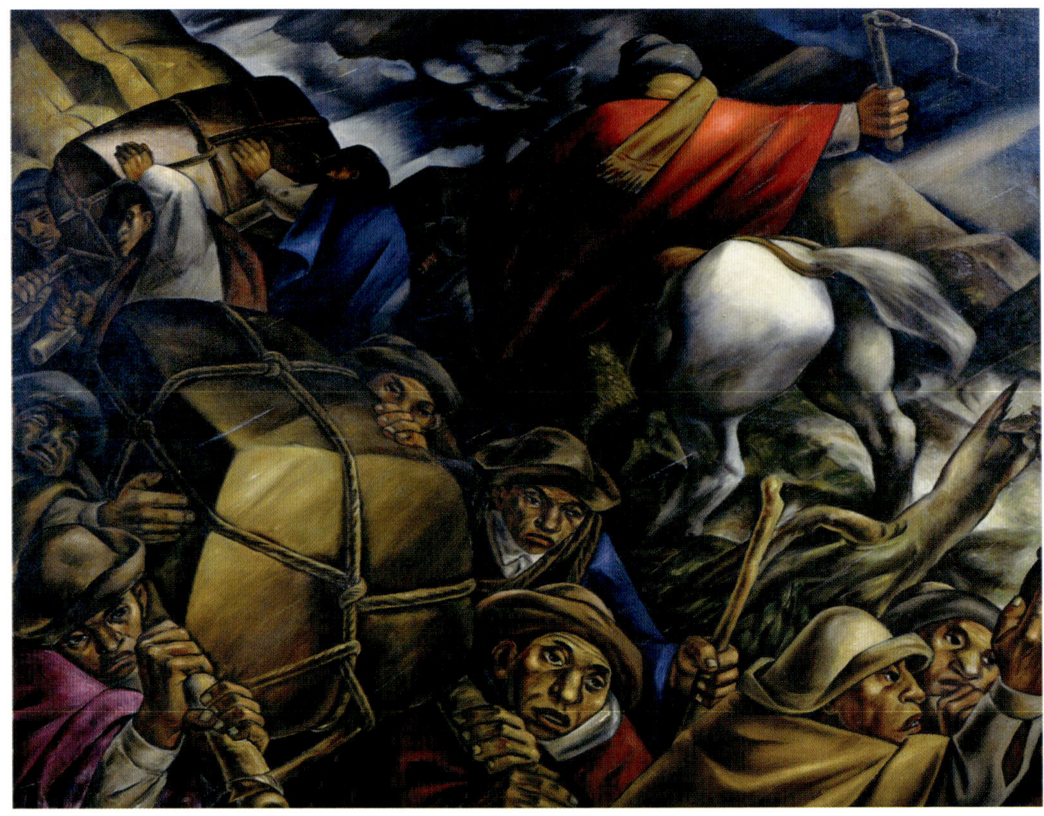

scarf. These garments add a note of vivid color to the otherwise monochromatic scene. There is a circular motion suggested in this composition, and we read the figures from the shape of the foreman's body riding a white horse, in a counterclockwise motion that encompasses the other men in the scene, all of whom are on foot. Ecuadorean writer Lenín Oña asserts that "[t]he spiral form of the exhausted group of men represents the circularity of unending exploitation."[37] Two enormous bundles are being carried by some of the workers (and indeed the picture's title comes from the indigenous Quechua, or Quichua, word for "carriers"). The objects are tied tightly with rope and evidently create an almost overbearing burden for the men. What are these objects? We cannot know, but their weight and the burden they represent serve as the vehicles for Kingman's underscoring of the oppression of the indigenous workers as they gloomily haul their heavy merchandise from one part of the country to another.

Exile and Migrations

The manual laborers of the Americas—Portinari's coffee worker, Tufiño's sugarcane cutter, or the men who bear the heavy burden of transport in Kingman's *Los Guandos*—all had progeny or other family members who could no longer exist in the economic and climatic conditions with which they were faced. Exile— the search for personal valorization and economic, political, or intellectual freedom—became more acute than ever as the century progressed. Fleeing from one country or regime to another became a hallmark of life throughout the world in the wake of the Depression, the threat of World War II, or a multitude of local events in the destabilized societies on virtually every continent. The daughters and sons of Portinari's workers left the interior and migrated to the coastal cities of Brazil. Those of Tufiño's field workers joined the great migration of Puerto Ricans that had started to move northward, especially to New York and other urban centers in the United States in the late 1940s and 50s, forming phalanxes of newcomers to Manhattan, Chicago, Hartford, and elsewhere, often living in difficult conditions in the *barrios* (neighborhoods) in their new cities, where they could survive (precariously) and be surrounded by familiar faces and words. The grandsons and great-grandsons of Kingman's carters form the core of the thousands of Ecuadorean workers doing often-dangerous construction jobs in contemporary New York City and other large urban centers, especially on the east coast of the United States. Their (often) undocumented status places them in a hazardous societal position.

Large-scale migrations of peoples from one part of the Americas to another in the first half of the twentieth century was a much wider phenomenon than can be even suggested here. U.S. artists, especially Jacob Lawrence (see Chapter 3), made some of their most dramatic images in attempts to evoke the trauma of the Great Migration of African-American populations from the South to the large cities of the North in the 1930s and 40s. In a larger context, the arrival to many large and small cities (Buenos Aires, Mexico City, Havana, Fort-de-France, Port-au-Prince) of European workers and intellectuals whose existence in their home countries was threatened in all manner of ways, provided the subject for the works of many photojournalists—works that offered the public graphic visual documentation of the effects on

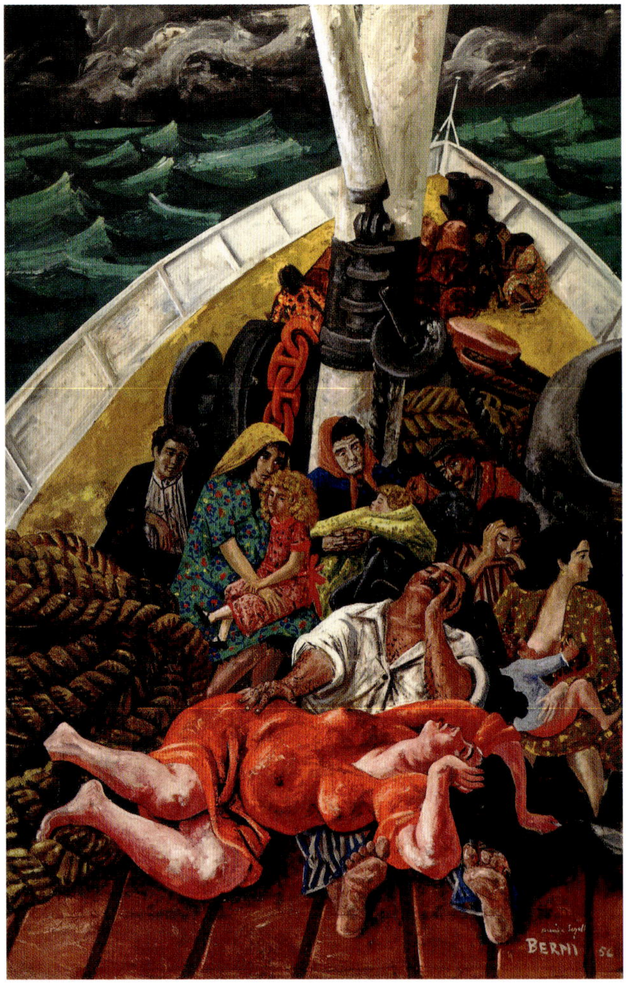

the hemisphere of the traumas of social disruption.

Argentinean artist Antonio Berni created an image that encapsulates and symbolizes the shock and disturbance of displacement. *Los Emigrantes* (The Emigrants) of 1956 (FIG. 5.16) employs the hallowed visual trope of the boat on a storm-tossed sea as metaphor for anxiety and fear. In this rendition we observe a group of hapless individuals from above as they occupy the deck of a small ship that plies its way through troubled waters, accompanied by a stormy sky. The picture's 16 figures are arranged in three configurations. Those closest to the viewer are huddled one upon another; some are awake and others are asleep. Three women of varying ages hold young children. A young boy at center left observes the scene despairingly, and in the foreground a young couple sleeps in a way that suggests exhaustion and troubled dreams. The man cups his head with his left hand and places the other on the thigh of a woman who is sprawled out over his lap. In voluptuous form and suggestive pose (like paintings of the female nude by Pablo Picasso, an artist much admired by Berni) she is in ironic opposition to the sad realities of the scene. Other figures inhabit the background, huddled against the floor of the deck. All are surrounded by oversized ropes, chains, and other mechanical forms that play as protagonic a role as the individuals themselves.

Berni derives his composition from the art-historical theme of the "ship of fools"—a metaphor of the difficulties of life (and exile) used by Western artists since the Middle Ages. He lends

Fig. 5.16
Antonio Berni
Los Emigrantes (The Emigrants), 1956, oil and mixed media on canvas, 118 x 75 in. (300 x 190 cm). Private collection.

this timeless subject a judiciously contemporary implication, referring, within a single dramatic image, to many chapters in the drama of migration and exile in the mid-century era. Berni's visual production since the 1930s had included images of urban and rural misery, sometimes suggested by photography of destitute Argentineans as they appeared in newsreels and other forms of mass communication. As his career unfolded, he became more and more attuned to social commentary in a way that employed scorchingly caricatural means, such as in his body of late work that focused on archetypes of the Buenos Aires suburbs.[38] During the 1950s Berni offered the public a series of expressionistic images, painted in thick impasto and with slashing, broken brushstrokes, of victims of the sociopolitical disturbances of the era. The government of President Juan Perón created instability in both the working and the intellectual sectors of the population. There was mass exile out of the country, as well as displacement of farm workers affected by the record-breaking droughts in the interior. Berni's hapless *emigrantes* may indeed be reflective of these specific realities.[39] It is also important to note that this painting (inspired in part by the 1939–41 composition *Ship of Emigrants* by Brazilian painter Lasar Segall) was done in Paris, where he and his family had gone in 1955, indicating that he had become sensitized to the continuing circumstances of post-war waves of immigration and exile. In a hemispheric sense we may interpret this painting as speaking eloquently of the ongoing shifts, as well as the physical and psychological dislocations, taking place throughout the Americas as the century progressed into its even more chaotic Cold War-dominated second half.[40]

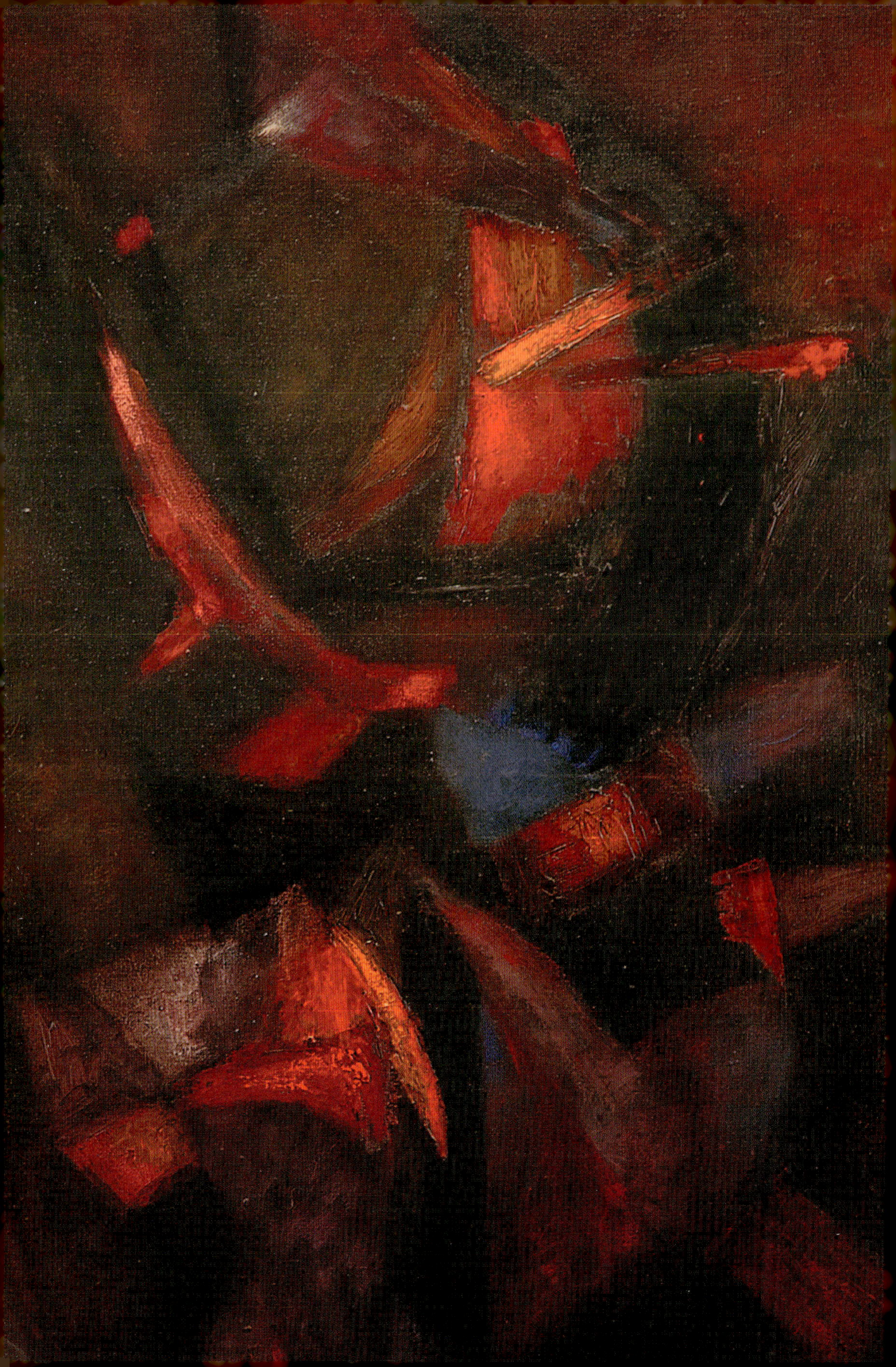

The Liberated Line:
Toward Abstracted Form

There are many forms of art created throughout the Americas in our time period that do not tell stories. Representational art may dominate in this series of fragmented histories of art in the western hemisphere from 1910 to 1960, yet there is a substantial portion of this chronicle that lies outside the realm of narration. The genesis and development of gestural or lyric abstraction is perhaps the most slippery and difficult picture to present in a cogent sequence of images. There are, to start with, many cultural myths that must be understood in order to relate this account. Perhaps of all of the artistic innovations of the later phases of our chronology, the development of Abstract Expressionism in the United States (and, specifically, in New York, where it was "born" in the 1940s) accounts for the most complex and conflicting chapter in the history of mid-twentieth-century art.

Gestural painting, action painting, or all-over painting (among its various titles) has generated a virtual sea of critical and interpretive writing, beginning with its most famous contemporaneous critics writing in English, Clement Greenberg and Harold Rosenberg (active in the 1940s to the 60s), who established varying paradigms of the New York School, as it became known, and a hierarchy of pictorial values often based on formal concerns and centering on a relatively small number of "founding fathers" of the movement.[1] In 1970 the American art historian Irving Sandler published his influential book *The Triumph of American Painting. A History of Abstract Expressionism*, which argued for the primacy of this mode of

Fernando de Szyszlo
Cajamarca, 1959
(detail).
See fig. 6.17.

art as a response to the trauma of World War II (while not minimizing the importance of the roots out of which artists like Jackson Pollock or Willem de Kooning [1904–1997] emerged, and the importance to them and others of Surrealism, Mexican muralism, and other sources).[2]

Among dozens of other important assessments of Abstract Expressionism, the 1999 study of alternate readings of the movement by Ann Eden Gibson was significant for its opening up of the parameters of scholarship on American abstraction by focusing on women artists, artists of color, and gay artists, almost all of

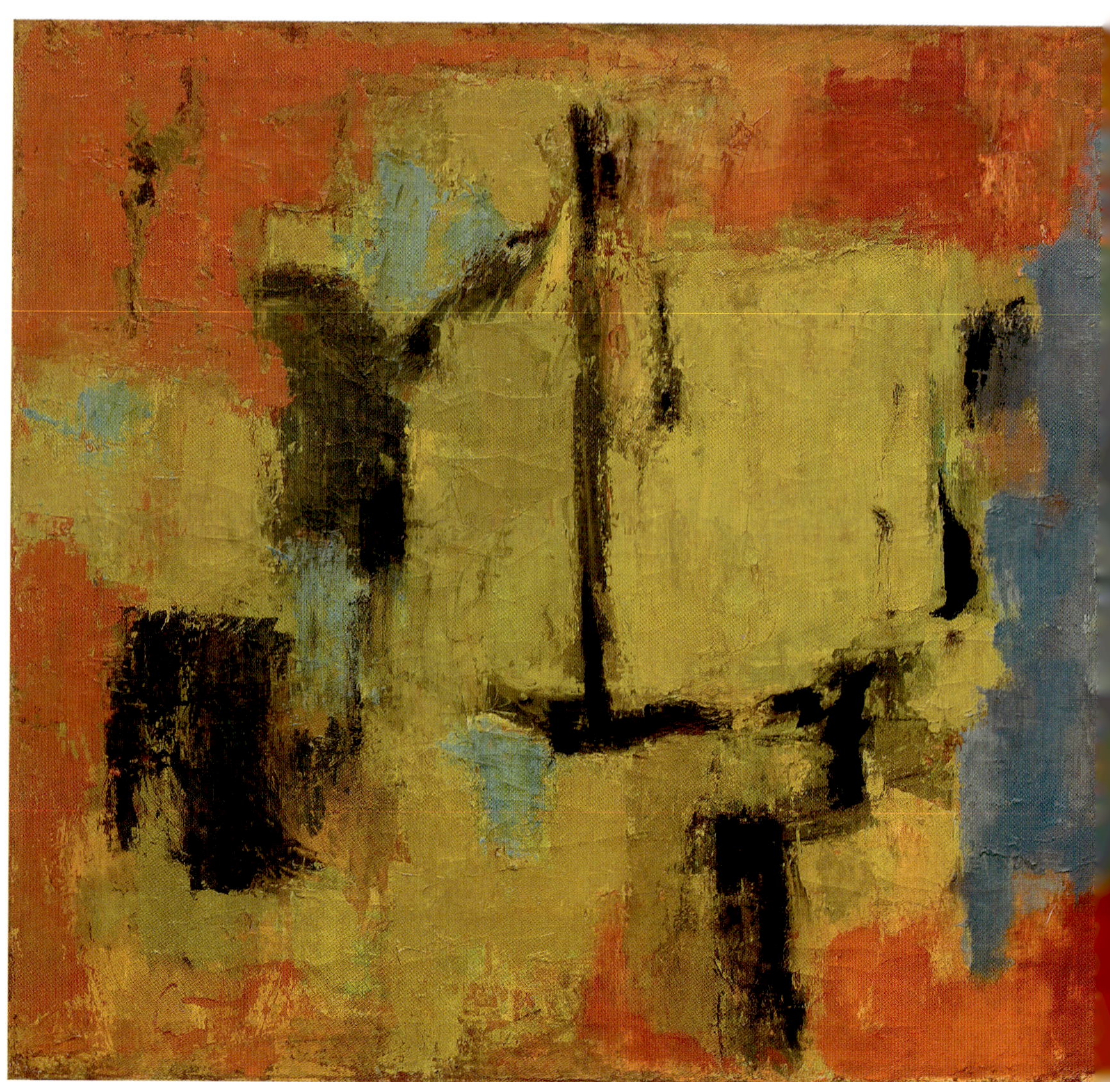

whom were either marginalized or ignored in previous writings on the subject.[3] This type of revisionist approach continues to this day, when exhibitions and books look again (or, in some cases, for the first time) at participants in the mid-century movement who were absent from the earlier texts but whose appearance on the scene deeply enriches what we know about this fundamental mode of artistic expression.[4] I suggest that we consider a work by Alma Thomas (1891–1978), one of the most celebrated African-American abstractionists, as a starting point for the discussion of non-geometric abstract art. *Yellow and Blue* of 1959 (FIG. 6.1) sets our stage for a series of alternative readings of gestural and other modes of non-geometric abstraction, as we will see below.

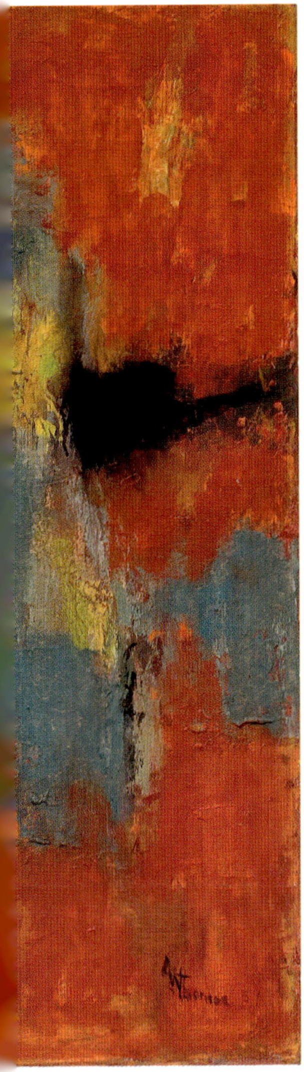

The hegemony of the U.S. form of Abstract Expressionism is itself a conundrum with which I must grapple in this series of remarks on art throughout the hemisphere. First of all, while the New York School of Abstract Expressionists (comprised of several generations and lasting well into the 1960s and beyond) may be the best known of the American nonobjective painter movements, it was by no means the only one. Gestural abstraction has a long and deep history throughout the Americas. There were also many phases of figurative art from the early 1900s and beyond that eventually led to the development of a large number of local approaches to the nonobjective form. Abstract art of a non-geometric mode is present throughout the Americas from as early as the 1910s, and the history of each region has its distinct genealogy. I will attempt to elucidate the individualities of hemispheric forms of abstraction within this and the following chapter.

Fig. 6.1
Alma Thomas
Yellow and Blue, 1959, oil on canvas, 28 x 40 in. (71.1 x 101.6 cm). Courtesy of Michael Rosenfeld Gallery LLC, New York.

Another myth is that concerning the supposed "influence" of U.S. abstraction upon artists in other parts of the Americas. Many artists from the Caribbean and Central and South America certainly came to the United States and eagerly looked to what the likes of the "canonical" painters of the first generation of Ab Ex artists (Pollock, de Kooning, Clyfford Still [1904–1980], Mark Rothko [1903–1970], Philip Guston, and Franz Kline [1910–1962], among others) were doing. But many more stayed home and saw (or not) reproductions of abstract works in publications and came up with their own solutions. The "anxiety of influence," to borrow a phrase from the title of a famous book by American critic Harold Bloom, stretches in many directions in visual terms throughout the two continents and the archipelagos that constitute the Americas.[5]

In many cases, abstract art developed in idiosyncratic and local forms that responded to historical conditions or aesthetic concerns deriving from circumstances unique to the areas that produced them. In other cases, artists from the Americas traveled to other parts of the world to witness at first hand what was happening in European centers such as Paris, Madrid, London, and elsewhere. European forms of abstraction, such as Spanish *Informalismo* or French *Tachisme* (both new modes of expression heavily imbued with, and resistant to, the profound distress of the immediate wartime past), were equally or even more significant in prodding the imaginations of young post-World War II artists throughout the Americas than the lure of Manhattan's galleries, studios, and museums. In addition, artists traveled from one hemispheric nation to another to study or observe what was happening in larger art worlds than their own. Cities like São Paulo, Rio de Janeiro, Buenos Aires, and Mexico City loomed large in the imaginations of artists from all over the Spanish- and Portuguese-speaking worlds. Internal artistic migrations also occurred with greater frequency in this period, with artists from smaller cities or towns gravitating to their nations' capitals or larger urban areas for art instruction. In addition, after World War II and the introduction in the United States of the G.I. Bill, which provided educational benefits for former soldiers to study in institutions of higher learning throughout the world, many art students made the journey to Mexico and beyond in search of inspiration. The internationalism of abstraction was further enhanced by the close ties between artists in Brazil of Japanese descent (or Japanese émigrés) in São Paulo and elsewhere, and the vibrant post-World War II movements in Tokyo and Kyoto such as Gutai, a distinctly Japanese form of both abstract and performance art that became well known in both Europe and the Americas in the 1950s.[6]

A further modern legend that must be dealt with in an assessment of the overall picture of abstraction in the hemisphere in our context is that of the hegemony of the figure. Stereotypical accounts of modern art in the Americas (outside of the United States and Canada) have long taken the dominance of the figure as conventional wisdom in explaining the genesis of modernism in the Americas. A reassessment of this supposed hierarchical position of figurative art has long been underway and it is abundantly clear from scholarly investigations and exhibition and gallery presentations over the last two decades that the supposed predilection for figurative art is, in fact, a fiction. Nonetheless, it bears repeating once again in our context that beginning early on in the century and continuing, especially after the 1940s, the myriad of abstract forms of art throughout the Americas become the often-dominant modes of visual expression, at least among those artists attuned to a variety of transnational art scenes.

As has been the case throughout this book, this chapter will attempt to present sometimes unexpected or perhaps even perplexing juxtapositions of a variety of options to abstraction, or what I might call "abstracting" art (art that stretches the definition of observed reality to its furthest point beyond which it would be unrecognizable in a conventional sense), in order to push the story of abstractions in the Americas well beyond the limits to which they have heretofore been subjected. While there have been recent attempts to broaden the interpretations as well as the definitions of abstraction in various parts of the hemisphere, there have been few endeavors to bridge the gaps between nations, regions, or continents to try and devise a transcontinental answer to the obvious questions posed when we look at this broad panorama with an open mind.

Alternative Histories

Beginning this section of my account at the opposite point of the chronological limits established for this book is an attempt to question and even to upend conventional opinions about the development and viability of gestural abstraction. The two works with which I start were painted in 1959 and 1960 respectively. The first is by Alma Thomas, with her painting *Yellow and Blue*. Thomas spent her career working in Washington, D.C. The other is by María Luisa Pacheco (1918–1982) from Bolivia. It is entitled *Composition* and was painted in 1960 (FIG. 6.2). Both paintings represent the artists' responses to visual trends that had enjoyed a long period of gestation since the 1940s, and there is, in both, an undeniable genealogy that links them, if somewhat tentatively, to the Abstract Expressionism of artists from New York and elsewhere in the United States that, by the late 1950s, had become much less experimental and less of a sign of aesthetic rebellion than during its era of initial

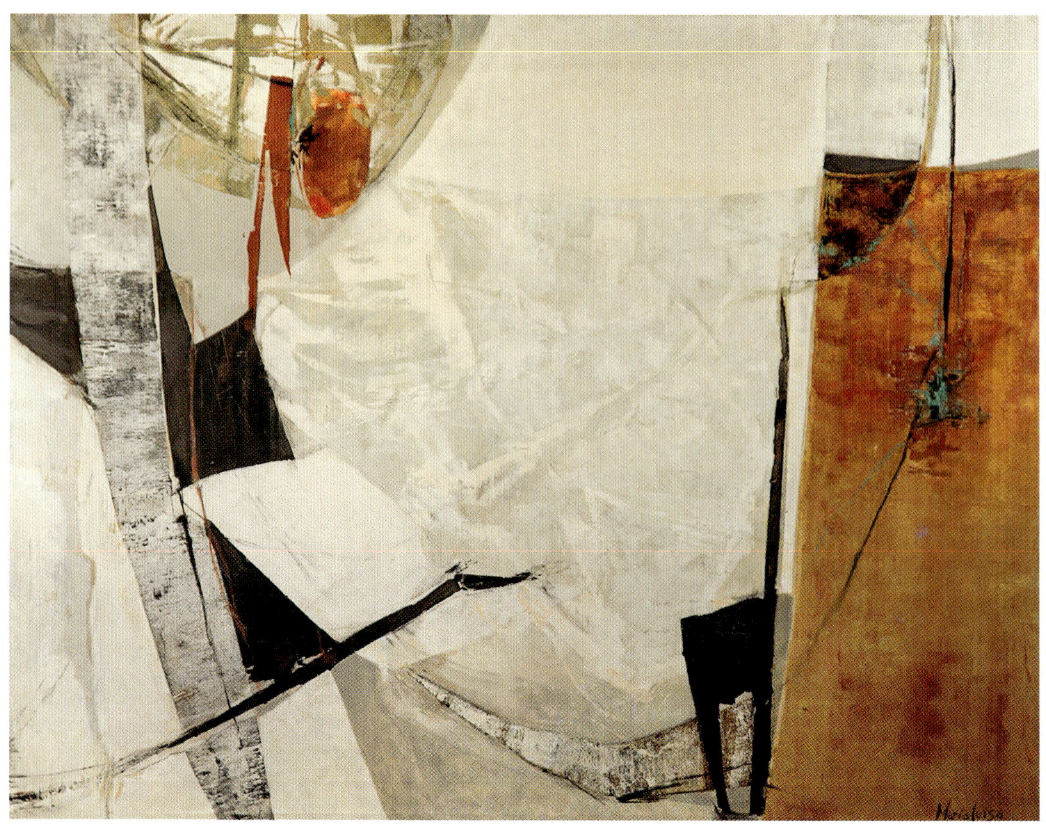

Fig. 6.2
María Luisa Pacheco
Composition, 1960, oil
on canvas, 48 x 61 in.
(122 x 155 cm). OAS Art
Museum of the Americas,
Washington, D.C.

192

gestation. In a clichéd manner of art-historical criticism, these two works by female artists might be placed in a category of "second tier" or "derivative." I argue here, however, that reusing the traditional cast of characters from the canon of New York abstract art as paradigms of originality and the progenitors of transnational gestural abstraction is simply perpetuating overused stereotypes that prevent us from moving forward with fresh assessments of the extremely broad reach of both the possibilities of and the uses of abstraction in (for our purposes) a hemispheric sense. Both Thomas and Pacheco, as well as the two other examples that I will discuss after looking at their art (Olga Albizu from Puerto Rico, and Esteban Vicente from New York via Spain and Puerto Rico—the only Spanish-born member of the first generation of New York Abstract Expressionists), offer different perspectives and serve to widen our doors of comprehension into the ongoing dialogues in an aesthetic sense between artistic expression and color and form.

Many artists throughout the region emerged into the light of abstraction, as it were, after lengthy periods of engagement with recognizable form. Such was the case with Alma Thomas. In many countries of the Americas, abstract art was not recognized as a viable option for serious artists until well past the mid-point of the twentieth century. Pacheco was a pioneer in her country, where the small art establishment did not admit purely abstract form as something acceptable to the public until the 1960s. While Brazilian or Argentinean artists were in the abstract vanguards of the 1930s and 40s and initiated experiments in both gestural and geometric abstraction before many of their more famous North American contemporaries, artists in places like Ecuador, Paraguay, or the Central American nations did not openly embrace nonobjective visualities until considerably later. A more nuanced review of gestural abstraction that I wish to argue for here (in a highly abbreviated way) is not merely a revisionist statement—it is, instead, meant to resist the by now less-than-useful traditional categories and the hegemony of certain paradigmatic figures as the principal (or the only) paragons of creativity.

When Alma Thomas painted *Yellow and Blue* in 1959, she had recently returned from her first trip to Europe. Visiting the major museums in such cities as London, Amsterdam,

Florence, and Rome, she was inevitably impressed by the Old Master art she saw there. Nonetheless, by the late 1950s Thomas was well on her way to a position of prominence among the Washington Color School painters, a group of abstract artists whose principal form of expression was in the area of broad washes or planes of pure color. Sam Gilliam (b.1933), Kenneth Noland (1924–2010), and Morris Louis (1912–1962) were also included within this group. This and several other related paintings from 1959 were breakout works for Thomas. She had long practiced figuration that had been stimulated to a certain degree by her membership in "The Little Paris School"—an artist's group that had been formed in part by Loïs Mailou Jones (whose work was discussed in Chapter 3). Thomas had studied at Columbia University's Teachers College and had previously received a fine arts degree from Howard University. Until 1960, she worked full-time as an art teacher at the Shaw Junior High School in her adopted city (to which she moved from Columbus, Georgia, in 1907), and it was only after her retirement that she was able to devote herself full-time to painting. Around 1958, Thomas, an admirer of Wassily Kandinsky, started her early incursions into the realm of pure abstraction, ultimately settling on a mode of pattern painting in which alternating colors formed regular shapes and overall designs on the canvas. Her career blossomed after this; Thomas became the first African-American woman to have a solo show at the Whitney Museum in New York (1972), and interest in her art has grown steadily in recent times.[7]

Yellow and Blue is a distinctive work and demonstrates the artist's deftness with both color and form. The colors of the title appear to float within a background of salmon red. The central yellow element is formed by the two planes of color that meet in the middle, creating a boxlike shape that reads as a cube or other quasi-architectonic structure. It is offset by the flatter sections of blue, and the overall appearance suggests what New York School artist Hans Hofmann (1880–1966, well known as a teacher of many younger abstractionists) called the "push and pull" effect.

María Luisa Pacheco's *Composition* embodies intimations of three-dimensional form analogous to those observed in the painting by Thomas. Here a central area of white is flanked by a large swath of brown at the right and by smaller areas of gray and black at the left. Solids and voids are delineated in a way that is reminiscent of a mountainous landscape. Like Thomas (whose work may well have been known to Pacheco, who spent considerable time in Washington, D.C.), the Bolivian artist had recently emerged from an early career as a creator of Indigenist subject matter, and many of her paintings up until the mid-1950s embody the themes and the melancholic mood evoked by the art of fellow Andean painters such as the Ecuadorean Eduardo Kingman (see Chapter 5). Yet prior to painting her first abstract compositions (of which this picture is one of the earliest) she had already embraced the power of nonrepresentational form when, in 1951, she received a scholarship from the government of Francisco Franco's Spain (eager to internationalize and show the West the progressive side of the dictatorship) to study at the Academia de Bellas Artes de San Fernando in Madrid. At that point Pacheco encountered and was impressed by the work of Catalan artist Antoni Tàpies (1923–2012), one of the premier members of the country's *Informalista* abstract group who was beginning to make a mark on the European art world with his "matter painting," composed of disparate elements (thickly applied paint, sand, mud, wood, rope, and so on) merged in unexpected combinations.

Pacheco's own New York experience began in 1956, and she lived there on and off until her death. Her familiarity with the developments in abstract art in the United States played a role in the development of her own aesthetic. Nonetheless Pacheco internalized these sources of inspiration in order to continue to create a corpus of work that embodied references (sometimes oblique) to the mountainous landscape of the Bolivian Andes. In effect, the colors that most frequently appear in Pacheco's abstract works—browns, rust, muted reds, and grays—are remarkably evocative of the dry, rugged landscape with which she was so directly associated during and after her life, so much so that a major retrospective exhibition of her art, held in La Paz and Santa Cruz de la Sierra (Bolivia's second city), was called *María Luisa Pacheco. Pintora de los Andes.*[8]

Olga Albizu (1924–2005) painted *Growth* (FIG. 6.3) in the same year as Pacheco's *Composition*. This Puerto Rican artist had left San Juan for Manhattan in 1948 and studied at the Hans

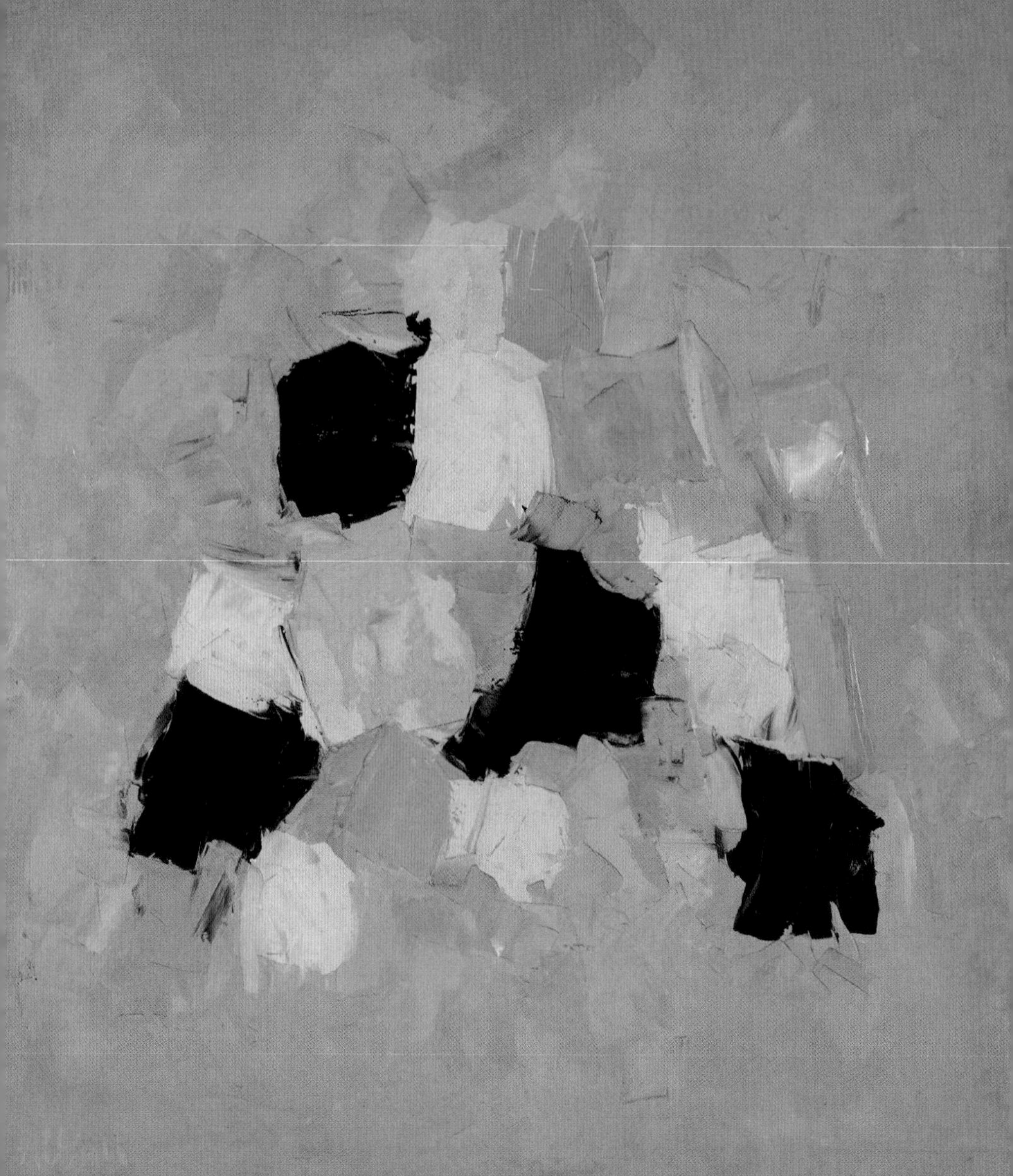

Hofmann School of Fine Arts and the Art Students League. She had received a degree in fine arts from the University of Puerto Rico only two years before, having studied with the Spanish-born artist Esteban Vicente (1903–2001), who taught at the university from 1945 to 1947. Vicente, whose impact on the artistic imagination of Albizu was decisive, would soon emerge on the New York downtown art scene himself, with paintings and collages that earned him a place in the first survey of the movement written by critic Thomas Hess.[9] Albizu's *Growth* plays, in a way not unrelated to Pacheco's painting, with positive and negative spaces, inevitably reminding us of the concept of Hofmann's theories of spacial construction. This all-over composition focuses on a central core of matter composed of semi-rectangular shapes of contrasting dark and light tones of black, tan, rust-orange, and yellow. This interior mass seems to float within a sea of variegated shades of yellow, applied with a loaded brush and palette knife.

I would suggest we examine the work of Albizu (who became well known in the 1960s for reproductions of her paintings on covers of jazz albums by Stan Getz) not simply as another example of a member of the New York abstract group of artists, but through the lens of her training and her Puerto Rican background. The art historian Abigail McEwen has written of the anomalies of Albizu's art as a reflection of her forging a personal identity that differs and, in fact, divorces her from the artistic context from which she came.[10] While there had been artists in Puerto Rico who embraced lyrical abstraction (such as Julio Rosado del Valle [1922–2008]), nonobjective art was a relatively rare commodity in the San Juan art world of the 1940s and 50s, and Albizu should be considered as one of its prime promoters.[11] As we saw in Chapter 5 in my discussion of the graphic work of Rafael Tufiño, socially concerned, realistic scenes of everyday life (especially in lithographs and woodcuts) were perhaps most representative of the production of the 1950s.

Given the Puerto Rican context of Albizu's training and initial career, *Growth* may be considered as a cry of liberation from even the indeterminate traces of popular identity or folklorisms. Throughout her productive career, Albizu forged a path of experimentation with abstract shapes in colors that became brighter as she progressed along her trajectory. She created a unique style and coloristic articulation. While she may be identified as a major Latina participant in a U.S.-based form of abstract art (she would certainly be considered a distinguished member of the second generation of Abstract Expressionists), Albizu never conformed to a single dominant trend.

Examining Albizu's work side by side with a consideration of a strictly contemporaneous piece by her teacher Vicente is especially useful. Esteban Vicente's *White, Black and Grey* (FIG. 6.4) is a collage made of hand-colored paper and charcoal on cardboard. Vicente had begun making collages during a summer teaching term at the University of California, Berkeley, where he had a small studio and less access to paint and canvas than in his more capacious downtown New York atelier.[12] With the application of seemingly random pieces of brown, gray, and beige paper, Vicente extends the implied three-dimensionality of Albizu's work, creating images that embody suggestions of physical structures that advance and recede into a virtual plane. Vicente's canvases of the 1950s embody similar principles of

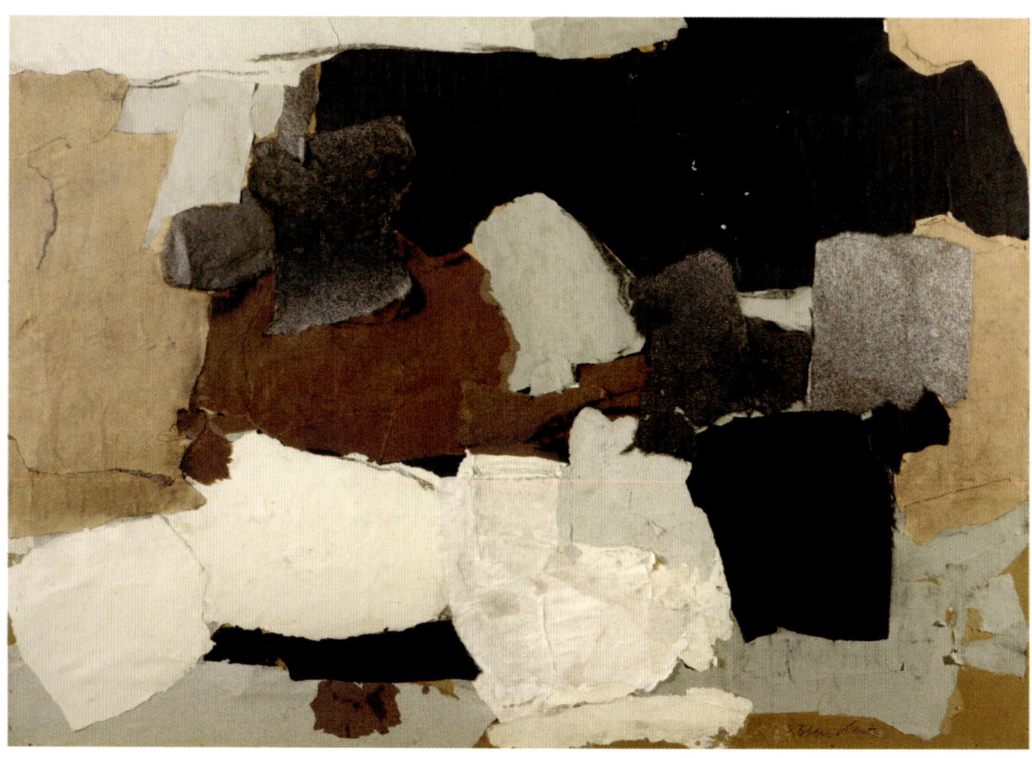

198

quasi-architectonic form and are, at times, vaguely reminiscent of landscapes. His early figurative work done in pre-Civil War Segovia, Madrid, and Barcelona, as well as Paris, reflected an engagement with the School of Paris artists such as Raoul Dufy (1877–1953) or Pierre Bonnard (1867–1947), yet the literal lyricism of his pre-American phase was soon replaced by a sobriety and technical concentration that reflected his deep admiration for the seventeenth-century Spanish painters, especially Francisco de Zurbarán (1598–1664) and Diego Velázquez (1599–1660), as well as twentieth-century artist Juan Gris (1887–1927), all of whom were masters of black and white contrasts.[13] Vicente's collages are subtler and more restrained than those of his New York Abstract Expressionist fellow artist Robert Motherwell (1915–1991) and come closer to the abstemiousness and color harmonies of another of his Ab Ex colleagues, Conrad Marca-Relli (1913–2000).[14] Vicente's cut-paper constructions of around 1950 to 1960 marked a turning point in his career and offered, as well, an antidote to the bravado and oversized boldness that are inherent in the works of the so-called A-list Ab Ex painters of the period.

Thus we see, in the preceding four interconnected stories of abstractionists working in various parts of the hemisphere, a web of affinities whose insertion within the larger panorama of abstract art reveals chapters and subtexts that go a long way toward enriching and expanding the often-told tale of gestural painting. The works of the African-American, Bolivian, Puerto Rican, and Spanish-U.S. artists described here form fundamental components of the many alternative histories that must be accounted for in order to reach a nuanced and even-handed comprehension of the complex history of this mode of visual expression. Yet the story cannot be properly related without referring to the progenitors of abstraction as well as the earlier forms of art that, from the 1910s onward, straddled the metaphorical fence between realism and nonobjectivity. This will occupy us in the following sections of this chapter.

Abstracted Nature

Chapter 1 traced some of the links that existed throughout the Americas in the first years of the twentieth century forged through a common fascination with the otherworldly or mystical in art. This was evidenced in the work of Kandinsky as well as other artists on both sides of the ocean who explored the possibilities of imbuing their art with an emotional inclination and a spiritual impulse that was achieved through pure abstraction, as well as in paintings or products of the graphic arts that blended the urge to create form based on gestures or the manipulation of light effects with embryonic or latent references to the figure. This section of my text will look at a few examples of artists who did both of these things in the spirit of tracing a gradually growing interest in, or engagement with, completely nonrepresentational imagery.

Perhaps the first Latin American artist to achieve absolute abstraction in his work was Emilio Pettoruti, son of Italian immigrants to Argentina. He reached artistic maturity through his long encounters with participants of the most avant-garde trends in the home country of his parents. This native of the city of La Plata (who had studied at the Academia Provincial there) left for Florence in 1913, not returning to Argentina (and to Buenos Aires) until the summer of 1924, after having also lived in Milan and exhibited throughout Italy. His experience in that country as a member of the artists' group known as the Famiglia Artistica, and his association with painters who would become the core of the Futurists (including Mario Sironi [1885–1961], with whom he was particularly close), marked his art in ways that would endure throughout his long career as a painter, educator, and museum director. From the early 1920s onward Pettoruti's work demonstrated an interest in Cubism and, at times, strict representationalism, yet the abstract experiments of the mid-1910s set the stage for the development of his mature artistic vocabulary.

Pettoruti's European experience (he lived out the years of the Great War in Italy) also included exhibitions in Paris and Berlin prior to his return to Argentina, accompanied by his friend and colleague Alejandro Xul Solar (see Chapter 1).[15] Among a series of charcoal-on-paper drawings that emerged in 1914 and 1915 is *Light in the Landscape* of 1915 (FIG. 6.5).

The forms are reminiscent of Pettoruti's interest in dynamic movement, with swirling lines creating a pattern of solids and voids that appear to suggest a vortex straining against the static confines of its frame. This image is somewhat more sensual than his straight-edged drawings of the same period, which often suggest the swift forward movement of a bird or a plane through space. *Light in the Landscape* also contains hints of biomorphism. The title itself suggests that it is a metaphor for the forces of earthly existence, an embodiment of the elements of nature.

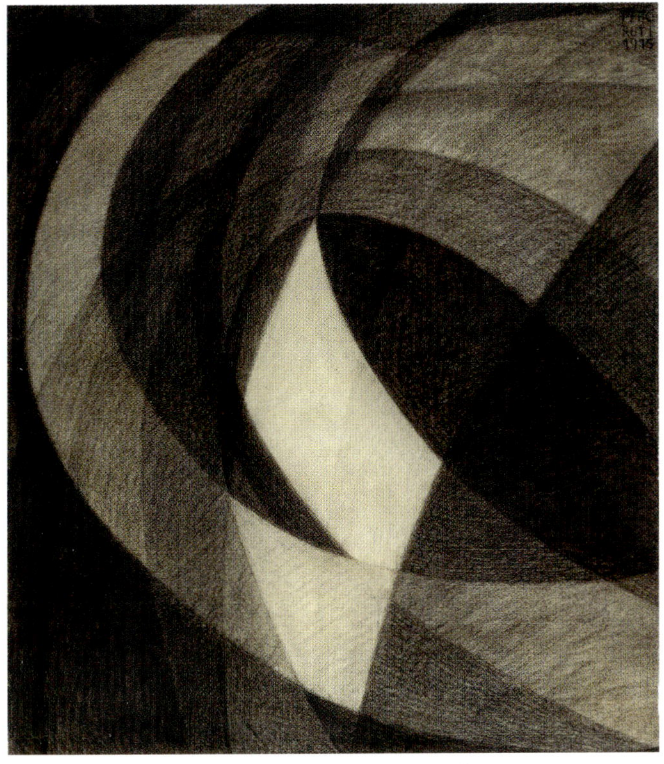

The dissolution of form through light is a thread that runs throughout modern painting, from the Suprematist forms of Kazimir Malevich (1878–1935) to the white-on-white paintings of Robert Ryman (b.1930), Hélio Oiticica (1937–1980), Jesús Rafael Soto (1923–2005), and others. The Brazilian poet Murilo Mendes (1901–1975) stated that "White is tamed light: the dynamic of our own contemplation."[16] Within the history of modern hemispheric painting there are few more trenchant examples than the "white" paintings of the Venezuelan painter Armando Reverón (1889–1954). Reverón is often remembered for his eccentric activities—a maker of a colony of lifelike dolls who inhabited a world with objects of daily use also fashioned by the artist, and a fashioner of Duchampian found objects. Sometimes called a mystic or, in more prosaic terms, a latter-day South American interpreter of Impressionism (although relatively few of his early works bear the stamp of that European movement), Reverón was one of the most original and idiosyncratic artists of his time. His art has been widely admired (and recently researched and exhibited) for its ingenious use of the effects of light and its distinctive

Fig. 6.5
Emilio Pettoruti
Luce nel paesaggion II (Light in the Landscape), 1915, charcoal on paper, 21½ x 18⅛ in. (54.6 x 46 cm). Museum of Modern Art, New York. Purchased with funds provided by Nelly Arrieta de Blaquier and by the Latin American and Caribbean Fund in honor of Edward Sullivan 1405.2007.

employment of materials (including rough burlap instead of canvas, and homemade paints and brushes).[17]

El Arbol (The Tree) of 1931 (FIG. 6.6) is a quintessential example of both the conquest of form by light (in this case, the searing heat of the Venezuelan coast) and the suggestion of an alternative type of artistic vision. This monochromatic image delineates a natural form through the use of slightly varying tones of white and cream as well as differing thicknesses of paint strokes and dabs. It suggests not a specific tree but an emblematic presence, a synecdoche of all trees and, in its farthest-reaching meaning, the generative force that stands for the energy of life itself.

Reverón's connection to wood, trees, and light is equally demonstrated in a 1927–29 untitled composition (FIG. 6.7) that depicts a female figure enclosed within the frame of an arbor. Her outlines are subtly suggested although principally dissolved in light. Those of the trees form a protective network of undulating branches that cover and embrace the unknown subject of

Fig. 6.6
Armando Reverón
El Arbol (The Tree),
1931, oil on canvas,
25½ x 31¾ in. (64.8
x 80.6 cm). Colección
Patricia Phelps de
Cisneros no. 1999.11.

202

this picture. The artist fashioned a roughly hewn wooden frame that carries out the conceit of the sheltering tree to a palpable degree, bringing the substance of the represented theme to life in a square enclosure surrounding this picture.

Armando Reverón's sense of light was defined by his reactions to, and evocations of, the hot sun's glare on the Caribbean coast where he lived for most of his life. Artists from more northerly regions evinced an entirely different sensibility in their abstractions or quasi-abstractions of natural forces. Particularly vivid contrasts are provided by paintings by contemporaries of Reverón working in New York and its environs. In Chapter 2 we considered Georgia O'Keeffe within the subject matter of urban painting. *New York Street with Moon* of 1925 (FIG. 6.8) is closely aligned chronologically with her view of Manhattan's harbor from the Shelton Hotel, where she was living with Alfred Stieglitz. Nonetheless it presents a stark contrast to that detailed city painting. In *New York Street*, nature, somewhat anomalously, reigns. O'Keeffe juxtaposes it with the built environment in such a way that the products of human intervention—both the hard-edge, Precisionist buildings and the almost-opaque nimbus of light from a street lamp—are subjugated by the evanescent illumination from the moon casting its glow over the midtown New York City landscape. The scene displays an actual place—the Chatham Hotel, built in 1916 as one of the city's most prestigious luxury hotels, located on Vanderbilt Avenue (adjacent to Grand Central Station) between 48th and 49th Streets. O'Keeffe, however, completely obliterates the individuality of the structure, using it mainly as a foil for the sensuality evoked by the undulating clouds (their ripples reminding us of Art Deco decorative forms). The tower boldly thrusts itself into the sky as if to challenge the softening effects of moonlight. Under the cover of

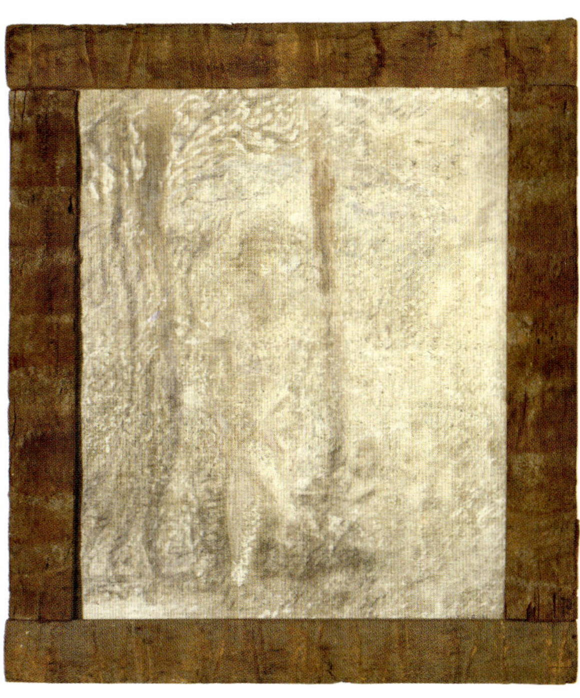

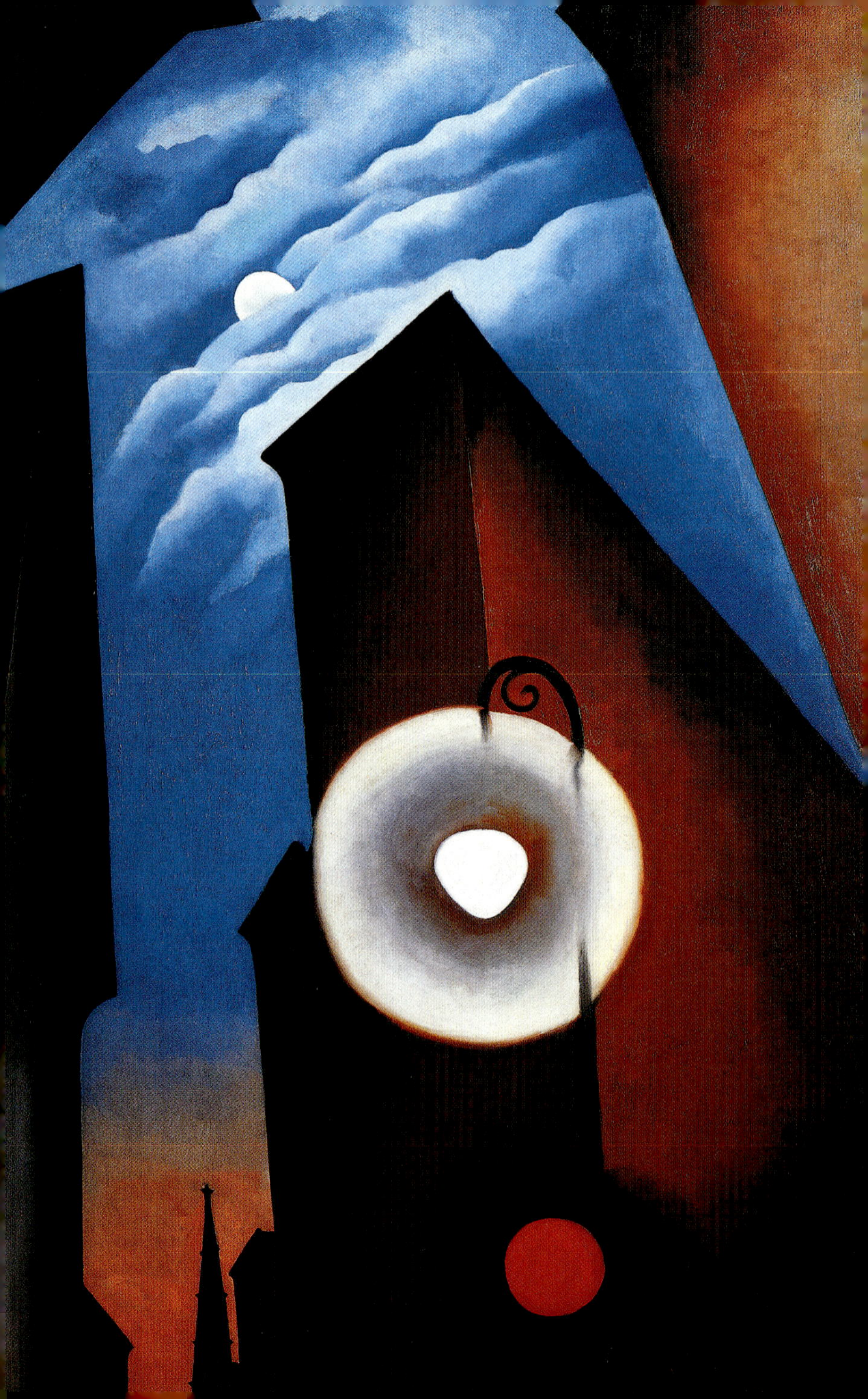

night, nature assumes hegemony and transforms all within its realm in a gesture of obscurity, foreshadowing the final darkness of death's arrival.

Helen Torr (1886–1967) knew Georgia O'Keeffe (although perhaps more as a rival than a friend) and also showed at Alfred Stieglitz's New York Gallery, an American Place, in 1933.[18] Her art has been somewhat overshadowed by that of her husband, the Precisionist and modernist pioneer Arthur Dove (1880–1946), who shares with Emilio Pettoruti the distinction of having created some of the earliest examples of pure abstract painting and drawing in their respective art environments.[19] Torr's work, nonetheless, plays a key role in the various projects of abstraction of natural forms that characterize hemispheric art of the 1920s and 30s. During the 1920s she and Dove lived on a 42-foot yawl (houseboat) anchored off the North Shore of Long Island, New York (moving to a nearby yacht club in winter). Torr was naturally attracted by the marine life and aquatic atmosphere around her. *Crimson and Green Leaves* of 1927 (FIG. 6.9) attests to Torr's interest in immersing herself within the natural life around her on the shore and the interior spaces of the place where she lived with Dove. In this painting the leaves form intersecting patterns of colors and shapes. The specific references to individual plant types virtually disappear as their outlines delineate an arrangement of intertwined, pulsating manifestations of nature's subtle sovereignty within the order of the world. As the art historian Anne Cohen DePietro has stated:

Helen Torr drew much of her subject matter from the natural world of Long Island. Her carefully painted still lifes of shells and leaves … as well as her nautical subjects with their evocation of the rhythms of nature, testify to her love of the Island.[20]

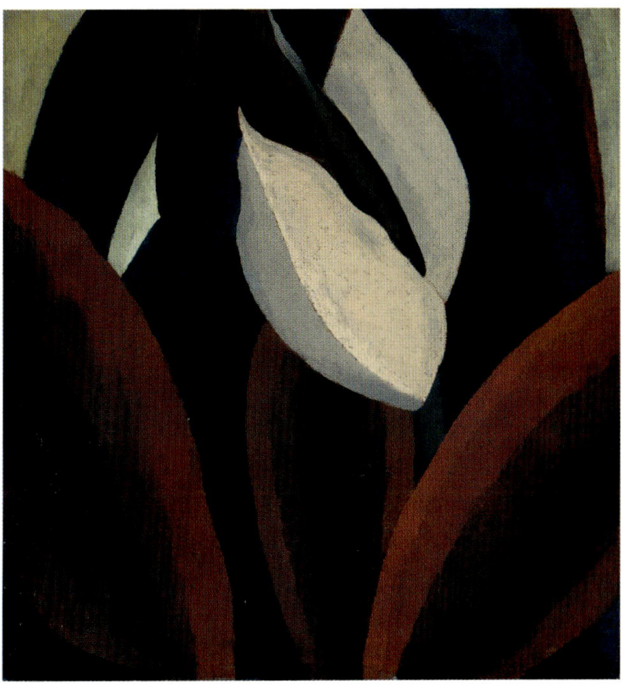

Fig. 6.9
Helen Torr
Crimson and Green Leaves, 1927, oil on plywood, 14⅛ x 12½ in. (35.9 x 31.8 cm). Metropolitan Museum of Art, New York. Gift of Carl D. Lobell, 1994. 1994.341.4.

Chapter 6 · The Liberated Line

The Pacific Northwest coast of the United States has both distinctive weather patterns and a characteristic school of painters whose contributions to the history of modernity are unique in their evocations of an often spiritually charged series of natural forces. We have already observed the art of Canadian painter Emily Carr (Chapter 2), who lived most of her life in British Columbia. The artists of the same time period who worked in the state of Washington, just south of the Canadian border, share, in many cases, a similar sensibility, incorporating references to the saturated air, rocky coasts, sea animals, and birds that they observed during the course of their daily existences. Morris Graves (1910–2001) belonged to a group of artists whose careers developed in Seattle as well as in more rural places throughout Washington and Oregon. He and some of his closest fellow painters of the Northwest School, like Mark Tobey (1890–1976),

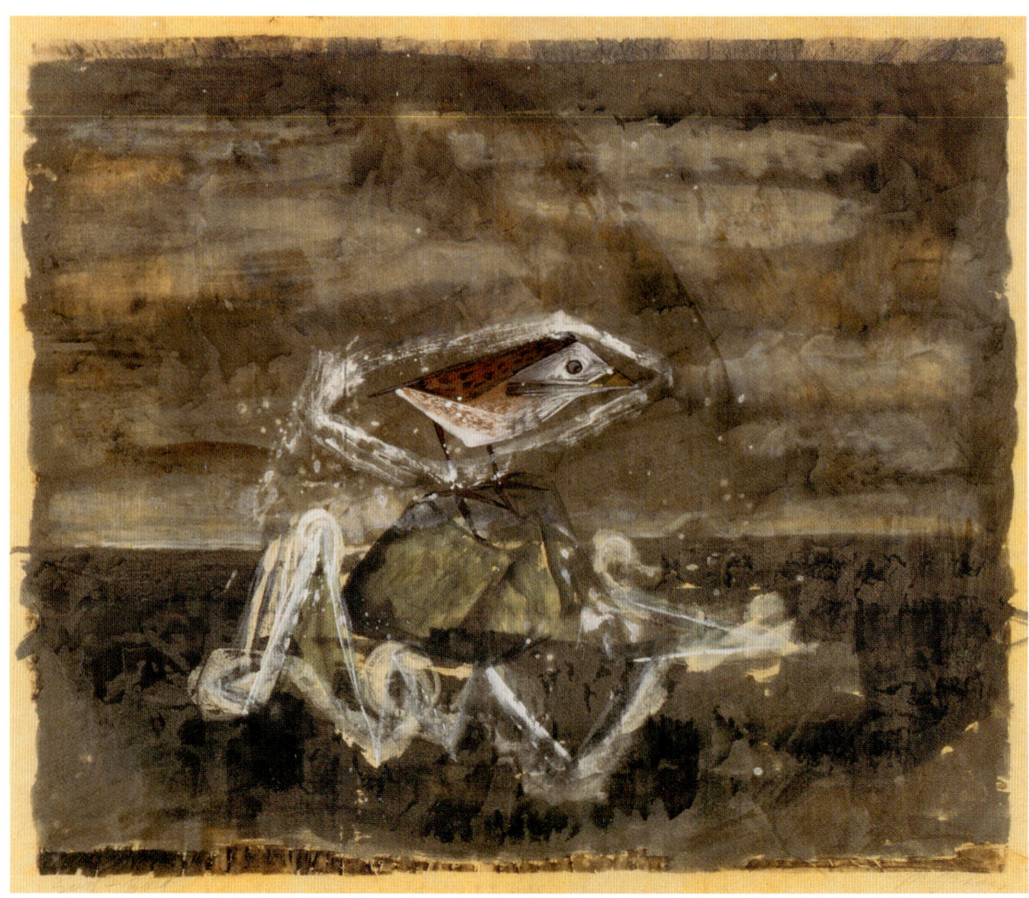

shared affinities for Asian art and philosophy (especially Zen Buddhism) and sometimes came close to the gestural techniques of the Abstract Expressionists without, for the most part, crossing over into the territory of pure abstraction.

Graves's gouache on paper of circa 1940 entitled *Surf and Bird* (FIG. 6.10) employs a subtle palette of browns, grays, and whites, referencing the sea and the transcendence of nature, convincingly incorporating natural forms within an ample field of vaporous sky and low horizon evoking the mystical aspects of the cycles of natural life.[21] Shortly after painting *Surf and Bird*, Graves participated in the exhibition *Americans 1942: 18 Artists from 9 States* organized by curator Dorothy C. Miller for New York's Museum of Modern Art. He showed a series of ten gouaches (a medium that by the late 1930s had become his favorite for what he considered its immediacy and potential to express intimacy). In the exhibition catalogue his artist's statement reveals a good deal to us about the emphasis he placed on attempting to capture his inner vision in his work:

I paint to evoke a changing language of symbols, a language with which to remark upon the qualities of our mysterious capacities which direct us to ultimate reality. I paint to rest from the phenomena of the external world—to pronounce it—and to make notations of its essences with which to verify the inner eye.[22]

Surrealism into Abstraction

The affinities between Surrealism and Abstract Expressionism have long been the subject of scholarly observation and commentary. Neither form of art can be said to embody a specific *style*. If any parallels may be articulated to link these two (very loosely associated) artistic movements, it would be their mutual interest in spontaneity and their dedication to evoking the imagination and unconscious thought. Chapter 8 examines a variety of American forms of Surrealism that succeeded in making cities from New York to Buenos Aires centers of Surrealist creativity in the late 1930s and into the mid-1940s. Many of these artists manifested their interest in the visionary or the private life of dreams through varying forms of abstract or semi-abstract art, and many of these émigré artists and their American counterparts throughout North and South America and the Caribbean connected on the level of mutual admiration for their intense visions of form, time, and space.

Few European-based artists active in the United States in the 1940s had such a significant impact on their newly adopted art world as the Chilean-born Roberto Sebastián Matta (1911–2002). Matta spent World War II and the immediate postwar years (1938–47) in New York, having left his previous home in Paris, where he had recently joined the Surrealist movement. During his time in the United States he created some of his best-known works. Those of the first half of the 1940s have been labeled "inscapes" and "psychological morphologies." The 1943 *La Lumière noire* (Black Light) (FIG. 6.11) is a quintessential example of Matta's creation of the illusion of vast spaces that seem to go on forever, guiding the eye and mind through an extraterrestrial existence permeated by globule forms, pinlike points of light, diaphanous floating shapes (vaguely reminiscent of creatures observed only in the greatest depths of the ocean), and skeins of thread winding their way through the surface of the image, connecting its disparate surfaces, objects, and gossamer forms. Matta's tonal sensibility in this painting brings to mind the poignant evocation by André Breton of the role played by color in the Chilean artist's work. Only a year after Matta painted *Black Light* Breton wrote that

Matta's richness consists in the fact that, from his earliest works onwards, he has been master of an entirely new range of colors: perhaps the only new one, and certainly the most fascinating one, offered to us since Matisse. This range, the gradation of which is based upon a by now famous quick-changing purple rose which Matta seems to have discovered … is arranged according to a complex prismatic pattern. Matta's prism, which is in fact composed of the prism of decomposition of solar light in free air combined with that of its decomposition through each cell of its cells, even goes so far as to correct itself by means of the scale of variations introduced by black light.[23]

Matta's connection to New York Abstract Expressionism has long concerned historians of the movement. American curator and art historian Lowery Stokes Sims has stated that

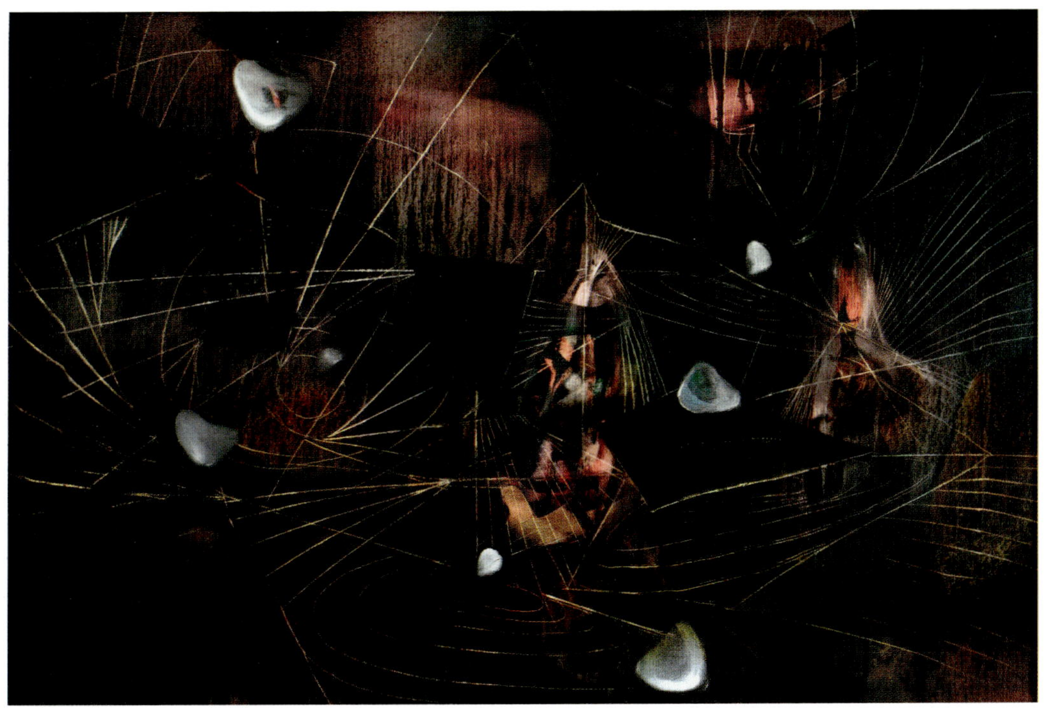

Matta's frequent suggestions of nether worlds of chaos and creation predicted the imagery of the Abstract Expressionists during the 1940s … his exercises of automatism that he organized in his studio in the early 1940s [are] credited with revolutionizing the work of [many of his contemporaries].[24]

Irving Sandler asserts, in addition, that more than any other artist Matta had the greatest impact on promoting automatism and the significance of chance elements in the art of the young New York School painters.[25] The "nether worlds of chaos" to which Sims alludes is evidently a reference to the trauma of the war from which Matta was fleeing. *Black Light*, while an elegant and captivating image, possesses, at the same time, suggestions of a world off-center, an existence turned upside down.

Matta moved with great ease (given his language abilities and contacts within the worlds of the social and intellectual elite of the major transatlantic capitals) in many of New York's art and social circles. Nonetheless, he was equally attracted to and desired contact with the Spanish-speaking parts of the hemisphere and the spring/summer of 1941, when he spent significant amounts

Fig. 6.11
Roberto Matta
La Lumière noire
(Black Light), 1943,
oil on canvas, 17 x 25
in. (45.1 x 63.5 cm).
Private Collection
Courtesy Mary-Anne
Martin Fine Art,
New York.

of time in Mexico, was critical for his art as well as for the artists with whom he came into contact. Matta traveled with Robert Motherwell to Mexico and lived for some time in Taxco, the colonial capital of silver production situated halfway between Mexico City and Acapulco. The landscape of the central plateau greatly impressed him, as did the constant threat of seismic activity in the volcanoes in the Valley of Mexico. In fact, several of his most well-known works from the early 1940s reference the potential tumult of these preternatural earthly forces in their most resplendent and deadly actions. Matta was also very captivated by the pre-Hispanic cultures of Mexico and studied the history and practices of the Aztecs and other indigenous groups, something that definitively marked his artistic production of the mid- and late 1940s. When he returned to the figure, scenes that suggested sacrificial rituals became staples of his artistic vocabulary, connecting him, at least in a historical sense, with a common past shared by persons living in the lands of the indigenous peoples formerly conquered by the Spaniards.

By the time the Austrian-born artist Wolfgang Paalen (1905–1959)—with whom Matta was closely associated in the early 1940s—arrived in Mexico City (1939), he had already distinguished himself in the circles of Surrealist painters and writers in Paris. His 1939 painting *Combat of the Saturnian Princes III* (FIG. 6.12) was executed in Paalen's distinctive medium of *fumage* (the smoke from a candle applied directly onto the canvas) mixed with oil. It presents a nightmarish image of a flying creature that appears to disintegrate while on its journey. It is an image that clearly straddles the border between grotesque figuration and expressive abstraction. Although many of the colors are jewel-like, the atmosphere of despair is redolent of the artist's fears of his upcoming exile (he was partly Jewish in a city threatened with invasion by the Nazis), which would be accomplished in 1939 when he and his wife, the French writer and painter Alice Rahon (1904–1987), and his patron, the Swiss filmmaker and photographer Eva Sulzer (1902–1990), left France for New York.

The threesome traveled through Canada, making their way to British Columbia where they studied and photographed the art of the First Nations peoples—images that later appeared in the magazine *DYN*, which Paalen published in Mexico between 1942 and 1944 and for which he wrote numerous articles of

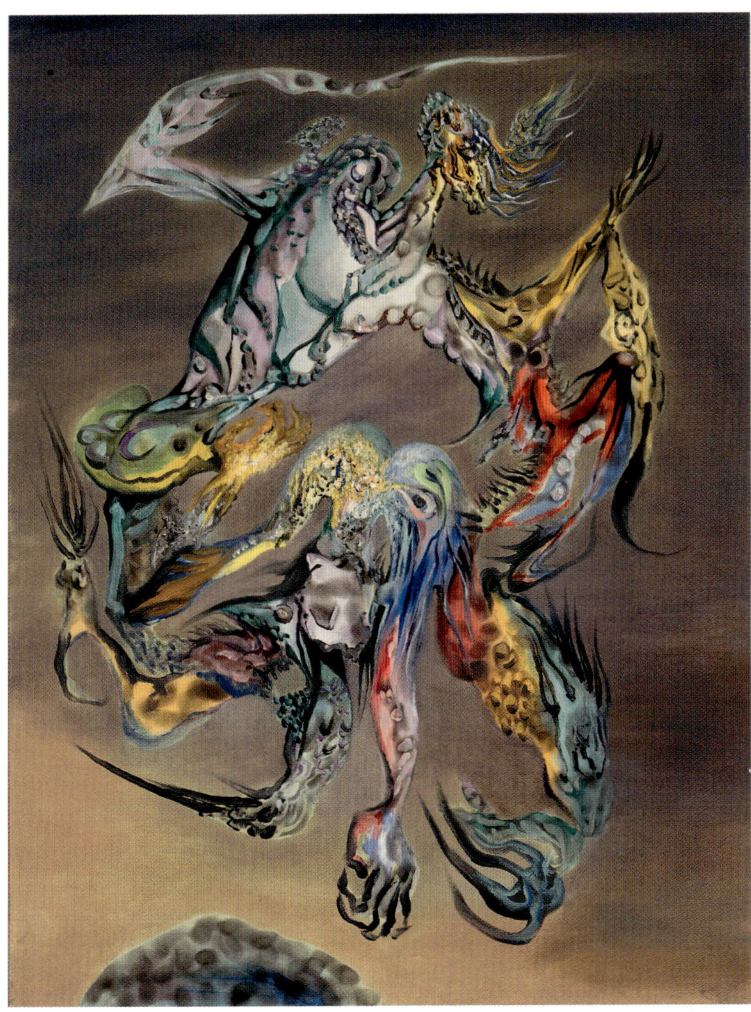

anthropological and artistic interest.[26] Paalen also included the work of Rahon (born Alice Philppot) in his magazine—appropriately so, as her art (which she began to do full-time after the couple arrived in Mexico City at the invitation of Frida Kahlo) was redolent of her intense interest in natural forms and was also steeped in the subject matter of both indigenous and ancient cultures on both sides of the Atlantic. As a child growing up in Paris, Rahon had spent summers at her grandparents' house in Brittany, a heartland of both Paleolithic and Celtic culture in France, where she would have seen prehistoric monuments on a regular basis. These experiences, as well as her travels with Paalen, whom she met in 1931, to the prehistoric caves at

211

Altamira in northern Spain as well as the ancient monuments of Greece in 1934 (the year of her marriage to the Austrian painter), reinforced her predilection for incorporating references to the mythic unknown in her poetry and, later, her art. In addition, as German art historian Andreas Neufert has pointed out, the book by James Frazer entitled *The Golden Bough: A Study in Magic and Religion* (first published in 1890) had a considerable impact on both Rahon and Paalen, as it did on many other artists and writers well into the middle years of the twentieth century.[27] Interestingly enough, Rahon's semi-abstract painting evinced relatively few direct references to ancient Mexican civilizations, even though she was keenly interested in the past of her new homeland.

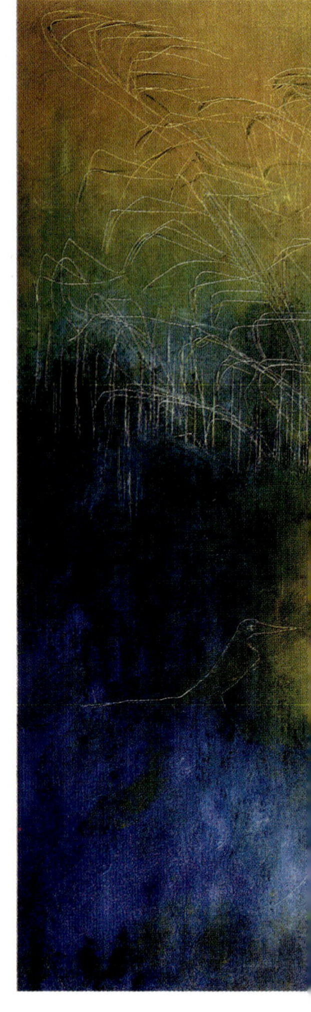

The Wind (1954) (FIG. 6.13) is a particularly representative and appealing example of Rahon's mature art. It is a symphony of blues and yellows, evoking the forces of nature and including, in lightly brushed-in forms in the lower part of the canvas, a series of birds as they are propelled through the air by the currents that transport them across the scene. Rahon was fascinated by the poetic potential of the air and the wind, and a number of her canvases of the 1940s and 50s suggest the evanescent element of nature in a manner that allows her to exercise her penchant for coloristic abstract forms in a powerful way.

Paalen's own art done in Mexico evolved in ways that evidenced his growing engagement with pure abstraction. He was, in addition, active for approximately a decade in California (beginning in 1948) among a group of U.S. artists that included Lee Mullican (1919–1998), who mined the iconic forms of various arts of mysticism derived from Asian religions and combined them with experiments in automatic writing. Mullican's *Quartet*

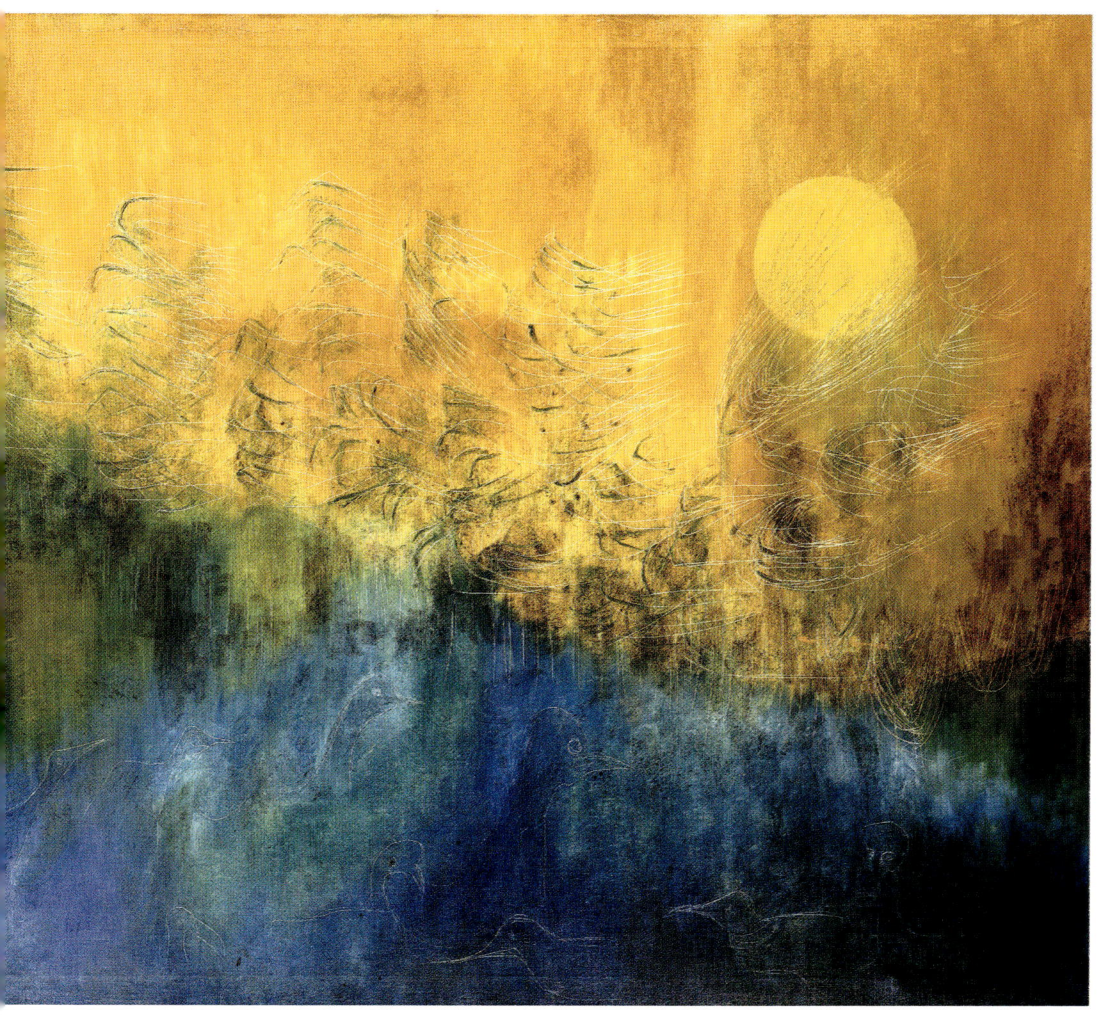

of Spider Sounds (FIG. 6.14) is a 1950 ink and charcoal drawing on paper. Its sinuous lines suggest organic forms and the energy of the insect creatures to which its title refers while remaining a completely abstract evocation of the dynamism of nature, not unlike certain examples of the most abstemious Japanese or Chinese ink paintings as well as ancient Southwest U.S. rock drawings so admired by the artist. This work is representative of the art produced by this group, which called themselves "Dynaton" (from the Greek for "things that are possible") and flourished in the San Francisco Bay area in the late 1940s, receiving a major exhibition at the San Francisco Museum of Modern Art in 1951 (organized by innovative museum director Grace

Fig. 6.13
Alice Rahon
The Wind, 1954, oil
on canvas, 42¾ x 70⅞
in. (108.4 x 180 cm).
Private collection.

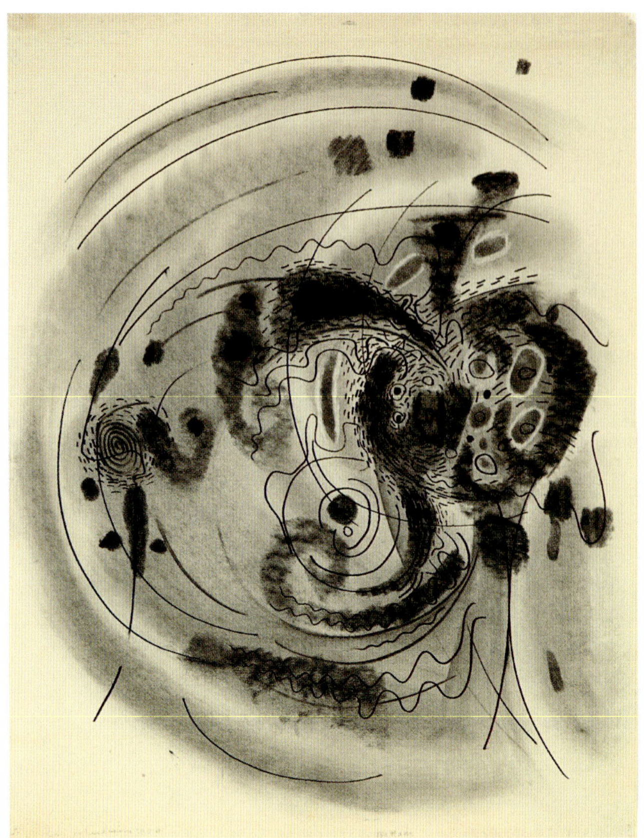

McCann Morley, whose efforts were definitive in introducing Californian audiences to Latin American and other forms of non-U.S. and European modern art). Paalen and Gordon Onslow Ford (1912–2003), who was also in Mexico from 1941 to 1947 and friendly with Paalen, Matta, Rahon, and other émigré artists, formed the group, with Mullican as the principal U.S.-born member (he originally came from Oklahoma).[28] Like the European Surrealist Max Ernst (1891–1976), who became entranced with native peoples in Arizona, the members of Dynaton included indigenous North American sources among their fountains of inspiration. Yet none were more avid absorbers of the mythic patterns, symbolic colors, and abstracted forms of the arts of such Northwest Coast groups as the Tlingit and Haida, or the Navajo, Hopi, and many others in the Southwest, than the "Indian Space Painters," a group of New York-based artists (discussed below) who had come to Manhattan from elsewhere and, during the 1940s, presented in their all-over abstractions with flat planes and often vivid colors, an alternative to the growing hegemony of the New York School Ab Ex painters.

Site-Specific Abstraction

In this final section of remarks on abstractions in the Americas I will consider the work of four artists who, on one hand, worked within visual vocabularies that paralleled those of many of their contemporaries but who, at the same time, sought to evoke specific places, times, objects, or social circumstances. The Indian Space Painters serve as our first example. This group of artists (whose coherence as an alliance was short-lived; they exhibited together only once, in 1946[29]) emerged from established New York institutions—mostly from the venerable Art Students League and the classes of Hans Hofmann. They were interested in (and wished to either surpass or transform) such common visual sources as Picasso's Cubism and the dynamism of many of his well-known compositions like the monumental 1937 *Guernica* (shown in New York shortly after it was painted), the brightly colored compositions of Paul Klee, or the biomorphism of Miró and late Kandinsky. Yet the Indian Space Painters' distinctive "voice" was achieved by the appropriation and reconfiguration of the flat colors and strong spatial divisions that they observed in Northwest Coast Indian blankets and wood carvings, the woven basket patterns and textiles of the Southwest native inhabitants, and the sand painting of tribes such as the Navajo, Hopi, and Zuni (which had also exerted a considerable force on the imagination of Jackson Pollock).[30]

Such sensitivity to what I call "site specific" bases of visual stimulus is neither folklorically clichéd nor exoticized. An artist such as Steve Wheeler (1912–1992), one of the principal figures within the Indian Space Painting movement, was conscious, like so many of his contemporaries, of the emotional and visual power of the art of peoples whose pictorial traditions emerged from sources other than those of the Western-oriented academies, or modes of graphic expression different from conventionally accepted forms of the so-called mainstream. In addition, such site-specific visualities served to confer a sense either of a specific place or of an affinity with what we would today called "Otherness." We will see in the next chapter how, for example, Joaquín Torres-García and those artists who emerged from his Workshop utilized symbols often derived from pre-Hispanic South American cultures to evoke identification, no matter how tenuous, with art makers and creators of images who had worked on the same continent hundreds of years before them. Visual affinities with other cultures (often those that had emerged in various American locales) served as a means to stabilize or "ground" the work of such painters or sculptors within a continuum of creativity that had origins in practices distinct from those that dominated in museums, academies, or sale rooms.

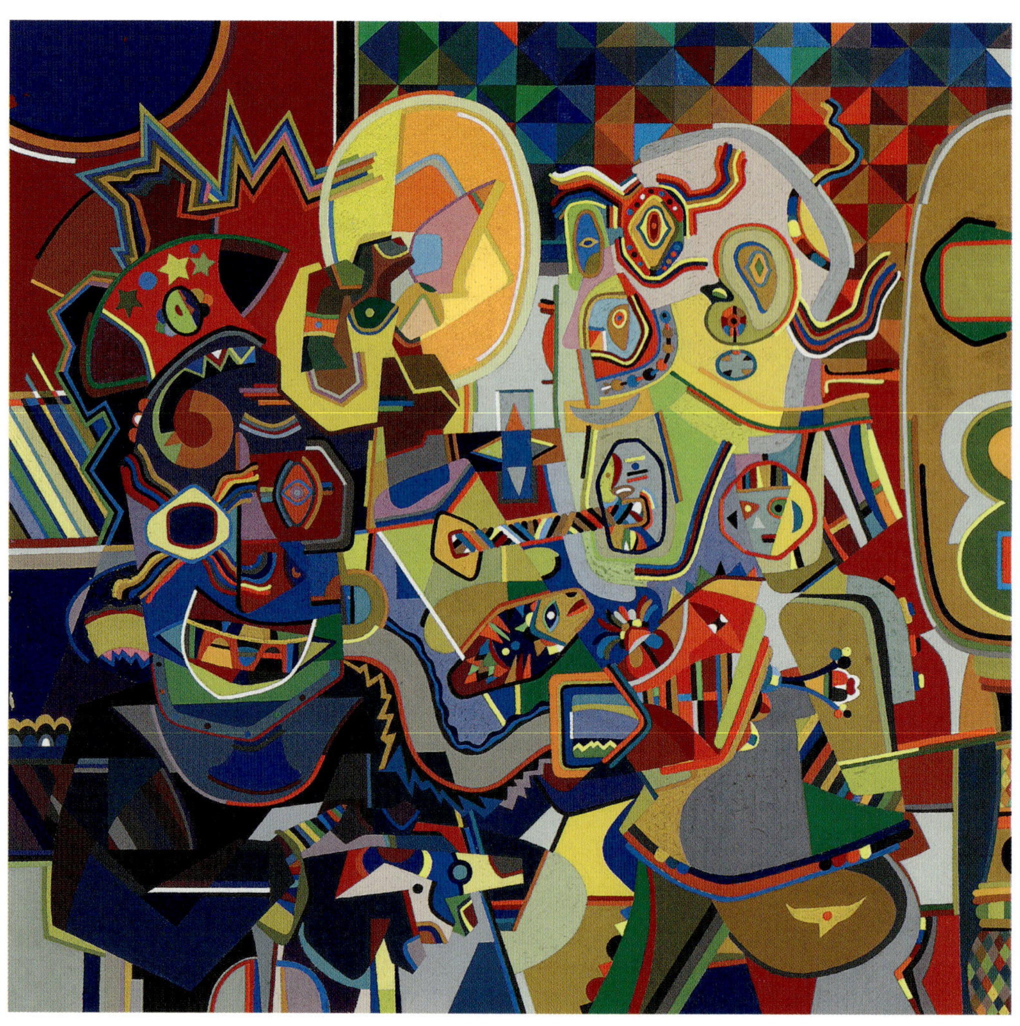

Wheeler's 1949 *Untitled W22 (Man Looking at a Pork Chop)* (FIG. 6.15) bears a characteristically amusing and ironic title but, at the same time, serves as an example of the use of overall pattern, intense engagement with color, and interest in fragmentation as well as order (a diamond pattern at the upper right is seemingly at odds with the "crazy quilt" nature of the rest of the composition) to create an image that, while suggesting certain recognizable forms (such as a face), also exudes a compelling aura of biomorphic movement. In this and other Indian Space Painting works by Wheeler and fellow members of the group (including Howard Daum [1918–1988], Peter Busa [1914–1985], and Will Barnet [1911–2012]), there is a synthesis of the forms of art they admired and from which they drew their stimulus, yet these have all been highly mediated, fashioned into a distinctly idiosyncratic and recognizably "American" form of abstraction.[31]

The oil on canvas painting entitled *Cenote* (Natural Sinkhole) (FIG. 6.16) of 1947 marks a turning point not only in the career of its creator, the Mexican painter Gunther Gerzso (1915–2000), but also within the trajectory of Mexican abstract art. Gerzso, born in Mexico City to émigré parents of Hungarian and German origin, had studied art history in Switzerland as a young man and worked for many years as a set designer for the Cleveland Play House in the United States. Although he was an essentially self-taught painter, he experienced considerable success on his return to Mexico, where he became friendly with Wolfgang Paalen and others in the abstract-Surrealist circles

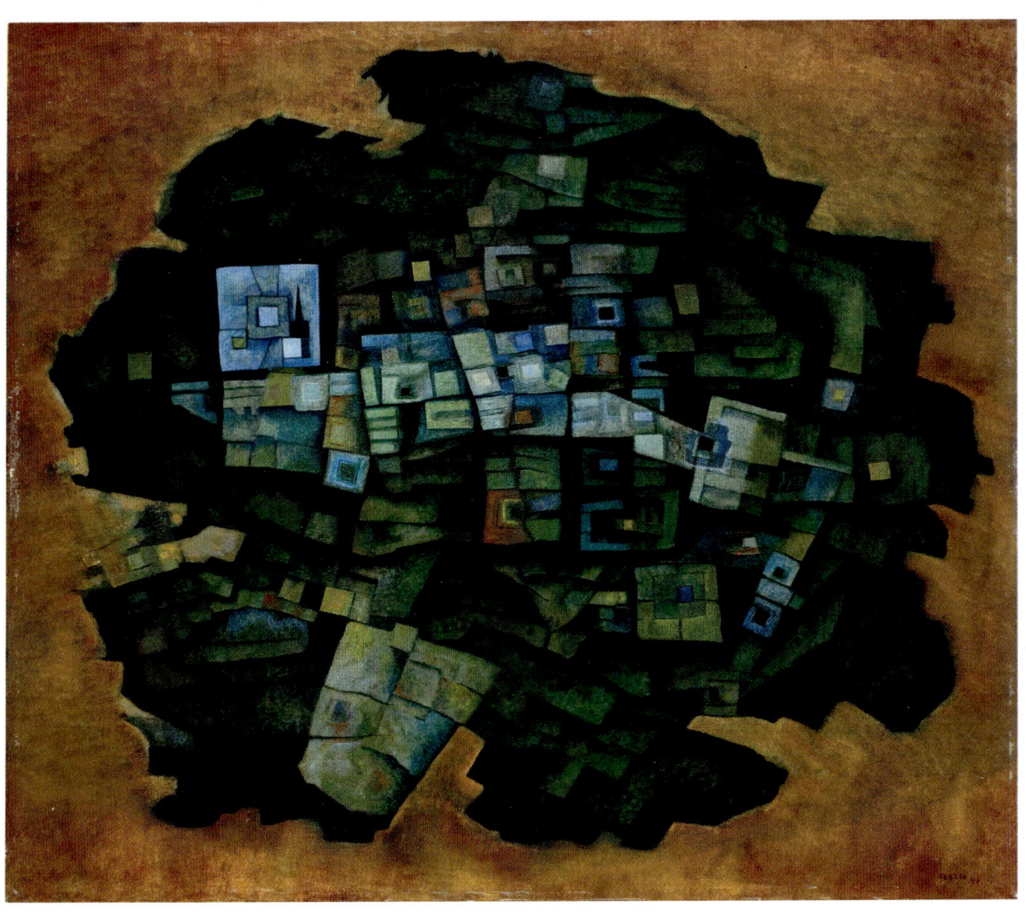

of native and foreign-born artists who made Mexico City one of the focal points of the hemisphere's art world in the 1940s. Although he was always attracted to ancient American history, art, and architecture, Gerzso's attention to pre-Hispanic art was undoubtedly strengthened by his links to Paalen and Rahon, among others, who utilized pre-Columbian forms in their own work.

Gerzso became a full-time artist in about 1940 and his initial compositions were located squarely within the realm of figurative Surrealism. However, by mid-decade he had set himself on a course from which he would rarely deviate, venturing into pure abstraction with images that were inspired by both ancient structures in Mexico and Peru, as well as natural forms that recalled the ancient-ness of the country of his birth. Such is the case with *Cenote,* an image that represents one of the most curious features of the topography of southern Mexico. Sinkholes are common features in the Yucatán Peninsula that extends into the Caribbean on Mexico's east coast, where literally thousands of these cavelike craters lead to underground bodies of water. The ancient Maya considered cenotes to be physical conduits to sacred realms, so for them they held magical connotations. Indeed, within Maya mythology there are many accounts of sacrifices (of both material riches and humans) being flung into a cenote as propitious offerings to appease a specific spirit or group of deities.

In *Cenote,* nonetheless, Gerzso employs his source of geological inspiration to create an image that, as art historian Diana Du Pont has noted, seems to peel away many layers of the earth's surface to reveal the architectonic substructure of the rock and magma below.[32] Gerzso's image is anything but representational, containing no indications of specific place, and yet it projects a sense of depth and secrecy that the viewer intuitively interprets as deriving from the realms of ancient people and places.

Cenote and related paintings of the mid-1940s by Gerzso marked a new chapter in the development of abstract art in Mexico. Although muralism had long held sway as a principal vehicle for both aesthetic and political expression, its moment of apogee had long since passed. A number of artists who came to prominence at this moment in Mexico City (and would collectively be referred to as members of *La Ruptura* [the Rupture] generation) moved far away from the literalism and the dominant figuration of muralism to embrace mainly gestural abstraction.[33] Gerzso's own abstraction was at least tangentially rooted in Cubism, and in *Cenote* we observe him constructing space by fragmenting the central mass of the picture into many small segments. His later work would eventually take on more monumental proportions, with broader intersecting planes of color as their characteristic feature.

Gerzso's "site specific" abstraction consists of his use of forms (here, a cenote) that had fundamental meanings for a specific group of people in his own country, and then removing the historical or geographical references to "cleanse," as it were, the field of vision. He succeeded in creating an original and influential mode of abstract visuality in Mexico. Du Pont states that "Gerzso emerges as the most important pioneer of Mexican abstraction ... [he] launched an unprecedented direction in Mexican painting ... he worked at the margins of modernism but furthered the development of international abstract art after World War II."[34]

Peruvian artist Fernando de Szyszlo (b.1925) has consistently developed a body of work throughout his long career (he works mainly in Lima but spent an important formative period from 1948 to 1955 in Paris and Florence) that utilizes free-form abstraction and inserts oblique references (through shapes or titles) to places and people of ancient Andean sites. The son of a Peruvian mother and a Polish father, Szyszlo has assiduously familiarized himself with Peruvian history and geography through his extensive travels and readings. He developed his characteristic style (which shares certain characteristics with the distinct brand of abstraction fashioned by Rufino Tamayo, with whom Szyszlo was friendly in his Paris years) in the 1950s, employing biomorphic forms that appear to float in a non-perspectival nether world. Peruvian novelist Mario Vargas Llosa has remarked that

One of the most highly praised aspects of Szyszlo's art is the way in which he brings together the ancient and the modern, bridging the gap between European abstraction and pre-Hispanic craftsmanship, traces of which linger in his paintings like an old memory or feeling of nostalgia.[35]

Yet Vargas Llosa goes on to reject any note of either traditional Indigenism or historical specificity in the images themselves.

Szyszlo's 1959 *Cajamarca* (FIG. 6.17) speaks to the binary in the artist's work pointed out by Vargas Llosa. This large canvas is a swirling mass of varying shades of red, oranges, and blacks. The shapes consist essentially of two masses: an upper form that is vaguely circular, with another more amorphous, boxlike shape below. They are anchored to the edges of the canvas by bands of black that function as restraints, locking the components of the principal composition in place, restricting the movement of elements that appear to embody forces of nature that desire to break the boundaries of the image before us. A few strategically placed

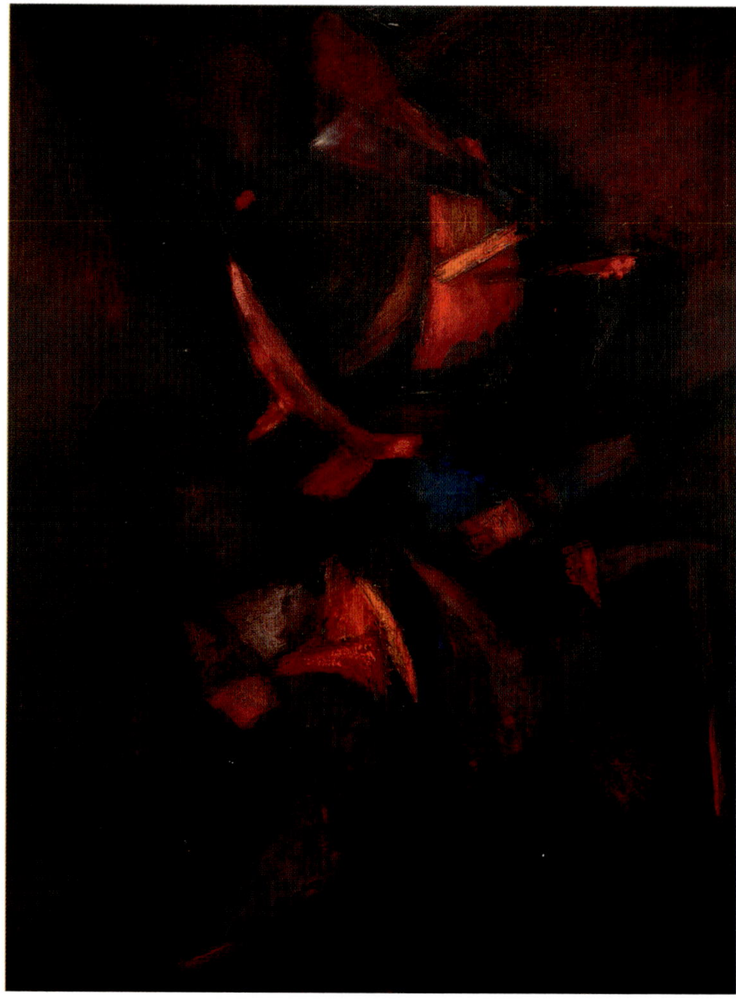

Fig. 6.17
Fernando de Szyszlo
Cajamarca, 1959, oil
on canvas, 50 x 36
in. (127 x 91.44 cm).
OAS Art Museum of the
Americas, Washington,
D.C.

220

patches of blue relieve the bloodlike crimson hues that predominate here. This painting is, on one hand, a study in pure form, a visual dissertation in barely contained mass and opposing stasis. Nonetheless, Szyszlo has always paid careful attention to the titles of his works and they often function as keys that suggest at least partial references to places and events. This picture bears the name of a city in northern Peru in the Andean highlands. Cajamarca is noted for its many preserved colonial monuments, but it was a significant site in pre-Hispanic times and was also the location of one of the most decisive and bloody events in the downfall of the Inca empire at the hands of the invading Spanish forces headed by Francisco Pizarro. It was in Cajamarca that Pizarro's troops captured and murdered the Inca emperor Atahualpa, effectively seizing the vast Andean region for Spain, creating the Viceroyalty of Peru that comprised most of the Spanish-speaking countries of the southern portion of modern South America. Szyszlo's painting may thus be understood on a number of levels. His art, especially that of the 1950s and 60s, created a pathway for Andean artists to avoid the restrictions of the socially conscious figurative tradition of Indigenism (discussed in Chapter 5). Yet it also adhered to a sense of history without falling into the trap of a literal form of essentialism or cultural nationalism. Szyszlo's affinities for Leftist causes are well known. He showed his work in post-revolutionary Havana in solidarity with the government of Fidel Castro and, among other graphic cycles, executed a series of lithographs in honor of the Peruvian poet César Vallejo, whose own political stance was decidedly Marxist.[36]

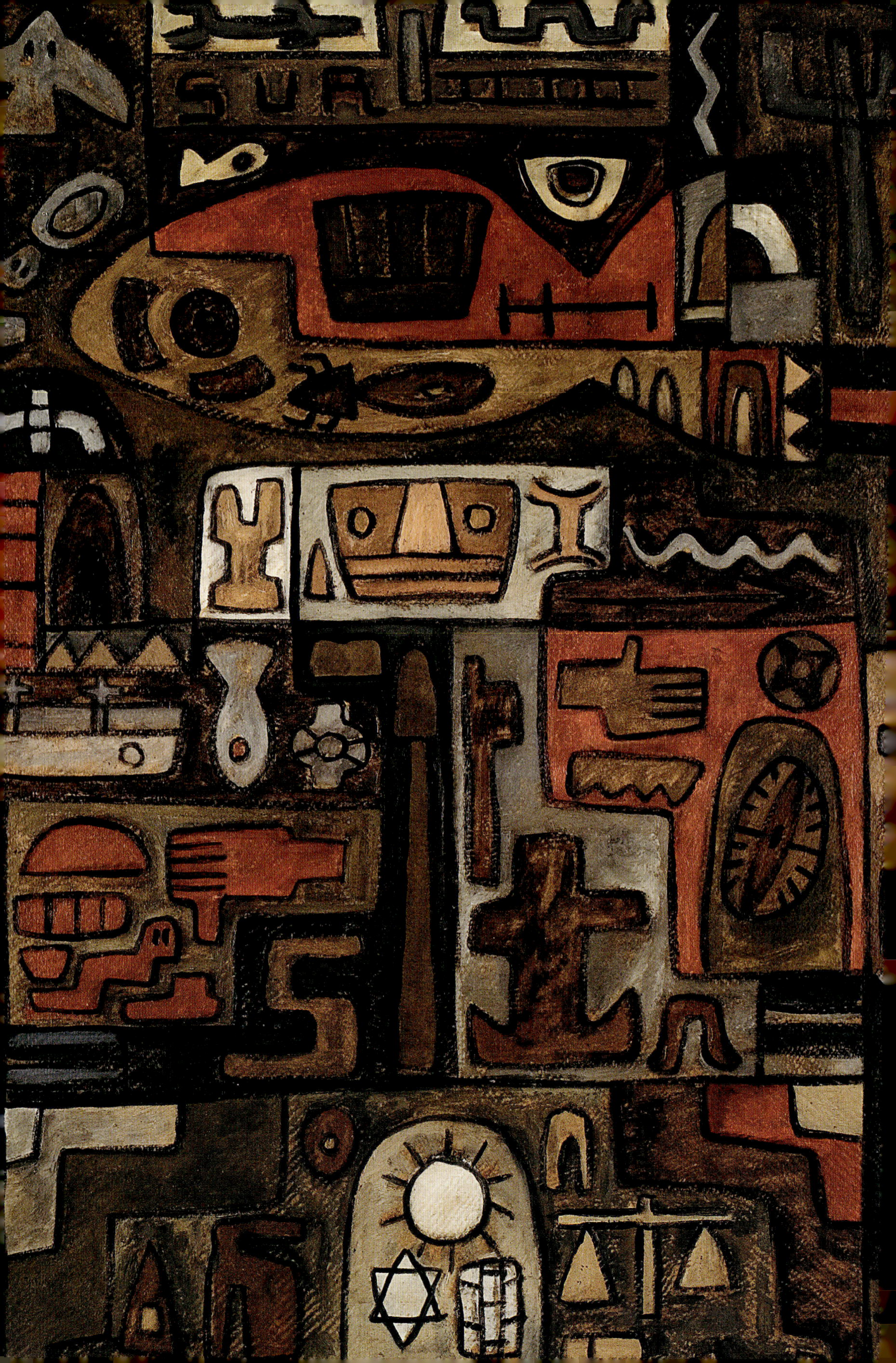

Chapter 7

The Cube, Sphere, and Cone:
Constructed Abstractions
in the Americas

I n recent decades there has been a pronounced interest on the part of scholars, students, collectors, and the art-cognizant public in geometric art from Latin America. This affinity has produced numerous essays, books, and exhibitions throughout the Americas and in Europe.[1] Such a shift in taste evidences a reaction against the type of figurative, identity-based art associated with the Spanish- and Portuguese-speaking Americas. A genuine desire to assess the achievements of Latin American artists within other criteria has created a veritable industry, with museums, publications, art fairs, and exhibitions promoting ordered, sometimes lineal, often monochromatic two- and three-dimensional art, principally dating from the post-1940 period. Many of the artists who have become of interest to a wide public will form part of this chapter, a partial inquiry into the role of geometric-based art in the western hemisphere which, in addition, places them in contrast to analogous trends in the United States and Canada.

When searching for the starting point of what could be called hard-edge abstraction in the Iberian-American world we usually have to look for it in the various "modernizing" events of the 1920s and later. Both São Paulo's *Semana de Arte Moderna* (1922) and Havana's *Exposición de Arte Nuevo* (1927) included paintings and sculptures that evidenced the impact of European forms of art employing geometry, symmetry, or compressed space as modes of constructing an image. It was not until the 1940s, however,

Rosa Acle
Norte (North), 1938
(detail).
See fig. 7.6.

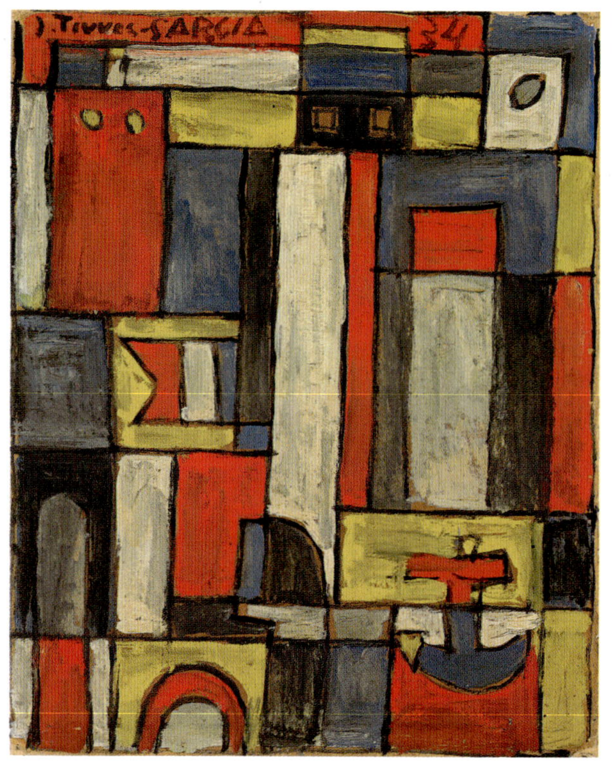

Fig. 7.1
Joaquín Torres-García
Navío constructivo
(Constructivist Ship),
1934, oil on board, 20
x 15¾ in. (51 x 40 cm).
Banco Itaú, Brazil.

that a large-scale geometric vogue (including such manifestations of Constructivism as Concrete and Neo-Concrete, or Kinetic art, for example) would come into being in many centers of Latin America. It was at that time, and especially after around 1950, that nonobjective, geometric art would take on, in many cases, characteristics specific to the places of their origin and would, by extension, link these visual productions to each other to produce a chain reaction, as it were, of art-making throughout the greater Americas, grounded in an interest in proportion and arithmetic ratios. While the heritage of European Constructivist movements (Russian Constructivism, Neo-Plasticism, and de Stijl, specifically) is undeniably a part of the collective artistic consciousness of the American abstract project, local manifestations of this spirit of creativity are central to the artistic developments that occurred as the Americas moved into the second half of the twentieth century.

As an introductory image to this complex story of hemispheric modernities we might turn to a work by Joaquín Torres-García that exemplifies the reconceptualization of the grid and the insertion of symbolic forms. His 1934 *Navío constructivo* (Constructivist Ship) (FIG. 7.1) employs vivid reds and yellows contrasted with white and earth tones to segment the canvas. An anchor at the lower right suggests the nautical theme, but far from presenting a conventional representation of a boat, this immensely influential artist (whose work is discussed at length below) departs from the strictly geometric forms of his contemporaries and friends, such as Piet Mondrian, to fashion a work where the handmade quality, the roughness of paint application, and the architectural substructure of the image are its predominant elements.

224

American Responses to Geometric Form, c.1910–1920

In a story such as this one, it is important to try and dig deeper into the genesis of interest in rational visual relationships of shapes and spaces. In the service of this quest, reverting to our starting point of circa 1910 may serve the purpose of telling the primal history of later forms of art that demonstrate an urge to simplify and abstract space and line according to principles of reduced shapes. In this pursuit of some of the earliest manifestations within the Americas of artists responding to the desire for experimentation with space by breaking it down and analyzing it according to proportion and arithmetical (or quasi-geometric) form, we should turn to a few key figures from the Americas who were working in Europe (as well as others who never made the journey) in the first decades of the century, absorbing and transforming the contributions of their Cubist and Futurist contemporaries in both completely abstract and semi-representational paintings and sculptures. We are particularly likely to find such practices in artists from Mexico, the United States, and the countries of the Southern Cone.

The year 1915 was a crucial one in the development of Diego Rivera's Cubism, as it witnessed the creation of what is arguably his signature work in this manner, a painting that (like his other Cubist images) presents recognizably geographic-specific signs to identify it as a work by an artist from Mexico.[2] The subject of *Zapatista Landscape* (FIG. 7.2) may, arguably, have been suggested by photographs of the Mexican revolutionary leader Emiliano Zapata.[3] This image reduces the figure of a man with a sombrero, gun, and *serape* (cloak) in a mountainous landscape to a series of interlocking semi-geometric shapes. The forms of the mountains in the distance are those of the two volcanoes near the Mexican capital. The figure itself is provided with a stylized hat that is more of a cone than a detailed rendition of a traditional Mexican workingman's headgear. Perhaps the most representational element is the gun. Although relatively few of Rivera's Cubist pictures contain the same obvious cultural references as the *Zapatista Landscape*, they sometimes appear in images whose subject has virtually nothing to do with the country's visual culture.

The term "Constructivism" or "Constructivist art" was widely known and had been used in writing about art and visual culture

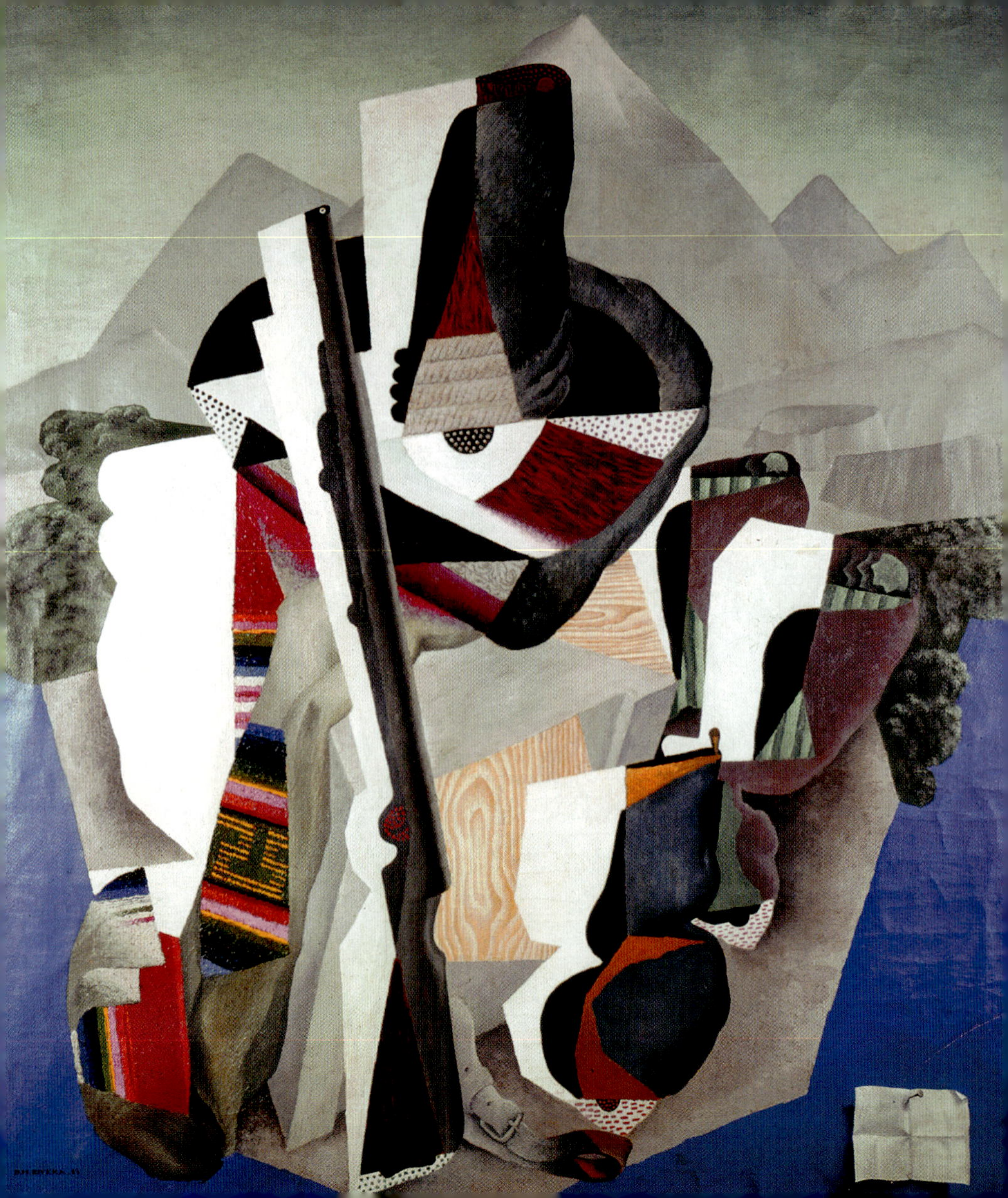

D.M. RIVERA. 15

in Mexico as early as 1921, when David Alfaro Siqueiros published his *Vida Americana* manifesto in Barcelona.[4] As art historian Sandra Zetina has remarked, it was used to denote the importance of geometric form in the conceptualization of works of art and also a type of pared-down architecture of strict geometric proportions that grew in popularity in Mexico, as it had in Europe shortly before 1920 when, in 1919, Walter Gropius (1883–1969) employed this term at the Bauhaus.[5] Siqueiros continued to be interested in geometric relationships in many of his works, and Orozco manifested close attention to constructed form in the prominence given to simple blocklike architecture or even purely geometric shapes in his murals. This is most notable in his paintings for The New School for Social Research in New York. José Clemente Orozco employed the theories of Canadian-born American artist Jay Hambridge (1867–1924) who, in the mid-1920s, published his book *Elements of Dynamic Symmetry*. Hambridge espoused the belief that the study of mathematical proportions of both natural forms (plants) and man-made objects (Greek and Roman architecture) could provide us with the arithmetical tools to create harmonious proportions in various forms of visual expression.[6]

Ángel Zárraga, Rivera's contemporary and fellow Mexican painter, also working in Paris in the 1910s, also strayed from his early Symbolist affinities (discussed in Chapter 1) and created a series of Cubist portraits, figure studies, and landscapes in the middle years of the decade. Meanwhile back in Mexico several years later, a group of young painters and writers banded together to create a highly influential, although short-lived movement in literature and art called *Estridentismo* (Stridentism), mentioned briefly in Chapter 2.[7] The first of several manifestos produced by the movement's members was published as a broadside in 1923. This text articulates the strong relationship between the language of *Estridentismo* and the absurdist language of the Italian Futurists. Its art (painting, and especially the highly distinctive graphic production) demonstrates a parallel dedication to the fragmentation of space and form along Cubist lines. A signature image of the *Estridentista* mode of analysis of form and space as dynamic orthogonals of semi-abstract form is *El Café de nadie* (No One's Café) of 1930 (FIG. 7.3) by Ramón Alva de la Canal. This work celebrates the gathering place of this group

Fig. 7.2
Diego Rivera
Paisaje Zapatista
(Zapatista Landscape),
1915, oil on canvas,
57¼₆ x 49¼ in. (145 x
125 cm). Museo Nacional
de Arte, Mexico City.

of like-minded artists and writers in Mexico City's Colonia Roma neighborhood. It is a perspectively compressed portrait of the movement's adherents, with many of the members of the association identified by fragments of paper collaged onto the surface of the canvas.[8]

We observed in Chapter 1 that Argentinean artists (and life-long friends) Emilio Pettoruti and Alejandro Xul Solar returned to Buenos Aires from their respective European sojourns in 1924 and made their mark on the Buenos Aires art world with works that displayed their interest in hard-edge (as well as gestural) abstract forms. The capitals of Argentina, Brazil, and Uruguay became the most open ports of reception to new ideas in the Americas well into the period under discussion here. The Barcelona–Madrid–Paris–Río de la Plata axis was of immense importance to the development of the sensibilities of many Latin American artists from the 1910s to the 1930s. Rafael Barradas (1890–1929) from Uruguay left his hometown of Montevideo in 1913 and the bulk of his career developed in the capitals of Spain, Catalonia, and France. Geometry and division of space conceived through the lens of Futurism

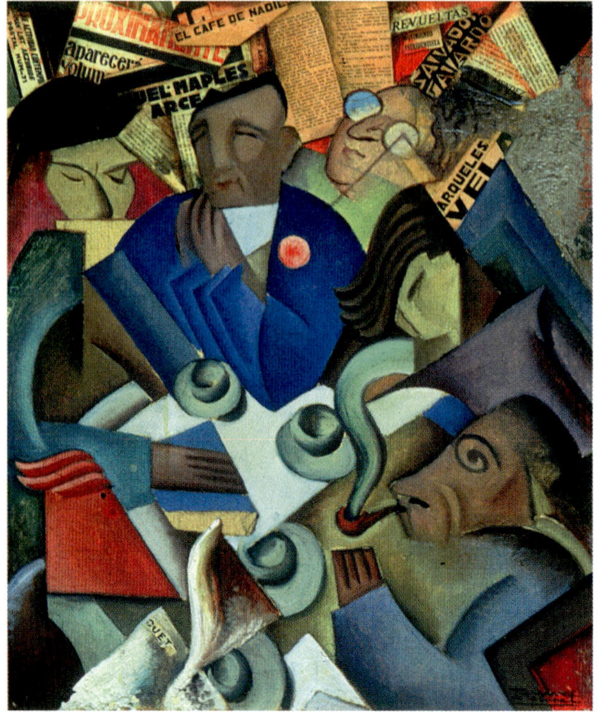

and Cubism characterize the work of this artist who codified his manipulation of constructed form under the title *Vibracionismo* (Vibrationism), referring to the inherent tensions of diverging spatial dynamics that characterize his views of rapidly accelerating urban life. Barradas's 1918 water-color evocation of the Catalan poet Joan Salvat-Papasseit (1894–1924) (FIG. 7.4), leader of an experimental group of Barcelona-based writ-ers, is a representative example of the aims of Barradas's painting in the 1910s either to reduce facial features and objects to interlocking shapes or to flatten them so radi-cally as to create a series of com-pletely abstract patterns.

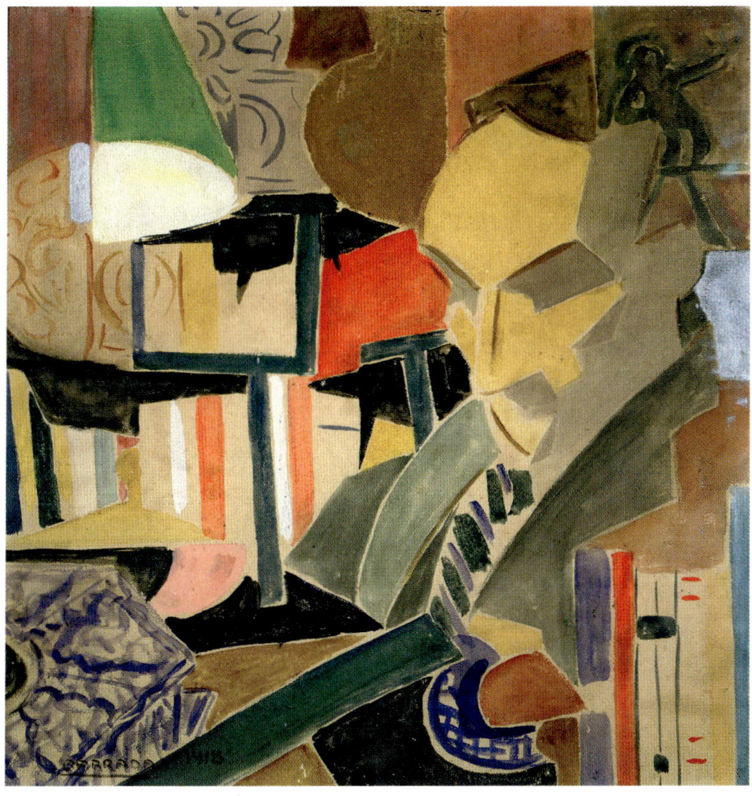

Joaquín Torres-García, the Torres-García Workshop, and Arithmetical Proportion

In 1934 (the year that *Navío constructivo* was painted) Torres-García returned to his native Montevideo after some 33 years abroad. There he played a critical role in the dissemination of Constructivist forms of art, first in the immediate circle of his students and disciples in Uruguay and Argentina. Later, his art would have an impact, both direct and indirect, on virtually all manifestations of two- and three-dimensional art made with an interest in proportion and geometry throughout Latin America.[9] The earliest indicators of his artistic talent arose in Barcelona where he worked in an Art Nouveau mode in a city that, along with Paris, Brussels, Glasgow, and Nancy, was one of the key centers for this form of painting, sculpture, architecture, and the decorative arts. He collaborated with Antoni Gaudí (1852–1926) on details of the cathedral at Palma de Mallorca, and executed many paintings and prints that evidenced an affinity for the art of those creators—including the young Pablo Picasso—who regularly gathered at the Barcelona café Els Quatre Gats around 1900.

Passing through a period of classical revival characteristic of many art centers in the period between the two world wars (the Catalan form of modern neoclassicism was called *Noucentisme*), Torres-García executed heroic murals in several venues in Catalonia, yet his art did not come into the sharp focus that defines his contribution today until he went to New York. The period 1920 to 1922 was critical for Torres; he became involved with some of the most avant-garde artistic circles of the time, becoming, for a brief period, an integral component in Manhattan's experimental arts movements (see a discussion of Torres in New York in Chapter 2). Joseph Stella, Stuart Davis (1892–1964), and other American friends were in dialogue with this versatile personality who, besides developing an impressive body of paintings, also created his first series of toys and wooden sculptures, which he called *maderas*. All of these forms of art manifested a strong interest in constructed shapes and a reliance on geometric proportion. A dedication to these principles is most clearly manifested in *Universalismo constructivo* (Constructive Universalism), published in Montevideo in 1944. This lengthy book was by no means the first manifesto published by Torres, who was, in fact, as significant as a writer and art theoretician as he was an artist; 1913 had witnessed the first such document, *Notes sobre art* (written in Catalan), while his autobiography, *Historia de mi vida* (Montevideo, 1939), followed his life story up to the time of his departure from Europe for South America. In fact, a number of his writings remain unpublished in the archives of the Torres-García Foundation in his native city.

Torres was a member of several Parisian artists groups, most notably Cercle et Carré (Circle and Square), which promoted the values of abstract art, specifically Constructivism and Neo-Plasticism, forms of art that principally embodied a geometric foundation. The legacy of Piet Mondrian, especially in the work of Theo van Doesburg (1883-1931), co-founder with Torres of the publication also called *Cercle et Carré* (which Torres later re-established in Montevideo as *Círculo y Cuadrado*), was instrumental in articulating the ongoing creative process of the Uruguayan artist while still in France. It was in Paris that Torres "discovered" the art of pre-Columbian peoples. The ancient Americas eventually held a magnetic attraction for him, and many of his later works contain overt or subtle references to Inca- or Nazca-inspired decorative models. In this regard Torres was also a pioneer within a Latin American context, as this fascination with the geometric design motifs of the ancient world would inspire artists on both sides of the Atlantic for decades to come.[10]

It is unlikely that Torres had any contact with art from the pre-1492 era while in Uruguay. The regions of the Río de la Plata were home to some indigenous groups, such as the Charrúa, but they were principally nomadic and left no monumental architecture and very few artifacts. The last of the Charrúa were exterminated in the early 1830s by Uruguayan authorities. There were also no public art institutions in the city where a young boy could observe what remained of the pre-Hispanic visual culture of his region. It was only through the work of his son Augusto (1913–1992), who in 1928 accepted a position at Paris's Musée d'Ethnographie (from 1938, the Musée de l'Homme), drawing and cataloguing ancient American (principally Andean) ceramics, that Torres conceived a fascination for the geometric forms that complemented his already well-established taste for mathematical proportion. In addition, the iconic qualities of the designs on the vessels, textiles, and other forms of art stimulated even further his interest in both the spiritual content and the communicative power of what he saw as archetypal symbols. Torres's dedication to recognizable subject matter, no matter how abstracted, caused a rift between him and the other members of Cercle et Carré, who were determined that only the purest form of abstract non-figuration could be tolerated as representative of their visual and psychological goals. Therefore a break with the group was inevitable and these strains, plus financial considerations, led to the artist's decision to return to South America.

Torres's most recognizable and characteristic paintings are the so-called Grid, Sign, and Pattern pieces (such as that seen in Fig. 7.1). They are works that he began in Paris and continued to paint during the continuation of his career in Montevideo. Torres's paintings in this manner anticipate the "pictograph" paintings of American artist Adolph Gottlieb (1903–1974) of the 1940s, and indeed the sensibilities of both artists are

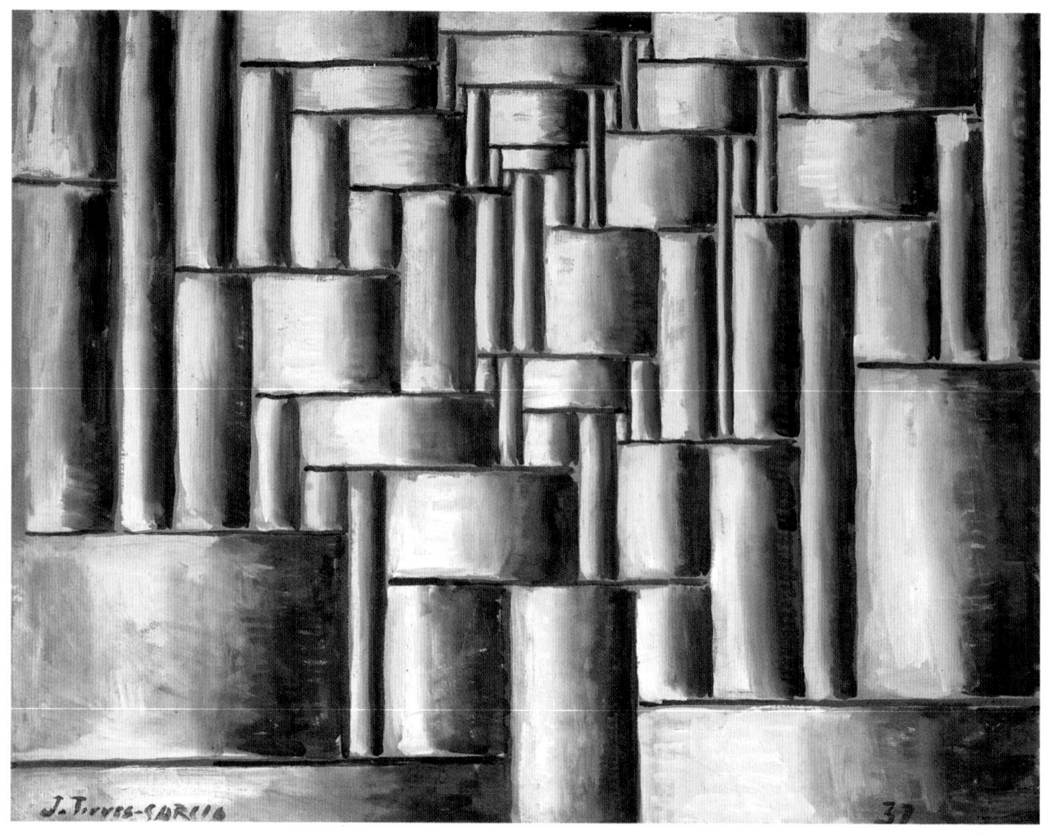

intimately connected. The use of the grid is fundamental, as is the inclusion of a series of what Torres called "universal symbols" to express elemental emotions. They include the heart, the sun, anchor, house, clock, schematic human figures, and others, mixed with more abstracted signs that represent an emblematic visual language indicating archetypal manifestations of the human responses to universal situations.

The 1937 *Tubular Abstract Composition* (FIG. 7.5) is one of the most outstanding examples of Torres's move to pure abstraction. We observe here a series of semi-spherical shapes radiating out from the inner portion of the canvas, becoming larger as they reach its outer limits. Each is of a different size; some are narrow and elongated, others squat like intersecting barrels or drums. The almost-monochrome tones of whites and grays are modulated by brushstrokes that create a series of lighter and darker portions of each of the many components of this wall-like image. Ultimately deriving from Torres's oblique engagement with the

Cubist technique of *passage* (demarcating different sections of a painting by using subtle gradations of color, forming shadowlike edges that lead the eye from one section to another), the painting represents a series of interlinked semi-tubular forms that suggest industrial shapes while at the same time appearing to embody the solidity of ancient structures.

Torres-García's theories and symbolic vocabulary had a profound impact on the circle of his immediate disciples in Montevideo and Buenos Aires. A prime example of the work of his followers is by Brazilian-born Uruguayan artist Rosa Acle (1916–1990). *Norte* (North) (FIG. 7.6) is a virtual compilation of the archetypal symbols whose significations transcend specific cultures. An architectural form, possibly inspired by Inca building types, is topped by a suggestion of a head with the sun's rays shining from it, a reference to Inti, the Inca god of the sun. In the body of the monolithic structure we observe individual niches inhabited by such iconographic pictographs as stylized humans, a boat, animals, masks, an eye, a fish, an anchor, and many other forms that derive from the artist's having cast her net far and wide in an attempt to suggest primal forms that would appeal to anyone who saw this image. Some of Torres's followers traveled to the Andean countries to absorb what they thought was an "authentic" American art in order to incorporate it into their Constructivist visual vocabulary. In a way this was an expression of an internal exoticism and a form of primitivist voyeurism. But, on the other hand, the use by Acle and her associates of such symbols was fully in synchronic accord with the lessons taught by Torres regarding cultural universalism.

In the end, however, it was the legacy of the nonspecific, unadulterated formal qualities of Torres-García's most abstract compositions, and not

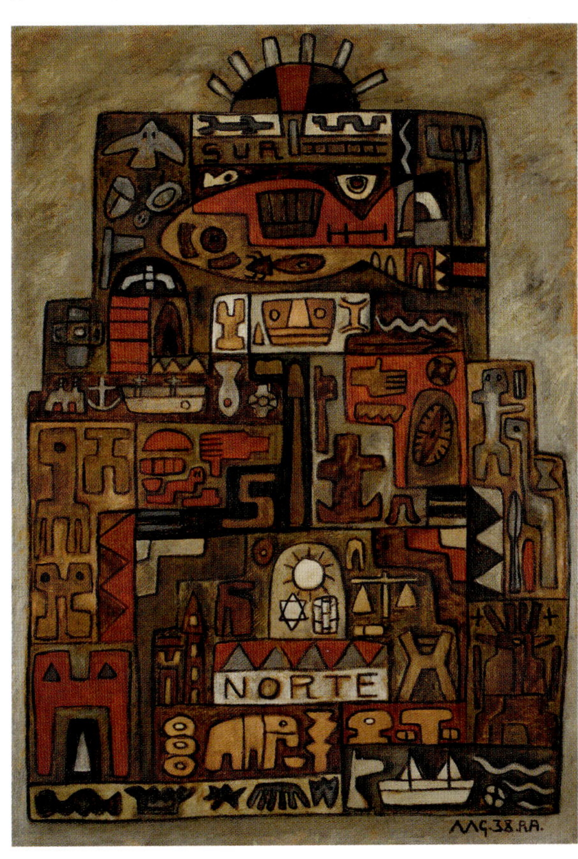

Fig. 7.6
Rosa Acle
Norte (North), 1938,
oil on paperboard,
39 x 27 in. (99.1
x 68.6 cm). Davis
Museum at Wellesley
College, Wellesley,
Massachusetts. Museum
purchase, The Mary
Clothier Slade Fund
2006.179.

his theoretical and philosophical systems of thought, nor his references to Americanist iconography, that had a transcendent impact on geometric art in the region and beyond, as we will see when we return to examine art in the Río de la Plata region in the 1940s.[11]

Geometric Manhattan

The introductory remarks to this book concerned, in part, the impact of several innovative and groundbreaking exhibitions throughout the Americas during the early phase of the period under question, in which new and often radical artistic tendencies were introduced to the public in places like Brazil, Cuba, Canada, and the United States. The 1913 Armory Show in New York represents, at least for an English-speaking public, one of the most memorable events in terms of providing a bridge between the older conservative tendencies and new forms of art. Although the exhibition contained work by many artists long since dead and consecrated within the pantheon of "masters" of the history of modern art (Francisco de Goya [1746–1828], Édouard Manet [1832–1883], Camille Pissarro [1830–1903], and many others) it was the production of the many artists linked to geometric analysis of space, form, and movement that played the critical and controversial roles. Pablo Picasso, Georges Braque (1882–1963), and other Cubists were included, yet the largest impact on the public (and artists') imagination was ultimately made by Marcel Duchamp (1887–1968) and Francis Picabia (1879–1953).

However, their paintings were bewildering for many and often ridiculed in the press, an indication of the slowness with which modernist artistic practices developed, even in the context of a city that prided itself on its openness to the new. Although the story of the Armory Show has been told in various subsequent exhibitions and academic studies, it is less well known that there were a number of innovative American artists included in this exhibition whose art forged new and critical directions for American painting and sculpture in the years following the exhibition.[12] One of them was Patrick Henry Bruce (1880–1936), who showed art that evidenced his engagement with Cubism and with Paul Cézanne's division of space. Bruce had also been aligned with the movement that represented the first attempts in the United States to paint in a mode that represented a synthesis of colors, contours, and spiritual qualities.

The Synchromist movement was an association of like-minded artists, most of whom had studied in Europe prior to World War I and sought to create modes of expression that embodied the spirit of synesthesia—the blending of the visual and emotional properties of both visual and musical stimuli. Bruce was associated with this movement (which was founded in 1912 and, while short-lived as a cohesive school, nonetheless had a serious impact on the development of American abstraction). The principal organizers were Stanton MacDonald-Wright (1890–1973) and Morgan Russell (1886–1953). While Wright's art tended to represent a free-form, almost gestural approach to space and line, Russell's abstractions (which, like those of his colleague, were linked to his knowledge of Cubism, although both artists vigorously denied this connection) were deeply involved with geometric form with reminiscences of architectural proportion. His painting entitled *Synchromy* of c.1914 (FIG. 7.7), painted in the year following the Armory Show, is a perfect example of interlocking solid shapes, each representing a series of color values, creating a harmonious union throughout the surface of the canvas.

The growth of a Machine Age sensibility of clean lines and dynamic forms (related to the later phases of Futurism in Italy, Vorticism in England, and many similar movements in the industrial arts and architecture that formed the core of the Art Deco sensibility) promoted the growth of various forms of hard-edge abstract painting and sculpture in the United States. Cities such as Los Angeles and Miami experienced the development of building projects by native and foreign architects that evidenced the impact of both Art Deco and the minimalist philosophies of the Bauhaus. Chicago held pride of place as a center for artistic experimentation within the realm of geometric abstraction. In the 1930s the Bauhaus was re-established there, and in 1937 the Hungarian-German artist László Moholy-Nagy (1895–1946) became its director. He became a key figure in the establishment of avant-garde modes of painting, photography, and design, and his influence was felt in Chicago well into the following decades.

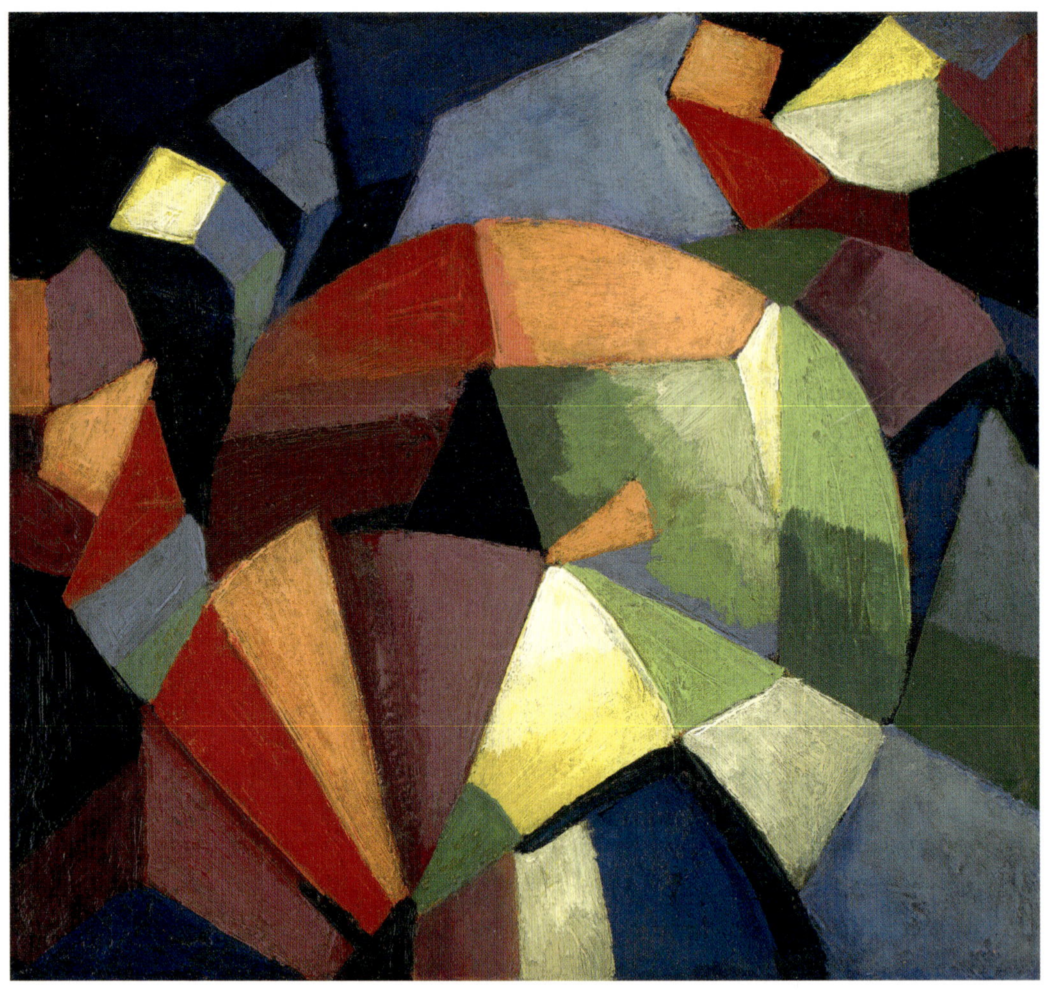

The importance of muralism and public art in the 1930s accounted for many approaches to large-scale visual expression. Although the social realist approach of those artists in the United States who were inspired by their Mexican colleagues (see Chapter 4) may be the best-known form of 1930s muralism, other modes included geometrically based murals for public and corporate spaces. The Russian-born artist Ilya Bolotowsky (1907–1981), for example, painted a series of murals during the years of his association with the Works Progress Administration. His four paintings on canvas (1936) for the walls of the Williamsburg Housing Project in Brooklyn, New York (now in the Brooklyn Museum), display his affinities for his primary source of inspiration—Mondrian and the

236

Neo-Plasticist movement, combined with the biomorphic approach of Joan Miró. Bolotowsky was also one of the founders of the Abstract American Artists (AAA) organization in 1936, a cooperative association (still in existence) that aimed to promote all forms of abstraction in the United States.[13] By the 1930s abstraction had fallen out of favor in the wider public sphere and was, to an extent, associated with foreignness and a European elitist sensibility.

Río de la Plata:
Beyond Torres—Experimentation in the 1940s
Taking up our story in the Río de la Plata we return to the personality and the phenomenon of Torres-García as a fundamental artistic figure, stimulator, and promoter of what would be for that city a new modernity that, Torres stated, would "surpass the art of Paris."[14] Torres-García had what, by all accounts, was an unstoppable energy. As soon as he returned to his native Montevideo he launched a one-man campaign of artistic reconfiguration that took the form of disseminating his philosophies of a pure, geometry-based art that contained the kernels of archetypal expression and was open to accepting the stimuli not only of the latest contemporary avant-garde trends but also those provided by the lessons of ancient American arts. Radio broadcasts, personal appearances at all manner of art events, dozens of publications, the creation of new art magazines such as *Círculo y Cuadrado* and *Removedor,* in addition to paintings, wood and stone sculptures, mosaics, murals, and plans for many other forms of artworks, characterized his inestimable contribution to the cultural life of his city and, eventually, that of Buenos Aires and beyond.

Torres soon established a group of disciples. Among these artists were his own sons Horacio (1924–1976) and Augusto. Torres flourished most when collaborating with others, and he went on to form several artists' associations. The first was the Asociación de Arte Constructivo (AAC) (1935–1942). Later, in 1944, an even longer-lasting organization, the Taller Torres-García (Torres-García Workshop), opened. This was an atelier, exhibition space, and a laboratory for experimentation in all forms of art, from painting and sculpture to furniture and utilitarian objects. The utopian spirit of the Bauhaus, with which Torres had been intimately familiar from his many years in the intellectually and artistically experimental circles of Europe, proved to be the greatest stimulus for the output of the Taller. It members, including (among many others) Rosa Acle, Julio Alpuy (1919–2009), Elsa Andrada (1920–2010), Gonzalo Fonseca (1922–1997), José Gurvich (1927–1974), Francisco Matto (1911–1995), and Manuel Pailós (1918–2005), all created two- and three-dimensional works, plus architectural projects, that carried the spirit of Torres well into the 1960s and beyond (the Taller closed in 1962, some 13 years after his death). Many of the Taller members moved from Montevideo to Europe; others, such as Gurvich and Alpuy, went to New York, where they formed a tight-knit circle of painters and sculptors in the 1970s whose art contributed to the heterogeneity of that city, and complemented the fast-increasing Latin American artistic presence in Manhattan that had begun to flourish after 1960 (although Latin American artists had made New York their home since the nineteenth century).

The enthusiastic embrace of experimentation and abstract art that took place in Montevideo after the homecoming of Torres was not repeated with quite so much enthusiasm in Buenos Aires, especially in the late 1930s, 40s, and beyond. In official circles during the administration of General Juan Perón, abstract art was considered unpatriotic, as indicated in a speech given by the Minister of Education Dr. Oscar Ivanissevich and reported in the newspaper *La Nación* on September 22, 1949. In it he stated the following: "Abstract art, there is no room among us for this unhealthy art ... There is no place among Peronists for fauvists, least of all cubists, abstract artists ..."[15] Despite this bias, however, Buenos Aires became, throughout the 1940s and well into the 1960s, one of the most progressive and experimental artistic centers in the hemisphere. Within its plurality of movements, many of which created a large-scale resistance to the conservative intellectual tendencies of officialdom, forms of painting, sculpture, and photography developed that, in many cases, anticipated the now better-known experiments carried out elsewhere considerably later.

The social history of Argentina during the 1940s presents a complex story of divided loyalties and multiple affinities. During most of World War II the country was neutral and, despite its strong cultural and political ties to Germany, there was a resistance to aligning with the Axis powers (even though President Perón did not block the emigration of many Nazis into the country throughout the mid- to later 1940s). In 1944 Argentina announced its allegiance with the Allies and ultimately declared war on Germany and Japan in the waning days of World War II. The nation's financial situation profited from the chaos of the war, as it was a supplier of vast amounts of raw materials to many countries, including Argentina's traditional rival, Great Britain. The 1940s also witnessed some extraordinary activity in the art world in Buenos Aires. There were smaller, innovative art movements in other parts of the country, but Argentina, like many other nations in Latin America, retained a strong centralist ideology, accounting for the capital as the principal venue for support of the efforts of artists on both a public and private level. Despite the official articulation of resistance to abstraction referred to above, the history of nonobjective art in the 1940s and 50s virtually dominated the development of the most forward-looking artistic achievements. While various forms of realism (including social realism) and Surrealism continued to flourish, the artists associated with a variety of abstract movements may be considered the chief pioneers of a new spirit in Argentine art at the time.

Although Torres-García's impact in the Río de la Plata by no means ceased in the 1940s, many younger artists both internalized his lessons of geometry and abstraction and rejected his persistent references to observed reality in his art, no matter how intangible those references may have been. The summer of 1944 witnessed the publication, in Buenos Aires, of a single-issue journal called *Arturo*. Although it reached a relatively small audience, its impact on what we could call an inner circle of young and restless artists was definitive. Despite the fact that its cover bore a gestural abstract print by Tomás Maldonado (b.1922), the magazine's main message was clear: pure abstraction, with a marked preference for geometric form, with no reference to concrete reality was the path of the future. Art was meant to be a reference only to itself. The flat canvas was a discrete object, not a synecdoche of anything beyond its own reality. The irregularly shaped frame and support underscored the uniqueness of

239

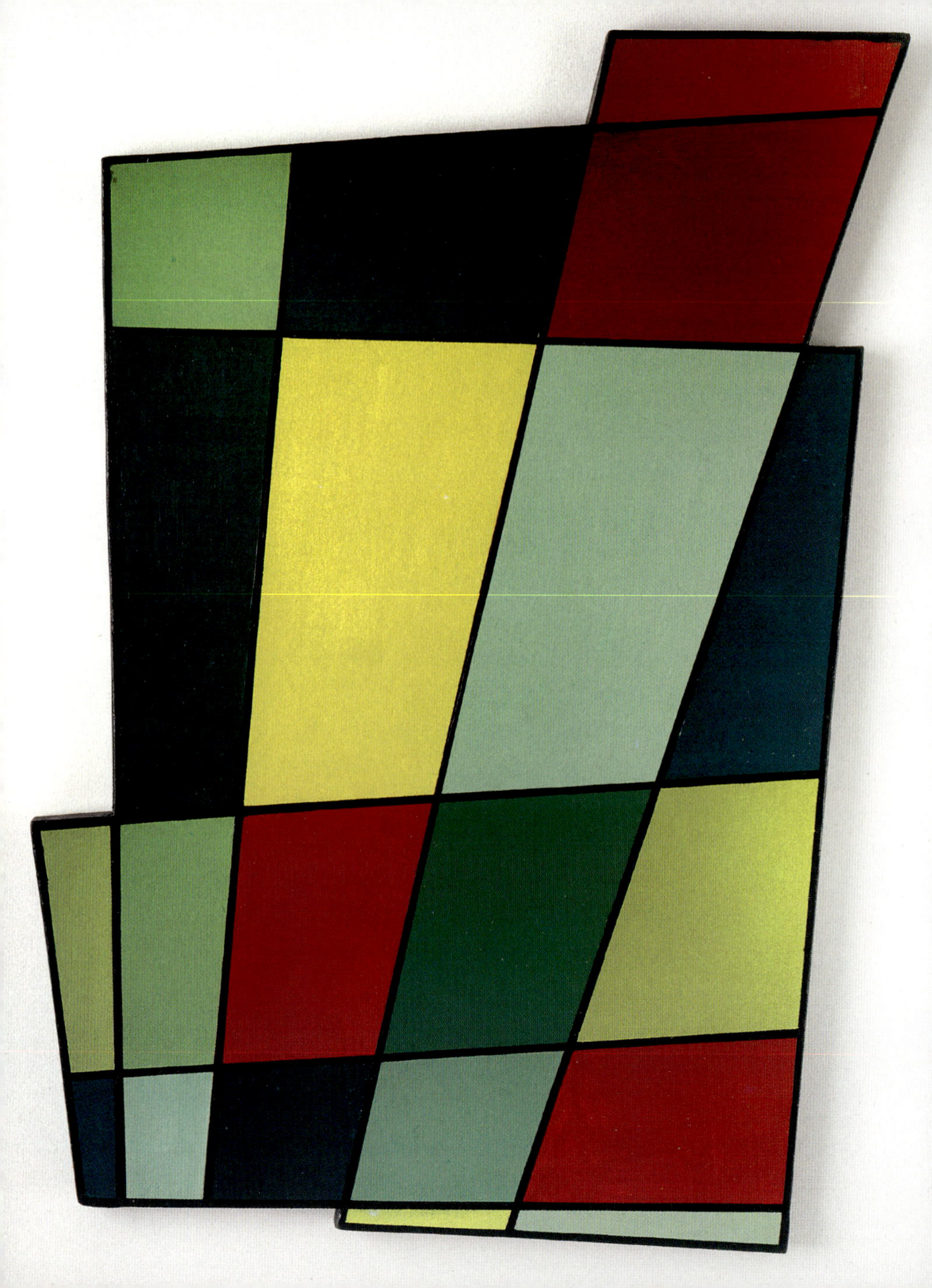

the picture as object and constituted the formal novelty of the magazine's message.[16]

The articles in *Arturo* manifested a new vision for art in the Southern Cone and may also represent an early mid-century articulation of an "art for art's sake" concept that resonates with other similar philosophical dicta guiding the creators of new imagery in many places throughout the hemisphere and across the Atlantic. Resonances of their ideas may be felt in the various forms of Concrete art that developed simultaneously or slightly later in Brazil, and, considerably later, the Minimalism and Post-Painterly Abstraction of artists in the United States.

Around the time of *Arturo*'s publication several significant artists' groups were forming that had considerable impact on the Buenos Aires art scene (and beyond). Among the most outstanding of these was the Asociación Arte Concreto-Invención, whose principal founder was Maldonado. Members held regular exhibitions (in 1945 there were two such shows held in private homes of the Swiss-Argentine psychiatrist Enrique Pichón Rivière [1907–1977] and of the noted photographer Grete Stern [1904–1999], herself a member of Arte Concreto). They were accompanied by manifestos that articulated the members' philosophies. In 1946 Juan Melé (1923–2012) joined the group. His painting from that year, *Irregular Frame No. 2* (FIG. 7.8), demonstrates one of Arte Concreto-Invención's major visual concerns, the importance of the shaped canvas. This dynamic object achieves its visual power through juxtapositions of unequal geometric sections, each constituting segments of pure, flat color. There are several shades of green interspersed with red, yellow, and blue. One of the series of subdivisions of the composition pierces space as it projects into the upper right, while the lower left and right portions of the composition also penetrate, although in a less energetic way, the flow of the area of the work's base. Argentinean art historian María Amalia García has described Melé's image as representing "an analytical systematization of the break with the conventional format of painting, a process that had its beginnings in the mid-1940s in Buenos Aires."[17]

Alfredo Hlito (1923–1993) was the son of Syrian immigrants to Argentina and a co-founder of Arte Concreto-Invención. He worked between Buenos Aires, Paris, and Mexico City.

In *Chromatic Rhythms III* (1949) (FIG. 7.9) the lines are contained within a strict rectangle. The innovation of this painting resides in its use of both a wide variety of bars and lines of color dividing the canvas into large fields of white. While the pictorial genealogy of *Chromatic Rhythms* evidently includes the Neo-Plastic conventions of Mondrian and his immediate followers, Hlito takes the play of colors and shapes in a markedly different direction, principally by relying on a broad range of tonal choices that vary between the primary colors red, yellow, and green, but then extending into more diverse shades of pink and gray.

Carmelo Arden Quin (1913–2010) was one of the artists whose writing made the short-lived journal *Arturo* so lively and controversial. This Uruguayan artist, active in Buenos Aires, and then for many years in Paris, took the most innovative aspects of Arte Concreto-Invención and carried them in new directions. Creating the movement known as Arte Madí in 1946, Arden Quin started a form of collective expression that soon incorporated many artists from both sides of the Plate River

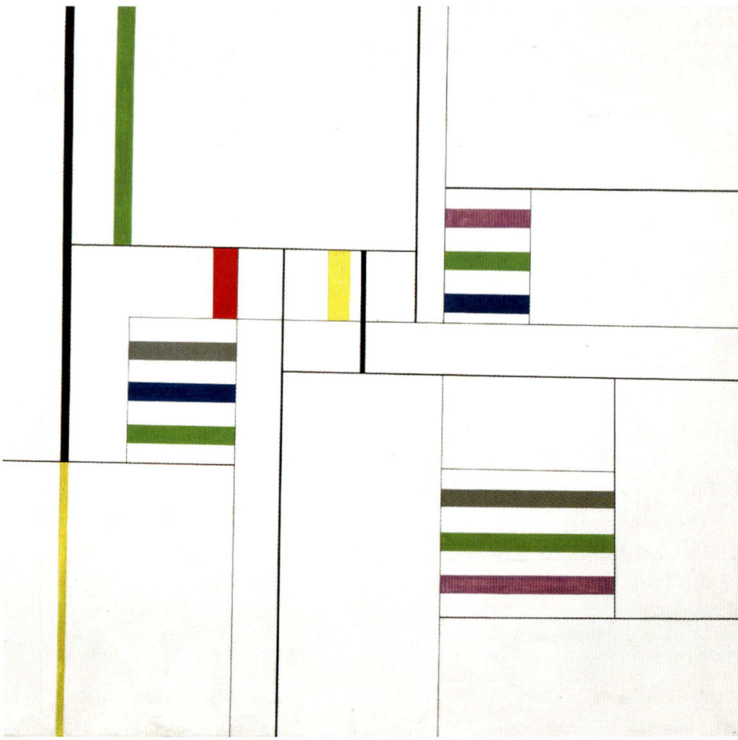

and, eventually, from many parts of the Western world as well as Asia. Arte Madí (the origins of whose name are both obscure and multifarious, not unlike the name "Dada," from earlier in the twentieth century) is perhaps the only one of the Vanguard artistic movements from South America, begun in the 1940s, to continue to the present. The Museum of Geometric and MADI Art in Dallas, Texas, has extensive holdings of several of the original members of the group, including Arden Quin, Rhod Rothfuss (1920–1969), and Martín Blaszko (1920–2011), as well as more recent artists from such far-flung places as Hungary, Pakistan, and the United States. Madí came into existence as a venue not only for painting (often with the Concreto-Invención's irregularly shaped frame) but also for sculpture, design motifs, and architecture. Madí was more of an aesthetic philosophy than a traditional artistic movement, although it produced many works of art that could be hung on a wall in a gallery or set up on a pedestal in a home.

Arden Quin, as well as some of his fellow Madí artists, including Gyula Kosice (1924–1916; an ethnic Hungarian from what is now the Czech Republic), was known for works that incorporated movement and light. Even in Arden Quin's nonmoveable compositions, such as the 1951 *Trio 2* (FIG. 7.10), intimations of spatial play and back-and-forth visual progression are present. In this painting, irregular geometry forms the substructure for an architectonic play of colors and shapes. The work is like many others by the artist, done on wood with varnish or other forms of industrial paint. These paintings and constructions by Arden Quin and other Madí practitioners often possess a high degree of polish, with little or no evidence of the art-ist's hand. This produces a sense of "purity" that allows the objects to appear as if they are artifacts of a robotically governed utopian (or dystopian) world where art is made by assem-bly lines composed of innumerable cyborgs acting in predetermined consort.

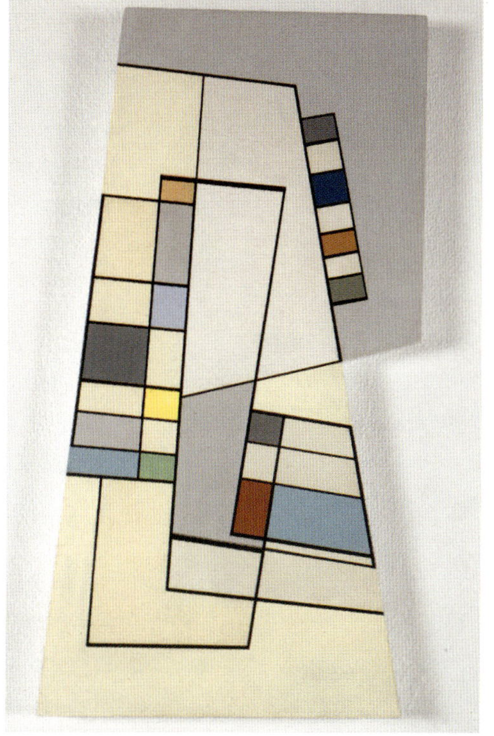

Fig. 7.10
Carmelo Arden Quin
Trio 2, 1951, varnish on wood, 20¼ x 14³⁄₁₆ x 1 in. (51.4 x 36 x 2.5 cm). Colección Patricia Phelps de Cisneros, New York.

Brazil Builds

The title of this section derives from a well-known and influential exhibition organized by architect Philip L. Goodwin for New York's Museum of Modern Art in 1943.[18] The exhibition had a lengthy tour, and its catalogue by G. E. Kidder Smith remained a standard reference tool for architects and architectural historians in both South and North America for decades. While the exhibition charted the course of Brazilian construction (domestic, ecclesiastical, and official) from the colonial era to the present, contemporary projects were featured too, by well-known architects such as Gregori Warchavchik (1896–1972), Henrique Mindlin (1911–1971), and, especially, Oscar Niemeyer (1907–2012), the most innovative and internationally famous figure of the time who, with Lúcio Costa (1902–1998) and Roberto Burle Marx (1909–1994), would go on to design Brasília. The creation of that city provides one of the terminus dates for this book, just as a number of other idealistic architectural projects in Latin America (including the new campuses of the universities in Caracas and Mexico City) provided a metaphorical end point for a period of optimism before a tidal wave of social unrest and terror (military dictatorships throughout South America, and student protest movements in Mexico, and the United States).[19]

The title of the MoMA show is used here because the majority of modern trends in Brazilian architecture in around 1940 echoed the growing receptivity and indeed the appeal to Brazilian audiences of constructed forms—whether they were the architectonic principles, based partly on the International Style of Le Corbusier (1887–1965) that were embraced and much transformed in major and minor cities in Brazil, or the modes of painting and sculpture (and related arts such as graphic and industrial design and photography) that accounted for the most forward-looking experiments of Brazilian artists, especially after around 1950.

One of the first wholesale manifestations of the taste for constructed form in the visual arts appeared at the first and, especially, the second São Paulo Biennial (1951 and 1953).[20] The Brazilian Biennial is the second oldest such exhibition in the world, following the Venice Biennale (founded in 1895). Moreover, its early editions (as well as a number of other innovative exhibitions throughout the 1950s and beyond) attested to the dedication on the part of artists from Rio de Janeiro and São Paulo—the country's two major centers of creativity (as well as exhibitions and collections)—to constructed form, which, like the achievements of contemporaneous architects, represented a dramatic local transformation of initial sources of inspiration from abroad.

The experimental arts connected with Constructivist tendencies were not embraced by all, even though judging by an early twenty-first-century version of Brazilian art history it may seem as if Concrete and Neo-Concrete art were by far the most salient manifestations of modernity in that country. Many conservative critics who continued to support figuration scorned geometric abstraction and other forms of nonfigurative art in terms that almost resembled religious zealotry. Nonetheless, it is precisely the names of such figures as Lygia Clark (1920–1988), Lygia Pape (1927–2004), and Hélio Oiticica who may be counted among the most pioneering artists of the 1950s, 60s, and 70s in the practice of the various forms of Constructivism that have survived as having most resonance with audiences in Brazil and throughout the world.

The complex and multivalent history of Constructivist art in Brazil cannot be told adequately within the framework of this text, but some of the main episodes of this narrative deserve mention. Brazilian Vanguard art of the 1950s and 60s was often a story of group activity. Individual careers are obviously the key markers of the story, yet many of these artists acted within the framework of affinities articulated by manifestos and other forms of group declarations. Among the earliest of these was the "Ruptura Manifesto" (1952) written by the artist Waldemar Cordeiro (1925–1973), who, along with Luis Sacilotto (1924–2003), Geraldo de Barros (1923–1998), and other São Paulo-based artists, represented the most orthodox form of painting based on often-rigorous geometric proportions (which would resonate with the nascent Minimalism in the United States) and the insistence on the rejection of any references to observed reality. In this the Grupo Ruptura artists evidenced a spirit of kinship with some of their Argentinean and Uruguayan contemporaries, such as those discussed above.

In answer to the severity of form and proportion, artists from Rio embraced a looser and more corporeally oriented, even sensual, form of abstraction (in its earlier phases, based upon arithmetic proportions). The Grupo Frente artists included Clark, Oiticica, Pape, Hercules Barsotti (1914–2010), and Willys de Castro (1926–1988), among many others. It should be remembered, nonetheless (as art historian Mónica Amor underscores), that the Rio-São Paulo binary between the approaches of these artists is essentially simplistic, since there were artists from both the Concrete and Neo-Concrete factions that came from elsewhere (for example, Clark was from Belo Horizonte, and Castro and Barsotti were São Paulo natives).[21]

The 1959 "Neoconcrete Manifesto" by Ferreira Gullar, one of the most important critics of the time, served as a compilation of the Neo-Concretists' desire to engage with the theories of, among others, French philosopher Maurice Merleau-Ponty, who advanced the concept of phenomenology, embracing the organic corporeality and sensuality of the work as a primary form of expression and communication.[22] Their Neo-Concrete art ultimately gave way, in some instances (especially in the cases of Clark, Oiticica, and Pape), to forms of expression that departed completely from two-dimensional formats to embrace performance, film, body art, and the type of group experience that was, in the 1960s and beyond, also occurring in Happenings and other free-form, participatory engagements in New York and elsewhere in the United States, developed by artists associated with Fluxus and other revolutionary participatory art movements, such as George Brecht (1926–2008), Allan Kaprow (1927–2006), John Cage (1912–1992), and Carolee Schneemann (b.1939).

It is in the works by the Rio de Janeiro Neo-Concrete artists from the 1950s that we can most directly observe both the tensions with their São Paulo contemporaries and their gradual departure from the arithmetically dictated lines and curves of the Concrete group and their embracing of a somewhat more idiosyncratic, "humanized," and personalized approach to abstract form. Lygia Clark's 1957 *Planos em superfície modulada no.5* (Planes on a Modulated Surface No.5) (FIG. 7.11) is representative of her painting in the 1950s before she left two-dimensional art altogether and began creating more organic three-dimensional objects. Nonetheless we sense the desire on the part of the artist to have her dynamic lines of energetic movement break out of the frame and connect with space beyond its confines.

Fig. 7.11
Lygia Clark
Planos em superfície modulada no.5 (Planes on a Modulated Surface No.5), 1957, alkyd and nitrocellulose paint on plywood, 31⅜ x 27½ in. (79.8 x 70 cm). Museum of Fine Arts, Houston.

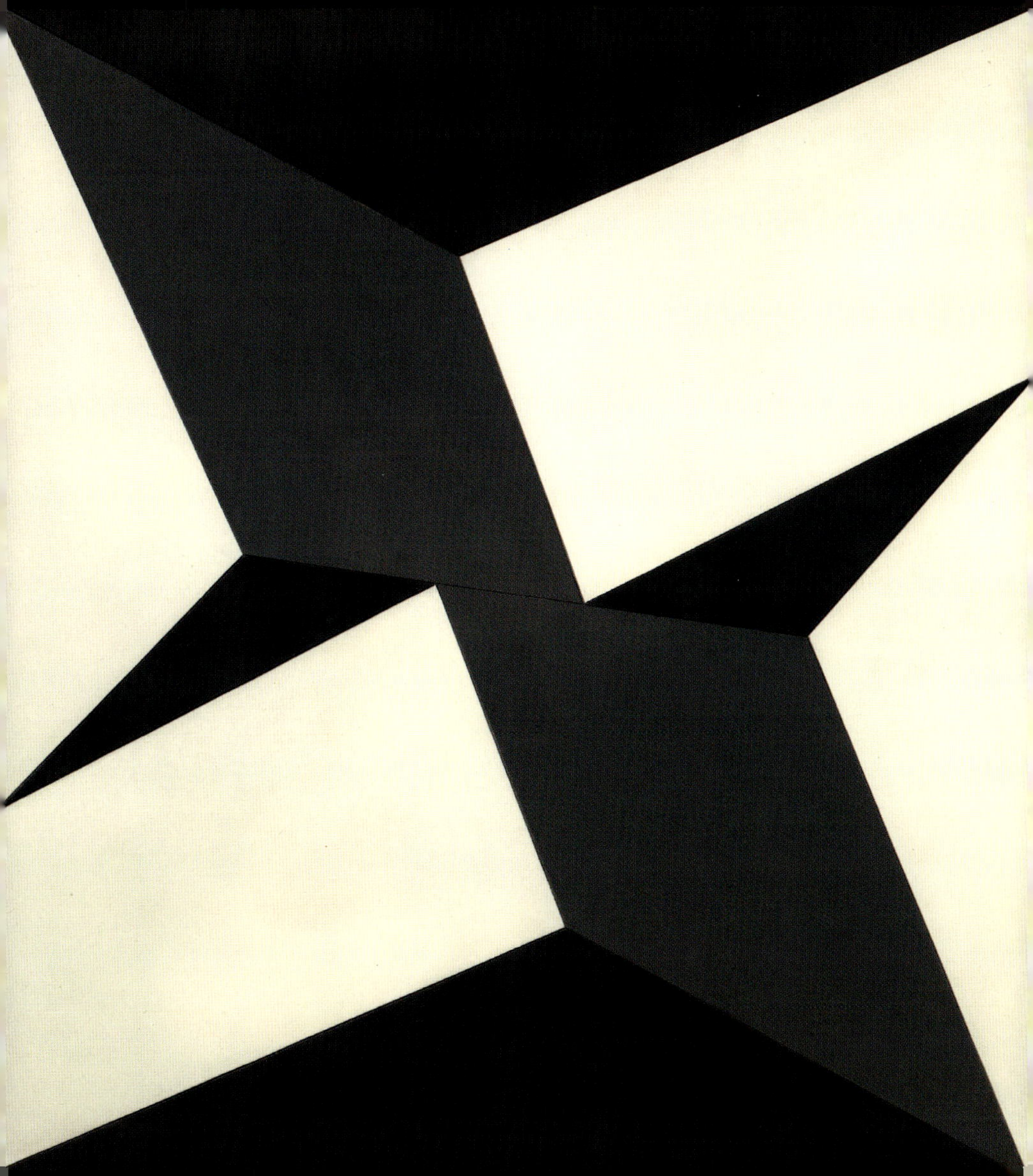

In a work by Clark's fellow artist and close friend Hélio Oiticica (who joined the Neo-Concrete group in 1960) called *Vermelho cortando o branco* (Red Cutting White) (FIG. 7.12) we observe the artist's growing passion for color, which would become the most integral component in his work in the 1950s and well into the 60s. This painting belongs to a series known as *Metaesquemas* (Metaschemes), a group of pictures painted on cardboard during 1957 and 1958, each of which suggests an interrupted grid. In this and other related works Oiticica experiments with the notion of the square and rectangle, throwing them off balance in a sort of inner dance where the redness of the cubic forms plays out against the stasis of the white background. Both tactility and movement are suggested here—elements that would soon become paramount features of his later production and remain as guiding principles until the end of his relatively short life.

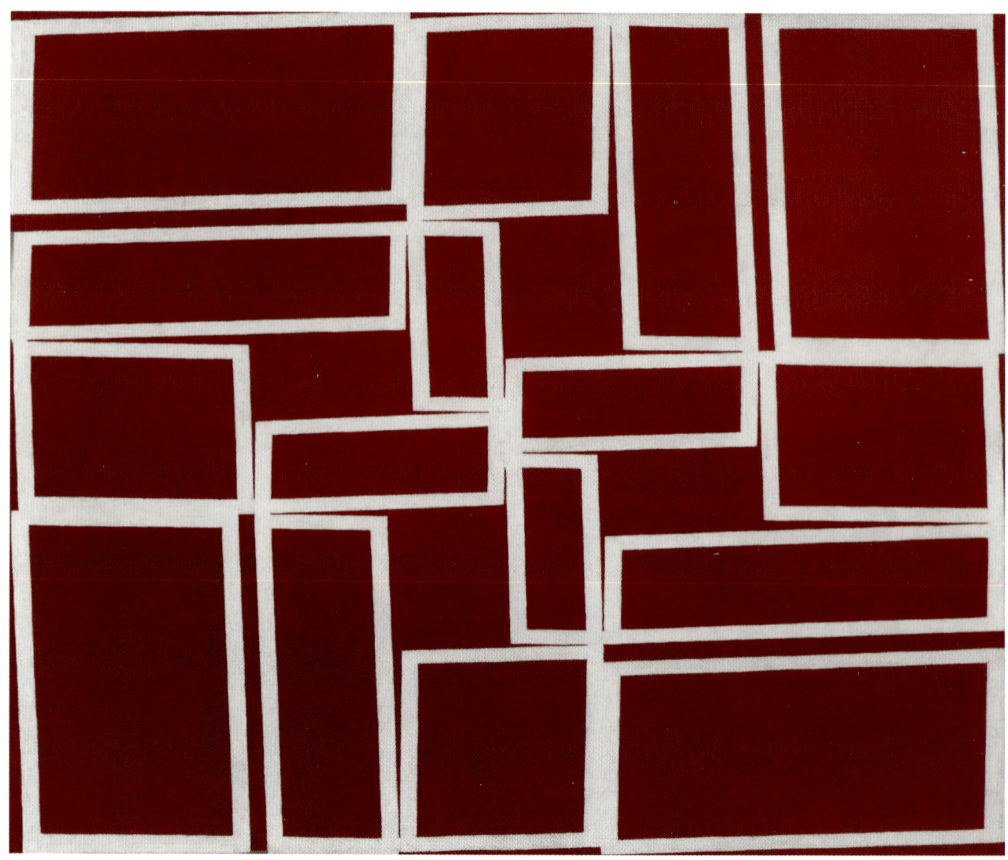

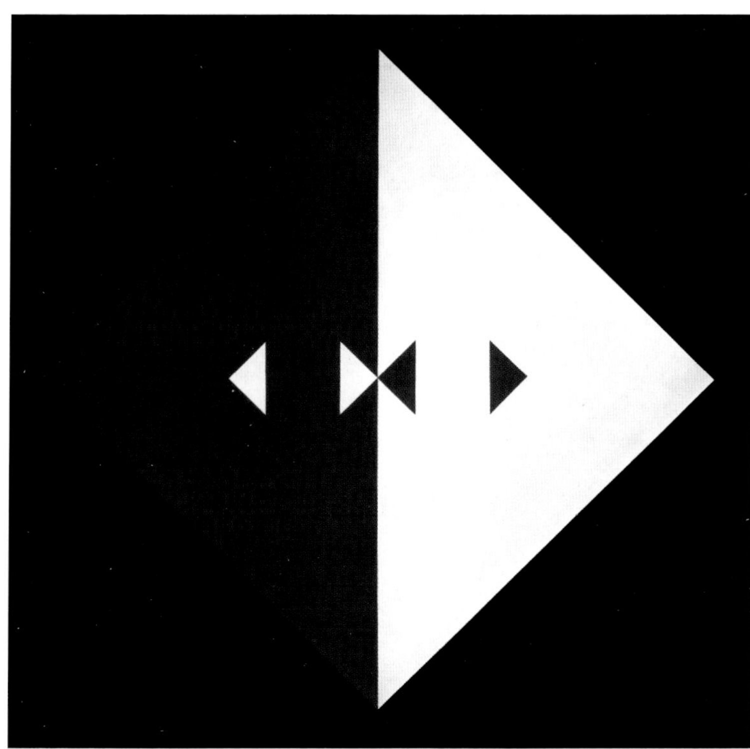

Fig. 7.13
Willys de Castro
Painting, 1958, oil
on canvas, 27½ x 27½
in. (69.9 X 69.9 cm).
Museum of Fine Arts,
Houston.

Willys de Castro is well known for his "active objects" (*objetos activos*), paintings on often unusually shaped canvases where the lines of pure color extend beyond the "front" of the work to the sides, making of them things that exist in and interact with the space around them. In his two-dimensional works, such as the 1958 *Painting* (FIG. 7.13), the white and green lozenge shapes with a black background appear to pulsate and yearn for a completion of their suggested three-dimensional form. It should be noted that Castro's dynamic use of green and white echoes a similar practice by Cuban artist Carmen Herrera, whose series of white and green pictures were done in New York at precisely the time Castro was painting his works in Rio (see the discussion below). While the two artists probably did not know of each other's art, the hemisphere-wide interest in geometric forms takes on a synergistic cast in many of the instances discussed in this text.

Also similar to Herrera's play of lines and dynamic form is the sensibility represented in paintings by Hercules Barsotti, whose close personal and professional relationship with Willys de Castro (with whom he founded the Estúdio de Projetos Gráficos, a well-known studio for graphic and textile design in São Paulo) served to stimulate the creation of images such as *White/Black* (1960, the year he joined the Neo-Concrete movement) (FIG. 7.14). In this painting an overwhelming space of white serves as the protagonist of this picture. Its movement is barely contained by the thin, irregular black lines of the periphery. To the right the black already breaks apart, driven by the inexorable force exerted upon it by the white field.

Havana–Paris–New York–Montreal

The art of the Caribbean, like that of Brazil and other places in the Americas in the first half of the twentieth century, is often, in the minds of many, mired in stereotypes. The clichés of "exoticism" and the hedonism of sun-drenched lands that are more often associated with pleasure and leisure have radically deformed our vision of Cuban and Brazilian art of the 1930s, 40s, and 50s, making it in the popular imaginary a manifestation of lively figuration, tropical settings, and exuberant color. Fortunately, recent scholarship, collecting practices, and probing exhibitions have effected a wholesale reform of our concepts of the visual production of Rio/São Paulo (as we have seen above), Havana, San Juan, Santo Domingo, and elsewhere in the mid-twentieth century.

Just as various forms of geometric-based Concrete and Neo-Concrete art dominated the Vanguard scene in Brazil, Argentina, Uruguay, and elsewhere in South America (including Colombia and Venezuela), the history of geometric (as well as gestural) abstraction in Cuba is still at a fairly early stage. Fortunately a series of exhibitions beginning in the 1980s in various Florida institutions began to reveal to the public the great variety of artistic options practiced in Havana beginning in the 1930s and continuing into the early post-revolutionary period of circa 1960.[23] More recently, exhibitions in Montreal, London, and New York have either included or focused specifically on the accomplishments of many of the Cuban abstract artists that form part of an extensive chain of artistic networks throughout the Americas whose art derives from their dedication to geometric form.[24]

At the height of the most intense political activity in mid-century Cuba, in the waning years of the dictatorship of Fulgencio Batista and the ascendency of the revolutionary era of Fidel Castro, Che Guevara, Camilo Cienfuegos, and other founders of the rebellion against the established social order, geometry-based art assumed a respected role in the elite art circles of the capital city. In 1958 artists including Rafael Soriano (1920–2015), José Mijares (1921–2004), Pedro de Oraá (b.1931), Sandú Darié (1908–1991), and Dolores (Loló) Soldevilla (1901–1971) banded together to create a group known as Los Diez Pintores Concretos (Ten Concrete Painters). Although they exhibited together only until 1961, they had a considerable impact upon the development of geometric art in their own country and in the greater Caribbean.[25] Unlike many artists of their generation who fled Cuba after the revolution, most of the members of Diez Pintores Concretos remained there, working on their own, while also showing abroad.

Loló Soldevilla was an especially multitalented member of this organization. She produced numerous paintings, sculptures, and kinetic objects. She was also an art historian and promoter of abstract art well into the later 1960s, when support from the revolutionary government for abstraction was nominally firm, but unreliable. Soldevilla had begun to exhibit in 1950 at the Lyceum (a private club and an important venue for art exhibitions and literary events) with a show of her sculptures. Soldevilla studied in Paris with geometric abstract artists Jean Dewasne (1921–1999) and Edgar Pillet (1912–1996), founders of the Atelier d'Art Abstrait. She also participated in the exhibitions of the Salon des Réalities Nouvelles, which promoted geometric abstract art and provided an important venue for many artists from Latin America (and elsewhere) to show their work.

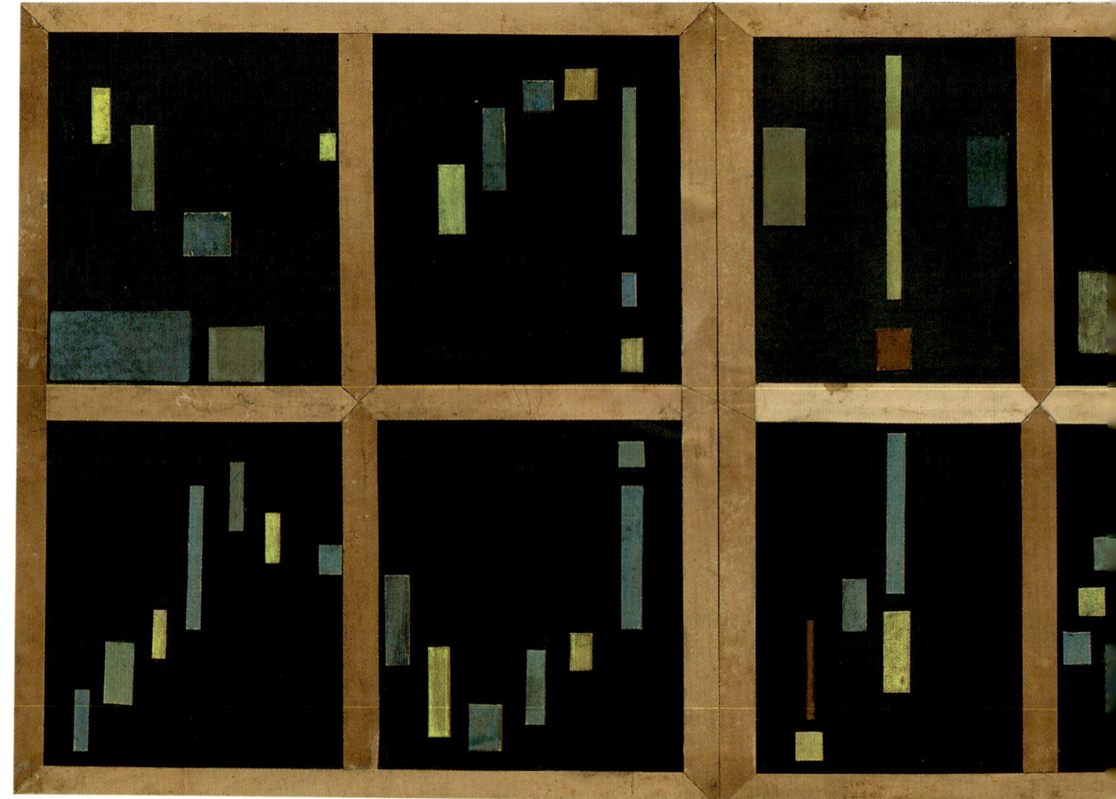

The 1958 *Untitled* composition (FIG. 7.15), in mixed media on wood, is larger than the often small-scale, discreet paintings that characterize Soldevilla's oeuvre. It is a triptych, with each component consisting of a windowlike structure of wood compartments separating space into four equal segments in each of the divisions. Through the window the observer sees various rectangular shapes, each of different proportions, punctuated in the two upper-right areas by triangles pointing to the left. The work creates a series of enigmatic patterns in reds, blues, yellows, and grays that appear to project outward from the dark brown background.

Among fellow Cubans to exhibit at the Salon des Réalités Nouvelles was Carmen Herrera (b.1915). Herrera's career developed in Havana, Paris, and New York (where she has spent most of her professional life). She is undoubtedly the most celebrated Cuban artist of the geometric abstract movement, having been the subject of gallery and museum exhibitions in both Europe

252

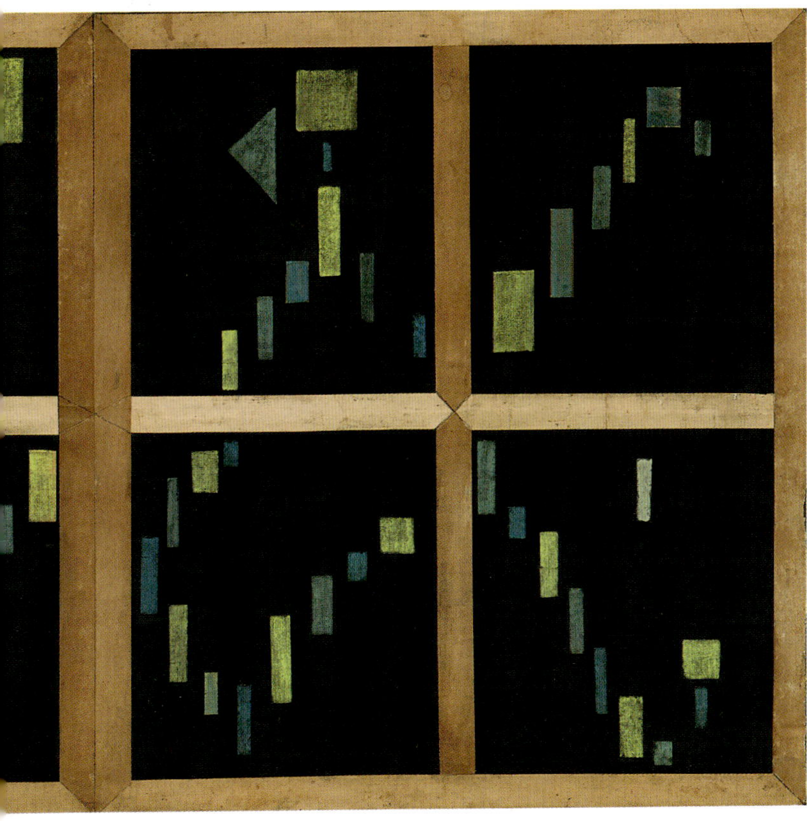

Fig. 7.15
Loló Soldevilla
Untitled, 1958, mixed
media on wood. 19¾
x 50 in. (50 x 127
cm). David Zwirner,
New York/London and
Tresart.

and the United States, including a notable retrospective show at the Whitney Museum of American Art in New York in 2016.[26] Her experiences as a young artist in Havana were critical, however, as art historian Gerardo Mosquera has pointed out.[27]

At the beginning of her career Herrera derived special stimulus from the art of Amelia Peláez (1896–1968), the most distinguished female artist of the First Vanguard Generation. Peláez had a conservative artistic background, working with Leopoldo Romañach (1862–1951) at the Academia de San Alejandro. It was, however, the six years that Peláez spent in Paris studying with, among others, the Russian Constructivist artist and stage designer Alexandra Exter (1882–1949) that turned her aesthetic in the direction of geometric proportion and Constructivist principles. Peláez never created purely abstract images, but her still lifes, views of inner rooms of Havana's domestic structures, and pictures of women (often playing a piano) make use of Cubist-derived proportions and divisions of space. This aspect of Peláez's work inspired Herrera's youthful interest in hard-edge form. One of Peláez's most accomplished still lifes, the 1943 *Fishes* (FIG. 7.16), presents the viewer with a dazzling array of color in its description of a lace tablecloth on which rests a plate containing four fish. Set against an iron grill-work window, a common feature of Havana's domestic architecture of the late nineteenth and early twentieth centuries, the scene is divided into individual segments reflecting the spatial divisions of the window, tabletop (dramatically tilted upward), and the cloth covering the table.

Carmen Herrera responded to the lessons learned from her older Cuban contemporary by preserving the theatrical effect of the color (while reducing it to only one or two contrasting tones) and regularizing the interlocking quasi-geometric forms, reducing them to the fewest possible elements to achieve her own signature mode, based on a more severe approach to the division of space and form. Art critic Juan Carlos Ledezma stated that "The way Herrera's linear composition fractures the support into distinct 'places' relates to Peláez's use of architectonic motifs to structure the expanse of the plane."[28] Herrera, who first met Peláez in 1935, admired her art, but "what inspired above all was

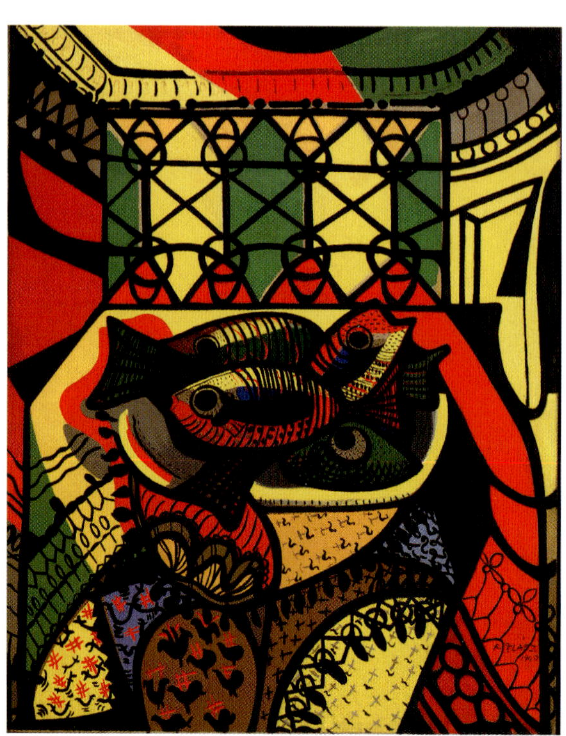

the example of a strong woman with a big personality devoted to art."[29]

After Herrera's initial contact with Peláez, she left Havana for New York, where she briefly studied in 1938 at the Art Students League before spending 1948 to 1953 in Paris. "We went to Paris as soon as we could after the war," Herrera has said.

I was showing with a group called the Réalités Nouvelles. It was an abstract salon … You would go in and show your painting, and they'd either accept it or not … When we returned to New York by boat, I took all my paintings with me. I cried. Paris at the time was like heaven.[30]

Indeed, the experience of the Salon was critical for nurturing her developing abstract manner (which, at this point, retained reminiscences of biomorphism combined with nascent geometric rigor). It also brought her into the orbit of many of the first wave of Latin American artists to arrive in Paris (often with travel subventions from the French government) soon after the end of World War II. As the art historian Estrellita B. Brodsky has noted, this younger generation of Latin American artists included

members of the Venezuelan Disidentes, the Brazilian Concretists, and the Argentine-founded Grupo Madí [who] exhibited in the Salon alongside established artists such as Josef Albers (1888–1976), Sonia Delaunay (1885–1979), Theo van Doesburg, Albert Gleizes (1881–1953), Fernand Léger, and Lászlo Moholy-Nagy.[31]

Of Herrera's Latin American contemporaries who regularly exhibited at the Salon in the early 1950s, the work of Venezuelan artist Jesús Rafael Soto (1923–2005)—who would later become known for his work in Kineticism—had particularly strong parallels with Herrera's concerns from the early 1950s onward.[32] Since 1948 Herrera has made Manhattan her home, and her career has developed in tandem with her North American contemporaries and friends of a similar geometric abstract tendency, especially Leon Polk Smith (1906–1996), who was until his death Herrera's closest artistic companion and fellow hard-edge abstractionist.

Herrera's *Blanco y Verde* (White and Green) of 1959 (FIG. 7.17) suggests back-and-forth movement in an area of serenity and calm. The mostly white canvas is bisected into two nearly equal fields by two green wedgelike shapes that almost touch at the middle point of the composition. This painting, one of a series of works by this artist in which stark green and white shapes form the only components in the visual field, is among the most severely simplified of the works of geometric abstraction discussed here. Nonetheless, the components of this and many of her related paintings (she did an extensive series of white and green works throughout the 1960s and into the early 70s) exude a sense of vigorous forcefulness. Herrera arrived at her signature style by the early 1950s after some experiments in gestural abstraction. By the mid-1950s, however, stark black-and-white paintings, or others that featured a limited number of tones, became her hallmark. Herrera has, throughout her career, also worked on three-dimensional wood sculptures that bear similar characteristics to her starkly bold paintings.

Among Herrera's other close associates and friends in New York during the 1950s and 60s was Barnett Newman (1905–1970). Associated as much with Abstract Expressionism as with geometric abstraction or Color Field painting, Newman's works, especially from the 1950s, bear a strong kinship with those of Herrera, and they were mutual sources of inspiration.[33]

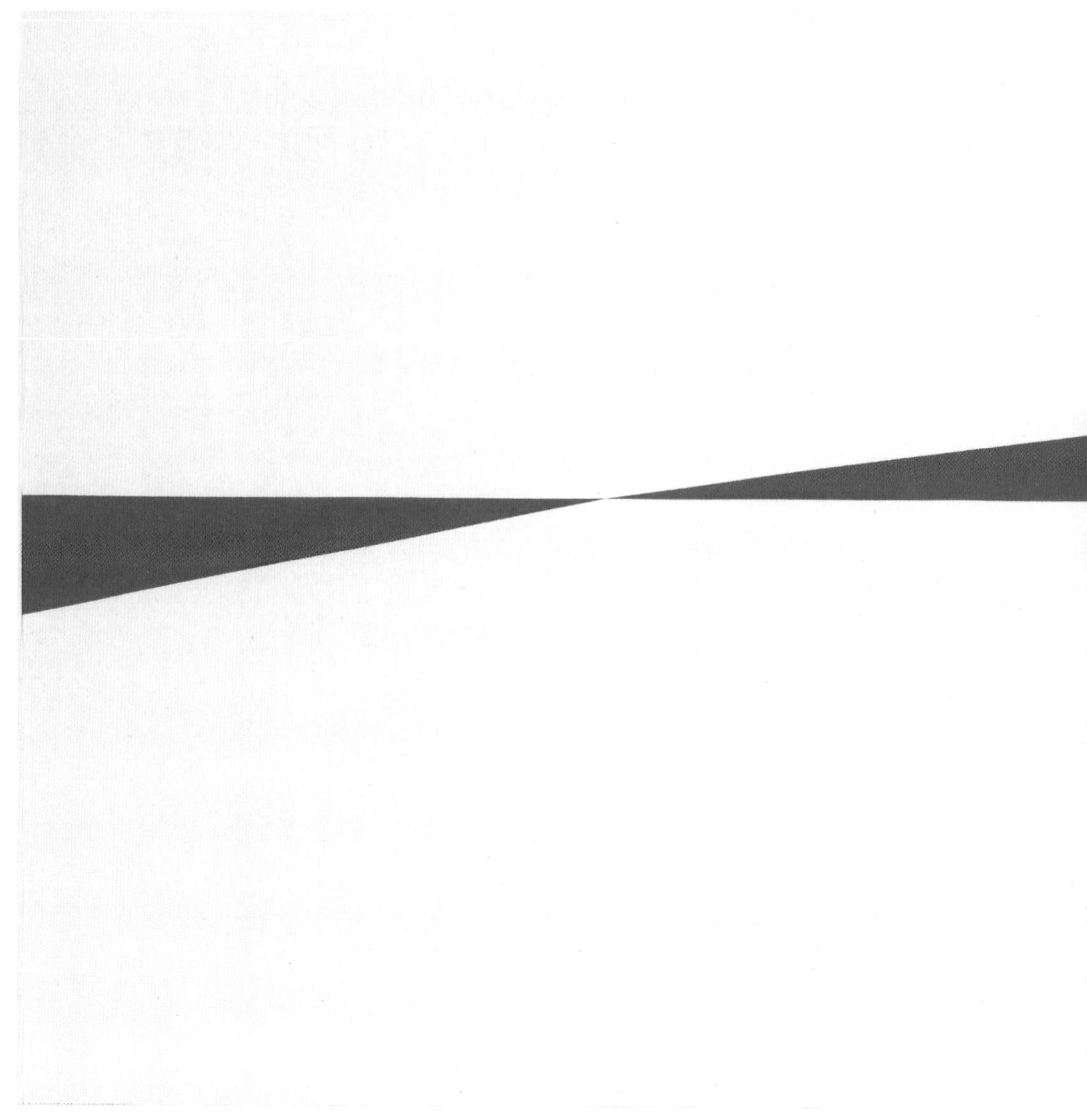

Take as an example Newman's 1955 oil on canvas entitled *Uriel* (FIG. 7.18). Here, Newman's famous "zip," the artist's distinctive lines of energy that, in this case, pulsate in parallel stripes on the right side of the canvas, also serves to separate discrete and equally powerful areas. Approximately two-thirds of the canvas is occupied by a serene field defined by a bluish-green tone, dramatically contrasting with the blackness of the right-hand portion of the picture. While we perceive this and other works by Newman as principally meditations on space, the artist often gave suggestive titles to his individual canvases or series. For *Uriel* he chose the name of an archangel from both the Hebraic and Christian traditions. A contemplative mood is established through the use of the contrasting colors with their respective intimations of the spheres and the abyss. Herrera, too, employed suggestive titles, but in a much more nonspecific way than Newman.

The title of Ellsworth Kelly's (1923–2015) painting *Seine* of 1951 (FIG. 7.19) speaks directly to the venue where it was created. It is a landmark work for this American artist who, like Herrera, was living in Paris in the late 1940s and early 50s (and their art created there and in New York in the later 1950s resonates clearly with similar stimuli).[34] One (or maybe the earliest) of his purely abstract works, this mesmerizing image was perhaps suggested by the effect of light reflected on the river that bisects the city. Kelly's early dedication to the power of intersecting forms and their suggestive force gives this painting its distinctiveness and authority. The artist's former archivist Eva Huber Walters has commented that "Kelly's work was influenced by light, shadow and chance … he was intrigued by the fragments in nature and objects which caught … his eye and how they interacted with the ground and space surrounding it."[35]

The year 1951 was, in fact, crucial for Kelly's experiments with both geometric form and color. Many of his most representative images of that and subsequent years are in stark black and white. He then expanded his repertory of forms to include large fields of (sometimes rounded) blue or green shapes. Shadows, plants, the outlines against the sky of hills and many other natural points of observation serve as points of departure for his unadorned ruminations on air, space, and nature. Kelly's mode of expression in the early 1950s (and beyond) was markedly different from the dominant Abstract Expressionist genre that, at the time, was capturing the attention of a broad audience in the United States. He found greater sympathy with his immediate cohort of artist friends in Manhattan, including Ad Reinhardt (1913–1967) and Agnes Martin (1912–2004).

Martin's abstemious geometry-based grid paintings (begun in the mid-1950s after a long period of gestation that included representations of abstracted natural forms) are perhaps the most rigorous manifestations of a taste for control and imposition of

258

serenity on nature.[36] In this they represent a spiritual kinship with both the restraint and the implicit celebratory quality of Carmen Herrera's work of the period. Geometric form mingles with color variations (much more sober in the case of Martin than in that of Herrera) to produce a state of meditative conjoining between the viewer's eye and the forms on the canvas. Martin's 1959 *Homage to Greece* (FIG. 7.20) is an early example of what would become her signature style. This is a combination of oil, collage, and nails on paper to form the grid, the visual element with which she experimented into the twenty-first century.

The grid was, of course, among the principal elements of modern expression that first surfaced within twentieth-century Russian experimental art such as the Suprematist canvases of Malevich, and the work of fellow Russian Constructivists Aleksandr Rodchenko (1891–1956) and Liubov Popova (1889–1924). Taken up later by Piet Mondrian, it resurfaced, as art historian Rosalind Krauss has famously declared, within the context of certain pioneers of contemporary art from the late 1950s and

into the 60s and 70s.[37] Martin's efforts in employing the grid as her singular form of expression within her mature career offer perhaps the most concrete case of this pattern's quintessential significance as a modernizing form within the later twentieth century's language of minimalist contemporaneity.

Agnes Martin was born in Canada (Macklin, Saskatchewan), but she left for the United States before she was 20. Her early educational and artistic formation took place in Washington State, New York, and New Mexico (a place with which she is most associated). While Canadian trends in abstraction had few consequences for the genesis of her career, they had a considerable place within the larger tendencies of nonobjective painting within a hemispheric context. Perhaps best known are the gestural abstractionists of the 1950s, especially those from Montreal—the group known as the Automatistes, which included Paul-Émile Borduas (1905–1960) and Jean-Paul Riopelle (1923–2002). Nonetheless, hard-edge geometric abstraction played an important role especially in Quebec (both in Quebec City and Montreal), where there was more interaction with events happening in the arts abroad, especially those in Paris, than was generally the case in western Canada.

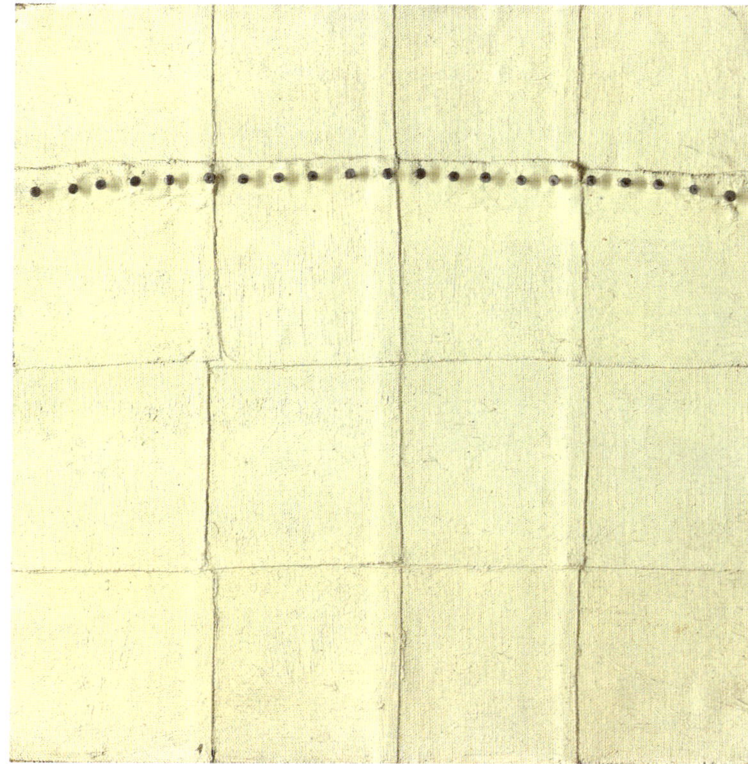

Fig. 7.20
Agnes Martin
Homage to Greece, 1959,
oil, canvas, and nails
laid down on paper,
12 x 12 in. (30.4 x
30.4 cm). Private
collection.

Guido Molinari (1933–2004) is representative of the strong current of geometric abstraction that developed in Montreal in the 1950s.[38] As a long-time teacher at Concordia University, Molinari was instrumental in tutoring a younger generation of Canadian abstract artists who carried his inspiration into the late years of the century. Although he is best known for his paintings done with industrial colors that feature vertical stripes of bright color, his early body of work derives from his initial attraction to Abstract Expressionism in New York, and *Tachisme* in Paris. By the mid-1950s he turned out a number of images that may be compared with the contemporaneous abstractions of Barnett Newman, whom he admired and whose art he studied in New York. *Noir Ascendant* (FIG. 7.21) of 1956, painted with Duco, is a good example of this aspect of Molinari's interests in minimalist form and monochromatic color relationships. There is a strong sculptural or even architectonic feel to this painting in which the white area gives the impression of a barrier superimposed on the black void, providing both a separation from nothingness, and a door and a window, should the idea of leaping into the abyss appeal to the beholder.

Fig. 7.21
Guido Molinari
Noir Ascendant, 1956,
duco, 26 x 20⅜ in. (66
x 51.9 cm). Art Gallery
of Ontario, Toronto.

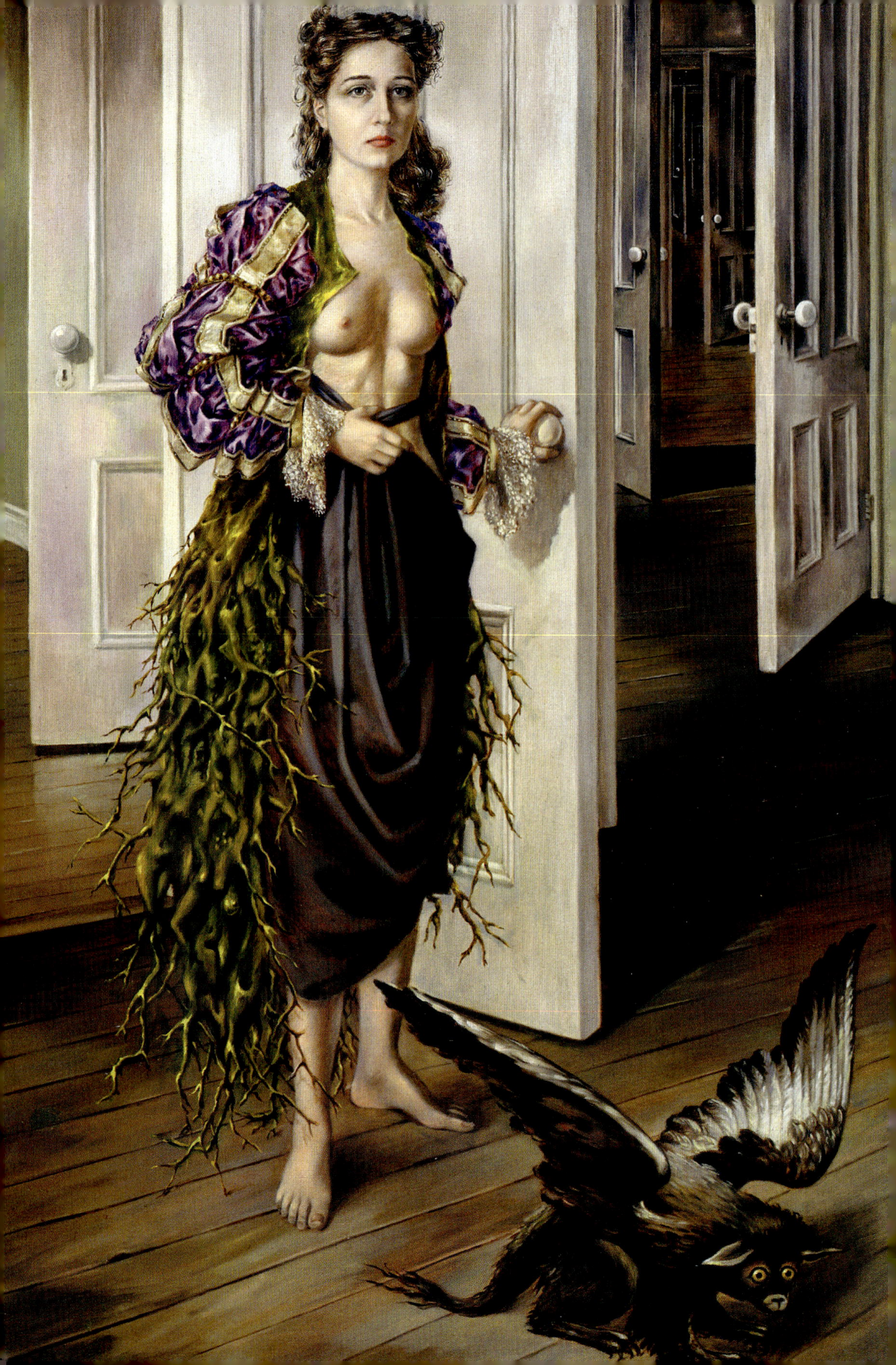

Modern Visionaries and the Intuitive Imagination

We return again to the realms of the subjective, to the territory of those forms of art created in the spirit of inquiry into the unconscious as well as to the arts made seemingly without the mediation of canonical art-world practices. Most of the Latin American "visionary" artists discussed in Chapter 1 had studied in Europe, and their sojourns abroad were critical in nurturing their imaginations. Their trips were also important in offering them models to both accept and reject—or refashion—in creating their own modes of modern sensibility in art. While Madrid, Milan, Berlin, and London were the sites of their training, it was inevitably Paris that attracted most of the Latin American artists who traveled abroad. By the early 1930s there were hundreds of Latin American artists working in the French capital, showing their work in Latin-only exhibitions and publishing their own journal to send back home to the cities of Latin America, large and small.[1]

This francophilia came to a forced halt by the mid-1930s when the threat of Fascism and ultimately war throughout the continent became a reality. It was then that the tables were turned. From the beginning of the Spanish Civil War (1936–39) and throughout the years of World War II and beyond, artists, composers, filmmakers, and writers joined the thousands of other European émigrés across the Atlantic. Some settled in the United States, but American immigration policy was such that great numbers of refugees, especially Jews, were not given visas or were even rejected as they approached the points of

Dorothea Tanning
Birthday, 1942
(detail).
See fig. 8.8.

entry on the eastern coast of the United States. In artistic terms, many of the cities of the Caribbean and mainland Latin America flourished, and the intermingling of émigré Surrealists (as well as artists of many other tendencies) with artists native-born to the region produced a particular model of what has been termed "New World Surrealism."[2] This is not to overstate the impact of the Europeans, however. The presence of Europeans during the 1930s and 40s had the effect of strengthening American Surrealist artistic production by encouraging the formation of a hybrid Surrealism and a sensitivity to the life of the inner mind that responded to local circumstances in terms of forms of narration, ethnicity, an absorption and reconfiguration of local myths and legends, and an intense interest on the part of both local and foreign artists in the material cultures and anthropological implications of indigenous forms of visual expression.

In December 1945 André Breton arrived in Haiti. One of his goals was to visit the newly organized (1944) Centre d'Art in Port-au-Prince. Founded by the American artist DeWitt Peters (who had been sent to teach English in Haiti as a conscientious objector during World War II) as a school, gallery, and artistic laboratory that welcomed artists who practiced a wide variety of forms of painting and sculpture, it soon became the "headquarters" for a group of self-trained artists who eventually constituted what became known as the "Haitian Renaissance."[3] Some of these painters and sculptors concentrated on images with religious subject matter, related to both Christianity and, more prominently, Vodou, the West African-based religion with links to other African-derived practices throughout the Americas. Hector Hyppolite (c.1891–1948) was, arguably, the best known of these artists, and he embraced the iconography of Vodou in many of his works. *Creator* or *Zombies* (FIG. 8.1) of circa 1945 depicts Baron Samedi, the Vodou spirit (*loa* or *lwa*) who serves as Guardian of the Graveyard, guiding two un-dead female figures out of a cemetery. The tomb, a skull, and various symbolic forms on the base of the grave (derived from African religious patterns called *vevés*) mark this as an evocation of religious beliefs regarding the afterlife.

Other artists of this group produced genre scenes or still lifes that were less spiritually infused. Those who exhibited and sold their work at the Centre d'Art soon became sought-after

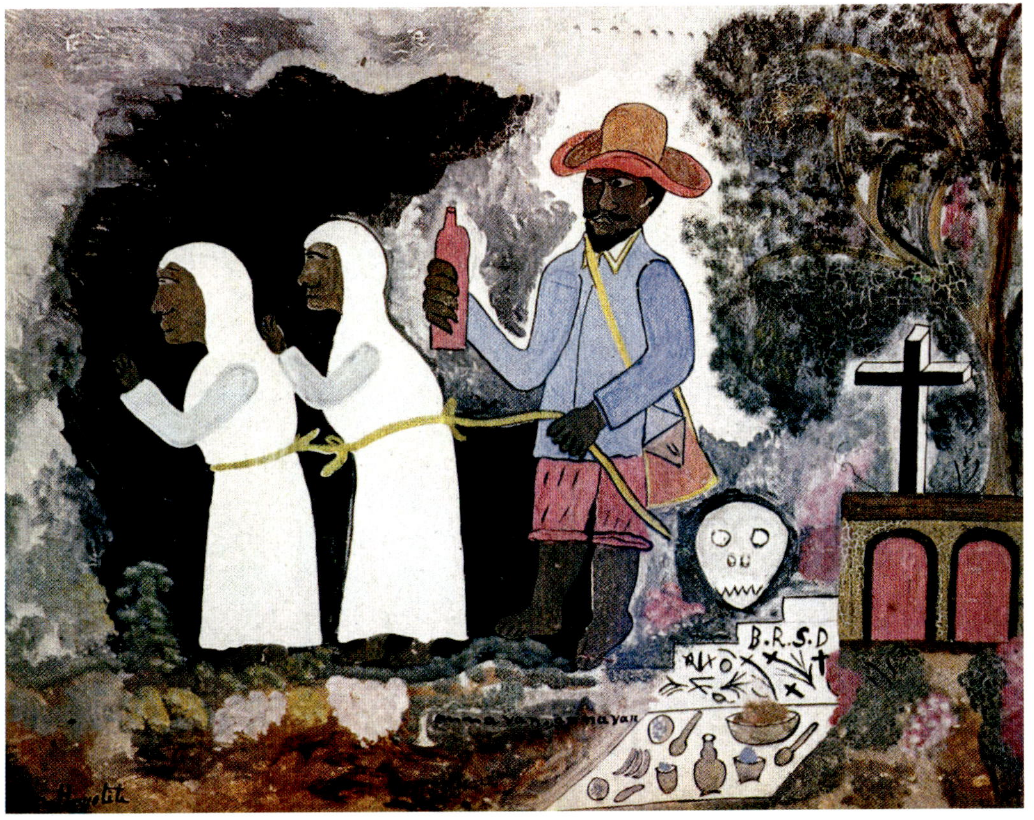

as individuals who represented a spirit of creativity free from the strictures of Western academic or avant-garde traditions. While their bright colors and sometimes fanciful subject matter later on devolved into the type of tourist art routinely sold today throughout the Caribbean, the first and second wave of Haitian artists of the 1940s and 50s represented a distinct bridge between visionary and so-called sophisticated forms of expression. Breton (who traveled only once to Port-au-Prince with Wifredo Lam and was ulti- mately expelled from the country for so-called subversive activity against the government) became interested in this group, and was a particular champion of the art of Hyppolite, whose paintings he exhibited in Paris in the late 1940s. Breton also purchased some five works by Hyppolite from the Centre d'Art for his personal collec- tion. About this artist he wrote glowingly, stating that Hyppolite's work was "Marked with the cachet of complete authenticity … Hyppolite's vision forms a point of conciliation between high class realism and a surrealism of complete exuberance."4

Fig. 8.1
Hector Hyppolite
Creator (also known as *Zombies*), c.1945, oil on board, 13⅞ x 10 in. (35 x 25.4 cm). Musée de Saint-Pierre, Port-au-Prince, Haiti.

In contemporary assessments of "intuitive" or "self-trained" artists there seems to be a gap between their place within the flow of the larger picture of modern art. There have also been debates regarding links between "visionary" art and Surrealism, with the received wisdom coming down on the side of Surrealism as a movement divorced from the imagination and production of artists such as Hyppolite. This compartmentalization was not always the case, judging from exhibition and collection histories of the 1940s and 50s. New York's Museum of Modern Art purchased notable examples of Haitian painting and, in the 1954–55 museum-wide *XXVIth Anniversary Collection. Paintings from the Permanent Collection*, exhibited some of them within the context of international modernism without separating them geographically.[5] In other exhibitions in the 1950s and 60s, Haitian art was shown within the context of art from Latin America and, again, was not singled out as being separate from wider artistic phenomena. Only later, with shifts in taste and the development of a specific market for "Outsider art," a phrase coined in the 1970s, did the work of painters like Hyppolite, Castera Bazille (1923–1966), Wilson Bigaud (1931–2010), Philomé Obin (1892–1986), and many others become unmoored from the larger frame of reference of modernist visual languages.

Trans-American Surrealism

In many cases Caribbean ports of entry became important centers of Surrealist artistic and literary activity in the early years of World War II. The group of Surrealists including Breton, Jacqueline Lamba (1910–1993), Wifredo Lam, the anthropologist Claude Lévi-Strauss, and others landed in exile at Fort-de-France, where Breton encountered the Martinican Paris-trained writer Aimé Césaire (1913–2008). Lam eventually made it back to his native Cuba, and during the war years he helped to make Havana another haven for the development of Surrealist art and literature, as was also the case in Santo Domingo, San Juan, and Port-au-Prince, where, as shown above, Breton "discovered" self-trained artists such as Hyppolite whom he branded "Surrealists."[6]

Many, if not all, of the European Surrealists had preconceived notions about what the Americas looked like and how American places figured in the Surrealist imaginary. As the art historian Louise Tythacott points out, as early as 1908 Guillaume Apollinaire (1880–1918) created an evocation of "primitive" and "savage" Mexico in a poem written in honor of Henri (Le Douanier) Rousseau (1844–1910), and contemporary writers and artists became increasingly fascinated with ancient American civilizations.[7] The Surrealists were great collectors who haunted both flea markets and galleries that sold ethnographic objects from "primitive" peoples throughout the world. In many cases anthropological "objects of wonder" formed part of their own collections, perhaps the most famous being that of Breton (unfortunately dispersed at auction in Paris in 2003). The Spanish-speaking Americas had been "revealed" to them through the collections of such institutions as the Musée d'Ethnographie (from 1938, the Musée de l'Homme) in Paris and other museums with non-Western collections. The arts of the Pacific West Coast indigenous peoples were also of particular fascination to artists like Wolfgang Paalen, Alice Rahon, and Eva Sulzer, who, as we saw in Chapter 6, had traveled in Alaska and British Columbia before coming to Mexico. Max Ernst made his home with fellow Surrealist Dorothea Tanning (1910–2012) during the 1940s in Arizona, where kachina dolls and other examples of the religious and material culture of the Navajo and Hopi peoples had particular appeal for them.

The transplanted Surrealists were constantly surprised at the novelties and "primitive qualities" they found, especially in places like Haiti and Cuba, but they were equally disappointed at the banalities of life in modern Latin American cities. The French artist and playwright Antonin Artaud (1896–1948), for example, lover of Mexican painter María Izquierdo (1902–1955), was shocked at what he considered the mundane modernity of Mexico City and sought the "real" Mexico among the Tarahumara Indians in the north of the country. The preconceived cultural notions of the Europeans also made for a rapport with their American and Latin American contemporaries and counterparts that did not always constitute a smooth relationship.

Surrealist activities in the Americas were dispersed throughout a wide range of locales, and each region and city eventually produced its own form of Surrealist expression. New York, Mexico City, and Buenos Aires all became Surrealist "hubs" with the comingling of foreign and native Surrealist artists. Surrealism was not, of course, a "style" of art. It originated (if we can trace its genesis at all) with Breton's Surrealist Manifestoes of 1924 and 1930, which were as much about politics, societal rebellion, and Freudian-based psychology as they were about artistic expression.[8] There were as many different forms of Surrealism as there were artists who practiced it. Thus we examine some of the ramifications of Surrealist activity here, as well as in other chapters, and especially that dedicated to non-geometric abstraction. The biomorphic images and the free-form paintings and drawings of such key figures in the American visual landscape as Lam, Arshile Gorky (1904–1948), Roberto Matta, Lee Krasner (1908–1984), or Jackson Pollock all adhere to, and derive from, modes of Surrealist experimentation. Surrealism itself was transgressive, breaking the boundaries of art as well as, in some cases, propriety. Thus Surrealist art is "modern" and "revolutionary" by its very definition.

The 1940s and 50s in Latin America: Surrealist Affinities
The presence of European visionaries or rebel-artists in Latin America, however, was not a late 1930s phenomenon. The nine-month visit by Marcel Duchamp to Buenos Aires in 1918–19 could be considered a preface to this story. If we consider Duchamp a Dadaist, even marginally, and Dada as a forerunner or prototype for Surrealism, we can look to this artist's sojourn as an early step in the development of an ethos of artistic imagination that arose from shared activities and shared spaces. In the case of Duchamp, however, this "step" was more symbolic than anything else, as we have scant evidence of his activities and only a few hints of the type of work he did in the Argentine capital before he left again. His letters to his friends and collectors the American couple Louise and Walter Arensberg provide us with some clues to his activities (working on his landmark piece *The Large Glass*, creating another work called *The Unhappy Readymade*, playing chess, and having fairly little to do with his fellow artists), and recent critics have endeavored to decipher and comment on some of his other pursuits.[9]

Yet there is a curious link between Duchamp in South America and the first Latin American Surrealist we will consider. Brazilian sculptor María Martins (1894–1973) was active in New

York in the 1940s and maintained a close romantic and artistic relationship with Duchamp, for whom she served as both muse and model. Martins worked in both Brazil and the United States under the professional name María. She was from the privileged elite of the white upper class (her husband, Carlos Martins, was Brazilian Ambassador to Washington during the years of the Getúlio Vargas dictatorship). However, Amazonian legends and Brazilian folk tales were of great interest to her, and important as sources for some of her most well-known works. In her fascination with the anthropological or ethnographic imaginary as expressed in themes related to (and often titled as) tropical places and creatures, Martins' work serves as a link with a similar interest on the part of Tarsila do Amaral. In addition, her presence and exhibitions in New York made Martins part of the connective tissue between émigré Surrealists and their North American counterparts of all artistic tendencies. Among the many artists in Martins' Manhattan circle were Yves Tanguy (1900–1955), Tanning, Léger, and Ernst. In 1943 she participated in a two-artist exhibition at New York's Valentine Gallery. Wealthy collectors bought Martins' sculptures with enthusiasm, while the paintings of Piet Mondrian, the other artist in the exhibition, remained unsold. (Martins purchased and was later responsible for the donation of Mondrian's now-iconic *Broadway Boogie Woogie* to the Museum of Modern Art.)

Martin's *Lacy* of c.1940 (FIG. 8.2) embeds a female figure within a complex web of heavily intertwined vegetal forms. She struggles to emerge from what threatens to overwhelm her. The tendrils of the inexorable tropical plants that we understand as Amazonian vegetation are her chief enemy as she struggles to overcome their choking force. The femme fatale of Symbolism has become the *femme victime* and, finally, *femme triomphante* of Surrealism, and we are reminded here, as in so many instances of Surrealist art by women, of the misogyny of the male participants in this movement and their notorious objectification of the female body.

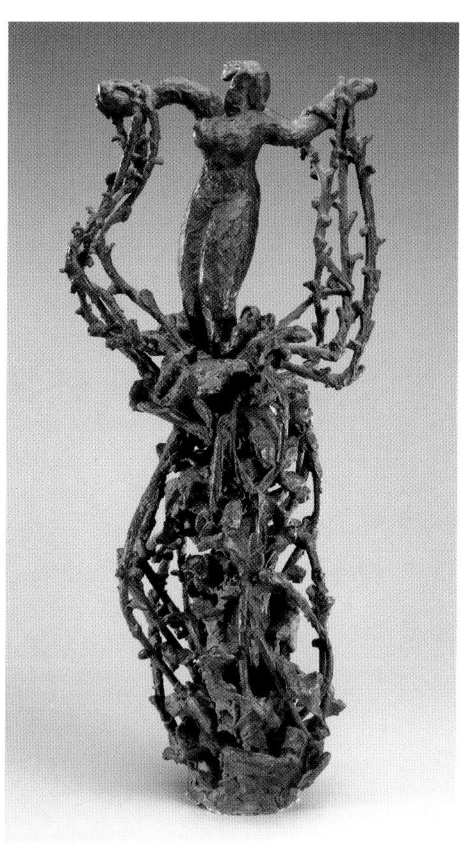

Fig. 8.2
María Martins
Lacy, c.1940, bronze, 30 x 8 in. (76.2 x 20.3 cm). Museum of Fine Arts, Houston.

Women Surrealists such as Martins resist this with projections of their own bodies, or surrogate bodies, in ways that place them beyond the servitude and abjectness into which they are often cast by their male counterparts, for whom they often served as sources of inspiration.

If we infer autobiographical references in the art of Maria Martins, they are more overt in that of Frida Kahlo. The majority of works by Kahlo are either self-portraits or images that have references to episodes in her life in Mexico City, New York, San Francisco, Detroit, or Paris. This observation, however, begs the question of the role of the stereotype of the autobiographical nature of the art of women Surrealists, or, in fact, that of art by women in general. While this is a theme more properly addressed in theoretical analyses, it should be a question that remains in our minds while discussing the art of many of the painters and sculptors presented in these chapters. Kahlo is something of an extreme case, as there has grown up around her personality a virtual cult of interest that includes her art but, much more palpably, bases itself upon the often dramatic events in her personal life. The episodes that have fascinated the public range from her childhood struggles with illness and physical disability, to the vicissitudes of her life as a woman artist in a gender-exclusive *machista* society, married to Diego Rivera, a larger-than-life figure whose own relationships with women were often tempestuous. Although well known during her lifetime, she has taken on an almost mythical persona since the late twentieth century, becoming the central character in novels, films, and countless lookalike contests. Kahlo played a central, if controversial, role within the development of Surrealism in the Americas and, specifically, what the Mexican art critic Ida Rodríguez Prampolini called "the Surrealist-saturated air of Mexico City" in the 1940s.[10]

Kahlo's 1940 *Self-Portrait with Thorn Necklace and Hummingbird* (FIG. 8.3) is an advantageous starting point for presenting some of the dilemmas inherent in her art. The work is rigidly frontal in the manner of the nineteenth-century Mexican provincial portraits that Kahlo and Rivera collected along with other types of popular paintings and objects. It displays the artist as she emerges from a profusion of tropical vegetation inhabited by insects. Her hair is piled atop her head and affixed with

Fig. 8.3
Frida Kahlo
Self-Portrait with Thorn Necklace and Hummingbird, 1940, oil on canvas, 24⅛ x 18½ in. (61.25 x 47 cm). Harry Ransom Center, University of Texas at Austin.

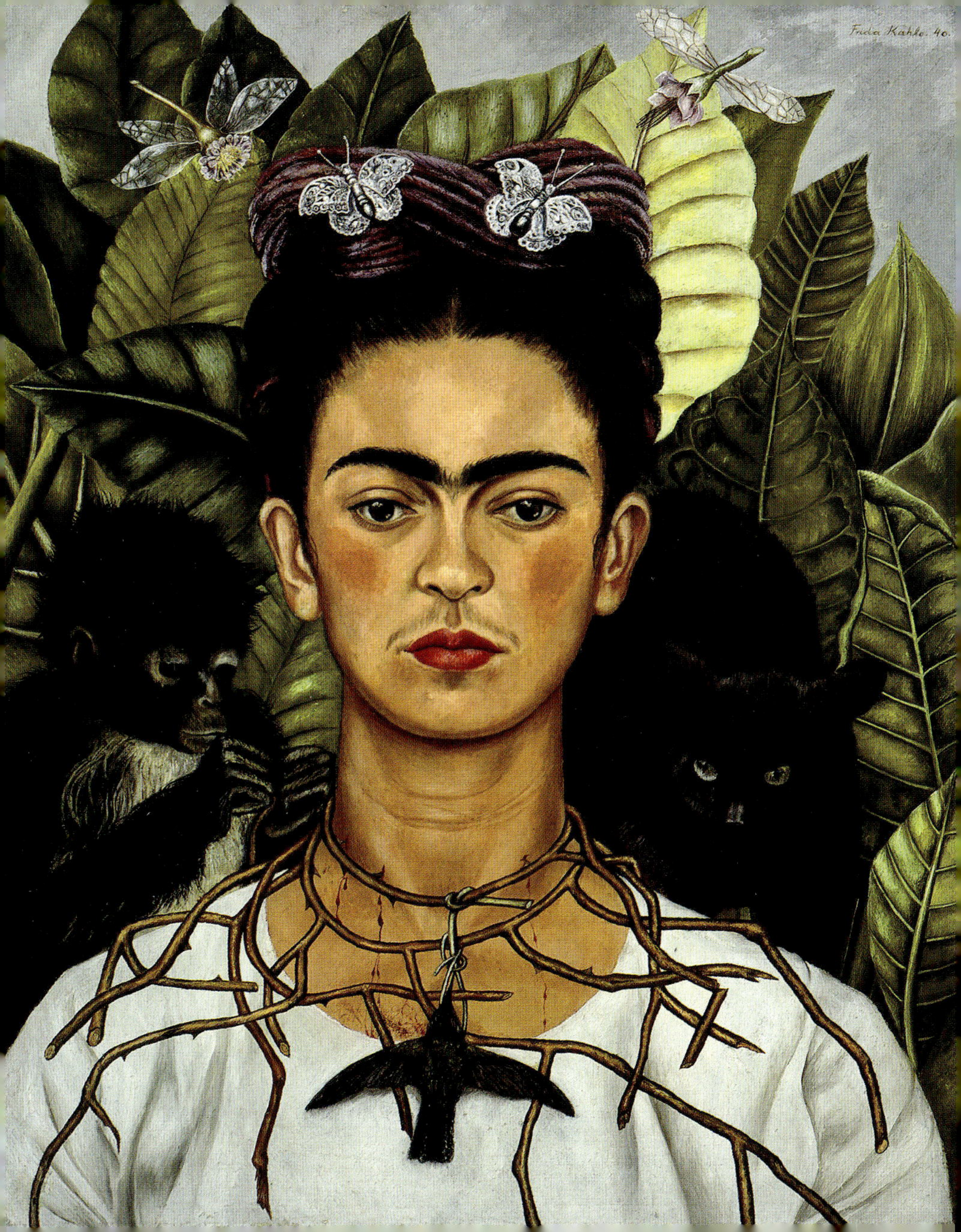

Frida Kahlo. 40.

ribbons and butterfly pins. Kahlo wears a simple white blouse that becomes the backdrop for an elaborate necklace of branches whose thorns pierce her skin, causing drops of blood to drip from her neck, eventually reaching the white cloth of her blouse. This display inevitably reminds us of the crown of thorns placed on Christ's head at the time of the Crucifixion, one of many such religious or quasi-sacramental references in Kahlo's art. Suspended from one of the thorn branches is a dead humming-bird, forming the center of a triumvirate of animal creatures that accompany the artist in her self-presentation. The other two are a monkey on her right shoulder and a black cat that stares out intently at the viewer on her left. Animals are often present in Kahlo's self-portraits and are connected with the occult concept of the "familiar" or the creature through which a human with extraordinary sensibilities communicates with the world beyond their own mundane reality.

Art historian Sarah Lowe is among many commentators on Kahlo's art who have offered interpretations of this picture. She has referred to Kahlo's "complex, idiosyncratic imagery" and has observed that

the artist draws from her Mexican heritage, making reference to Aztec divinatory rituals entailing self-mortification with maguey thorns. The dead hummingbird around her neck and the butterflies in her hair are Aztec symbols that signify the souls of dead warriors.[11]

Other significations of this painting that would be clear to anyone familiar with the artist's biography include references to the health challenges she faced throughout her life, and the emotional impact of her divorce from her husband the year before this picture was created. Kahlo's self-portrait is similar to many others she made throughout her life in its projection of personal information and the inclusion of clothing, flora and fauna, and other objects of obvious Mexican derivation.

Combining recognizably Mexican accouterments within an oneiric setting to evoke a Surrealist atmosphere is a trait found in many of the works of Kahlo's female contemporaries in Mexico, including María Izquierdo and the photographer Lola Álvarez Bravo. Izquierdo's *Sin título (Escena dramática)* (Untitled, Dramatic Scene) 1938 watercolor (a genre in which she did

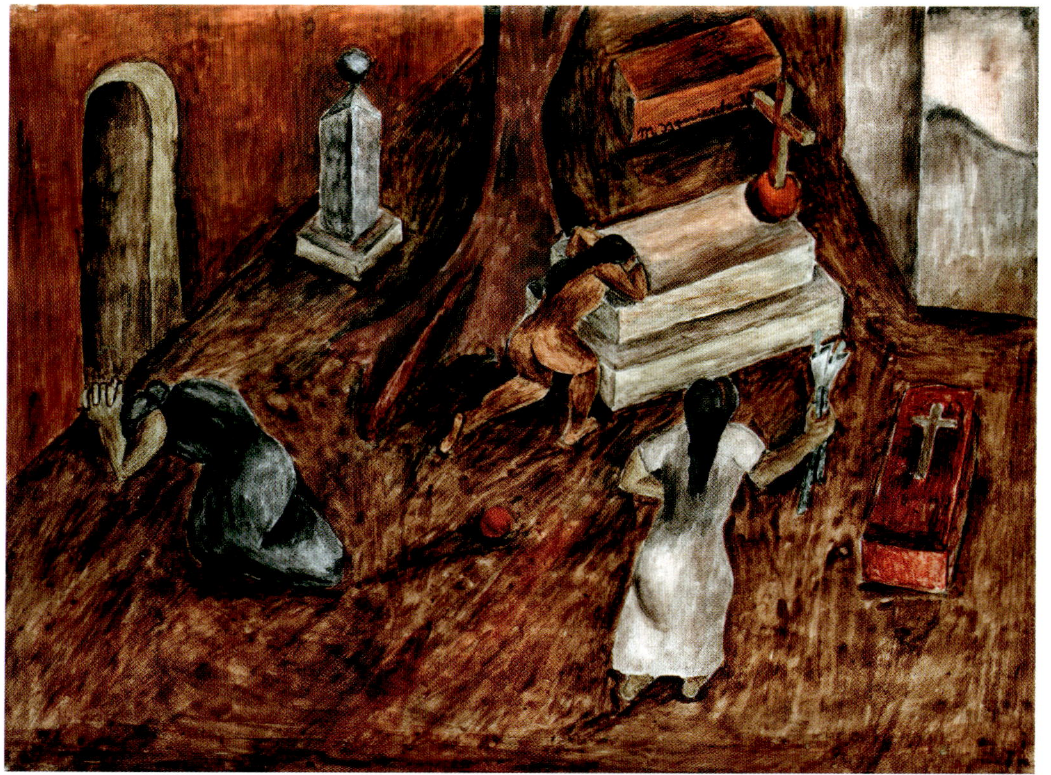

some of her most impressive small-scale works) shows a Mexican country graveyard (FIG. 8.4). Women weep the loss of a dead family member and are performing various acts of mourning in the composition. Izquierdo is a key member of the history of Surrealism in Mexico and her art, like that of Kahlo, has been widely researched and exhibited in the recent past.[12] Borrowings from the idiom of naïve Mexican painting of the nineteenth century and a deep interest in folk arts are at the heart of many of Izquierdo's works, thus linking her to the many popular or even visionary traditions that I argue inform the development of various modes of modern expression throughout the hemisphere in the first half of the twentieth century.

In the case of such personal and culturally specific art as that of Frida Kahlo we might ask ourselves what is, in fact, the relationship to international Surrealism in her painting? The answer is a complex mixture of seemingly conflicting ideas. While I do not wish to embrace the essentially clichéd notion of much Mexican modern art as inherently Surrealist,

Fig. 8.4
María Izquierdo
Sin título (Escena dramática), (Untitled, Dramatic Scene), 1938, watercolor on paper, 8½ x 11 in. (21.6 x 27.9 cm). Courtesy of Mary-Anne Martin Fine Art, NY.

as Breton said of the country itself, it is nonetheless obvious that one cannot understand the art of Kahlo, or that of many other American Surrealists (and particularly Surrealists from Latin America), without recognizing the extent to which their referential points of departure offer cultural clues and appropriations of visual tropes of their own past (both personal and, especially, national).[13]

Throughout her career Kahlo voiced her skepticism regarding her association with Surrealism, even though her first one-artist show had taken place in November 1938 at New York's Julien Levy Gallery, a venue that had been strongly associated with Surrealist art since the early 1930s.[14] Breton, who had written the essay in the Levy catalogue, then organized the exhibition *Mexique* at the Galerie Renou et Colle in Paris in spring 1939 that featured works by Kahlo (as well as photographs by Manuel Álvarez Bravo) in juxtaposition with pre-Columbian, colonial, and popular Mexican arts (further underscoring the pseudo-genesis of Mexican Surrealism as springing from an "innate spirit," starting in the pre-Hispanic era and continuing through the visual production of untutored artists of the modern era). Kahlo, who famously stated that she did not know she was a Surrealist until Breton came to Mexico to give her the news, also had, like many of her Mexican artist contemporaries, a conflicted relationship with the foreign artists (many of whom were Surrealist fellow travelers) who flocked to Mexico in the World War II period.

Kahlo painted the self-portrait described above in the same year as a landmark event in the Mexican art world. The *International Exhibition of Surrealism* was held at the Galería de Arte Mexicano (then Mexico City's premier art gallery) in 1940. It was organized by Rivera, Wolfgang Paalen, and the Peruvian Surrealist artist and poet César Moro (1903–1956). Following similar exhibitions in Paris, London, and Amsterdam, the Mexican version of the Surrealist show presented a wide panorama of mostly European art to the Mexican public. Few Mexican artists' works were actually included. Among the outstanding contributions were two of Kahlo's largest paintings, *Las dos Fridas* (The Two Fridas, a double self-portrait) and *La Mesa herida* (The Wounded Table, a composition displaying a table with bleeding legs, portraits of Kahlo and her niece and nephew, and images of large-scale skeletal figures called *Judas* images; this painting was last seen in Warsaw in 1955 and is perhaps lost).[15]

Among the visitors to the exhibition at the Galería de Arte Mexicano was Juan Soriano (1920–2006), a young painter who became closely associated with the Surrealist artists and writers in Mexico City and who played a major role in the Surrealist developments in Mexican visual and dramatic arts (as a designer of stage sets) between 1940 and 1950. While Soriano did not exhibit any of his paintings at the *Exposición*, his dramatic 1938 image entitled *Niña muerta* (The Dead Girl) (FIG. 8.5) matched the spirit of the Surrealist show. This painting was inspired by an experience the artist had had earlier in 1938 in the city of Veracruz, when he and the photographer Lola Álvarez Bravo happened upon the large front window of a house in which was displayed the corpse of a recently deceased child prior to her burial. Soriano, moved by this incident, and aware of the long-standing tradition in paintings and photographs of child post-mortem images—particularly strong in Mexico (and elsewhere in Latin America)—returned to his studio in Mexico City and painted several versions of this scene.[16]

The work illustrated here is the most dramatic and otherworldly of the series. The dark-skinned girl is dressed in a dull-brown garment and is shown from a curious perspective:

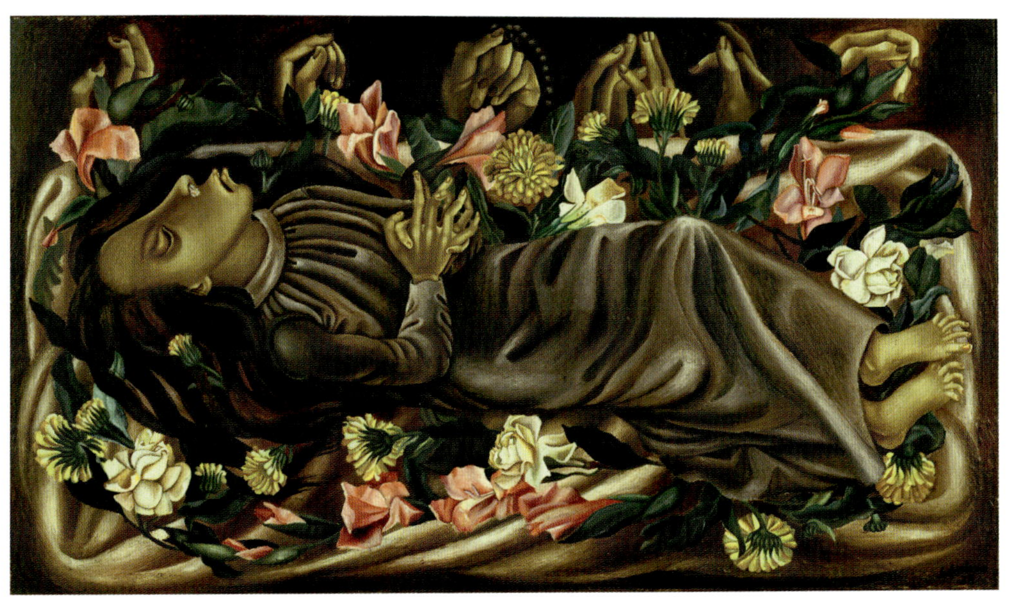

Fig. 8.5
Juan Soriano
Niña muerta (The Dead Girl), 1938, oil on panel, 18½ x 31½ in. (47 x 80 cm). Philadelphia Museum of Art.

the tabletop or coffin in which she rests is tipped up almost perpendicular to the picture plane. Her features are elongated; her intertwined hands and her feet appear to be more like claws than human appendages. A piece of cotton has been placed in the child's nose to prevent fluids from leaking out of the corpse and to retard the onset of the odor of decomposition. Around the child's body are combinations of roses, lilies, and marigolds— referred to by their Aztec name, *cempasúchil,* and long associated with death in pre- and post-Conquest Mexico. Barely noticeable at first, but strikingly dramatic once observed, the disembodied hands of six praying women are seen at the upper portion of the picture. One of them clasps a rosary and all of them pray for the swift journey of the souls of the *angelito* (the child who dies without sin) to heaven. Death, suffering, and salvation as Surrealist topics are here mingled with traditions derived from centuries of daily life in Mexico. The eeriness of the presentation in Soriano's small drama removes it from quotidian or "informational" representations of dead children, as in the case of post-mortem infant photography such as that by Romualdo García (1852–1930), who created multiple images, sometimes on postcards, to be sent to family and friends announcing the death of a child.

Soriano's *Dead Girl* is now in the Philadelphia Museum of Art, an institution that has a particularly distinguished collection of Mexican modernist painting. This is mainly owing to the efforts of Inés Amor, owner of the Galería de Arte Mexicano (the venue for the Surrealist exhibition discussed above), and Henry Clifford, who served for many years as Chief Curator in Philadelphia. Amor, in fact, facilitated the introduction of many Mexican artists (many of whom were associated with Surrealism) into U.S. private and public collections. She curated the 1943 exhibition *Mexican Art Today* for Philadelphia. It traveled to numerous other U.S. and Canadian museums, strengthening the enthusiasm and taste for Mexican painting as one of the most potent sources of modernization of the American art scene in the 1940s. This and similar shows (like MoMA's *Twenty Centuries of Mexican Art,* 1940) served as conduits through which many Vanguard artists in New York and throughout the United States and Canada were able to observe large displays of modern Mexican art at first hand. Such exhibitions became, in part, the strengthening catalysts for an interest in Mexican art in the United States that had started as early as the beginning of the 1930s, with an appreciation for Mexican muralism. U.S. artists of a wide variety of stylistic tendencies who were searching for new stimuli to "modernize" their work were profoundly nurtured by the Mexican art that they saw in museums and they came to understand more deeply through the presence of many Mexican artists in major cities throughout the country.[17]

In Mexico City in the 1940s and later, a divide existed between many of the foreign Surrealists and their Mexican counterparts. While they certainly were aware of each other's work they did not often, generally speaking, keep company on a social basis. One of the links between the various émigré groups and the Mexican-born artists was Soriano. As a garrulous and youthfully charismatic individual he served as a galvanizing force within the art world of the Mexican capital at the time. One of his closest foreign-born friends was the British Surrealist painter Leonora Carrington (1917–2011). Carrington's arrival in Mexico in 1942 followed a long and tumultuous period of fleeing both World War II and her tyrannical family. After a long romantic association with Max Ernst in Europe (whose work she first saw in the 1936 version of the International Surrealist Exhibition in London) she made Mexico City her home for the rest of her long life (with a considerable hiatus in New York in the late 1960s and 70s). In Mexico, Carrington developed a style that bore little relationship to the manner of her Mexican contemporaries and there are few instances in which anything approaching Mexican subject matter is observable in her art.[18] Instead, she turned her attention to methods of traditional medieval and Early Renaissance painting (such as egg tempera), creating a large body of paintings (and, later, prints and sculptures) that attested to her profound knowledge of the occult, mystical literature, and many other numinous sources. As art historian Gloria Orenstein has stated:

Alchemy, Celtic mythology, Kabbalah, Tibetan Buddhism, Gnosticism, magic, shamanism, Jungian psychology, the prepatriarchal Goddess religion, and the tarot – these are just some of the many sources of Carrington's inspiration, cultivated through years of intense personal investigation.[19]

Carrington's 1946 painting *Tuesday* (FIG. 8.6) embodies many of the characteristics that typify her art of the period. The art historian and Carrington biographer Susan L. Aberth has described the work's essential qualities. The painting was done, says Aberth,

when she was working with tempera as a magical substance [eggs] and also going back to the Renaissance paintings she loved so much … The background textures that make up the cave-like "architecture" are reminiscent of the decalcomania of Max Ernst, although more delicate. There are multiple dimensions, a subterranean realm with water, turtles swimming, miniature horses in a corner as if seen through a lens onto another time and place. Animals turn into trees, women walk or sail with cats, the moon is full, there are crows … the witching hour is upon us.[20]

Carrington was at the center of a circle of European Surrealist artists and writers in exile in Mexico City that included the Hungarian-born photographer and photojournalist Kati Horna (1912–2000), who had documented the Spanish Civil War. It also included the extraordinary figure of Edward James (1907–1984), British poet, art collector, and promoter of Surrealist art

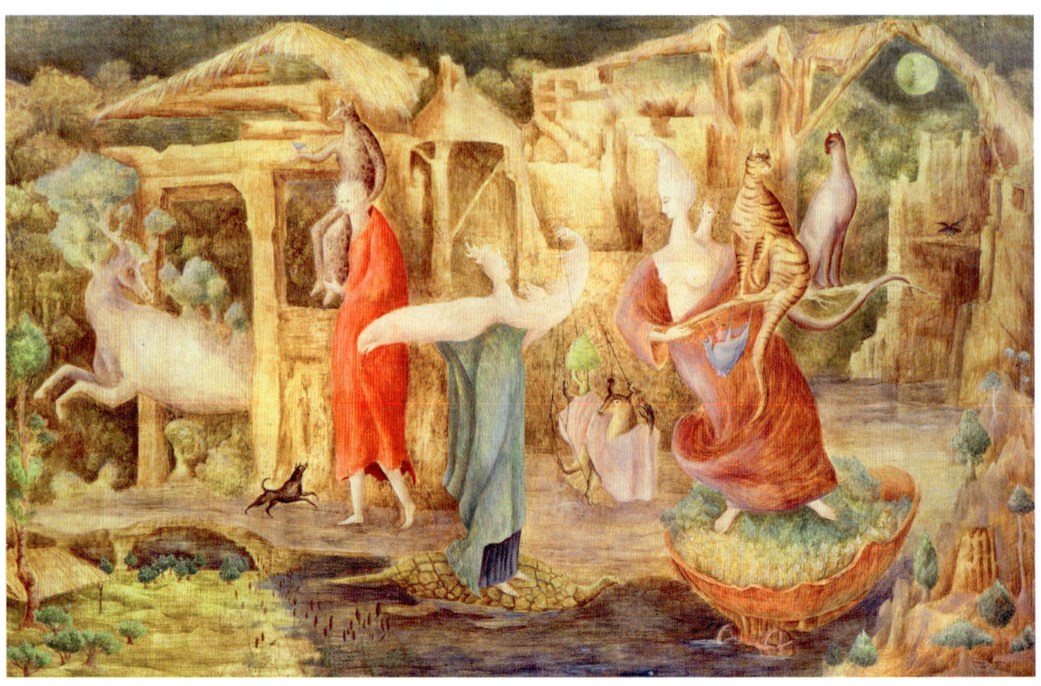

on both sides of the Atlantic. During the 1940s James, who had been instrumental in supporting the career of, among many Surrealists, Salvador Dalí (1904–1989), spent the war years between New York and Hollywood where he made a major impact on the film industry. James eventually moved to New Mexico and then to Mexico where he built a Surrealist fantasy property near the town of Xilitla (in the state of San Luis Potosí). Decorated with fantastical sculptures and water features (the house is called "Las Pozas," or The Pools) it became a retreat for James and some of his Surrealist friends, including Carrington.

Equally crucial to the coterie of émigré Surrealists, and closest friend of Carrington in Mexico, was the Spanish painter Remedios Varo (1908–1963). Varo had come to Mexico as a "double exile." During the Spanish Civil War she left Barcelona when the city was threatened by the invasion of the troops of General Francisco Franco, who ultimately triumphed and became dictator of Spain until his death in 1975. Varo fled to Paris with her French husband, the Surrealist poet Benjamin Péret (1899–1959), and ultimately, with the further threat of the German invasion at the start of World War II, she abandoned the French capital, arriving in late 1941 in Mexico City, where she stayed until her death. Varo lived in a ramshackle apartment building on Gabino Barreda Street in the San Rafael neighborhood, close to downtown Mexico City.[21] One of her neighbors was Carrington and they soon formed an alliance that extended beyond their mutual interests in the arts of the occult and fantasy, to include culinary experiments and trawling the streets of the city for inspiration from the detritus of everyday life. Varo also brought with her from her upbringing in Spain the entire repertory of images of visionary arts she had seen there, from the trove of works by Hieronymus Bosch (1450–1516) in the Prado Museum to the Mannerist twists and turns of the often tortured compositions by El Greco (1541–1614) to the dark fantasy worlds created by Francisco de Goya in his Black Paintings or his print series. All of these artists served as a collective storehouse of subjects and individual motifs for Varo's art.

Varo was fascinated by psychoanalysis and wrote imaginary letters to a psychiatrist.[22] She often exorcised (or buried) her anxieties in her painting. *Woman Leaving the Psychoanalyst* of 1960 (FIG. 8.7) is a representative example of this. The scene takes place in a patio of what appears to be an ancient (medieval or Renaissance) building with a small fountain in the center. It is a claustrophobic space that closes in upon the sole participant in the scene, as well as upon the viewer. An enigmatic female figure, certainly a reference to Varo herself, veiled and clothed in a pale green robe, carries a small basket of unidentifiable objects in her right hand. Her left hand holds a disembodied head with a long beard. The protagonist carries the head by the tip of this white goatee and is about to deposit it in the waters of the fountain. This woman has emerged from a doorway shrouded in darkness. Nonetheless we can perceive the inscription "Dr. FJA" inscribed on the door. The initials stand for the names of the "three great ones" of the history of psychoanalysis: Freud, Carl Jung (1875–1961), and Alfred Adler (1870–1937). The head may be that of Varo's father, or her husband, Péret.[23]

I mentioned in Chapter 1 the importance in Mexico of the theories of Sigmund Freud; the popularity of various forms of analysis became only more widespread during the angst-ridden years of the mid-twentieth century. Judging from the admiration for Freudian themes in high as well as popular culture in Mexico after 1950, Varo is following the lead of many of her erudite contemporaries, such as the poet Octavio Paz (1914–1998) and the psychoanalyst Erich Fromm (1900–1980), who held a teaching position at the National Autonomous University from 1949 to 1965 and at the Mexican Society of Psychoanalysis until 1974.[24] Varo's use of a theme related to the inner workings of the mind aligns her with many of her fellow Surrealists in Mexico and beyond, yet she was one of the few to make such direct reference to Freud's theories as she does here and in other related works of 1960. In this affinity for Freudian symbolism, Varo expresses a kinship with film director Alfred Hitchcock (1899–1980), whose movie *Vertigo*—a work driven by the director's concern with Freudian principles—premiered only two years before Varo painted her vision of psychoanalysis. Hitchcock's work was well known in Mexico, and Hitchcock himself deeply admired the (then waning) golden age of Mexican "noir" movies. Varo created mini-dramas in each of her paintings and we could indeed call her overall work cinematic. Her affinities with the medium of film bring her art into a wider arena of popular expression.

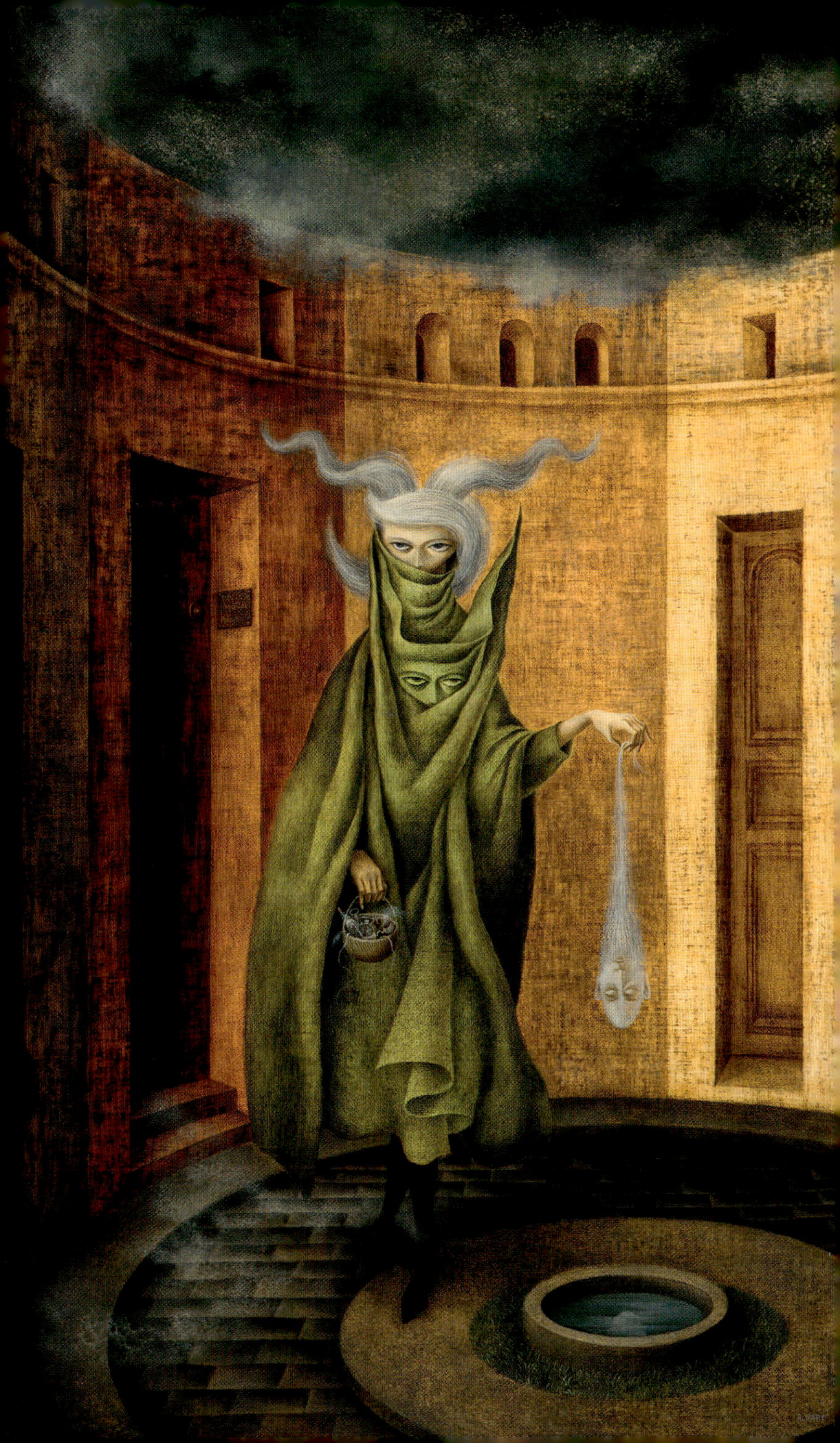

Self-portraiture among women of the Surrealist movement often reveals much more than the simple physical description of the painting's (or photograph's, or even sculpture's) subject. As a tool for self-investigation and self-affirmation, the auto-image, as we have seen so palpably in the case of Frida Kahlo, allowed the artist to create and refashion her often stultifying world of marginalization and debasement within the framework of the male-dominant cultural scene. Varo's *Woman Leaving the Psychoanalyst* is a perfect example of a narrative that concentrates more on the mind than on the physicality of the artist. The same may be said for a well-known 1942 self-portrait called *Birthday* (FIG. 8.8) by Dorothea Tanning, the American artist who is often considered to be a U.S. counterpart of Carrington and Varo.

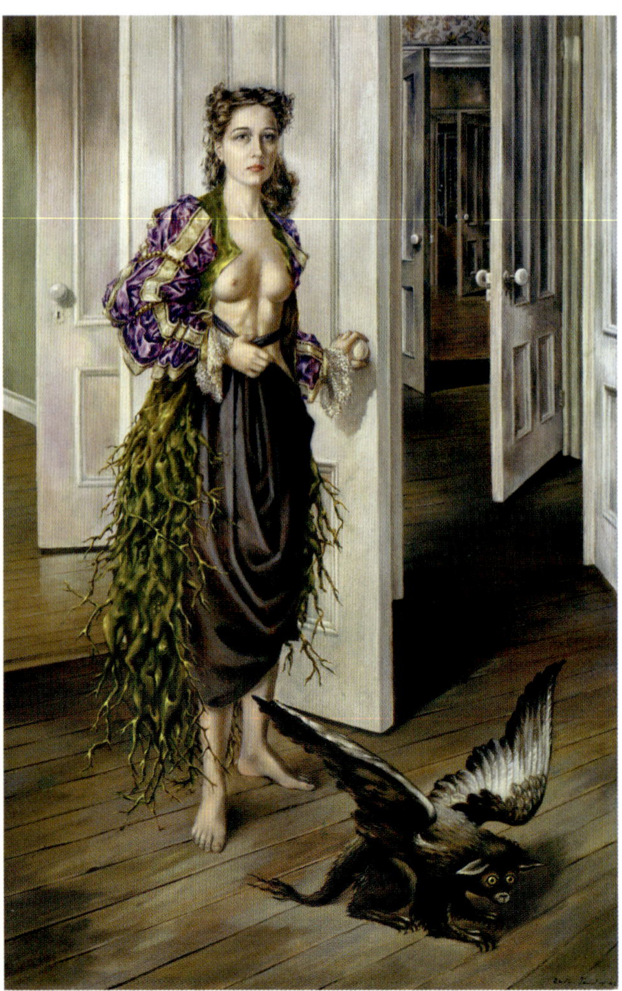

In Varo's *Woman*, doors play a major role. There are two doors, both closed. Entrance or exit appears impossible. Tanning's picture also represents doors, but they have different meanings from those of Varo. Instead of closing in the protagonist, they are all open, allowing the artist potential egress in any direction—all of which seem to be disquieting or even threatening in their own ways. Tanning presents herself to the public in this painting (whose title was suggested by Max Ernst, former lover of Carrington and future husband of Tanning) as dressed in an odd combination of garments. A courtier in a Renaissance palace might have worn the fancy purple jacket. Tanning's skirt is a mauve drapery partially covered by vegetal forms that resemble skeins of seaweed. The artist's chest is bare and her feet are unshod. This, combined with the disquieting look on her face, suggests a distinct sense of insecurity. Perhaps most disturbing is the creature at her feet, a composite animal that would not be out of place in either a description of an upside-down world by the Surrealists' hero Hieronymus Bosch, or a fantasy narrative by Tanning's contemporary Carrington. Dawn Ades has identified this beast as a winged lemur, "a nocturnal animal found only in Madagascar, where it has long been associated with night and spirits of the dead."[25] Its dark aura and elaborately upswept wings remind us of the bat described in the Symbolist relief sculpture by Marco Tobón Mejía with which I opened this book. In that work, however, the creature represented the decadent and objectified woman. In Tanning's self-portrait it is a surrogate for the artist herself, perhaps ready to defend her from predators or perform supernatural feats that the human subject of the picture could accomplish only in her fantasy life.

From Mexico to Manhattan and Beyond

The cosmopolitan Mexico City art world of the 1930s to the 50s was composed of artists from many places of origin. The North American painters Philip Guston and Marion Greenwood, the sculptor Isamu Noguchi (1904–1988), the photographers Paul Strand and Edward Weston, and many others began arriving en masse from the 1930s, in many cases to participate in mural projects, as we examined in Chapter 4. In other cases, like that of Milton Avery (1885–1965), who was there in 1946, artists were attracted more by a more folkloric image of the country and sought to incorporate it into their work.[26] During the 1930s and 40s Mexican painting set an example for many local developments throughout Latin America as Mexican artists traveled throughout the hemisphere during this time, either in political exile or to fulfill commissions for murals. David Alfaro Siqueiros was one such peripatetic artist. His travels to New York and Buenos Aires in the 1930s, and to Havana and Chillán, Chile, in the 1940s, had pronounced consequences for the development of experimental art forms in those places. There was a constant back and forth between artists from Mexico and those from elsewhere in the hemisphere during and after World War II.

One of the principal representatives from Central America to work much of his life in Mexico City was the Guatemalan artist Carlos Mérida (1891–1984). After early training in Guatemala

City Mérida left for Paris where, between 1910 and 1914, he painted a series of images of indigenous peoples from the Maya highlands of his home country in a Cubist idiom. His 1919 *Motivo Guatemalteco* (Guatemalan Motif) (FIG. 8.9) divides the background into wedge shapes while the main figure appears in a series of triangular and other geometric forms, offset by the multicolored series of embroidered motifs on her traditional *huipil* (mantle).

During the 1930s Mérida became actively interested in Surrealism and found the philosophies of Bretonian Freudianism compatible with his deep dedication to the indigenous literature and folk traditions of the Maya. A principal source for Mérida's art was the *Popol Vuh*, the compendium of Maya legends and information about both practical and spiritual matters, an original pre-Hispanic manuscript that managed to survive the depredations of Spanish domination of Guatemala and has ever since served as inspiration for contemporary Maya peoples as well as anyone else interested in the customs of the people of the former Quiche Kingdom. Mérida's series of illustrations for the *Popol Vuh* included numerous paintings as well as a series of ten lithographs called the "Estampas del Popol Vuh" (1943) that had wide dissemination in Mexico and abroad, especially after their publication in the Surrealist magazine *DYN*. The style of these works is in accord with the broad interest among many of the Surrealists in biomorphic semi-abstraction. Figures, recognizably derived from the repertory of stylized Mayan images and glyphs on ceramics, architectural reliefs, and wall paintings, inhabit the

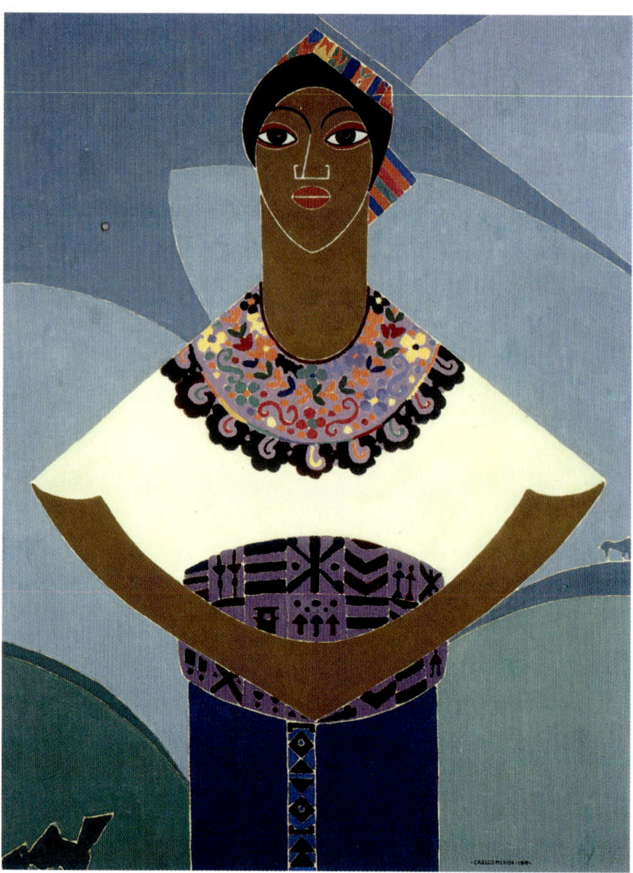

space and float in the air in the paintings and prints. They are often circular forms, appearing like bubbles or clouds within the frame of the image. Not all of these paintings, watercolors, and prints were related directly to the Maya text. Mérida, who wished to avoid what he considered the clichéd folklorisms of many of his Mexican contemporaries, would employ references to indigenous subjects and infuse them with the biomorphic mode of his Spanish counterpart Joan Miró, as art historian Courtney Gilbert has pointed out.[27]

In 1940 Mérida participated in the *International Exhibition of Surrealism* at the Galería de Arte Mexicano. Mérida became one of the best-known Central American artists in the United States, showing widely in galleries in New York such as the Valentine Gallery, a bastion of modernism and Surrealism, and the venue for the exhibition of Picasso's *Guernica* in 1939. In Los Angeles Mérida exhibited at the Stendhal Galleries, where his Mexican contemporary Siqueiros had had a significant show in 1932. Throughout his life Mérida had over 40 exhibitions in the United States.

By the late 1930s Mérida's surrealizing art took on a new aspect when he created a series of paintings with automaton-like figures inhabiting a severe, barren landscape. *Temptation* of 1940 (FIG. 8.10) is representative of this phase of his enigmatic modernism. A nude couple (Adam and Eve?) is set in high relief against a vivid red background with ominous gray cloudlike forms at the left. The ground on which the male figure reclines and the female stands is a vivid yellow. Their bodies are flat, matte color, but the face of the man takes on a strange yellow hue. Both faces are masklike and the bodies are more like those of puppets than humans. The male is the submissive character here; he reaches his left arm up to the woman in a gesture of protest in order to fend off her advances. This is an interesting reversal of the dominant male figure so associated with the Surrealist vocabulary, yet the female's aggressive attitude reinforces the femme fatale stereotype. Two simple vessels—small red pans, perhaps for food—are the only other elements in this picture. There is a detached, odd theatricality to this work. The figures remind us of dancers in an abstract choreography. In fact a suggestion of dance in this work by Mérida is completely in keeping with one of the artist's lifelong obsessions.

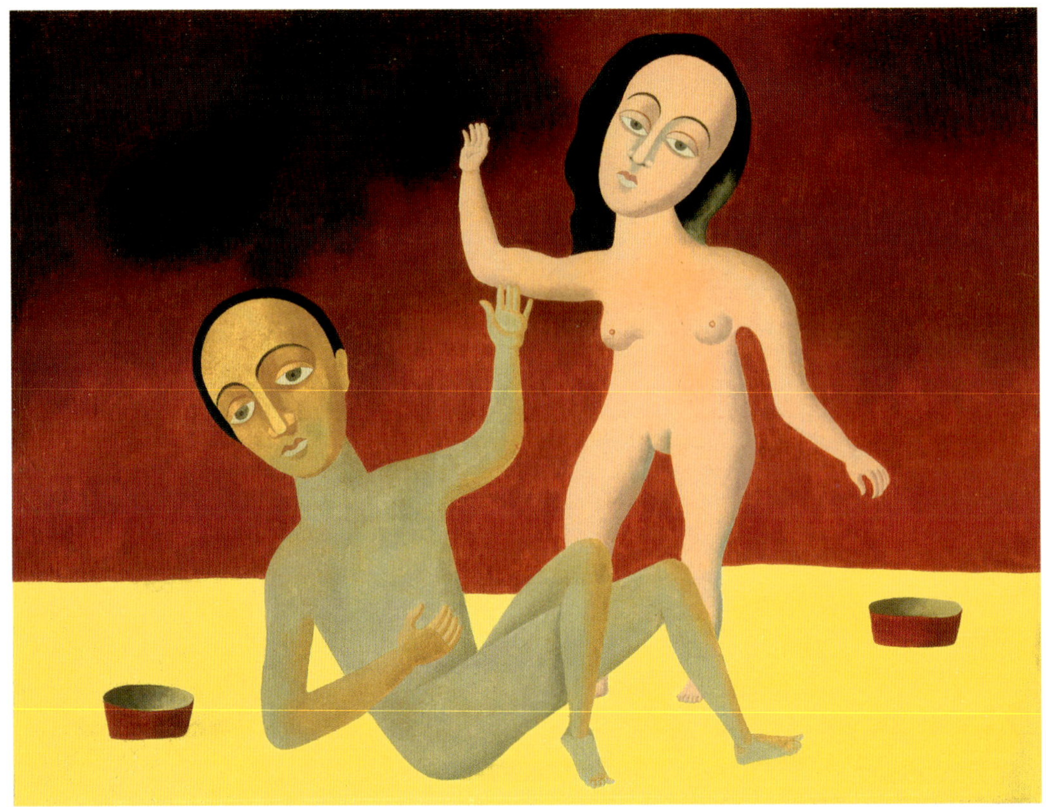

From his youth in Guatemala, Mérida studied indigenous music and dance, and he remained interested in various forms of choreographed movement all his life. He put this fascination into practice in his profession and many of his paintings show people dancing. Mérida served as Director of the School of Dance of the Secretariat of Public Education in Mexico City from 1932 to 1935. During the 1930s he worked on plans for a ballet based on ethnographic dance forms of Mexico, and throughout his career he worked for the dance theater, creating sets, costumes, and props for 22 choreographed works. His suite of prints known as the "Danzas de México" (Dances of Mexico) of 1937 serves as a virtual encyclopedia of dance forms in his adopted country. Mérida's daughter Ana Mérida (1922–1991) became a famous dancer who also co-founded the Academia Mexicana de Danza with composer Carlos Chávez (1899–1978) in 1947.

I wish to emphasize Mérida's intense involvement with dance and the development of dance companies and schools in Mexico in the 1930s, 40s, and beyond for several reasons. One of them has to do with the role of the dance revival in Mexico at the time, and the promotion and recovery of many forms of indigenous and popular dance to enhance the cultural profile of the country in a modern mode that incorporated traditional performative idioms. Dance, like painting, was viewed not only in Mexico but also throughout the hemisphere as an instrument of instruction and promotion of national values.[28] In Mexico this sentiment culminated in the creation of the Ballet Folklórico de México by Amalia Hernández in 1952.

Dance, Visual Art, and Visionary Modernity

There were close synergies and collaborations between the creators of modern dance and the visual arts in the period under consideration here, and correlations between choreographic history and the development of painting and other forms of art serve to underscore the dynamic nature of this interchange. In Argentina, the huge success of tango during its "golden age" (1935–55) is associated with the art form itself, but also with the modernization and economic flourishing of Buenos Aires. In Cuba, Havana's tourist industry took off in the 1930s and 40s, causing, in part, a financial boom that had much to do with visitors wishing to experience at first hand the rhythms of such fantastically successful performers of the *charanga* (big band) movement as Tito Puente (1923–2000) and Celia Cruz (1925–2003), who would perform in spectacular cabaret venues such as the fabled Tropicana Nightclub.

In 1935 the African-American choreographer Katherine Dunham (1909–2006) arrived in Haiti for the first of many visits, later buying a home in Port-au-Prince and entering the same artistic circles as her visual artist contemporaries. She initially went to Haiti to research her Master's thesis on Haitian dance and the intersections with Vodou for the University of Chicago under the direction of Melville Herskovits (1895–1963, a student of the anthropologist Franz Boas [1858–1942], and the teacher of such foundational anthropologists as Margaret Mead [1901–1978]). Later, however, Dunham realized her desire to form a dance troupe and, ultimately, a school for the promotion of knowledge of Caribbean, and especially Haitian, dance. Her company enjoyed great success throughout the United States in the 1940s and beyond, well into the 1960s, providing stimulus for the popularity of Afro-Caribbean dance forms in North America. Examining the repertory of visual artists who were concerned with (and painted or photographed) forms of dance, including both contemporary and regional forms, or who worked directly with choreographers and dance impresarios in the first half of the twentieth century, reveals another powerful source and mutual stimulus for the modernization of both modes of artistic expression.

In 1936 Lincoln Kirstein, who worked directly with Alfred Barr at MoMA to create the museum's Latin American and Caribbean collection, founded the Ballet Caravan in New York to present modern works for young dancers on specifically American themes (such as *Billy the Kid*). American choreographers such as Agnes de Mille (1905–1993) staged works like *Rodeo* (1942; with a score by Aaron Copland, 1900–1990). Two years later Martha Graham (1894–1991) created the emblematic ballet *Appalachian Spring*, also with a Copland score, a work that has been pointed to as a high point of choreographic creativity in a distinctly American regional idiom. This piece entered the American dance repertory and has never left, regularly revived by the Martha Graham Company many years after the choreographer's death. This work incorporated folk idioms of the American Southeast in a thoroughly experimental and path-breaking way, creating a new space for dance as an art form that heralded "the new" while reviving the traditional. *Appalachian Spring* also represented one of the many collaborations between Graham and her friend the Japanese-American sculptor Noguchi, who created the starkly spare sets for the piece.

Noguchi was one of the principal American Surrealists of the 1930s and 40s. His art includes many objects designed as components of stage sets for Martha Graham's dances, beginning in 1935 and continuing throughout the 1940s. These may be considered as stand-alone biomorphic sculptures whose oneiric suggestions complemented the radically contemporary movements of Graham's dancers. The interaction between sculptural objects and dancers helped to create of the Graham performances a "total work of art." Noguchi designed the sets for *Appalachian Spring* in 1944, a series of highly stylized objects and structures suggesting interior and exterior spaces. A photograph of a staging of this dance classic at the Library of Congress in Washington, D.C. (FIG. 8.11), attests to the artist's interest in highly abstracted form. Yet the inclusion of a highly stylized Shaker-style chair in this scene in which Graham and her dance partner Stuart Hodes (in a production from circa 1955) appear in the foreground also serves as an indication of Noguchi's interest in folk traditions.

There is, as well, a specific connection with Carlos Mérida and Mexico in the work of Noguchi. In 1936 he was in Mexico City participating in the decoration of the newly erected Abelardo Rodríguez Market (discussed in Chapter 4, one of many such public facilities that replaced the ambulant vendors that clogged the streets of Mexico City until the 1930s). The market served, in part, as a laboratory for varying types of public art. The majority of works were large-scape murals painted by both Mexican and American artists (including Marion and Grace Greenwood and Pablo O'Higgins). Noguchi's contribution was an abstract three-dimensional mural with political, anti-Fascist references. Noguchi was friendly with Mérida and visited him during the Guatemalan artist's frequent journeys to New York, and both artists had close connections to Surrealism and the world of dance and the theater on both sides of the U.S–Mexico border.

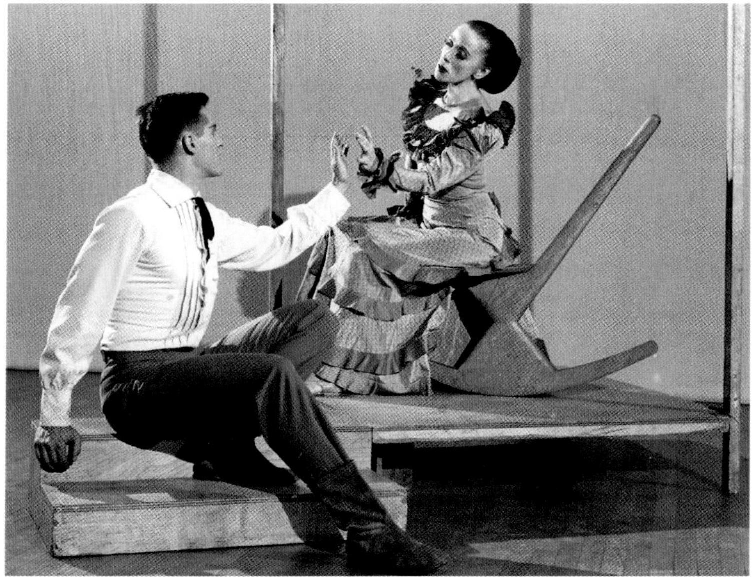

Fig. 8.11
Unknown photographer
Martha Graham and
Stuart Hodes in
Appalachian Spring
choreographed by Martha
Graham, c.1955, with
Isamu Noguchi Shaker
chair.

Popular Arts, the Intuitive Eye, and Modernity

The mention above of an example of American popular arts—a Shaker chair in the context of Noguchi's sets for Graham's ballet—brings us to a theme related to the larger issues of this chapter and this book. I would like here to consider the role of the popular, folk, untutored, or intuitive arts within the panorama of Surrealist-related or visionary arts of the Americas and their role within the making of a modern vision for the hemisphere.

The art historian Wanda Corn has discussed the significance of U.S. artists' appreciation for and collecting of "Americana" in the 1910s through the middle part of the twentieth century. In the 1920s, artists such as Charles Sheeler, the sculptor Elie Nadelman (1882–1946) and his wife, Viola Spiess Nadelman (1878–1962), and others became enthusiastic collectors of so-called Early Americana as well as American folk art. The Nadelmans even created their own museum in the Riverdale section of New York City in 1926 to house their collection.[29] Their tastes in collecting informed the styles of Elie Nadelman's art. By the 1930s there was a broader taste for folk art and it became identified more closely with a sense of nationalism. This played itself out within the contexts of pre-World War II isolationism as well as a search for "national roots" and a pursuit of visual symbols of American exceptionalism.[30] Nadelman's wood sculpture entitled *Pianiste* (FIG. 8.12), representing a woman seated at a stylized piano, her head turned to face the viewer and her hands caught in midair as she plays the instrument, combines incipient Art Deco sinuous lines with the more prominent reference to simple country wood carvings of untrained artisans of an earlier era.

Members of the Rockefeller family and curators like Alfred H. Barr Jr. contended that many of the roots of North American modernism derived from the "simplicity" and "clean lines" of art and architecture from the colonial and nineteenth-century United States. They promoted the admiration for both Early American art and folk art to a wide general public. Museums such as the Metropolitan Museum of Art and the Museum of Fine Arts in Boston opened series of galleries dedicated to American art from the colonial era to the nineteenth century. These invariably featured reconstructed rooms from Early American homes equipped with the objects (and folk art) that would have originally been seen within them.

In the 1920s to the 40s the vogue for restored colonial towns produced the popular tourist attraction of Old Sturbridge Village in Sturbridge, Massachusetts, one of the country's first such restorations. Much better known and more ambitious was the reconstruction as a vast museum of the colonial city of Williamsburg, Virginia. This project was financed and supported by the Rockefeller family, beginning in the 1920s. Work continued throughout the 1930s and 40s. Abby Aldrich Rockefeller (wife of John D. Rockefeller and one of the founders of the Museum of Modern Art) was particularly interested in this enterprise and oversaw much of the adornment of the colonial houses in the city.[31] Among the antiques she purchased for Colonial Williamsburg were Spanish colonial objects obtained in Mexico when she visited there with her son Nelson (who later formed one of the world's most distinguished collections of Mexican popular arts) in 1933.

The widespread interest in folk art and the connections between folk and art nationalism were by no means phenomena limited to the United States. In Mexico the promotion of what was labeled *artes populares* had a distinctly politicized cast. Almost immediately after the Mexican Revolution the government sponsored large-scale exhibitions of folk art both at home and abroad and helped to revive many folk traditions in arts, crafts, dance, cookery, and other areas.[32] Popular arts were considered artifacts of living nationhood and as a tool within a (not always successful) utopian project to involve working classes, both urban and rural, in the role of building a reconfigured society after ten years of warfare. In Mexico as well as other places in Latin America, popular motifs that began appearing in the arts were also dependent upon archaeological excavations being carried out in the early years of the century. The revival of

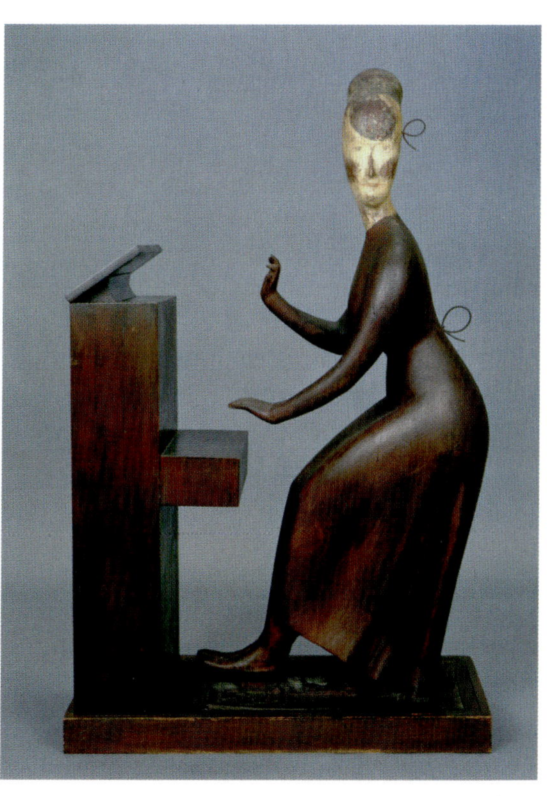

Fig. 8.12
Elie Nadelman
Pianiste, c.1924, wood, 35¾ x 22 x 11⅜ in. (90.8 x 55.8 x 28.8 cm). Fogg Art Museum, Harvard University, Cambridge, Massachusetts.

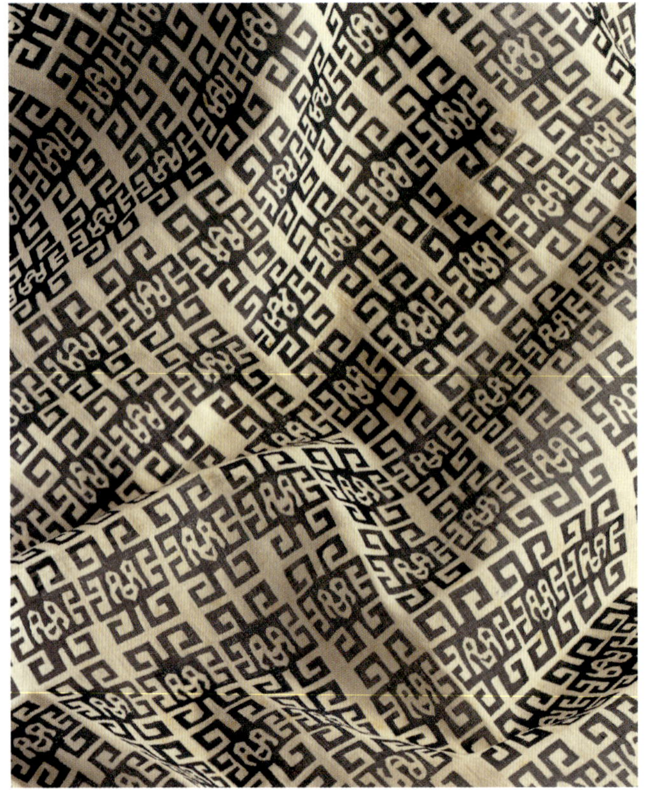

folk art was also part of a concerted effort on the part of the Mexican government to present an image of the country as "timeless" and an appropriately "exotic" venue for both local and foreign tourism.

In Peru the artist, designer, and educator Elena Izcue (1889–1970) played a significant role in disseminating knowledge about ancient art of the Incas and other indigenous groups. Her 1926 book *El Arte peruano en la escuela* was used as an instruction manual in schools throughout the country. It discussed the nation's ancient artistic patrimony and promoted the making of new works of art based on ancient patterns and designs.[33] Izcue, who spent a formative decade in Paris, also became famous for her clothing and textile designs based on patterns observed in ancient textiles that were found in many excavations in both the Andes and the coastal lowlands of Peru.[34] One of Izcue's fabrics (FIG. 8.13), datable to between 1928 and 1936 (her years in Paris), amply demonstrates, through its geometric black-and-white patterns and stylized suggestions of figures, the artist's careful study of Inca cloth patterns and Nazca ceramics employed for use in a modern context, as well as fulfilling the then-current trend for exoticist or primitivist cultural references.

Folk art is often an anonymous production. Nonetheless, many self-taught artists whose names are well known are considered "folk," "intuitive," or (in a more recent denomination) "Outsider" artists. All of these categories comprise terms that are unwieldy and in the end do not offer a satisfactory description for art production done by individuals (or groups) who did not emerge from a school or academy. From the 1920s onward, self-trained or folk art and artists appealed to the Surrealists who praised their ability to "see" and visualize things beyond the realm of empirical observation. I am interested here in posing a question about untutored artists within the realm of both Surrealism and American modernity. What makes a self-taught artist compelling to Surrealists and what, at the same time, sets their work apart from the discourse of modern art and leaves it within a realm of its own, outside of the "flow" of art-historical developments? This question has a large bearing on cultural phenomena in many areas of the western hemisphere during the twentieth century, and in the space remaining in this chapter I would like to point out some of these instances and suggest some paths of thought and possible forms of reconsidering the modernity or radical nature of the art of the intuitives throughout the Americas.

The following concluding remarks take up the theme of the slippage between what is in the vanguard and what constitutes the marginal. In many instances the self-taught artists negotiate both worlds either consciously or through the ways in which their works are written about, collected, and displayed by critics, galleries, museums, and collectors. Since the late 1970s the term "Outsider art" has gained currency. I will not use the term, both because its origins fall outside the chronological strictures of this book, and because it is a designation that constitutes, in itself, a form of marginalization. Nonetheless it should be understood that my position with respect to the art of all of the categories included in the "Outsider art" appellation (untutored artists, institutionalized persons, children, and others) is that their contributions to the process of modernization in the visual experience of the twentieth century were absolutely critical to its progress.

In 1937 Alfred H. Barr Jr. organized a one-artist show of the sculpture of William Edmondson (c.1874–1951) at the Museum of Modern Art.[35] This exhibition, the first accorded at this museum to an African American, was one of the first of several manifestations of Barr's interest in untutored American artists. In 1939 Sidney Janis, the art dealer and Chairman of MoMA's Art Committee, organized a show for the museum entitled *Contemporary Unknown American Painters* that included two works by retired tailor and self-taught painter Morris Hirshfield (1872–1946). Hirshfield was given a solo show at the museum in 1943.[36] Most of the other artists in Janis's 1939 exhibition are now obscure names, with the exception of Anna Mary Robertson Moses (1860–1961), commonly known as Grandma Moses (whose profession was listed in the checklist as "Housewife"), who was represented by three paintings. Grandma Moses is now lionized as one of America's most representative intuitive painters and her works fetch considerable prices at auction.[37] Edmondson's exhibition was of double significance for its acknowledgment of the black artist's accomplishment and for his inclusion within Barr's concept of the evolution of modern art. As Barr stated, "… certain of our self-taught [artists] can hold their own in the company of their best professionally trained compatriots."[38]

Edmondson's career as a sculptor paralleled that of his other positions as a railroad worker and janitor in Nashville, Tennessee, not far from where he was born to formerly enslaved parents. The bulk of his art was religious. He affirmed that he had received a vision from God instructing him to create images of saints, angels, and other sacred beings (along with some secular themes, such as sports figures and a portrait of Eleanor Roosevelt). His work eventually became known far beyond his native city and was recorded in photographs such as that of the artist's sculpture garden outside his studio in Nashville taken by Edward Weston in 1941 (FIG. 8.14). We read the inscription on the sign on the side of the building: "Tomb stones for sale, Garden Adornments, Stone Ware." In the foreground we observe many pieces representing angels, children, the Lamb of God, and other figures done in Edmondson's characteristic bulky, solid manner. He was clearly an artist who realized the commercial potential of his visionary creations (yet he never became wealthy from his sales). Following his death Edmondson's work fell out of view, but there was a revival of interest in the 1980s and 90s. This continues into the present, yet almost completely within the confines of the world of collectors of intuitive arts.[39]

Mardonio Magaña (1865–1947) was the foremost member of what has been termed the Mexican School of sculpture (the counterpart in three-dimensional terms to the Mexican School of painting that included those artists of the 1920s–40s whose work, like that of Rivera, often depicted themes of working-class life and expressed strong social convictions). Magaña's sculptures

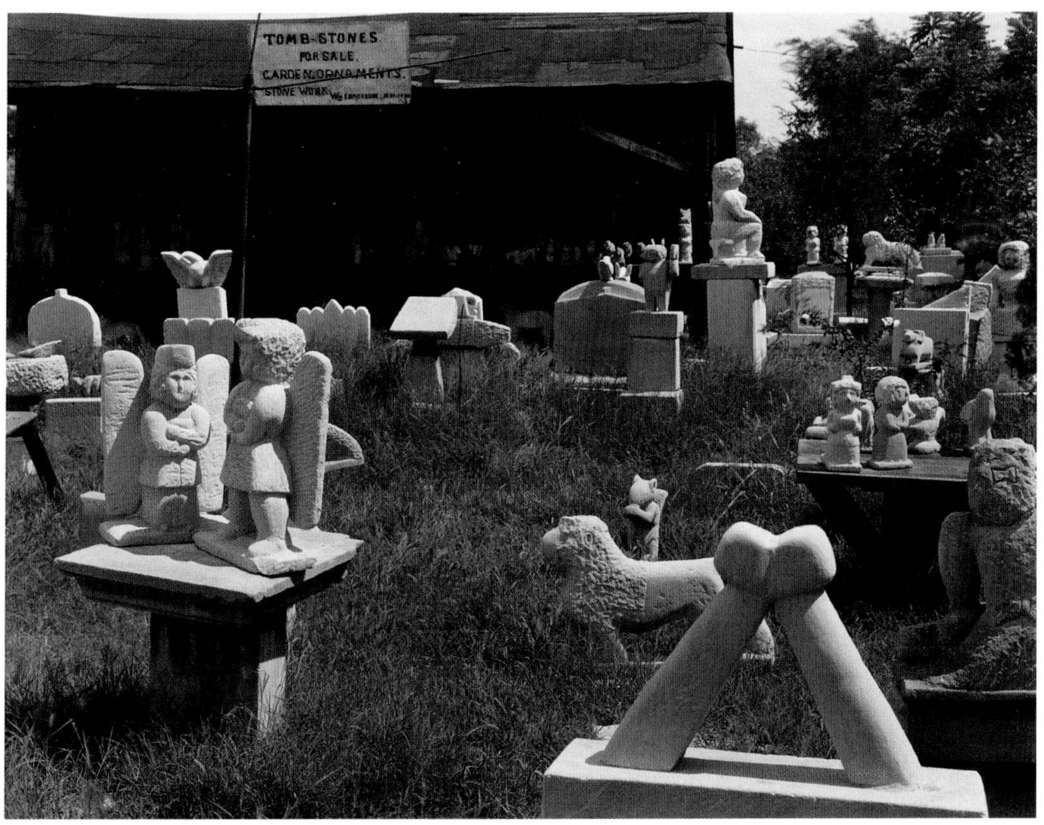

of varying sizes done in wood and stone, pose the same questions that we have considered in the case of Edmondson. Magaña's *Crucifixion* of circa 1930 (FIG. 8.15) epitomizes the strength of the rough-hewn carving that sometimes characterizes his work (other examples, principally those in wood, are elegantly cut with highly polished sophistication)—an almost-medieval feeling that transmits the pain of Christ, his mother Mary, and Mary Magdalen. Yet Magaña, a native of a rural part of the state of Guanajuato whose career developed in Mexico City and who never studied art, was taken up as an example of the innate talent possessed by the modern Mexican artist in the sentiments expressed by Diego Rivera, who "discovered" him and wrote an essay in the journal *Mexican Folkways* in 1930 (at the time he created the piece illustrated here), hailing him as the greatest living Mexican sculptor. In 1948 Rivera reiterated his admiration for the singular talent of Magaña, referring to him as an heir of the national traditions intrinsic to Mexican sculpture since

Fig. 8.14
Edward Weston
William Edmondson's Sculpture, Nashville, Tennessee, 1941, gelatin silver print, 71¼ x 91¼ in. (19.1 x 24.2 cm). Art Institute of Chicago, Gift of Max McGraw, 1959-809.

297

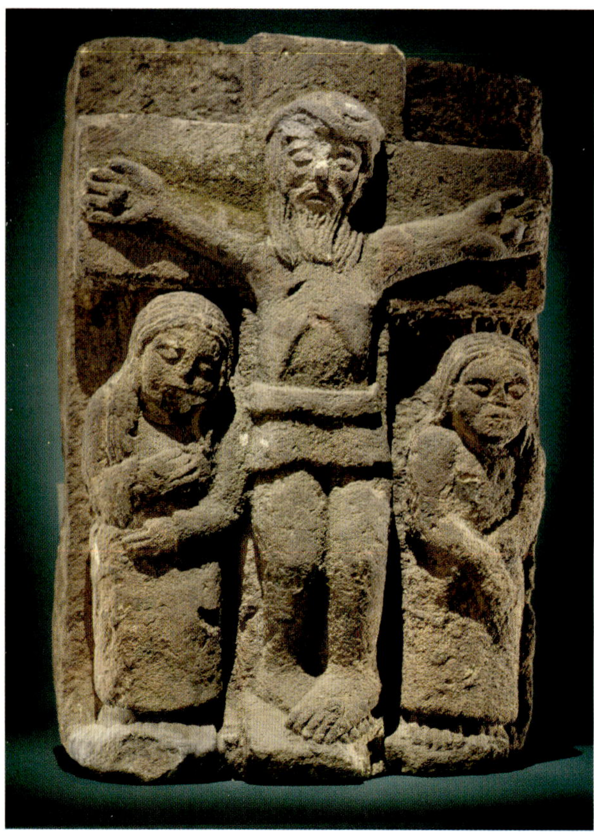

Aztec times.[40] While Magaña's art cannot be called "visionary," it nonetheless possesses the straightforwardness and candor that mark pieces by Edmondson. Its context is different, however, as the story of Mexican modern art differs from that in the United States. While racial and class distinctions were as present and as pernicious in the art world in Mexico as they were in the United States, Magaña was fortunate enough to have been supported by the elite powers from the beginning of his artistic career (Edmondson was only partly successful in this regard).

The final example to which we might turn to complicate the task of situating self-taught artists within the realm of contemporary art movements is taken from a Brazilian context. Agnaldo Manoel dos Santos (1926–1962) was from the state of Bahia and developed his career as a sculptor in the city of Salvador, where he received instruction from the abstract sculptor Mário Cravo Júnior. Agnaldo, as he is popularly known, created the *Man with a Pipe and Hat* (FIG. 8.16) sometime during the 1950s, one of the many wood images of the type for which he is widely known in his native country. While he was not self-taught like the artists discussed above, he absorbed far less from his teacher than from his own study of the traditional wood-carving techniques of Brazil, especially those associated with the nineteenth-century tradition of wood figurehead carvings on ships that plied the waters of the São Francisco, Amazon, and other of the vast networks of rivers in Brazil. The *carrancas*, as these figureheads were known, were derived partly from African inspiration as enslaved persons did many of them, and the memories of African carving types inform the manner of the works that most impressed Agnaldo. Therefore he is clearly associated with the anonymous

298

traditions of the century previous to his own. His work, with its powerful suggestions of iconic forms (his sculptures often possess squat proportions and are carved in dark wood), may also be associated with the beliefs of Candomblé, the syncretistic Afro-Brazilian religion. Agnaldo's art is principally connected to, exhibited, and collected with the context of "Afro-Brazilian art" and is generally seen as representing a high point in that racially segregated category. I will end by stating that all of the artists discussed here represent a confluence of spiritual, visionary, and emotionally engaged sentiments in their work, yet according to the circumstances of their birth, race, and class they are separated in the (shifting) canons of modern art into individual and sometimes frustratingly limited classifications.

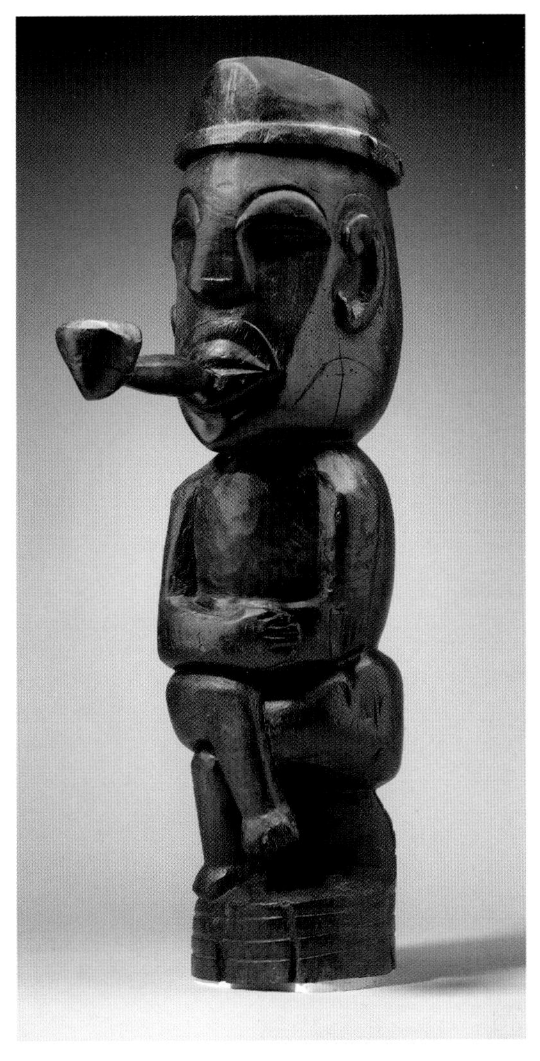

Fig. 8.16
Agnaldo Manoel dos Santos
Man with a Pipe and Hat, 1950s, 32¼ x 7 x 7 in. (82.1 x 17.8 x 17.8 cm). Museum of Fine Arts, Boston. The John Axelrod Collection – Frank B. Bemis Fund and Charles H. Bayley Fund (2011.1844).

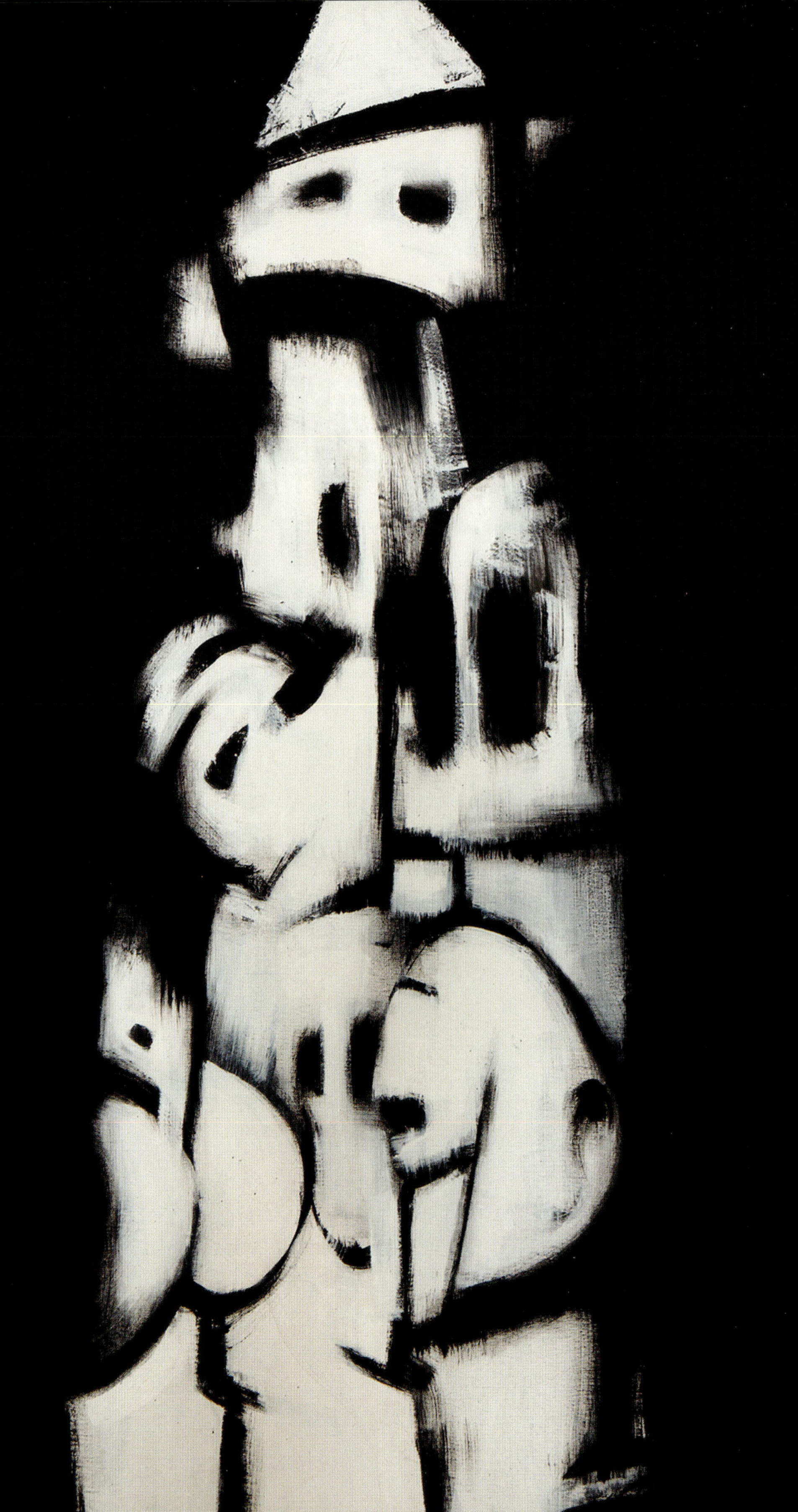

Into the Future

The art discussed in these eight chapters represents a variety of American approaches to ideas and circumstances. The discussions of each "story" are arranged to convey some of the principal points of artistic expression throughout the Americas from the 1910s through the 50s. While social and political events determined a great deal about the aesthetic and psychological atmosphere in which the work was produced, these were not, of course, the only determining factors. In this brief epilogue I wish to suggest merely some ideas of the divergent ways of seeing that artists developed and continued to exploit as the decade of the 1960s—a time of universal turmoil in so many hemispheric societies—proceeded to unfold. I do not by any means wish to suggest in a few pages a panoramic vision of what happened after the time frame that defines this text, yet by means of a handful of images I might suggest a few of the paths that would continue to progress throughout the decade and beyond.

Pop Art and Revolution

In his color lithograph (FIG. 9.1) entitled *Cuba* (1969), Raúl Martínez (1927–1995) celebrates the tenth year of what is called in the island nation the "triumph of the revolution." In January 1959 Fidel Castro's troops overthrew the dictatorship of Fulgencio Batista, the culmination of a struggle that had started in the mid-1950s. This image contains the portraits of Castro, Ernesto (Che) Guevara, and Camilo Cienfuegos, the three principal protagonists in the project that resulted in a wholesale redirection of Cuban society, economy, and political affinities.

Norman Lewis
American Totem, 1960
(detail). See fig. 9.9.

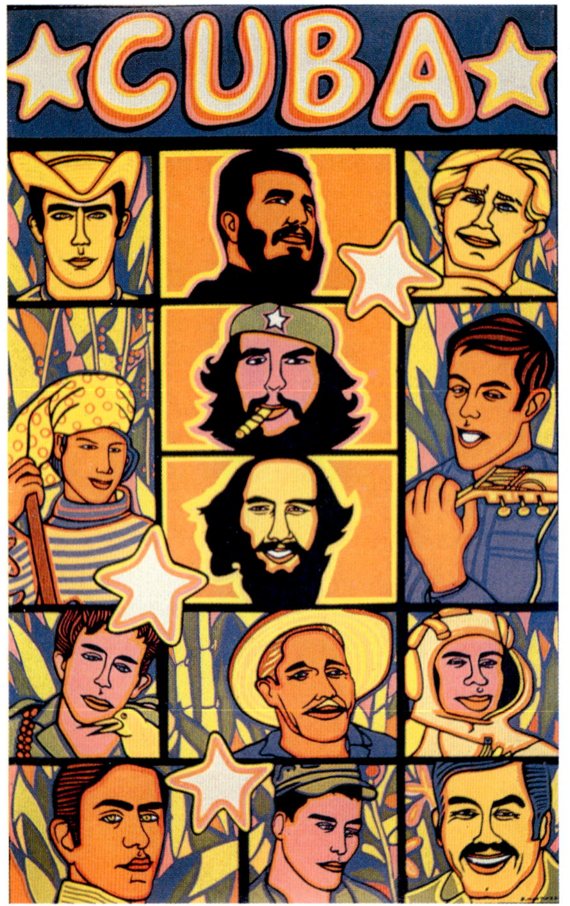

The Cuban Revolution serves as one of the markers of the time frame of this book. It had many consequences for cultures and societies throughout the Americas and served to redirect the sociopolitical priorities of virtually every nation in the hemisphere. It represented for many a victory over capitalist imperialism and, especially, a rebuff of the hegemony of the United States, a nation that had held sway over the economic fortunes not only of Cuba but also of many other countries of the Caribbean, Central America, and beyond. The Cuban Revolution also unleashed a wholesale fear of Communist influence throughout the Americas and obliged the United States to devise many plans to destabilize what it considered an overwhelming threat.

The image itself is what concerns us most here, however. It is an appropriate barometer of a trans-American interest in forms of art that celebrate the appropriation of popular imagery and the adaptation of visual tropes often related to advertising. In the United States the phenomenon of Pop Art is widely considered to be one of the most characteristic forms of visuality of the 1960s. It was developed by artists such as Andy Warhol (1928–1987) and Roy Lichtenstein (1923–1997), among many others, although its roots may also be traced to the experiments in collage and juxtaposition of popular advertising motifs by British artist Richard Hamilton (1922–2011) and his contemporaries, such as Eduardo Paolozzi (1924–2005), in the 1950s.[1] Pop has a long and complex international story that has been explained through reference to simultaneous centers of its production in Asia, Europe, and Latin America as well as the United States. Martínez, an artist who began his career as a practitioner of a vigorous mode of gestural abstraction, turned his attention to Pop's flat colors, repetition of form, and glorification of everyday culture. In a Cuban revolutionary context, "everyday culture" involved political propaganda as an integral component of the visual landscape of the country, especially in the urban centers. Posters and billboards representing compelling images of revolutionary heroes, as well as the urban and rural proletariat, were the mainstays of what every Cuban would see during her or his daily routine. We should also stress the fact that in Cuban Pop, as in the manifestations of this mode of two- and three-dimensional art that developed throughout the Americas during the 1960s, particular attention was paid to politically oriented imagery.[2] In Brazilian, Argentinean, or Colombian Pop or Pop-related art, a social message was either paramount in the meaning of the artwork, or existed just below its surface appearance.[3] Far from being a means of distancing themselves from the ideological content of art of previous decades, as might be the case with images created by some U.S. Pop artists, many of those in Latin America placed their political and social views front and center.

Coca-Cola 3 of 1962 by Andy Warhol (FIG. 9.2) represents the quintessential subject matter of North American Pop Art.[4] An icon of everyday commercialism, the image of this popular soft drink was repeated by Warhol in numerous prints and paintings in configurations that, most often, represented the artist's fascination with seriality and repetition—a facet of aesthetic expression that finds its corollary in such other arts as music, as in the compositions of Philip Glass (b.1937), for example. Andy Warhol created of himself an exemplar of the artist as celebrity and the artist as commodity. His fame, and his personal

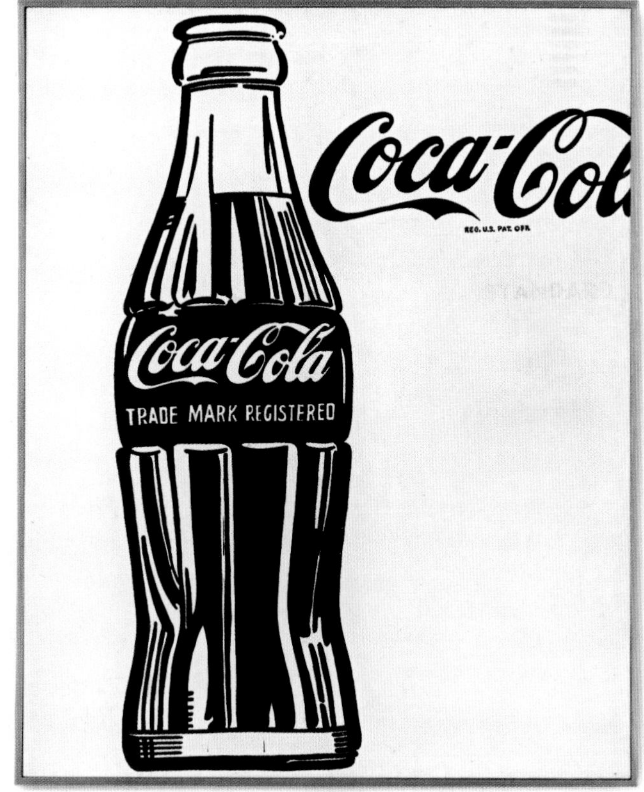

and artistic impact on art throughout the world (and especially the Americas), was affirmed by images of the artist as subject in the work of painters and sculptors in the 1960s and beyond. The Venezuelan sculptor Marisol Escobar (called 'Marisol') (1930– 2016) was born in France and spent much of her career in New York, yet her art—especially her large-scale wood carvings—had roots in her interest in Latin American colonial statuary as well as in the many forms of contemporary visualities that she had absorbed in the United States. Her 1962–63 wood sculpture (with graphite, oil, and plaster) *Andy* (FIG. 9.3) monumentalizes the figure of Warhol, a close friend of the artist, celebrating his fame and, at the same time, encasing him in a sculptural form that echoes the laconic nature of his well-known personality, characterized by terse verbal expression.[5]

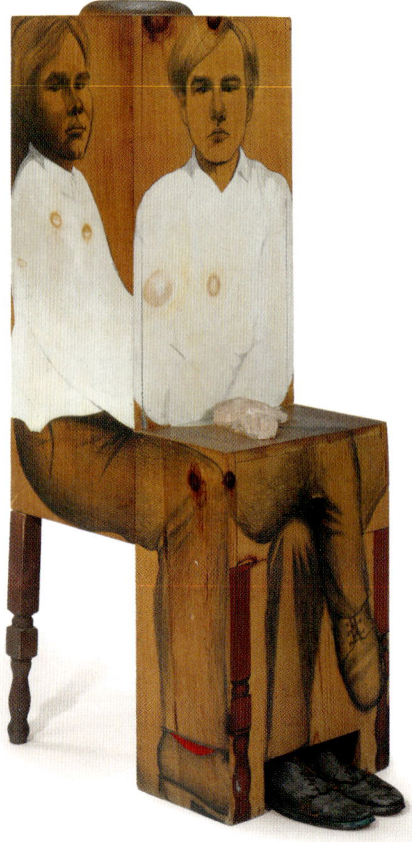

The use of found materials characterized many phases of twentieth-century art following Marcel Duchamp's exaltation of such mundane objects as urinals, snow shovels, and bicycle wheels; his radically subversive Dada-related sculptures formed the ultimate basis of Conceptualism and other forms of expression in the later phases of the century. The Colombian artist Beatriz González (b.1938) earned a reputation for (among many other forms of painting and prints) installations that included cheap metal or wood furniture that she purchased in the markets of Bogotá. She then repurposed these with painted images in order to erase all references to their original use (while still preserving the integrity of the objects themselves).[6] On the other hand, these pieces made allusions to either sacred iconography or celebrated historical moments in her nation's political trajectory in order to juxtapose them ironically with the banality of the support on which they were depicted. González's 1971 *Gratia plena* (FIG. 9.4) employs a dressing table and chair. In the place where the mirror would normally appear she painted (in flat

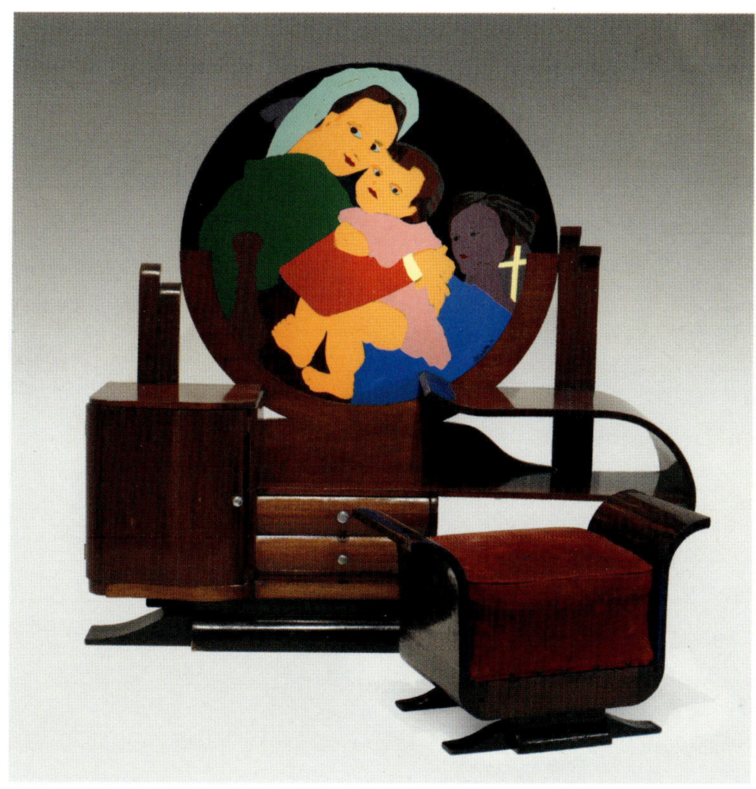

primary colors with enamel paint on a round sheet of metal) an appropriated version of Raphael's famous *Madonna della sedia* (Madonna of the Chair) of 1513–14, an ironic secularization of a well-known religious painting in the context of a mundane household accouterment associated with personal vanity. This work has various levels of meaning and artistic reference. González was one of Colombia's foremost practitioners, during the 1960s and 70s, of a Pop visual vocabulary. With her use of found (or, in this case, purchased) objects, she referenced the Dadaist past and the future of installation art. This composition, in addition, is self-referential. The artist is a distinguished art historian and art critic with a long trajectory in the art and art-history departments of major universities in Colombia (Universidad de los Andes), and former curator of the art and historical collections at the National Museum.

Current events, catastrophes, politics, scientific investigation, and art history are all components in the cacophonous composition of *Skyway* (1964) by Robert Rauschenberg (1925–2008)

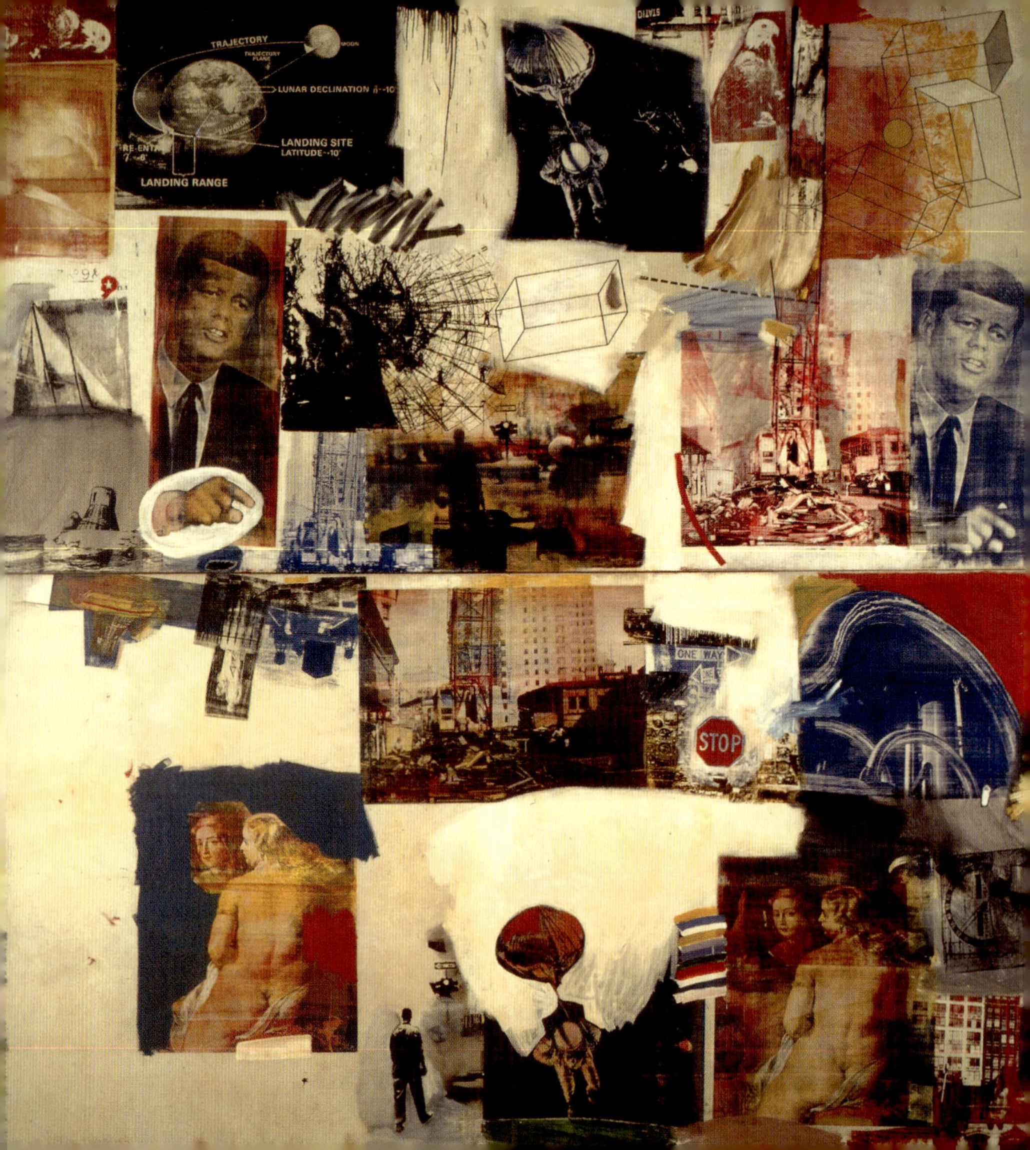

TRAJECTORY
TRAJECTORY PLANE
MOON
LUNAR DECLINATION
LANDING SITE
LATITUDE
RE-ENTRY
LANDING RANGE
ONE WAY
STOP

(FIG. 9.5), an oil and silkscreen on canvas that testifies to the ironic, sometimes jarring, and always intensely provocative imagination of this American artist. The composite nature of this work of the 1960s grows out of his earlier experiments with found objects, often affixed to a support that was itself a "throwaway" item. His complex three-dimensional assemblages known as "combines," begun in the 1950s (including painting, sculpture, and things retrieved from street trash), were revolutionary for their seemingly chaotic concatenations of unexpected things in surprising juxtapositions. This sense of freedom, to pick and choose images and objects from any time period, or from the throwaway culture of mid-century America, grew out of Rauschenberg's deep involvement with a wide variety of artistic manifestations—from performance (dance, music) to painting, photography, and assemblage.[7]

While *Skyway* is a two-dimensional image (with its montage of photographs of John F. Kennedy—assassinated three years before—views of urban destruction, and multiple repetitions of Peter Paul Rubens's *Venus Before the Mirror* of 1614–15, reminding us of González's appropriation of the painting by Raphael), it possesses all of the suggestions of multiplicity of space and time observed in his more ambitious three-dimensional pieces. *Skyway* was also created in the same year that Rauschenberg won the Grand Prize for Painting at the 32nd Venice Biennale, causing a sensation in both positive and negative terms. It was considered by many to be a verification of the hegemony of Pop on the international scene, as well as an indication of the ascendancy of American art within a European setting.

Art for All

Only two years after Rauschenberg won his prize at Venice, the Argentinean kinetic and installation artist Julio Le Parc (b.1928) earned the same accolade at the 33rd Biennale for works that were dramatically different from the Pop imagery of his U.S. contemporary. Le Parc's early formation took place in Buenos Aires (although he is a native of Mendoza). He moved to Paris in 1958 and from then on his aesthetic credo centered on the significance of art as a collective enterprise. In 1960 he participated in the founding of an artists' collective known as GRAV

(Groupe de Recherche d'Art Visuel), which included five other artists from both sides of the Atlantic. As Estrellita B. Brodsky, who has examined the impact of Le Parc's work in both an American and a French context, writes,

Le Parc's fundamental notions of art as a participatory act and means of empowering the viewer was well established during his formative years in Argentina, before he moved to Paris. ... [C]ritics have commended his collaborative endeavors and his use of light and ludic elements [yet] they have tended to disregard the provocative social and political aspects of his art.[8]

Le Parc, and other members of GRAV, created works of art that demanded the participation of their audiences, whether on the street or in a museum or gallery setting. The idea of art as something to reconfigure and transform the body became a major issue in the 1960s as artists throughout the Western world responded to the interest in phenomenology and experiential engagement with both traditional and nonconformist materials and substances as the bases for artworks.

Le Parc's *Continuel-lumière mobile* (1960–66) (FIG. 9.6) is a mobile comprised of hanging elements that shimmer, turn, and reflect on each other in a dark space illuminated by spotlights. Every viewer perceives the work in a different way; the beholders' perceptions change constantly as the metallic disks, rectangles, and elliptical shapes turn and literally dance in space. This work is characteristic of Le Parc's desire to engage the senses and create an atmosphere that goes well beyond the conventional art-viewing experience in the white cube gallery. This piece is not meant to be viewed by an isolated individual, but rather by ever-changing groups of visitors to the place where it is exhibited. The idea of "group experience," which, in the mind of the artist, has the effect of galvanizing the participants in a visual drama, is central to Le Parc's aesthetic. It is also important to remember that his many works of a participatory nature were developed and elaborated during the 1960s and evidence a growing sense of communal spirit within cultural circles on both sides of the Atlantic. The notion of group perception as a way of organizing what would otherwise be chaotic movement is behind the creation of these pieces.

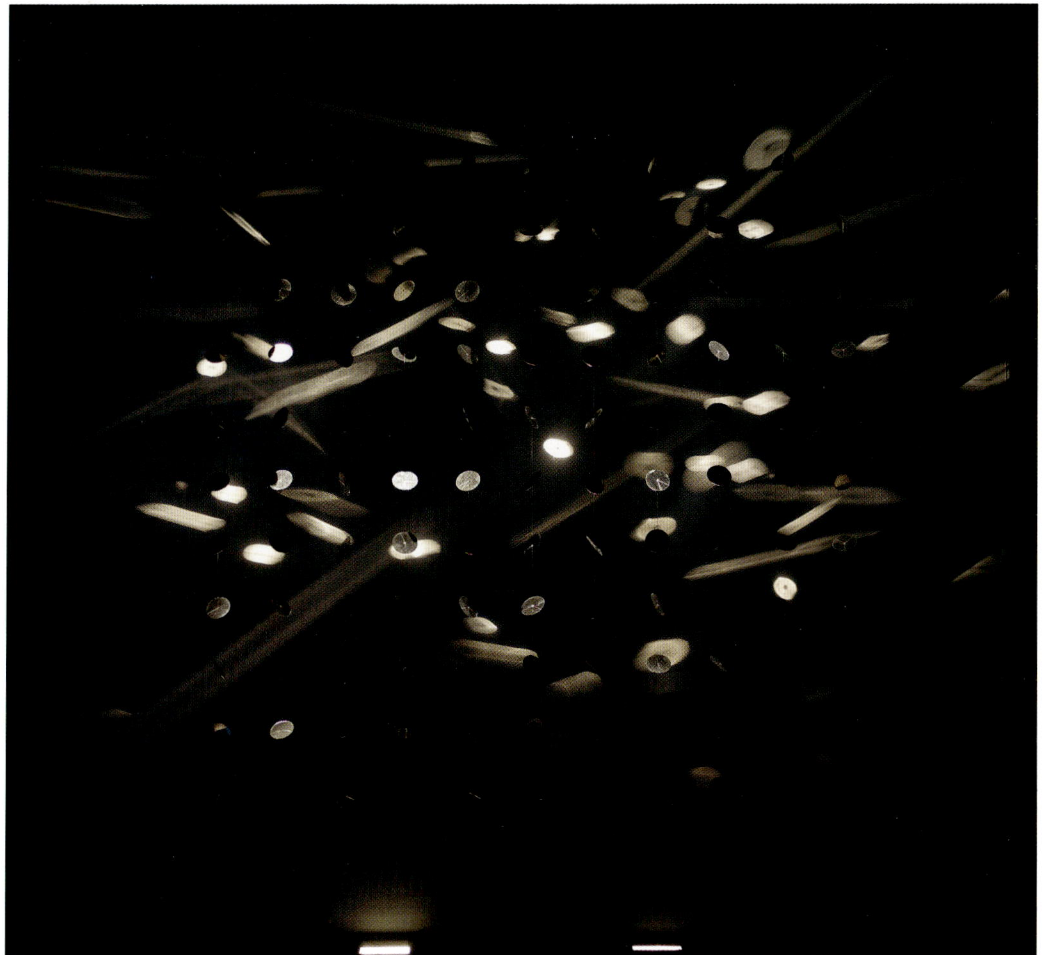

Fig. 9.6
Julio Le Parc
Continuel-lumière mobile, 1960-66, light piece, dimensions variable. Museum of Fine Arts, Houston.

Artistic projects such as these became politically more poignant as the 1960s progressed on its long march to greater social activism in the face of trauma and turmoil represented by such events as the student uprising in France in May 1968 and in Mexico City several months later, or the international mass demonstrations against the Vietnam War. Their creation during a period that witnessed the worldwide development of many movements of resistance to the status quo or opposition to repressive political movements adds a weight of additional meaning to the art of Le Parc and the many other artists throughout the Americas (as well as in Europe and Asia) who became increasingly conscious of art as a collective experience. The work produced at this time, in this vein, always has a strong underlying political ramification, whether it be related to a specific movement (such as the work created in many South American countries during a decade that witnessed the rise of military dictatorships) or, as in the case of Le Parc, a more ethereal statement of popular engagement within a common cause of perception that extends the awareness of the participants to realms that transcend the depredations of political or social oppression.

Environments and Total Participation

In 1969 the German-born Venezuelan artist Gertrud Goldschmidt, known as Gego (1912–1994), astonished audiences in both Caracas and New York with the installation of her room-filling web of wires and metal tubes woven together in an intricate net. Audiences gathered in the Venezuelan capital's Museo de Bellas Artes and New York's Center for Inter-American Relations (now called the Americas Society), the two venues where *Reticulárea* (FIG. 9.7) was first displayed. The word is derived from the Spanish for "net" and refers to a complex web of wires and filaments joined together to create an all-enveloping environment.

Audiences were drawn into the vortex of the *Reticulárea*'s movement, shadows, and light plays created on the walls of the gallery by the light and constantly, subtly moving elements of this monumental installation. Even more than in the case of Le Parc, the viewers became accomplices in energizing the work. *Reticulárea* was the opposite of a static work; it became a complete whole only when the viewers became complicit in its physicality and created the effects of bodily intervention with the movements of the piece's components. Art historian Mónica Amor has affirmed, "The *Reticulárea* rehearsed a paradigm of artistic production that, in its refusal of the conventions of sculpture (mass, volume, surface), made lines and space the means for a critique of architectural enclosure and sculptural monumentality."[9] Although many such works from this period in the twentieth-century story of participatory and bodily oriented art are no longer displayed in their proper condition (they are often shown as art-historical relics with which the public cannot interact), the memory of the original purpose lingers within the aura of such works' afterlives, creating in our imaginations reminiscences of a specific time and place.

Fig. 9.7
Gego (Gertrud Goldschmidt) *Reticulárea*, 1969, stainless-steel wire, variable measurements. Photo by Paolo Gasparini showing participants at the Museo de Bellas Artes, Caracas, 1969. Fundación de Museos Nacionales, Caracas, Venezuela. © Fundación Gego.

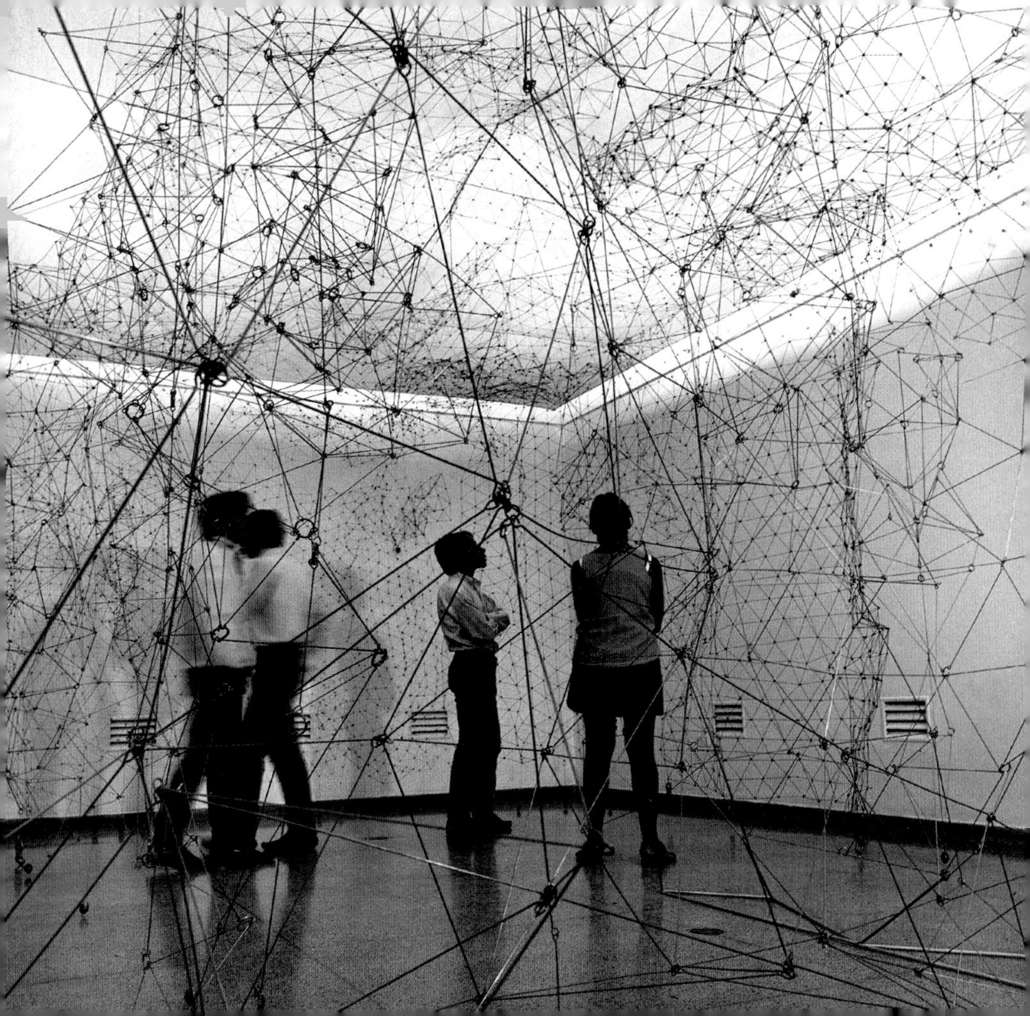

Art and Terror

If Gego's *Reticulárea* or Le Parc's *Continuel-lumière* captivate us with their sensual networks of forms, shapes, and shadows, many of the more directly politically oriented works by hemispheric artists living daily in what I could describe as Zones of Terror in the 1960s era of military repression (Brazil, Argentina, Uruguay, Paraguay, and, later, Chile) appeal not for their conventional beauty but for the visceral impact of their forms and messages. Portuguese-born Brazilian conceptualist Artur Barrio (b.1945) is one of the most notable cases of artists who purposefully abandoned both the modes of conventional art practice and the circuit of promotion and display of art to formulate, in often abject and sometimes visually disturbing pieces, direct action statements against the fear and aura of authoritarianism that became the daily norm in Brazil between 1964 and 1985.[10]

In the late 1960s and early 70s Barrio embarked on a series of street interventions in Brazilian cities such as Rio and Belo Horizonte that proved to be among the most powerful of the long history of conceptual art-making in the Southern Cone at this point. The overall name for his project was *Situações* (Situations). Among the most notorious manifestations of his noncommercial, non-site-specific creations were the *trouxas*, or bloody bundles. These would represent a combination of objects that could range from household garbage to cast-off clothing, animal skin, bones, and teeth, or any other such wretched substances, all tied up in rags that were often soaked with animal blood and left surreptitiously on street corners or in public parks to provoke fear and anxiety among the passersby, who would sometimes look in fascination or confusion at the bundles, or quickly pass them by lest they be terrorist devices of an unknown sort.

Many photographs of Barrio's *Situações* (FIG. 9.8) display the anxiety on the faces of those who encountered them in random configurations. The photographer was often Barrio himself. He would mingle with the crowd gathered around the unknown objects, secretly photographing them and their observers—an act that he considered an integral part of the creative process. These *trouxas*, powerful metaphors for the wretched and fear-inducing quality of much of daily life in military-dominated Brazil, were sometimes left to rot in situ, or were simply disposed of by

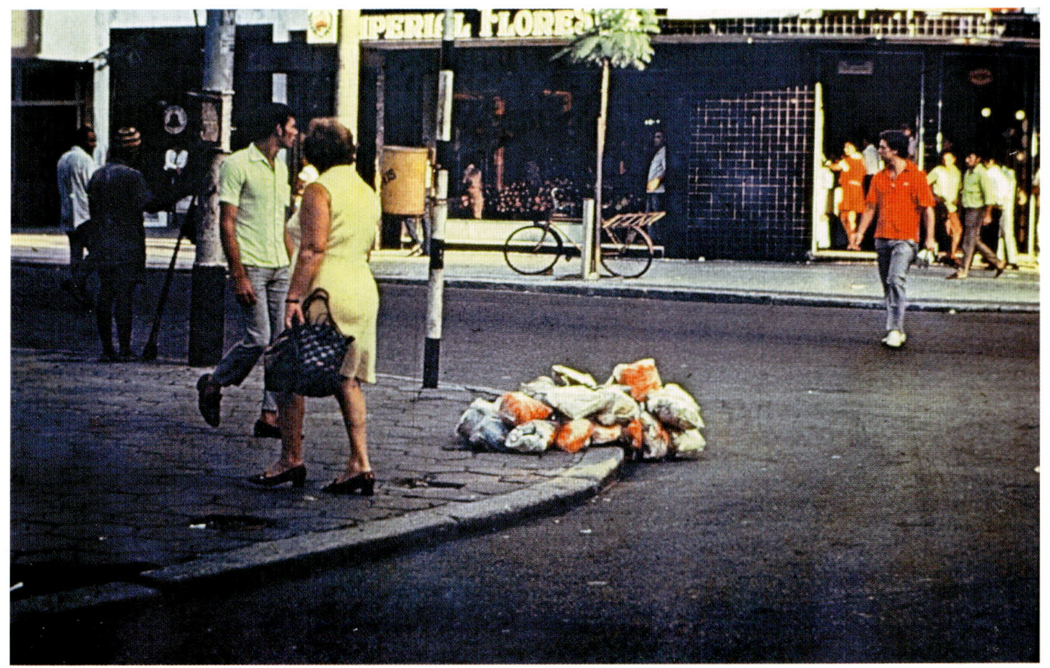

the municipal waste-removal squads. The artist had no intention of preserving any of them, as their decomposition was an essential characteristic of their creation.

Our last stop on this retrospective pathway into the future—beyond the confines of the rest of this book—brings us once again before a distinguished African-American artist, Norman Lewis (1909–1979). Lewis played a crucial role in the development of abstract art. His training and the progress of his career took place principally in New York where, in the early 1960s, he was a leading member of a short-lived but influential group of African-American artists who made up the membership of the Spiral Gallery, founded in Manhattan's Greenwich Village in 1963 and whose membership included (among others) Romare Bearden and Hale Woodruff (both discussed in Chapter 3).[11]

Our last image takes on poignant as well as premonitory connotations for the realities that the readers of this book will have experienced in the sociopolitical realm as dominating many aspects of our own lives in the late 2010s. *American Totem* (FIG. 9.9) returns us, albeit through a single, ghostly, shrouded figure, to the traumatic landscape of racial and religious prejudice, segregation, and bigotry. This and a series of related works from the

Fig. 9.8
Artur Barrio
Photograph of his
DEFL Situação +S+ Ruas,
April 1970. Rio de
Janeiro.

313

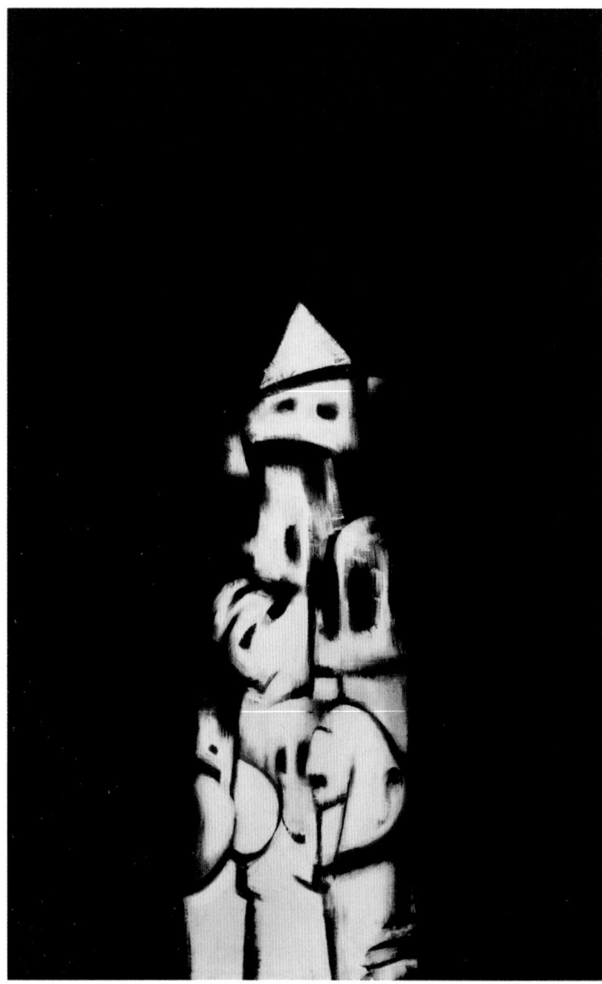

early 1960s represents an important example of Lewis's return to the figure and a reaffirmation of his constant (although often veiled) anxiety caused by the difficulties and societal hurdles presented to the African-American population of the United States, and, by extension, to all inhabitants of color throughout the Americas.[12] Against a black background a composite creature of stark white, whose form is made up of many facets and many positive and negative shapes, stands as a looming presence before us. The salient feature of this man's figure is the conical shape on his head and the white hood or mask that covers his face, allowing us to see only the holes through which his eyes are observing us, the viewers—an unmistakable reference to the sinister menace of the Ku Klux Klan (whose nefarious activities were discussed in Chapter 5).

This threatening presence was painted (along with other related pictures by Lewis in the early 1960s) at a moment in U.S. history when lynching still represented a specter of horror for black people. While the last "officially recorded" lynching happened in 1968, this abhorrent form of racially motivated torture and death almost certainly continued covertly for years beyond that time. The ominous, threatening manifestation of the nemesis of the imagination of Norman Lewis and of all people of black skin, the oppressor, is embodied in this image. Painted in the years preceding the signing of the Civil Rights Act by President Lyndon Johnson in 1964 and the murder of civil rights leader Dr. Martin Luther King Jr. on April 4, 1968, *American Totem* brings us back to collective memories of the era of the 1965 Freedom March from

Fig. 9.9
Norman Lewis
American Totem, 1960,
oil on canvas, 74 x 45
in. (188 x 114.3 cm).
© Estate of Norman
W. Lewis. Courtesy
of Michael Rosenfeld
Gallery LLC, New York.

Selma to Montgomery, Alabama, the Freedom Rides in the early 1960s throughout the American South, the years of struggle for a place at the front of the bus in virulently segregated societies, to the Watts riots in Los Angeles of August 1965, provoked by the (likely unlawful) arrest of a black motorist by a white California Highway Patrolman, as well as all of the other hundreds of events redolent of trauma and anxiety that have played themselves out in the first two decades of the twenty-first century. The more recent iteration of protest against inequality, the Black Lives Matter movement, has made many positive strides, yet, at the same time, it has been minimized and its adherents psychologically emasculated by a generation of officials claiming authority in the political and social spheres.

Lewis's image stands as an artistic evocation of historical realities and a prefiguration of their future permutations. Yet it is a picture of clear resistance that speaks not only to one sector of society but also to all inhabitants of the hemisphere who must still confront their own "totems" of violence, forced migration, ridicule, prejudice, rejection, and blind dismissal by segments of societies everywhere who lay their own claims to "ownership" and the "right" to govern at the expense of so many of their fellow humans.

Endnotes

Chapter 1

1 I am grateful to Susan L. Aberth for discussing this imagery with me. Email correspondence with the author, July 15, 2016.

2 Álvaro Medina, *Procesos del arte en Colombia. Tomo I (1810–1930)* (Bogotá: Universidad de los Andes, 2014), p. 381.

3 Marta Traba, *Art of Latin America, 1900 to 1980* (Washington, D.C.: Inter-American Development Bank, 1994), p. 6.

4 For Andrés de Santa María see Eduardo Serrano, *Andrés de Santa María* (Bogotá: Museo de Arte Moderno, 1988) and the recent writings of Halim Badawi including his essay "La vida secreta del paisaje: Andrés de Santa María, la Hacienda El Vínculo, la propiedad de la tierra y los inicios de la pintura de paisaje en Colombia," in Subgerencia Cultural. *Decir el lugar: Testimonios del paisaje colombiano* (Bogotá: Banco de la República, 2017) pp. 115-131.

5 For literary contexts see Vicky Unruh, *Latin American Vanguards. The Art of Contentious Encounters* (Berkeley and Los Angeles: University of California Press, 1994).

6 See the essays on Mexican Symbolism by Roxana Velásquez Martínez del Campo and Fausto Ramírez in the exhibition catalogue *El espejo simbolista. Europa y México, 1870–1920* (Mexico City: Museo Nacional de Arte, 2005).

7 See Rivera's introduction to Frances Toor (ed.), *Monografía: Las obras de José Guadalupe Posada, grabador mexicano* (Mexico City: Mexican Folkways, 1930).

8 Jean Charlot, "José Guadalupe Posada. Printmaker to the Mexican People," *An Artist on Art* (Honolulu: University Press of Hawaii, 1972), pp. 162–173. Originally printed in *The Magazine of Art*, 1945.

9 Ramón Favela, *El joven e inquieto Diego María Rivera (1907–1910)* (Mexico City: Editorial Secuencia, 1991).

10 Georges Rodenbach, *Bruges-La-Morte* (Paris: Librairie Marpon & Flammarion, 1901). See the modern edition with commentary published by Actes Sud/Labor, Brussels, 1986.

11 *Modernidad y modernización en el arte Mexicano 1920–1960*, exhibition catalogue (Mexico City: Museo Nacional de Arte, 1991), p. 108.

12 Rubén Gallo has studied the impact of Freud in *Freud's Mexico. Into the Wilds of Psychoanalysis* (Cambridge, MA, and London: MIT Press, 2010).

13 *La Raza cósmica* was first published in Mexico in 1925. (See English translation published in 1997, Baltimore: Johns Hopkins University Press). It is a complex and dense tract that proposes a number of theories of race that to many of today's readers seem questionable. One of the principal messages of this book is the importance of racial blending, or *mestizaje*, as the chief component of the fully developed modern Mexican citizen who can trace her/his lineage to a combination of white Spanish and indigenous backgrounds. Vasconcelos was important for, among many other reasons, his position as first Secretary of Public Education in post-revolutionary Mexico and, arguably, as the mastermind of the modern Mexican mural movement.

14 See the commentary on this painting by Fausto Ramírez in *Mexican Modern Painting from the Andrés Blaisten Collection* (Mexico City: Universidad Nacional Autónoma de México, 2011), p. 40.

15 On representations of homoerotic figures in Latin American art of the nineteenth and early twentieth centuries see Rudi Bleys, *Images of Ambiente: Homotextuality and Latin American Art, 1810 to Today* (London and New York: Continuum, 2000), pp. 37–53, and Adolfo Mantilla Osornio, "Una Genealogía del cuerpo masculino en el arte mexicano," in the exhibition catalogue *El hombre desnudo. Dimensiones de la masculinidad a partir de 1800* (Mexico City: Museo Nacional de Arte, 2014), pp. 45–55.

16 Andrew Wilton and Tim Barringer, *American Sublime. Landscape Painting in the United States 1820–1880* (Princeton: Princeton University Press, 2002). On Inness see Rachel Ziady DeLue, *George Inness and the Science of Landscape* (Chicago: University of Chicago Press, 2004).

17 Charles C. Eldredge, *American Imagination and Symbolist Painting* (New York: Grey Art Gallery and Study Center, 1979).

18 Annie Besant and C. W. Leadbeater, *Thought-Forms* (London: Theosophical Society, 1925). I am grateful to Susan Aberth for discussing the significance of this volume on American art in the early twentieth century. The most recent edition is the 2014 publication (Createspace Independent Publishing Platform).

19 Michael Duncan, "American Surrealism Outside of New York: Membership Open," in Isabelle Dervaux (ed.), *Surrealism USA* (New York: National Academy Museum, 2005), p. 38.

20 Alfred H. Barr, *Fantastic Art, Dada, Surrealism* (New York: Museum of Modern Art, 1936), pp. 213, 252.

21 See Michael Zakian, *Agnes Pelton, Poet of Nature* (Palm Springs: Palm Springs Desert Museum, 1995), pp. 23–26.

22 Ana Maria Belluzzo, "Trans-positions," in *XXIV Bienal de São Paulo: Núcleo Histórico: Antropofagia e Historias de Canibalismos* (São Paulo: Bienal de São Paulo, 1998), p. 78. For a larger discussion of the cultural ramifications of cannibalism see Thomas B. F. Cummins, "To Serve Man: Pre-Columbian Art, Western Discourses of Idolatry and Cannibalism," *Res*, 42 (Autumn 2002), pp. 109–130.

23 The manifesto was first published in the *Revista de Antropofagia*, São Paulo, no. 1, May, 1928. For the English-language version see Dawn Ades, *Art in Latin America. The Modern Era, 1820–1980* (London and New Haven: Yale University Press, 1989), pp. 312–313.

24 Emilio Pettoruti, *Un pintor ante el espejo* (Buenos Aires: Librería Histórica, 2004), p. 100.

25 Patricia M. Artundo, "With the Eyes of the Spirit: Borges Imagines Xul Solar," in *Xul Solar and Jorge Luis Borges. The Art of Friendship* (New York: Americas Society, 2013), pp. 46–47. Borges spoke of Xul and Blake in one of the Norton Lectures he delivered at Harvard University on March 20, 1968.

26 The most complete account and analysis of Tarsila's life and work is Aracy Amaral, *Tarsila. Sua obra e seu tempo* (São Paulo: Editora da Universidade de São Paulo/EDUSP, 2003). For a succinct English-language résumé of Amaral's career see Fatima Bercht, "Tarsila do Amaral," in Rasmussen (ed.), *Latin American Artists*, pp. 52–59.

27 Mário de Andrade, *Macunaíma* (English-language translation) (New York: Random House, 1984).

28 These debates on "exoticism" in the criticism of Latin American art are well represented in the essays comprising the anthology edited by Gerardo Mosquera, *Beyond the Fantastic: Contemporary Art Criticism from Latin America* (Cambridge, MA: MIT Press, 1996).

Chapter 2

1   See Peter John Brownlee, Valéria Piccoli, and Georgiana Uhlyarik (eds.), *Picturing the Americas. Landscape Painting from Tierra del Fuego to the Arctic* (Toronto: Art Gallery of Ontario, 2015).

2   Joseph R. Hartman, *Modern Dreams. Building Machado's Cuba, 1925–1933*, PhD dissertation, Dallas: Southern Methodist University, 2016, chapter 3.

3   For Blanes Viale's working methods during the six months he spent at the Iguazú Falls see Joana Sureda Trujillo, *El pintor P. Blanes Viale* (Palma de Mallorca: El Tall Editorial, 1992), pp. 62–67.

4   An English-language version appears in the anthology *Looking North. Writings from Spanish America on the U.S., 1800 to the Present*, ed. John J. Hassett and Braulio Muñoz (Tucson: University of Arizona Press, 2012), pp. 21–29.

5   Ibid., pp. 227–229. For the original Spanish see Rubén Darío, *Obra poética* (Madrid: Fundación José Antonio de Castro, 2011), pp. 420–421.

6   Ilene Susan Fort, *The Flag Paintings of Childe Hassam* (Los Angeles and New York: Los Angeles County Museum of Art and Harry N. Abrams, 1988).

7   Theodore Roosevelt, *Fear God and Take Your Own Part* (New York: George H. Duran Co., 1916), is a lengthy rumination on freedom and American exceptionalism. In it Roosevelt refers directly to the Mexican Revolution and specifically to the "outrage" of the incursion by Pancho Villa into American territory earlier in 1916 at Columbus, New Mexico (see text above). Roosevelt stresses American sovereignty and, by extension, the need for American intervention in the current war in Europe.

8   Roberta Cozzalino, Anne Claussan Knutson, and David M. Lubin (eds.), *World War I and American Art* (Philadelphia: Pennsylvania Academy of the Fine Arts, 2016).

9   Discussions of Collivadino's working methods and his views of urban Buenos Aires are found in Laura Malosetti Costa, *Collivadino* (Buenos Aires: Editorial Ateneo, 2006), chapter 5, pp. 101–119. Collivadino's career was influenced by his 1890–98 trip to Rome and Venice, where he was immersed in a classical mode of art instruction and production. He became a decorative (mural) painter and a theater set designer, as well as a realistic portrayer of the urban scene in the Argentine capital. He was, after the first decade of the twentieth century, a member of the Nexus group, artists whose work was directly concerned with nationalist values. For a variety of texts analyzing the cultural and social phenomena of the "modernizing" Argentine capital in the early twentieth century see Margarita Gutman and Thomas Reese (eds.), *Buenos Aires 1910. El imaginario para una gran capital* (Buenos Aires: Editorial Universitario de Buenos Aires, 1999).

10 The *Semana Trágica* involved anarchist activity and protest against British companies and factories in La Boca and elsewhere in the city. For a discussion of Collivadino's images of the new urban fabric of the Argentine capital see the exhibition catalogue *Collivadino. Buenos Aires en construcción* (Buenos Aires: Museo Nacional de Bellas Artes, 2013).

11 Angel Kalenberg, *Arte uruguayo y otros* (Montevideo: Edición Galería Latina, 1990), p. 103. See also Raquel Pereda, *José Cuneo. Retrato de un artista* (Montevideo: Edición Galería Latina, 1982), pp. 65–67.

12 Raquel Pereda, *José Cuneo. Correspondencia entre artistas y amigos* (Montevideo: Gráfica Mosca, 2012), pp. 91–92.

13 Gabriel Peluffo Linari, "José Cúneo [sic] Perinetti. The Stream 1914," in Brownlee et al., *Picturing the Americas*, p. 206.

14 José Hernández, *The Gaucho Martín Fierro* (Albany: State University of New York Press, 1967).

15 Domingo Faustino Sarmiento, *Facundo. Civilization and Barbarism* (intro. by Ilan Stavans) (New York: Penguin Books, 1998).

16 See, for example, Wanda M. Corn, *The Great American Thing. Modern Art and National Identity, 1915–1935* (Berkeley: University of California Press, 1999), especially chapter 1. Celeste O'Connor, *Democratic Visions. Art and theory of the Stieglitz Circle, 1924–1934* (Berkeley: University of California Press, 2001), and Heather Hole, *Marsden Hartley and the West. The Search for an American Modernism* (New Haven and London: Yale University Press, 2007).

17 Artists had begun traveling to Taos and other places in the region as early as the 1890s, and the roots of what became known as the Taos School of painters started then. Its earlier members, such as Ernest L. Blumenschein (1874–1960), did romantically realistic pictures of Native Americans and sun-drenched landscapes, while later artists who gravitated to the region, such as Hartley, Georgia O'Keeffe, or John Marin (1870–1953), adapted modernist techniques of semi-abstraction and fracturing of space in their art.

18 Hole, *Marsden Hartley and the West*, p. 101.

19 Donna Cassidy, Randall Griffey, and Elizabeth Finch, *Marsden Hartley's Maine* (New York: Metropolitan Museum of Art, 2017).

20 Suzan Campbell, *In the Shadow of the Sun: The Life and Art of Rebecca Salisbury James*, PhD dissertation, Albuquerque: University of New Mexico, 2002.

21 The Spanish Colonial Arts Society's museum was founded in 1930, and the Harwood Museum in 1923 by the collectors Burt and Elizabeth Harwood, whose efforts were supported by Mabel Dodge Luhan. These institutions were influential for the spread of knowledge of the distinctive forms of New Mexican colonial furniture, painting, tin and wood sculpture, and other types of art that became popular with transplanted residents to the area and throughout the western part of the United States in the 1920s and 30s as a regional manifestation part of a nationwide colonial revival in art and architecture.

22 The other members were Franklin Carmichael (1890–1945), A. Y. Jackson (1882–1974), Frank Johnston (1888–1949), Arthur Lismer (1885–1969), J. E. H. MacDonald (1873–1932), and Frederick Varley (1881–1969).

23 Ann Davis, *The Logic of Ecstasy. Canadian Mystical Painting 1920–1940* (London, Ontario: London Regional Art and Historical Museums, 1990).

24 Joseph R. Wolin, "Introduction," in Andrew Hunter, *Lawren Stewart Harris. A Painter's Progress* (New York: Americas Society, 2000), p. 8. See also *The Idea of the North. The Paintings of Lawren Harris* (Toronto: Art Gallery of Ontario and New York: DelMonico Books/Prestel, 2015).

25 It should be noted that there are numerous affinities between the art of Harris and Scandinavian landscapists whose work was featured in the *Exhibition of Contemporary Scandinavian Art*, and seen by Harris in the company of fellow Group of Seven painter J. E. H. MacDonald in January 1913 at the Albright Art Gallery in Buffalo, New York. See Raold Nasgaard, "The Mystic North," in John O'Brian and Peter White (eds.), *Beyond Wilderness. The Group of Seven, Canadian Identity, and Contemporary Art* (Montreal and Kingston, Ontario: McGill-Queen's University Press, 2007), pp. 251–253.

26 Fred Housser, *A Canadian Art Movement: The Story of the Group of Seven* (Toronto: Macmillan, 1926).

27 Doris Shadbolt, *Emily Carr* (Seattle: University of Washington Press, 1990).

28 See, for example, the essays that comprise chapter 5 of O'Brian and White (eds.), *Beyond Wilderness*.

29 Emily Carr, *Hundreds and Thousands: The Journals of Emily Carr* (Toronto: Clark, Irwin, 1966).

30 Ibid, p. 126. Quoted in Shadbolt, *Emily Carr*, p. 181.

31 Gerardo Murillo, "Dr. Atl," in *Las artes populares en México* (Mexico City: Cultura, 1921).

32 Anna Indych-López, *Muralism Without Walls. Rivera, Orozco, and Siqueiros in the United States, 1927–1940* (Pittsburgh: University of Pittsburgh Press, 2009), pp. 88–89.

33 Cuauhtémoc Medina, "El Dr. Atl y la aristocracia: monto de una deuda vanguardista," in the exhibition catalogue *Heterotopías. Medio siglo sin-lugar: 1918–1968* (Madrid: Museo Centro de Arte Reina Sofía, 2000), pp. 77–83. See also Olga Sáenz, *El símbolo y la acción. Vida y obra de Gerardo Murillo, Dr. Atl* (Mexico City: El Colegio Nacional, 2005), pp. 462–466.

34 Geaninne Gutiérrez-Guimarães, "Spirit of America: Joaquín Torres-García in New York, 1920–1922," in Luis Pérez-Oramas, *Joaquín Torres-García. The Arcadian Modern* (New York: Museum of Modern Art, 2015), p. 43.

35 Leah Dickerman and Anna Indych-López, *Diego Rivera. Murals for the Museum of Modern Art* (New York: Museum of Modern Art, 2011).

36 Stella was attracted to the type of Futurism practiced by artists such as Boccioni, Giacomo Balla (1871–1958), Gino Severini (1883–1966), and others that he had seen in Paris on a return trip to Europe that began in 1909. Stella formed part of the larger Futurist movement, and because of his reliance on images of industrialized America, he is also considered a member of the Precisionist group. See Vivien Greene (ed.), *Italian Futurism: Reconstructing the Universe 1909–1944* (New York: Solomon R. Guggenheim Museum, 2014).

37 On the art program at The New School see Anna Indych-López, "Making Nueva York *Moderna*: Latin American Art, the International Avant-Gardes, and The New School," in Edward J. Sullivan (ed.), *Nueva York 1613–1945* (New York: New-York Historical Society and Scala Publishers, 2010), pp. 234–255. On Benton's murals see Randall Griffey et al., *Thomas Hart Benton's America Today* (New York: Metropolitan Museum of Art, 2015).

38 Tamayo's industrial paintings became known on a wider basis through their publication in magazines of the era. The *Estridentista* journal *Horizonte* published in its first volume a similar work by Tamayo entitled *Factory*, probably painted in 1925. See Tatiana Flores, *Mexico's Revolutionary Avant-Gardes. From Estridentismo to 30–30!* (New Haven and London: Yale University Press, 2013), pp. 215–216. A recent reassessment of the development of Tamayo's early career and his connection to the international avant-garde is found in the essays in the exhibition catalogue *Construyendo/Constructing Rufino Tamayo, 1922–1937* (Mexico City: Consejo Nacional para la Cultura y las Artes, 2013).

39 See Martin Cooper, *Brazilian Railway Culture* (Newcastle upon Tyne: Cambridge Scholars Publishing, 2011), pp. 188–197, for a discussion of Tarsila's depictions of the railroads. Between 1924 and 1925 Tarsila painted at least five works with railway themes.

40 Ibid, p. 192.

41 For an analysis of Tarsila's Pau-Brasil period and a discussion of the significance and history of this and her other paintings of transport, see Aracy Amaral, *Tarsila. Sua obra e seu tempo* (São Paulo: Editora da Universidade de São Paulo/EDUSP, 2003), pp. 143–169.

Chapter 3

1 Dawn Ades, "The Image of the Black in Latin America," in David Bindman and Henry Louis Gates Jr. (eds.), *The Image of the Black in Western Art. The Twentieth Century Volume V part 1* (Cambridge, MA, and London: Belknap Press of Harvard University Press, 2014), pp. 195–260. On colonial art and artists of color see Edward J. Sullivan, "The Black Hand: Notes on the African Presence in the Visual Arts of Brazil and the Caribbean," in Joseph J. Rishel and Suzanne Stratton-Pruitt (eds.), *The Arts in Latin America 1492–1820* (Philadelphia: Philadelphia Museum of Art, 2006), pp. 39–55, and Edward J. Sullivan, *From San Juan to Paris and Back: Francisco Oller and Caribbean Art in the Era of Impressionism* (New Haven and London: Yale University Press, 2014), chapter 1.

2 Since the 1870s, well before abolition took place in 1888, Brazilians have regularly been classified for census purposes into various racial categories that include "white," "brown," "black," "yellow," and "indigenous." The discourse on race in Brazil is immense and continues to produce important analyses of the conundrum of racial classifications in the country. On black art in Brazil see Emanoel Araújo, *A Mão afro-brasileira: significado da contribução artística e histórica. The Hand of the Afro-Brazilian: The Significance of its Artistic and Historical Contribution* (São Paulo: Museu Afro Brasil, 2010).

3 *Anita Malfatti e seu tempo* (São Paulo: Museu de Arte Moderna de São Paulo, 1996).

4 Aracy Amaral reproduces the catalogue for the *Semana de Arte Moderna* in *Arts in the Week of '22* (São Paulo: BOVESPA, 1992), pp. 136–137.

5 Various critics have suggested that Tarsila's painting derives from her knowledge of Afro-Brazilian representations of the Yoruba deity Yemanjá. For a summary of these arguments see Fatima Bercht, "Tarsila do Amaral," in Waldo Rasmussen (ed.), *Latin American Artists of the Twentieth Century* (New York: Museum of Modern Art, 1993) p. 53 and p. 59, note 15.

6 See, for example, Jorge de Lima, Mário de Andrade, and Mario Bandeira, *Mangue* (Rio de Janeiro: Revista Acadêmico Editora, 1943). Segall executed the prints for this book in 1941.

7 Stephanie D'Alessandro, *Still More Distant Journeys. The Artistic Emigrations of Lasar Segall* (Chicago: Smart Museum of Art, University of Chicago, 1997).

8 Woss y Gil founded her own academy in the mid-1920s after her return from New York and was influential in the establishment of the National Academy of Fine Arts in Santo Domingo in 1942. See Edward J. Sullivan, Jeanette Miller, Marianne de Tolentino, and Elizabeth Ferrer, *Modern and Contemporary Art of the Dominican Republic* (New York: Americas Society, 1996), and M. Guerrero and Danilo de los Santos, *Mujer y arte dominicano hoy. Homenaje a Celeste Woss y Gil* (Santo Domingo: Voluntariado de las Casas Reales, 1995). The most recent study of this artist's work is Marianne de Tolentino, *Celeste Woss y Gil en Bellas Artes* (Santo Domingo, Galería Nacional de Bellas Artes, 2016). I am especially grateful to Dr. de Tolentino and to the kindness of Francis Woss y Gil for their help in providing information and permission to publish the work of Celeste Woss y Gil.

9 See the exhibition catalogue *Víctor Patricio Landaluze (1830–1889)* (Bilbao: Museo de Bellas Artes, 1989) and E. Carmen Ramos, "A Painter of Cuban Life: Víctor Patricio Landaluze and Nineteenth Century Cuban Politics," PhD dissertation, University of Chicago, 2011. The definitive edition of *Cecilia Valdés* by Cirilio Villaverde was published in 1882 (it had originally appeared in a Havana newspaper). See the English translation by Helen Lane, *Cecilia Valdés or Angel Hill* (New York: Oxford University Press, 2005).

10 For Pedro Figari see Raquel Pereda, *Pedro Figari* (Montevideo: Edición Fundación Banco de Boston, 1995); María L. Battegazzore and Nancy Carbajal, *Pedro Figari: Tradición y utopia* (Montevideo: Psicolibros, 2010); and Miguel Carbajal, *Pedro Figari* (Montevideo: BBVA, El País, Testoni Studios, 2011). On Figari's depictions of blacks in Montevideo see Lyneise E. Williams, "A Different Shade of Modernism: Difference and Distinction in Pedro Figari's Representations of Black Bodies," in Mary D.

Sheriff (ed.), *Cultural Contact and the Making of European Art since the Age of Exploration* (Chapel Hill: University of North Carolina Press, 2010), pp. 177–201.

11 On the broader sociopolitical history of the black populations in Latin America see Henry Louis Gates Jr., *Black in Latin America* (New York: NYU Press, 2011).

12 On African-American artists in Paris see Tyler Stovall, *Paris Noir: African Americans in the City of Light* (Boston: Houghton Mifflin, 1996), and Petrine Archer-Straw, *Negrophilia: Avant-Garde Paris and Black Culture in the 1920s* (New York: Thames and Hudson, 2000). See also the essays on the relationship between black artists and modernity in Bindman, "Le 'New Negro' et la Harlem Renaissance. Art, Jazz, Primitivisme et Communisme," in Daniel Soutif (ed.), *The Color Line. Les Artistes Africains-Américains et la Ségrégation* (Paris: Musée du Quai Branly Jacques Chirac/Flammarion, 2016), pp. 155–167.

13 The most complete monograph on Colson is the exhibition catalogue *Colson errante* (Santo Domingo: Museo Bellapart, 2008).

14 Ramón Vázquez Díaz, *Víctor Manuel* (Madrid: Ediciones Vanguardia Cubana, 2010). On the first and second generations of the Cuban Vanguard see Juan A. Martínez, *Cuban Art and National Identity. The Vanguardia Painters, 1927–1950* (Gainesville: University Press of Florida, 1994).

15 Alejandro Anreus, "Historical Close-Up: *Modern Cuban Painters* at MoMA, 1944," April 1, 2014, www.cubanartnews.org/news/historical-close-up-modern-cuban-painters-at-moma-1944.

16 Richard Powell, *Black Art and Culture in the Twentieth Century* (New York: Thames and Hudson, 1997), chapter 1.

17 Among the many studies of the Harlem Renaissance, Samella Lewis, *African American Art and Artists* (Berkeley, Los Angeles, and London: University of California Press, 2003), put this phenomenon into the larger context of the development of black arts in the United States since the seventeenth century. See also Mary Schmitt-Campbell, David Driskell, David Levering Lewis, and Deborah Willis Ryan, *Harlem Renaissance: Art of Black America* (New York: The Studio Museum in Harlem and Harry N. Abrams, 1987), and Deborah Cullen, "Out of the Shadows: The Harlem Renaissance and New York's Afro-Caribbean Diaspora," in Deborah Cullen and Elvis Fuentes, *Caribbean. Art at the Crossroads of the World* (New York: El Museo del Barrio, 2012), pp. 243–259.

18 Richard Powell (ed.), *Archibald Motley. Jazz Age Modernist* (Durham, NC: Nasher Museum at Duke University, 2014).

19 Richard Powell, "Becoming Motley, Becoming Modern," in ibid., p. 120.

20 Veerle Poupeye, *Caribbean Art* (New York and London: Thames and Hudson, 1998), p. 74.

21 David Boxer, *Edna Manley: Sculptor* (Kingston: National Gallery of Jamaica and the Edna Manley Foundation, 1990).

22 Poupeye, *Caribbean Art*, p. 71.

23 Among the most noteworthy of the early Intuitives, whose work David Boxer has studied in depth, are John Dunkeley (1891-1947), Gaston Tabois (1924-2012), Everald Brown (1917-2003), and Mallica "Kapo" Reynolds (1911-1989). The 1979 exhibition at the National Gallery of Jamaica was the first effort to categorize and display the breadth of these Afro-Jamaican artists. See David Boxer and Rex Nettleford, *The Intuitive Eye* (Kingston: National Gallery of Jamaica, 1979), and David Boxer, "Introducing Fifteen Intuitives," in Cullen and Fuentes, *Caribbean*, pp. 201–220.

24 For arguments about this problematic discourse of Otherness in the arts of this period see the essays in William Rubin and Kirk Varnedoe (eds.), *"Primitivism" in 20th Century Art." Affinity of the Tribal and the Modern* (New York: Museum of Modern Art, 2002). Among the earliest articulations of this subject is Robert

Goldwater, *Primitivism in Modern Painting* (New York: Harper, 1938). The attitudes expressed in the writings of these authors have been highly contested over the years. For a summary of the arguments surrounding the Eurocentric analyses of "the primitive" see Sieglinde Lemke, *Primitivist Modernism: Black Culture and the Origins of Transatlantic Modernism* (Oxford and New York: Oxford University Press, 1998). In particular see Hal Foster, "The 'Primitive' Unconscious of Modern Art," *October*, 34 (Fall 1985), pp. 45–70.

25 White also painted another important series of murals for the Chicago Public Library in 1939 depicting "Five Great American Negroes." This series has unfortunately been lost.

26 Carla M. Hanzal, *Loïs Mailou Jones. A Life in Vibrant Color* (Charlotte, NC: Mint Museum, 2009). See also Tritobia Hayes Benjamin, *The Art and Life of Loïs Mailou Jones* (New York: Pomegranate Art Books, 1994).

27 "Remembering Albert Huie (1920–2010)," January 31, 2010, *National Gallery of Jamaica Blog*. www.nationalgalleryofjamaica. wordpress.com/2010/01/31/remembering-albert-huie-1920-2010.

28 Sharecroppers were both black and white. See the following chapter and my discussion of the image of an indigent white sharecropper by Texas artist Jerry Bywaters.

29 Melanie Anne Herzog, *Elizabeth Catlett: An American Artist in Mexico* (Seattle: University of Washington Press, 2005). See also Herzog, *Elizabeth Catlett: In the Image of the People* (Chicago: Art Institute of Chicago, 2005).

30 Melanie Anne Herzog, "Elizabeth Catlett: Inheriting the Legacy," in Amy Helene Kirschke, *Women Artists of the Harlem Renaissance* (Jackson, MS: University Press of Mississippi, 2014), p. 217.

31 Daniel Soutif, "La Marche des Artistes. Romare Bearden, Elizabeth Catlett, Norman Lewis, Reginald A. Gammon Jr., Alma Thomas," in Soutif (ed.), *The Color Line*, pp. 282–283.

32 Elizabeth Alexander, *Jacob Lawrence: The Migration Series* (New York: Museum of Modern Art, 2015).

33 Ibid., p. 160.

34 Among many sources on Lawrence see Ellen Wheat, *Jacob Lawrence: American Painter* (Seattle: University of Washington Press, 1990), and Elizabeth Hutton Turner, Patricia Hills, Paul J. Karlstrom et al., *Over the Line: The Art and Life of Jacob Lawrence* (Seattle: University of Washington Press, 2001).

35 "The Negro's War," *Fortune*, vol. 25, no. 6 (June 1942), pp. 77–80, 157.

36 Ruth E. Fine, *The Art of Romare Bearden* (Washington, DC: National Gallery of Art, and New York: Harry N. Abrams, 2003).

37 Lowery Stokes Sims, *Wifredo Lam and the International Avant Garde, 1923–1982* (Austin: University of Texas Press, 2002), and Catherine David (ed.), *Wifredo Lam* (London: Tate, 2016).

38 Los Once showed together only a few times and the number of its members varied over time. For a thorough discussion of this and related abstract movements see Abigail McEwen, *Revolutionary Horizons: Art and Polemics in 1950s Cuba* (New Haven and London: Yale University Press, 2016), and Christoph Singler, *Guido Llinás. Parisian Works. His Friendship with Wifredo Lam* (Paris: Handpick/JP AKA, 2015).

39 Guido Llinás, letter to Vicente Báez, April 22, 1987, quoted in ibid., p. 14.

40 Severo Sarduy, "Black Signatures: Night of Ink," quoted in ibid., p. 30.

41 See, among many other sources, Araújo, *A Mão*; Mikelle Smith Omari, *From the Inside to the Outside: The Art and Ritual of Bahian Candomblé* (Los Angeles: University of California Press, 1984); and Kimberly Cleveland, *Black Art in Brazil: Expressions of Identity* (Gainesville: University Press of Florida, 2013).

Endnotes

42 See *Rubem Valentim: Construção e símbolo* (Rio de Janeiro: Centro Cultural Banco do Brasil, 1994), and Bené Fonteles and Wagner Barja, *Rubem Valentim: artista da luz* (São Paulo: Edições da Luz, 2001). On Valentim in a wider context of Afro-Brazilian art see Roberto Conduru, *Arte Afro-brasileira* (Belo Horizonte: Editora C/Arte, 2007), especially chapter 4; Joëlle Busca, "L'Image d'un Espace de la Mémoire," in Christiane Falgayettes-Leveau, *Brésil. Heritage Africaine* (Paris: Musée Dapper, 2005), pp. 191–215; and Tanya Barsun and Peter Gorschlüter (eds.), *Afro-Modern. Journeys Through the Black Atlantic* (Liverpool: Tate Liverpool, 2010).

43 Rubem Valentim quoted in Fonteles and Barja, *Rubem Valentim*, p. 28 (translation by the author).

Chapter 4

1 Mexican art history of the post-revolutionary period witnessed a rise in the study of the archaeological remains of the Aztecs, Maya, and many other indigenous peoples whose public buildings were painted. See the many texts by Manuel Gamio and others on this subject. In addition, scholars like Manuel Toussaint, who began his long career as historian of Mexican colonial art in the late 1920s, also investigated the role of colonial-era murals.

2 See José Vasconcelos, *The Cosmic Race/La raza cósmica* (bilingual edition) (Baltimore: Johns Hopkins University Press, 1979).

3 Elizabeth Ferrer, *Lola Alvarez Bravo* (New York: Aperture, 2006), and James Oles and Adriana Zavala (eds.), *Lola Alvarez Bravo and the Photography of an Era* (Mexico City: Consejo Nacional para la Cultura y las Artes, 2012).

4 Anita Brenner was an immensely influential figure within the panorama of the Mexican/U.S. cultural world in the 1920s and 30s (and beyond). Her most famous book was *Idols Behind Altars* (New York: Payson and Clarke Ltd., 1929), in which she attempted to translate the synergies between ancient and modern aesthetic in Mexico for an English-speaking audience. On Brenner see Susannah Joel Glusker, *Anita Brenner: A Mind of Her Own* (Austin: University of Texas Press, 1998), and Susannah Joel Glusker (ed.), *Avant Garde Art and Artists in Mexico: Anita Brenner's Journals of the Roaring Twenties* (Austin: University of Texas Press, 2010).

5 Tina Modotti, "On Photography," *Mexican Folkways*, vol. 5, no. 4 (October–December 1927). See also Margaret Hooks, *Tina Modotti. Photographer and Revolutionary* (San Francisco: Pandora, 1993), p. 153.

6 A broad assessment of the political situation in the United States as it is reflected in figurative art is found in Judith A. Barter "Introduction," *America After the Fall. Painting in the 1930s* (Chicago: Art Institute of Chicago, 2016), pp. 14–25.

7 Sarah Lowe, *Tina Modotti Photographs* (New York: Harry N. Abrams, 1995), pp. 16–17.

8 James Oles, *Art and Architecture in Mexico* (London: Thames and Hudson, 2013), p. 240. On the revolutionary character of the SEP murals see also David Craven, *Art and Revolution in Latin America 1910–1990* (New Haven and London: Yale University Press, 2002), pp. 37–45.

9 The visual sources for fictive banderoles such as the one seen here ultimately may be traced back to medieval and Early Renaissance paintings where words can be seen emanating from the mouths of the participants in the picture's drama or as a commentary on the action represented.

10 The story of the Detroit murals is most fully detailed by Linda Bank Downs in *Diego Rivera. The Detroit Industry Murals* (Detroit: Detroit Institute of Arts, 1999).

11 Irene Herner de Larrea, *Paradise Lost at Rockefeller Center* (Mexico City: EDICUPES, 1987).

12 Bertram Wolfe, *The Fabulous Life of Diego Rivera* (New York: Stein and Day, 1963), p. 306. The first edition of this book appeared in 1939.

13 James Oles, *South of the Border: Mexico in the American Imagination 1914–1947* (Washington, D.C.: Smithsonian Institution Press, 1993).

14 Among the projects to bring realist, socially concerned art to those who could not afford more expensive paintings was the Associated American Artists (AAA), an organization founded in 1934 that commissioned prints from many of the most well-recognized U.S. artists of the day such as Thomas Hart Benton, Georgia O'Keeffe, and Grant Wood. See the exhibition catalogue *Art for Every Home. Associated American Artists* (Manhattan, KS: Beach Museum of Art and Yale University Press, 2015). For more extensive studies of socially concerned art at this time in the United States see (among many other sources) Richard D. McKinzie, *The New Deal for Artists* (Princeton: Princeton University Press, 1973); Francis V. O'Connor, *Art for the Millions: Essays from the 1930s by Artists and Administrators of the WPA Federal Art Project* (New York: New York Graphic Society, 1975); Belisario R. Contreras, *Tradition and Innovation in New Deal Art* (Lewisburg: Bucknell University Press, 1983); and Roger G. Kennedy and David Larkin, *When Art Worked* (New York: Rizzoli, 2009). A model case study of the impact of Mexican muralism in wall painting in California is found in Antony W. Lee, *Painting in the Left. Diego Rivera, Radical Politics and San Francisco's Public Murals* (Berkeley, Los Angeles, and London: University of California Press, 1999).

15 Hawaii and Vermont were also independent countries in the eighteenth and nineteenth centuries.

16 Gerald Bywaters, "Diego Rivera and Mexican Popular Art," *Southwest Review*, vol. 13, no. 4 (1927), pp. 475–480. Bywaters became professor of art and art history at Southern Methodist University in Dallas, where he was also in charge of the Owens Art Gallery (forerunner to the present Meadows Museum). His directorship of the Dallas Museum of Fine Arts (today the Dallas Museum of Art) was marked by a major expansion of the collections and a new building. See Francine Carraro, *Jerry Bywaters. A Life in Art* (Austin: University of Texas Press, 1994), and Sam Deshong Ratcliffe (ed.), *Jerry Bywaters. Interpreter of the Southwest* (College Station: Texas A&M University Press, 2007).

17 Ellen Landau, *Mexico and American Modernism* (New Haven and London: Yale University Press, 2013). See chapter 2 for a discussion of the Morelia mural by Guston and Kadish.

18 Dorothy Seckler, "Oral History Interview with Marion Greenwood, 1964, Jan. 31," www.aaa.si.edu/collections/interviews/oral-history-marion-greenwood-11871 (accessed October 21, 2016). This interview, sponsored by the Archives of American Art, concentrates on Greenwood's experience in Mexico, describing in detail her work for the Mexico City Market. See also James Oles, *Las hermanas Greenwood en México* (Mexico City: Consejo Nacional para la Cultura y las Artes, 2000).

19 *Seven American Women: The Depression Decade* (Poughkeepsie: Vassar College Art Gallery, 1976), p. 22.

20 On the Chapingo murals see Susana Quijano Pliego, *Los murales de Diego Rivera en Chapingo: Naturaleza fecunda* (Mexico City: Universidad Autónoma de México, 2015).

21 A case in point was the decoration of the Centro Escolar Revolución (Revolutionary Teaching Center), a school in downtown Mexico City, by members of the LEAR (League of Revolutionary Artists and Writers) in 1937 in which the principal themes of the mural cycle deal with education. The six artists included the Colombian painter Ignacio Gómez Jaramillo (1910–1970) and the first Mexican woman muralist, Aurora Reyes (1908–1985). I am grateful to Juanita Solano for her (unpublished)

work on this fresco cycle and her discussion of it with me. See also Dina Comisarenco Mirkin, "Aurora Reyes's *Ataque a la maestro rural*: The First Mural Created by a Mexican Female Artist," *Women's Art Journal*, vol. 26, no. 2 (Autumn 2005–Winter 2006), pp. 19–25.

22   The title of the mural is *The Making of a Fresco Showing the Building of a City*.

23   See Sharon Lorenzo, "The Walls of My Dreams. The Commissioning of José Clemente Orozco's Mural *The Epic of American Civilization* at Dartmouth College," in Mary K. Coffey et al., *Men of Fire. José Clemente Orozco and Jackson Pollock* (Hanover, NH: Hood Museum of Art, 2012), pp. 55–63.

24   For a discussion of the ideology within this mural complex see Héctor Jaimes, *Filosofía del muralismo mexicano: Orozco, Rivera y Siqueiros* (Mexico City: Plaza y Valdés, 2012), pp. 87–89.

25   Olivier Debroise, "Arte acción: David Alfaro Siqueiros en las estratégias artísticas e ideológicas de los años treinte," in the exhibition catalogue *Siqueiros. Retrato de una década* (Mexico City: Instituto Nacional de Bellas Artes, 1997), p. 46.

26   James Oles, *Diego Rivera, David Alfaro Siqueiros, José Clemente Orozco* (New York: Museum of Modern Art, 2011), p. 23.

27   For the relationship between Pollock and the Mexican artists, especially Siqueiros, see Robert Storr, "A Piece of the Action," in Pepe Karmel (ed.), *Jackson Pollock: New Approaches* (New York: Museum of Modern Art, 1999), pp. 33–70.

28   Barry Bergdoll et al., *Latin America in Construction: Architecture 1955–1980* (New York: Museum of Modern Art, 2015).

29   Mary K. Coffey, *How a Revolutionary Art Became Official Culture. Murals, Museums, and the Mexican State* (Durham, NC, and London: Duke University Press, 2013), p. 109.

30   A good example of this is his mural *Portrait of the Bourgeoisie* of 1939–40 in the Electricians Union Building in Mexico City.

31   For a summary of the controversy see Coffey, *How a Revolutionary Art ...*, pp. 109–119.

32   *Hale Woodruff: 50 Years of His Art* (New York: The Studio Museum in Harlem, 1979). Woodruff's most famous series of six large-scale murals (oil on canvas) in a higher-education context are the paintings for Talladega College in Alabama (begun 1938), charting the history of the slave ship *Amistad*, a vessel that witnessed an uprising of its slave cargo. Woodruff illustrates this and the subsequent story of the trial of its instigators in New Haven, Connecticut. See Stephanie Meyer, *Rising Up: Hale Woodruff's Murals at Talladega College* (Atlanta: High Museum of Art, 2012).

33   Alain Locke, *The New Negro* (New York: Albert and Charles Boni, 1925).

34   Hale Woodruff, artist's statement, www.cau.edu/art-galleries/murals.html (accessed February 19, 2017).

35   Lizetta LeFalle-Collins, "Redefining the African-American Self," in LeFalle-Collins and Shifra Goldman, *In the Spirit of Resistance. African-American Modernists and the Mexican Muralist School* (New York: American Federation of Arts, 1996), pp. 27–67.

Chapter 5

1   In 1952 Siqueiros worked with the African-American printmaker and sculptor Elizabeth Catlett to make this image into a lithograph. (For more on Catlett see Chapter 3.)

2   German-Mexican artist Hugo Brehme bases the composition on an early twentieth-century photograph. Circulated as a postcard, this photograph served a touristic value that is completely undermined in the Siqueiros painting. It was owned

for many years by lyricist Ira Gershwin (1896–1983) and was likely commissioned of the artist by George Gershwin, whose portrait (now in the collection of the Harry Ransom Center of the University of Texas at Austin) Siqueiros painted in the same year as *Niña madre*. See Jürgen Harten, *Siqueiros/Pollock, Pollock/Siqueiros* (Dusseldorf: Kunsthalle Düsseldorf, 1995), vol. 1, p. 82, and James Oles, "Catálogo de obra," in *Siqueiros. Retrato de una década* (Mexico City: Museo Nacional de Arte, 1996), p. 176.

3   Matthew Affron, Mark A. Castro, Dafne Cruz Porchini, and Renato González Mello (eds.), *Paint the Revolution. Mexican Modernism 1910–1950* (Philadelphia: Philadelphia Museum of Art, 2016), illustrated on p. 175.

4   Oles, "Catálogo," asserts that *Child Mother* was painted in February 1936, shortly before Siqueiros left for New York, even though the painting embodies the techniques he would teach at the Experimental Workshop.

5   See the discussion of this print in Harten, *Siqueiros/Pollock*, p. 148.

6   Oles, "Catálogo," p. 178.

7   There is a certain ambiguity regarding the origin of this term. Jim Crow was a character in nineteenth-century American musical (minstrel) theater, in which white actors appeared in blackface for white audiences, mimicking and exaggerating the songs and dances of African Americans.

8   "Housepainter," *Time*, vol. 25, no. 22 (June 3, 1935), p. 32. Quoted in M. Melissa Wolfe, "Joe Jones, Worker-Artist," in Andrew Walker (ed.), *Joe Jones. Radical Painter of the American Scene* (Saint Louis: Saint Louis Art Museum, 2010), p. 44.

9   Ibid.

10   The story of the event is recounted in Cynthia Carr, *Our Town: A Heartland Lynching, A Haunted Town and the Hidden History* (New York: Crown Publishers, 2006). On lynching photography see James Allen et al., *Lynching Photography in America* (Santa Fe: Twin Palms Press, 2000), and Dora Apel and Shawn Michelle Smith, *Lynching Photographs* (Berkeley: University of California Press, 2007).

11   See Anthony W. Lee, "Introduction," in ibid., especially p. 6. According to all accounts of this event and the photograph that documents it, *Lynching in Marion, Indiana 1930* served as the stimulus for New York poet and composer Abel Meeropol to write the lyrics to what became the famously melancholy popular song "Strange Fruit," a tune that shocked large swaths of the U.S. listening population when African-American singer Billie Holiday performed and recorded its most famous version in 1939. Meeropol himself has an important place within activist politics. He was a New York City high-school teacher and member of the Communist Party. Sympathetic to the infamous couple Julius and Ethel Rosenberg, who were executed in 1951 (at the height of the anti-Communist panic in the United States) for allegedly spying for the Soviet Union, he and his wife, Anne, adopted the Rosenbergs' children, Robert and Michael, after their parents' death. The boys then took their adopted parents' surname.

12   Byrna R. Campbell, "Anti-Lynching Activism," in Walker (ed.) *Joe Jones*, p. 40.

13   The influence of Goya's prints was decisive for both Goitia and Orozco.

14   A discussion of Goitia's painting within a larger context of art during the Mexican Revolution is found in Laura González Matute, "L'École mexicaine de peinture," in Agustín Arteaga (ed.), *Mexique 1900–1950. Diego Rivera, Frida Kahlo, José Clemente Orozco et les avant-gardes* (Paris: Réunion des Musées Nationaux, 2016), pp. 81–91.

15   Patricia Hills, *Alice Neel* (New York: Harry N. Abrams, 1983), p. 61.

16 Petra Gördüren, "Emotional Value. Alice Neel and the American Reception of German Art," in Jeremy Lewison (ed.), *Alice Neel. Painter of Modern Life* (Brussels: Mercatorfonds, 2016), p. 30, discusses Neel's painting and its stylistic and thematic relationship to German Expressionism.

17 Emily Genauer writing in the *New York World-Telegram*, September 12, 1936. Quoted in www.aliceneel.com/biography/1930–2shtml (accessed November 4, 2016).

18 This print has been given the alternative titles of *Lo que puede venir* (That Which Could Come), *Amenaza sobre México* (Menace Over Mexico), and *Visión* (Vision). Deborah Caplow, *Leopoldo Méndez. Revolutionary Art and the Mexican Print* (Austin: University of Texas Press, 2007), the most complete monograph on the artist in English, accepts the title I use here and discusses the alternatives on p. 271, note 30.

19 A comprehensive history of the modern print in Mexico is found in John Ittmann (ed.), *Mexico and Modern Printmaking. A Revolution in the Graphic Arts, 1920 to 1950* (Philadelphia: Philadelphia Museum of Art, 2006). The social implications of Mexican printmaking are analyzed in John Lear, *Picturing the Proletariat. Artists and Labor in Revolutionary Mexico, 1908–1940* (Austin: University of Texas Press, 2017).

20 See Helga Prignitz-Poda, *El Taller de Gráfica Popular en México, 1937–1977* (Mexico City: Instituto Nacional de Bellas Artes, 1992). Among the foreign-born artists associated with the Taller were Elizabeth Catlett and Paul (Pablo) O'Higgins (who, together with Méndez and Luis Arenal, were the group's founders).

21 Caplow, *Leopoldo Méndez*, p. 187.

22 Roland Barthes, *Camera Lucida. Reflections on Photography* (New York: Hill and Wang, 1980).

23 Edward J. Sullivan, *The Language of Objects in the Art of the Americas* (New Haven and London: Yale University Press, 2007), p. 140.

24 Carleton Beals. *The Crime of Cuba* (Philadelphia: J. B. Lippincott, 1933).

25 This tradition goes back to at least the end of the sixteenth century, when Annibale Carracci (1560–1609) created his series of drawings (later published as a print series) called the *Arti di Bologna*, documenting a wide variety of street vendors and other types of urban workers in that Italian city. There are numerous other examples through the ages. By the twentieth century this had become a photography tradition. Perhaps the best-known examples are the series of single images of workers and merchants by the German photographer August Sander (1876–1964), who executed a well-known series called "People of the 20th Century," begun in 1911.

26 Parks also became well known as a composer and film director, in addition to a photographic career that included not only photojournalism but also portrait and landscape photography.

27 Gordon Parks quoted in Paul Roth, "The Storyteller," in *Gordon Parks* (London: Thames and Hudson, 2013), n.p. Parks refers in the title he gave to the photograph to the American painter Grant Wood's most famous composition of 1930, in which a white middle-class farm couple is portrayed standing in front of their modest new-Gothic house. The husband of the couple holds a pitchfork in his hand. The painting is the embodiment of white Middle America, and thus creates an ironic precedent for the title of Parks's image.

28 Gordon Parks stated that "[She] divulged that her life had been full of misery," www.pdngallery.com/legends/parks/photo_01_set.shtml (accessed November 18, 2016). Watson's father had been the victim of lynching when she was a youth. See www.loc.gov/pictures/collection/fsa/docchap7.html (accessed November 18, 2016).

29 Jacqueline Barnitz, *Twentieth Century Art of Latin America* (Austin: University of Texas Press, 2001), p. 87.

30 The Domino Sugar Company's refinery in Brooklyn stands today. The original plant dated from 1854. The Havermeyer Family, famous as art collectors, were the developers of this industry that made their fortune and produced more sugar than all other such factories in the United States

31 Teresa Tió, "El portafolios gráfico o la hoja liberada," in *La hoja liberada. El portafolios en la gráfica puertorriqueña* (San Juan: Instituto de Cultura Puertorriqueña, 1966), p. 14.

32 Teresa Tió, "Rafael Tufiño. The Art of Self," in *Rafael Tufiño. Pintor del pueblo* (San Juan: Museo de Arte de Puerto Rico, 2001), p. 198.

33 See José Trías Monge, *Puerto Rico. The Trials of the Oldest Colony in the World* (New Haven and London: Yale University Press, 1997).

34 Michele Greet, *Beyond National Identity. Pictorial Indigenism as a Modernist Strategy in Andean Art, 1920–1960* (University Park: Pennsylvania State University Press, 2009), p. 1.

35 Andrea Moreno Aguilar, *Eduardo Kingman Riofrío* (Quito: Banco Central del Ecuador, 2010), p. 107.

36 Kingman's penchant for both social commentary and forms derived from German Expressionism's use of orthogonal lines and strident colors may be connected to his friendship with George Grosz in New York in 1930–40. Kingman had gone to New York to participate in the decoration of the Ecuadorean Pavilion at the 1930–40 World's Fair. See ibid., op. cit., pp. 94–95.

37 Lenín Oña, "Ecuador," in Edward J. Sullivan (ed.), *Latin American Art in the Twentieth Century* (London: Phaidon, 1996), p. 183.

38 For Berni's later career see Mari Carmen Ramírez and Marcelo Pacheco, *Antonio Berni. Juanito y Ramona* (Houston: Museum of Fine Arts, 2013).

39 A visual repertory of Berni's paintings of rural migration and exile is found in *Antonio Berni. Obra pictórica 1922–1981* (Buenos Aires: Museo Nacional de Bellas Artes, 1984).

40 Argentinean art historian Cristina Rossi discusses this painting as paradigmatic of specific national social concerns in "Hacer para resistir, La SAAP en la dinámica de confrontación," in Rossi (ed.), *Antonio Berni. Lecturas en tiempo presente* (Buenos Aires: Editorial de la Universidad Nacional Tres de Febrero, 2010), p. 67.

Chapter 6

1 See John O'Brian, *Clement Greenberg. The Collected Essays and Criticism*, Vols. 1-4 (Chicago: University of Chicago Press, 1988–95), and Harold Rosenberg, *Art on the Edge. Creators and Actions* (New York: Macmillan, 1975).

2 Irving Sandler, *The Triumph of American Painting. A History of Abstract Expressionism* (New York: Praeger, 1970). This book has had numerous re-editions. See also Sandler's most recent assessment of the New York art world and the social-artistic milieu of the 1940s and beyond in *Swept Up by Art. An Art Critic in the Post-Avant-Garde Era* (Brooklyn: Rail Editions, 2015).

3 Ann Eden Gibson, *Abstract Expressionism. Other Politics* (New Haven and London: Yale University Press, 1999).

4 Joan Marter (ed.), *Women of Abstract Expressionism* (Denver: Denver Art Museum, 2016).

5 Harold Bloom, *The Anxiety of Influence. A Theory of Poetry* (Oxford: Oxford University Press: 1973). This volume deals with the burden faced by poets in their inevitable response to their predecessors. This theory has long been appropriated by critics to

refer to this problem in larger arenas of creativity including the visual arts.

6   See the exhibition catalogue *Nipo-Brasileiros: Mestres e Alunos em 50 Anos* (São Paulo: Pinacoteca do Estado de São Paulo, 1984).

7   The Whitney Museum's exhibition (*Alma W. Thomas*) was a modest show with only 13 paintings and 6 works on paper. The same year the Corcoran Gallery of Art, Washington, DC, mounted a larger exhibition (*Alma W. Thomas. Retrospective Exhibition*), which included 40 paintings and 9 works on paper. More recently, much larger exhibitions have been organized by the Fort Wayne (Indiana) Museum of Art (1998) and the Frances Young Tang Teaching Museum and Art Gallery at Skidmore College (Saratoga Springs, New York) and the Studio Museum in Harlem, New York (2016). See Ian Berry and Lauren Haynes, *Alma Thomas* (New York: Studio Museum in Harlem, DelMonico Books/Prestel, 2016). Her art was also featured in the 2016–17 exhibition *Women of Abstract Expressionism* (Denver Art Museum). Thomas was the first African-American woman artist to enter the collection of the White House. See Mayer Rus, "Executive Order," *Architectural Digest*, December 2016, pp. 78–83.

8   *María Luisa Pacheco. Pintora de los Andes* (La Paz: La Papelera, 1993). See also *Tribute to María Luisa Pacheco of Bolivia, 1919–1982* (Washington, D.C.: Museum of Modern Art of Latin America, 1986).

9   Thomas B. Hess, *Abstract Painting: Background and American Phase* (New York: Viking, 1951), pp. 142–143. From 1965 to 1972 Hess was the editor of the prestigious *ARTnews* magazine, and at the end of his life (he died in 1972) he was curator of contemporary art at the Metropolitan Museum of Art.

10 Abigail McEwen, "Olga Albizu and the Borders of Abstraction," *American Art*, vol. 29, no. 2 (Summer 2015), pp. 87–111.

11 Vicente had two exhibitions at the Ateneo Puertorriqueño, San Juan (1945 and 1946). The second of these exhibitions was a landmark for the development of abstract art in the island.

12 Lynn Gumpert, Ana Martínez de Aguilar, and Edward J. Sullivan, *Concrete Improvisations: Collages and Sculpture by Esteban Vicente* (New York: Grey Art Gallery, 2011).

13 The most complete account of Vicente's early career is in Elizabeth Frank, *Esteban Vicente* (New York: Hudson Hills Press, 1995). On Vicente's affinities for Spanish art see the exhibition catalogue *Zurbarán, Juan Gris, Esteban Vicente. A Spanish Tradition of Modernity* (Segovia, Spain: Museo de Arte Contemporáneo Esteban Vicente, 2003).

14 Daniel Haxall, "Unlimited Possibilities: Esteban Vicente and the Art of Collage," in Gumpert et al., *Concrete Improvisations*.

15 Edward J. Sullivan and Nelly Perrazzo, *Emilio Pettoruti (1892–1971)* (Buenos Aires: Fundación Pettoruti, Asociación Amigos del Museo Nacional de Bellas Artes and La Marca Editora, 2004).

16 Murilo Mendes, "Texto branco," in *Transitor* (Rio de Janeiro: Editora Nova Fronteira, 1980), pp. 371–372, quoted in Paulo Herkenhoff, "Monocromos," in *XXIV Bienal de São Paulo. Núcleo histórico: antropofagia e histórias de canibalismos* (São Paulo: Fundação Bienal de São Paulo, 1998), p. 192.

17 John Elderfield, Luis Pérez Oramas, and Nora Lawrence, *Armando Reverón* (New York: Museum of Modern Art, 2007).

18 Anne Cohen DePietro, "This Unity of Interest is Marvelous: Arthur Dove and Helen Torr in Halesite," in *Arthur Dove and Helen Torr: The Huntington Years* (Huntington, NY: Heckscher Museum, 1989), p. 24. See also Ellen E. Roberts, Samantha Niederman, and Gregory Nosan, *O'Keeffe, Stettheimer, Torr, Zorach: Women Modernists in New York* (West Palm Beach: Norton Museum of Art, 2016).

19 Arthur Dove created a series of pastels in 1912 that has been called "the first body of distinctly nonrepresentational art shown by an American." Ann Lee Morgan, "Prelude and Prologue. The Early Work of Arthur Dove," in DePietro, *Arthur Dove and Helen Torr*, p. 12.

20 Anne Cohen DePietro, "Beyond Abstraction. The Late Work of Arthur Dove," in ibid., p. 57.

21 *Morris Graves. Falcon of the Inner Eye: A Centennial Celebration* (New York: Michael Rosenfeld Gallery, 2010).

22 Dorothy C. Miller (ed.), *Americans 1942: 18 Artists from 9 States* (New York: Museum of Modern Art, 1942), p. 51. For a discussion of the impact of East Asian art on Graves (who lived in Japan in 1930) see Theodore F. Wolff, "Morris Graves. Precipitating an Epiphany," in *Morris Graves. The Early Works* (La Conner: Museum of Northwest Art, 1998), pp. 9–39.

23 André Breton, "Matta. La perle est gatée à mes yeux ..." in *André Breton. Le Surréalisme et la peinture* (Paris: Gallimard, 1965), pp. 187–188. English translation reproduced in Curtis L. Carter and Thomas R. Monahan, *Matta. Surrealism and Beyond* (Milwaukee: Patrick and Beatrice Haggerty Museum of Art, 1997), pp. 27–28.

24 Lowery Stokes Sims, "New York Dada and New World Surrealism," in Luis R. Cancel et al. (eds.), *The Latin American Spirit. Art and Artists in the United States, 1920–1970* (New York: Bronx Museum of the Arts and Harry N. Abrams, 1988), p. 160.

25 Irving Sandler, *The Triumph of American Painting. A History of Abstract Expressionism* (New York: Harper & row, 1976) pp. 37–38.

26 Andreas Neufert, "Wolfgang Paalen: The Totem as Sphinx," in Dawn Ades, Rita Eder, and Graciela Speranza (eds.), *Surrealism in Latin America. Vivísimo muerto* (Los Angeles: Getty Research Institute, 2012), pp. 111–129, and Annette Leddy and Donna Conwell, *Farewell to Surrealism. The DYN Circle in Mexico* (Los Angeles: Getty Research Institute, 2012). The major monograph in English on Paalen is Amy Winter, *Wolfgang Paalen. Artist and Theorist of the Avant-Garde* (Westport, CT, and London: Praeger, 2003). See also *Wolfgang Paalen. Retrospectiva* (Mexico City: Museo de Arte Alvar y Carmen T. de Carrillo Gil, 1994).

27 Andreas Neufert, "Celos, miedo y delirio en el signo de la Luna," in *Alice Rahon. Una surrealista en México* (Mexico City: Instituto Nacional de Bellas Artes/Consejo Nacional para la Cultura y las Artes, 2009), p. 105.

28 Carol S. Eliel, *Lee Mullican. An Abundant Harvest of Sun* (Los Angeles: Los Angeles County Museum of Art, 2005).

29 The group exhibited together in New York's Galerie Neuf in 1946.

30 W. Jackson Rushing, "Semiology," *Art Journal*, vol. 51, no. 2 (Summer 1992), p. 97, argues for an acceptance of a wider body of sources for the Indian Space Painters.

31 Sandra Kraskin, *The Indian Space Painters. Native American Sources for American Abstract Art* (New York: Sidney Mishkin Gallery, Baruch College, City University of New York, 1991).

32 Diana C. Du Pont, "Gerzso: Pioneering the Abstract in Mexico," in Du Pont (ed.), *Risking the Abstract: Mexican Modernism and the Art of Gunther Gerzso* (Santa Barbara: Santa Barbara Museum of Art, 2003), p. 119.

33 *Ruptura. 1952–1965* (Mexico City: Museo de Arte Alvar y Carmen T. de Carrillo Gil, 1988). The essays in the exhibition catalogue *Desafío a la estabilidad. Procesos artísticos en México 1952–1967/Artistic Processes in Mexico 1952–1967* (Mexico City: Universidad Nacional Autónoma de México, 2014) analyze in a complex and thought-provoking way the dramatic changes taking place in the Mexican art world in those years.

34 Du Pont, *Risking the Abstract*, p. 105.

Endnotes

35 Mario Vargas Llosa, "Szyszlo," in *Szyszlo in His Labyrinth* (Washington, D.C.: Art Museum of the Americas, 1996), p. 20.

36 See the discussion of Szyszlo's work in this vein in Claire F. Fox, *Making Art Panamerican. Cultural Policy and the Cold War* (Minneapolis and London: University of Minnesota Press, 2013), p. 27 and chapter 2.

Chapter 7

1 Yve-Alain Bois et al., *Geometric Abstraction. Latin American Art from the Patricia Phelps de Cisneros Collection* (Cambridge, MA: Harvard University Art Museums, 2001); Gabriel Pérez-Barreiro (ed.), *The Geometry of Hope. Latin American Abstract Art from The Patricia Phelps de Cisneros Collection* (Austin: Jack S. Blanton Museum of Art, 2007); Osbel Suárez and María Amelia García, *Cold America. Geometric Abstraction in Latin America (1934–1973)* (Madrid: Fundación Juan March, 2011); Joe Houston et al., *Geometric Abstraction since 1950. A Global Exchange/Abstracción geométrica desde 1950: un intercambio global* (Buenos Aires: Museo de Arte Contemporáneo de Buenos Aires, 2013).

2 Michael Govan and Diana Magaloni, *Picasso and Rivera* (Los Angeles: Los Angeles County Museum of Art, 2016).

3 James Oles, *Art and Architecture in Mexico* (New York: Thames and Hudson, 2013), p. 232, states that "the felt sombrero, rifle, and colorful serape in the still life may not have originally referenced Zapata, at least not explicitly; at the time, Rivera referred to the picture only as his 'Mexican trophy.' The current title, which overtly politicizes the subject, seems a retrospective attempt by Rivera to bolster his populist credentials." See Oles's extended discussion of Rivera's painting and its meanings in Oles, "Rivera's Trophy," in Goven and Magaloni, *Picasso and Rivera*, pp. 147–161.

4 David Alfaro Siqueiros, *Vida Americana* (single-issue magazine), Barcelona, May 1921. See English translations of the texts in Dawn Ades, *Art in Latin America. The Modern Era, 1820–1980* (London and New Haven: Yale University Press, 1989), pp. 322–323.

5 Sandra Zetina, "Experimentación formal de la Vanguardia. Técnicas y ocultamiento," in Renato González Mello et al., *La Vanguardia en México 1915–1940* (Mexico City: Museo Nacional de Arte, 2013), p. 161.

6 Jay Hambridge, *Elements of Dynamic Symmetry* (Lowell: The Courier Corporation, 1926). For The New School as a laboratory for Vanguard art in 1930s and 40s New York see Anna Indych-López, "Making Nueva York *Moderna*: Latin American Art, the International Avant-Gardes and The New School," in Edward J. Sullivan (ed.), *Nueva York 1613–1945* (New York: New-York Historical Society and Scala Publishers, 2010, pp. 235–255.

7 Tatiana Flores, *Mexico's Revolutionary Avant-Gardes. From Estridentismo to 30–30,* (London and New Haven: Yale University Press, 2013).

8 Lynda Klich, "Mexico Estridentista," in Matthew Affron, Mark A. Castro, Dafne Cruz Porchini, and Renato González Mello (eds.), *Paint the Revolution. Mexican Modernism 1910–1950* (Philadelphia: Philadelphia Museum of Art, 2016), pp. 301–309. Klich discusses the painting and clarifies that the 1930 work is based on a now-lost 1926 original.

9 Among the principal general sources on Torres-García's painting and sculpture are Mario H. Gradowczyk, *Torres-García: Utopía y transgresion* (Montevideo: Museo Torres-García, 2007); Mari Carmen Ramírez et al., *Joaquín Torres-García: Constructing Abstraction with Wood* (Houston: Menil Collection and Museum of Fine Arts, 2009), and Luis Pérez-Oramas et al., *Joaquín Torres-García. The Arcadian Modern* (New York: Museum of Modern Art, 2015).

10 César Paternosto, *The Stone and the Thread: Andean Roots of Abstract Art* (Austin: University of Texas Press, 1996), and *Abstraction: The Amerindian Paradigm* (Brussels: Société des Expositions du Palais des Beaux-Arts, 2001). See also Barbara Braun, *Pre-Columbian Art in a Post-Columbian World: Ancient American Sources of Modern Art* (New York: Harry N. Abrams, 1993).

11 Aracy Amaral, "Abstract Constructivist Trends in Argentina, Brazil, Venezuela, and Colombia," in Waldo Rasmussen (ed.), *Latin American Artists of the Twentieth Century* (New York: Museum of Modern Art, 1993), p. 98.

12 Marilyn S. Kushner et al., *The Armory Show at 100: Modernism and Revolution* (New York: New-York Historical Society, 2013).

13 The early history of the AAA is recounted by Susan C. Larsen, "The American Abstract Artists: A Documentary History 1936–1941," *Archives of American Art Journal*, vol. 14, no. 1 (1974), pp. 2–7.

14 Cecilia Buzio de Torres, "The School of the South: The Asociación de Arte Constructivo, 1934–1942," in Mari Carmen Ramírez et al., *El Taller Torres-García. The School of the South and Its Legacy* (Austin: University of Texas Press, 1992), p. 7.

15 Nicolás Guagnini, "Sustracción del naufragio," in the exhibition catalogue *Esteban Lisa de Arturo al Di Tella (1944–1963)* (Buenos Aires: Ruth Benzacar Galería de Arte, 2002), p. 26. (Buenos

16 Mario H. Gradowczyk and Nelly Perazzo, "Abstract Art from the Río de la Plata: Buenos Aires and Montevideo, 1933–1953," in the exhibition catalogue of the same name (New York: Americas Society, 2001), p. 39.

17 María Amalia García, "Juan Melé 'Marco recortado no. 2,'" in Pérez-Barreiro (ed.), *The Geometry of Hope*, p. 101.

18 Philip L. Goodwin, *Brazil Builds. Architecture Old and New 1652–1942* (New York: Museum of Modern Art, 1943).

19 See Barry Bergdoll, *Latin America in Construction: Architecture 1955–1980* (New York: Museum of Modern Art, 2015).

20 Adele Nelson, "Monumental and Ephemeral: The Early São Paulo Bienais," in Mary Kate O'Hare (ed.), *Constructive Spirit. Abstract Art in South and North America 1920s–1950s*, exhibition catalogue (The Newark Museum, 2010), pp. 127–142; Isobel Whitelegg, "The Bienal Internacional de São Paulo: A Concise History, 1951–2014," *Perspective. La Revue de l'INHA*, 2 (2013), pp. 380–386.

21 Mónica Amor, *Theories of the Nonobject. Argentina, Brazil, Venezuela, 1944–1969* (Berkeley: University of California Press, 2016), p. 251, note 113.

22 Ibid., pp. 91–136.

23 Among these exhibitions were *Amelia Peláez* (Miami: Cuban Museum of Art and Culture, 1988) and *Guido Llinas and Los Once After Cuba* (Miami: Art Museum at Florida International University, Miami, 1997).

24 *Cuba: Art and History from 1868 to Today* (Montreal: Montreal Museum of Fine Arts, 2008); *Concrete Cuba* (exhibition at David Zwirner Gallery, London, September–October 2015, and David Zwirner Gallery, New York, January–February 2016); *Constructivist Dialogues in the Cuban Vanguard: Amelia Peláez, Loló Soldevilla and Zilia Sánchez*, Galerie Lelong, New York, May–June 2016; and *Adiós Utopía: Dreams and Deceptions in Cuban Art Since 1950* (Houston: Museum of Fine Arts, 2017).

25 See Abigail McEwen, *Concrete Cuba* (New York: David Zwirner Gallery, 2016) and *Revolutionary Horizons: Art and Polemics in 1950s Cuba* (London and New Haven: Yale University Press, 2016), and Abigail McEwen and Susanna Temkin, *Concrete Cuba: Cuban Geometric Abstraction from the 1950s* (New York and London: David Zwirner Books, 2016).

26 Dana Miller (ed.), *Carmen Herrera. Lines of Sight* (New York: Whitney Museum of American Art, 2016).

27 Gerardo Mosquera, "Carmen Herrera: Cuba, Inside and Out," in ibid., pp. 43–53.

28 Juan Carlos Ledezma, quoted in Mosquera, "Carmen Herrera," p. 47.

29 Ibid.

30 Carmen Herrera, "Heavenly Paris," *Art in America*, November 2015, p. 7.

31 Estrellita B. Brodsky, "Relocating the Dislocated: Collage, Décollage, and Assemblage in the Work of Jesús Soto," in *Soto: Paris and Beyond, 1950–1970* (New York: Grey Art Gallery, 2012), p. 1.

32 For Herrera's work in a context of Latin American geometric abstraction see Edward J. Sullivan, "Carmen Herrera: South to North," in Miller (ed.), *Carmen Herrera*, pp. 69–81.

33 Ann Temkin (ed.), *Barnett Newman* (Philadelphia: Philadelphia Museum of Art, 2002).

34 On Kelly see Yve-Alain Bois, Jack Cowart, and Alfred Pacquement, *Ellsworth Kelly: The Years in France, 1948–1954* (Washington, D.C.: National Gallery of Art, and Munich: Prestel, 1992); Diane Waldman (ed.), *Ellsworth Kelly. A Retrospective* (New York: Solomon R. Guggenheim Museum, 1996); and Yve-Alain Bois, *Ellsworth Kelly: Catalogue Raisonné of Paintings, Reliefs and Sculpture. Volume One, 1940–1953* (Paris: Cahiers d'Art, 2015).

35 Eva Huber Walters, email correspondence with the author, May 26, 2017.

36 Briony Fer and Frances Morris (eds.), *Agnes Martin* (London: Tate, 2015), and Nancy Princenthal, *Agnes Martin: Her Life and Art* (New York: Thames and Hudson, 2015).

37 Rosalind Krauss, "Grids," *October*, vol. 19 (Summer 1979), pp. 50–64.

38 Sandra Grant Marchand, *Guido Molinari. Une Rétrospective* (Montreal: Musée d'Art Contemporain de Montréal, 1995).

Chapter 8

1 See "Transatlantic Encounters," the website dedicated to the history of Latin American artists in Paris between the two world wars: www.chnm.gmu.edu/transatlanticencounters (accessed July 20, 2016).

2 Lowery Stokes Sims, "New York Dada and New World Surrealism," in the exhibition catalogue *The Latin American Spirit: Art and Artists in the United States, 1920–1970* (New York: Bronx Museum of the Arts, 1988), pp. 152–183. Among other sources that treat American Surrealism in a transnational sense see *El Surrealism entre viejo y nuevo mundo* (Madrid: Fundación Cultural MAPFRE Vida, 1990); Martica Sawin, *Surrealism in Exile and the Beginning of the New York School* (Cambridge, MA: MIT Press, 1997); Anke Birkenmaier, *Alejo Carpentier y la cultura del surrealismo en América Latina* (Madrid: Iberoamericana, 2006); *Territorios del diálogo. 1930–1945. Entre los realismos y lo surreal* (Mexico City: Museo Nacional de Arte, 2006); and Dawn Ades, Rita Eder, and Graciela Speranza (eds.), *Surrealism in Latin America. Vivísimo muerto* (Los Angeles: Getty Research Institute, 2012).

3 On the genesis of the Haitian Renaissance see Michel-Philippe Lerebours, *Haïti et ses Peintres de 1804 à 1980. Souffrances et Espoirs d'un Peuple* (Port-au-Prince: Bibliothèque Nationale d'Haïti, 1989); Gérald Alexis, *Peintres Haïtiens* (Paris: Éditions Cercle d'Art, 2000); and Carlo A. Célius, *Langage Plastique et énonciation identitaire. L'Invention de l'art Haïtien* (Quebec: Les Presses de l'Université Laval, 2007). For a more romanticized version of this story see Selden Rodman, *Renaissance in Haiti. Popular Painters in the Black Republic* (New York: Pellegrino and Cudahy, 1948), and Rodman, *Where Art Is Joy. Haitian Art: The First Forty Years* (New York: Ruggles De Latour, 1988).

4 André Breton, "Hector Hyppolite," in *Le Surréalisme et la Peinture* (Paris: Gallimard, 1979), pp. 308–312. On Hyppolite see also *Hector Hyppolite 1891?–1948* (Paris: Éditions de Capri, 2011).

5 During the late 1940s and early 50s the museum purchased important works of the first generation of the Haitian Renaissance, including paintings and prints by Bazille, Obin, and Bigaud. The 1954–55 exhibition featured several of these. In the 1967 exhibition *Latin American Art 1931–1966*, Bigaud was included with artists from Mexico, Central and South America, and other parts of the Caribbean. The 1966 exhibition at the Art Institute of Chicago entitled *The United States Collects Pan-American Art* included Haitian works alongside others from throughout the Americas. On the role of "primitive" art within the collection of MoMA see Miriam Basilio, "Evolving Taxonomies at The Museum of Modern Art in the 1930s and 40s and the Definitions of the 'Latin American Collection,'" in Edward J. Sullivan (ed.), *The Americas Revealed. Collecting Colonial and Modern Latin American Art in the United States* (University Park: Pennsylvania State University Press, 2018).

6 On the complex story of Surrealism in the Caribbean see Michael Richardson (ed.), *Refusal of the Shadow. Surrealism and the Caribbean* (London and New York: Verso, 1996), and María Clara Bernal Bermúdez, *Más allá de lo real maravilloso: El surrealismo en el Caribe* (Bogota: Universidad de los Andes, 2006).

7 Louise Tythacott, *Surrealism and the Exotic* (London and New York: Routledge, 2003), p. 175.

8 André Breton, *Manifestoes of Surrealism* (Ann Arbor: University of Michigan Press, 1972).

9 Lori Cole, "Revisiting the Vanguard: Duchamp in Buenos Aires," in Renée M. Silverman (ed.), *The Popular Avant-Garde* (Avant Garde Critical Studies) (Leiden: Brill, 2010), pp. 77–93, and Graciela Speranza, "Out of Field (Fuera de Campo) Marcel Duchamp in Buenos Aires," *Journal of Surrealism and the Americas*, vol. 4, no. 1 (2010), pp. 1–14.

10 Ida Rodríguez Prampolini, *El Surrealismo y el arte fantástico en México* (Mexico City: Universidad Nacional Autónoma de México/Instituto de Investigaciones Estéticas, 1969), p. 90.

11 Sarah M. Lowe, *Frida Kahlo* (New York: Universe, 1991), pp. 55, 57.

12 Adriana Zavala, *Becoming Modern. Becoming Tradition. Women, Gender and Representation in Mexican Art* (University Park: Pennsylvania State University Press, 2009), especially chapter 5, and Paulina Bravo Villareal, "Artistes femmes, femmes puissantes," in Agustí Arteaga (ed.), *Mexique 1900–1950. Diego Rivera, Frida Kahlo, José Clemente Orozco et les avant-gardes* (Paris: Réunion des Musées Nationaux, 2016), pp. 159–167.

13 See Daniel Garza Usabiaga, "André Breton, Surrealism and Mexico 1938–1970. A Critical Overview," *Arara*, no. 10 (2011). Online journal, www.essex.ac.uk/arthistory/research/pdfs/arara_issue_10/usabiaga.pdf. See also Fabienne Bradu, *André Breton en México* (Mexico City: Fondo de Cultura Económica, 2012).

14 See Ingrid Schaffner and Lisa Jacobs, *Julien Levy. Portrait of an Art Gallery* (Cambridge, MA: MIT Press, 1998).

15 On the exhibition see Luis Castañeda, "Surrealism and National Identity. Changing Perspectives, 1940–1968," *Journal of Surrealism and the Americas* vol. 3, no. 1 (2009), pp. 9–29.

16 Edward J. Sullivan, *Fragile Demon: Juan Soriano in Mexico 1935–1950* (Philadelphia: Philadelphia Museum of Art, 2007), p. 47.

17 The literature on the relationship of modern Mexican art and the U.S. avant-garde is extensive and much of it is summarized in Ellen G. Landau, *Mexico and American Modernism* (London and New Haven: Yale University Press, 2013), and Anna Indych-López, *Muralism Without Walls. Rivera, Orozco, and Siqueiros in the United States, 1927–1940* (Pittsburgh: University of Pittsburgh Press, 2009).

18 There is a principal exception to this rule. In 1963 Carrington was commissioned to do a mural for the new National Museum of Anthropology in Mexico City. The subject she chose was "The Magic World of the Mayas." To prepare for this large-scale work the artist spent considerable time in San Cristóbal de las Casas in the state of Chiapas. She familiarized herself with the sacred book of the Mayas, the *Popol Vuh*, and created an evocative painting that recalls ancient and modern blending of mysteries and spiritual practices of the survivors of the ancient indigenous group. See *Leonora Carrington. The Mexican Years, 1943–1985* (San Francisco: The Mexican Museum, 1991).

19 Gloria Feman Orenstein, "Down the Rabbit Hole. The Art of Shamanic Initiations and Mythic Rebirth," in Ilene Susan Fort and Tere Arcq (eds.), *In Wonderland. The Surrealist Adventures of Women Artists in Mexico and the United States* (Los Angeles: Los Angeles County Museum of Art, and New York: DelMonico Books/Prestel, 2012), p. 178.

20 Susan L. Aberth, email correspondence with the author, July 8, 2016. See also Aberth, *Leonora Carrington: Surrealism, Alchemy and Art* (London: Lund Humphreys, 2004).

21 A well-known painting of 1944 entitled *Los días de la calle Gabino Barreda* (The Days of Gabino Barreda Street) (private collection) by Gunther Gerzso, a Mexican artist whose work in the 1940s was closely associated with Surrealism, constitutes a symbolic portrait of the residents of the building. It includes Varo, Carrington, Péret, and the Spanish painter Esteban Francés.

22 Janet A. Kaplan, *Unexpected Journeys. The Art and Life of Remedios Varo* (New York: Abbeville Press, 1988), p. 155.

23 Jennifer Mundy (ed.), *Surrealism. Desire Unbound* (Princeton: Princeton University Press, 2001), p. 306.

24 Rubén Gallo, *Freud's Mexico. Into the Wilds of Psychoanalysis* (Cambridge, MA, and London: MIT Press, 2010), pp. 109–114. See also Néstor A. Braunstein, "Las pinturas superrealistas y el psicoanálisis," in the exhibition catalogue *Surrealismo. Vasos comunicantes* (Mexico City: Museo Nacional de Arte, 2012), pp. 175–217.

25 Dawn Ades, "Dorothea Tanning. Birthday," in Mundy (ed.), *Surrealism*, p. 197.

26 James Oles, *South of the Border: Mexico in the American Imagination 1914–1947* (Washington, DC: Smithsonian Institution Press, 1993). On Avery see Edward J. Sullivan, "Milton Avery and the Allure of Mexico," in *Milton Avery's Mexico. Paintings and Watercolors* (Scottsdale: Reva Yares Gallery, 2009), pp. 4–8.

27 Courtney Gilbert, "Negotiating Surrealism. Carlos Mérida, Mexican Art and the Avant-garde," *Journal of Surrealism and the Americas*, vol. 3, nos. 1–2 (2009), p. 38.

28 Alberto Dallal, *La Danza en México* (Mexico City: Universidad Nacional Autónoma de México, 1986).

29 On this important collection, which inspired Nadelman himself in the creation of many of his sculptures, see Margaret K. Hofer and Roberta J. M. Olson, *Making It Modern: The Folk Art Collection of Elie and Viola Nadelman* (London: D. Giles, 2015). It should be noted that the Nadelmans also included many examples of European folk art along with examples of North American popular traditions in their collection. I am grateful to Cynthia Nadelman for clarification of this fact. Email correspondence, May 15, 2017.

30 I am grateful to Marci Kwon for her views on the changing roles of folk art within the developments of modernism in the U.S. Conversation with the author, July 27, 2016.

31 James Oles, "For Business or Pleasure. Exhibiting Mexican Folk Art, 1820–1930," in Susan Danly (ed.), *Casa Mañana. The Morrow Collection of Mexican Popular Arts* (Albuquerque: University of New Mexico Press, 2002), p. 24. This study focuses on the large collection of Mexican folk art that the Morrow family collected for their house in Cuernavaca, Mexico, and is now housed at the Mead Art Museum of Amherst, Massachusetts. Morrow was American ambassador to Mexico from 1927 to 1930.

32 Oles has written several other important studies of the impact of the enthusiasm for Mexican folk art among modern artists and collectors in the United States. See *South of the Border*, pp. 108–144, and *De artesanos y arlequines. Forjando una colección de arte mexicano* (Mexico City: Museo Nacional de Arte, 2005).

33 Elena Izcue, *El Arte peruano en la escuela* (2 vols.) (Paris: Editorial Excelsior, 1926).

34 *Elena Izcue. Lima–Paris. Années 30* (Paris: Musée du Quai Branly, 2008). The principal essay by Natalia Majluf and Luis Eduardo Wuffarden, "Elena Izcue. L'art précolombien dans la vie moderne" (pp. 10–41), is an essential study of the artist and, in broader terms, the phenomenon of pre-Columbian art's position in developing modernity in South American art of the 1920s and 30s. On Izcue and pedagogy see pp. 22–23.

35 *Sculpture by William Edmondson*, October 20–December 1, 1937. The checklist of the exhibition lists 12 works exhibited. As was the case in many MoMA exhibitions at the time, most of the works were for sale. Half of the works sold, according to the annotated checklist in MoMA's archives, along with other pieces not included in the show. See www.moma.org/calendar/exhibitions/2019 (accessed March 17, 2017).

36 Barr's enthusiasm for self-taught art and artists was one of the factors in his dismissal (1943) from the directorship of MoMA by the board of directors, who found his exhibitions of this material inimical to the mission of the museum. He thereafter served as Curator of Collections.

37 *Contemporary Unknown American Painters*, October 18–November 18, 1939.

38 Alfred H. Barr, foreword to Sidney Janis, *They Taught Themselves: American Primitive Painters of the Twentieth Century* (New York: Dial Press, 1942), p. xx.

39 In January 2016 Edmondson's sculpture *The Boxer* was sold at a Christie's auction of "Outsider and Vernacular Art" for a record price of $750,000.

40 Diego Rivera, "Mardonio Magaña," *Espacios*, no. 1, (September 1948), p. 6. Earlier, in 1930, Rivera had written an essay on Magaña for *Mexican Folkways* (vol. 6, no. 2, July 1930) in which he stated: "This authentic peasant sculptor is thought by all to be a simple man, but these irremediably ignorant people do not know that artistic culture is organic knowledge, not simple copying by apprentices." Quoted in *La Escuela mexicana de escultura: maestros fundadores* (Mexico City: Consejo Nacional para la Cultura y las Artes, 1990), p. 84.

Epilogue

1   Thomas Crow, *The Long March of Pop: Art, Music and Design, 1930–1995* (New Haven and London: Yale University Press, 2015).

2   See Rachel Weiss, *To and From Utopia in the New Cuban Art* (Minneapolis: University of Minnesota Press, 2011) and *Adiós Utopia: Dreams and Deceptions in Cuban Art Since 1950* (Houston: Museum of Fine Arts, 2017).

3   Jessica Morgan and Flavia Frigeri, *The World Goes Pop* (London: Tate, 2015), and Darsie Alexander et al., *International Pop* (Minneapolis: Walker Art Center, 2015).

4   Joseph D. Ketner, *Andy Warhol* (London: Phaidon, 2013).

5   Douglas Dreishpoon, "The Voice Behind the Silence," in Maria Pacini (ed.), *Marisol. Sculptures and Works on Paper* (Memphis: Brooks Museum of Art, and New Haven and London: Yale University Press, 2014), p. 115.

6   Benjamín Villegas (ed.), with texts by Holland Cotter, Carmen María Jaramillo, and María Margarita Malagón, *Beatriz González* (Bogotá: Villegas Editores, 2005).

7   Leah Dickerman and Achim Borchardt-Hume (eds.), *Robert Rauschenberg* (New York: Museum of Modern Art, 2016).

8   Estrellita B. Brodsky, "Julio Le Parc: Form into Action," in Brodsky (ed.), *Form into Action: Julio Le Parc* (Miami: Pérez Art Museum Miami, and Munich, London, and New York: DelMonico Books/ Prestel, 2016), p. 11.

9   Mónica Amor, *Theories of the Nonobject. Argentina, Brazil, Venezuela, 1944–1969* (Berkeley: University of California Press, 2016), p. 172. See also Iris Peruga et al., *Gego. Obra complete. 1955–1990* (Caracas: Fundación Cisneros, 2003), and Mari Carmen Ramírez (ed.), *Gego, Between Transparency and the Invisible* (Houston: Museum of Fine Arts, and Buenos Aires: Fundación Eduardo F. Costantini, 2007).

10   See Claudia Calirman, *Brazilian Art Under Dictatorship. Antonio Manuel, Artur Barrio, and Cildo Meireles* (Durham, NC, and London: Duke University Press, 2012), and Anna Katherine Brodbeck, *Parallel Situations: Artur Barrio, Brazilian Art and International Exchange in the Post-Studio Era (1969–1974)*, PhD dissertation, New York University, 2014.

11   Ruth Fine (ed.), *Procession: The Art of Norman Lewis* (Berkeley: University of California Press, 2015).

12   Ruth Fine, "The Spiritual in the Material," in ibid. (p. 80), examines this series of Ku Klux Klan paintings, which include both black-and-white images such as *Totem* and others done in red on white. These were shown in a Spiral Gallery group exhibition organized between May and June 1965 in a rented space on Christopher Street in New York's Greenwich Village. The catalogue's preface reads, in part: "we hoped with our art to justify life…. What is most important now, and what has great portent for the future, is that Negro artists, of divergent backgrounds and interests, have come together on terms of mutual respect."

Further Reading

Please note that the following is an abbreviated list of books in English, or bilingual editions, that are relatively easy to find in libraries or by other means. It is limited to volumes that examine broad areas of information related to the content of this book, and does not pretend to be comprehensive in any way. It does not contain monographs on individual artists. I refer readers, in this case, to the endnotes for each chapter, in which I have attempted to include at least one source on the individual artists discussed in the text.

Ades, Dawn, et al. (ed.), *Art in Latin America. The Modern Era, 1820–1980* (New Haven and London: Yale University Press, 1989)

——— Rita Eder, and Graciela Speranza (eds.), *Surrealism in Latin America. Vivísimo Muerto* (Los Angeles: Getty Research Institute, 2012)

Adiós Utopía. Art in Cuba Since 1950 (Miami: The Cisneros Fontanals Art Foundation, 2017)

Affron, Matthew, Mark A. Castro, Dafne Cruz Porchini, and Renato González Mello (eds.), *Paint the Revolution: Mexican Modernism, 1910–1950* (Philadelphia: Philadelphia Museum of Art, 2016)

Alberro, Alexander, *Abstraction in Reverse: The Reconfigured Spectator in Mid-Twentieth Century Latin American Art* (Chicago and London: University of Chicago Press, 2017)

Anreus, Alejandro, et al. (eds.), *Mexican Muralism: A Critical History* (Berkeley: University of California Press, 2012)

Archer Straw, Petrine, and Kim Robinson, *Jamaican Art. An Overview with a Focus on Fifty Artists* (Kingston: Kingston Publishers Limited, 1990)

Barnitz, Jacqueline, and Patrick Frank, *Twentieth-Century Art of Latin America* (revised ed.) (Austin: University of Texas Press, 2015)

Barter, Judith A. (ed.), *After the Fall: Painting in the 1930s* (Chicago: Art Institute of Chicago, 2016)

Basilio, Miriam, et al. (eds.), *Latin American and Caribbean Art: MoMA at El Museo* (New York: The Museum of Modern Art and El Museo del Barrio, 2004)

Biller, Geraldine P. (ed.), *Latin American Women Artists: 1915–1995* (Milwaukee: Milwaukee Art Museum, 1995)

Bindman, David, Henry Louis Gates Jr. et al. (eds.), *The Image of the Black in Western Art*, vols. 4 and 5 (Cambridge, MA: Belknap Press of Harvard University Press, 2014–2015)

Bois, Yve-Alain, et al., *Geometric Abstraction: Latin American Art from the Patricia Phelps de Cisneros Collection* (Cambridge, MA: Harvard University Art Museums, 2001)

——— (ed.), *Cuba: Art and History from 1868 to Today* (Montreal: Montreal Museum of Fine Arts, 2009)

Bondil, Nathalie, and Victor Pimentel (eds.), *Peru: Kingdoms of the Sun and Moon* (Montreal: Montreal Museum of Fine Arts, 2015)

Boxer, David, and Veerle Poupeye, *Modern Jamaican Art* (Kingston: Ian Randall Publishers, 1998)

Brownlee, Peter John, Valéria Piccoli, and Georgiana Uhlyarik (eds.), *Picturing the Americas: Landscape Painting from Tierra del Fuego to the Arctic* (New Haven and London: Yale University Press, 2015)

Camnitzer, Luis, *New Art of Cuba* (Austin: University of Texas Press, 2003)

Cancel, Luis R., et al. (eds.), *The Latin American Spirit: Art and Artists in the United States, 1920–1970* (New York: Bronx Museum of the Arts and Harry N. Abrams, 1988)

Coffey, Mary K., *How a Revolutionary Art Became Official Culture: Murals, Museums, and the Mexican State* (Durham, NC, and London: Duke University Press, 2012)

Corn, Wanda M., *The Great American Thing: Modern Art and National Identity, 1915–1935* (Berkeley: University of California Press, 2001)

Craven, David, *Art and Revolution in Latin America 1910–1990* (New Haven and London: Yale University Press, 2002)

Cullen, Deborah (ed.), *Nexus New York: Latin/American Artists in the Modern Metropolis* (New Haven and London: Yale University Press, 2009)

———, and Elvis Fuentes (eds.), *Caribbean: Art at the Crossroads of the World* (New Haven, London, and New York: El Museo del Barrio, 2012)

Dossin, Catherine, *The Rise and Fall of American Art, 1940s–1980s: A Geopolitics of Western Art Worlds* (Farnham: Ashgate, 2015)

Eder, Rita (ed.), *Desafío a la estabilidad. Procesos artísticos en México 1952–1967. Defying Stability. Artistic Processes in Mexico 1952–1967* (Madrid: Turner, 2014)

Fernández, Segundo J., Juan A. Martínez, and Paul Neill, *Cuban Art in the 20th Century: Cultural Identity and the International Avant Garde* (Tallahassee: Florida State University Museum of Fine Arts, 2016)

Flores, Tatiana, *Mexico's Revolutionary Avant-Gardes: From Estridentismo to 30-30!* (New Haven and London: Yale University Press, 2013)

Folgarait, Leonard, *Seeing Mexico Photographed: The Work of Horne, Casasola, Modotti and Alvarez Bravo* (New Haven and London: Yale University Press, 2008)

Fort, Ilene Susan, and Tere Arcq, *In Wonderland: The Surrealist Adventures of Women Artists in Mexico and the United States* (Los Angeles: Los Angeles County Museum of Art, and New York: DelMonico Books/Prestel, 2012)

Foster, Hal, et al., *Art Since 1900: 1900–1944* (London: Thames and Hudson, 2011)

Fox, Claire F., *Making Art Panamerican: Cultural Policy and the Cold War* (Minneapolis and London: University of Minnesota Press, 2013)

Frank, Patrick (ed.), *Manifestos and Polemics in Latin American Modern Art* (Albuquerque: University of New Mexico Press, 2017)

——— (ed.), *Readings in Latin American Art* (New Haven and London: Yale University Press, 2004)

Giunta, Andrea, *Avant-Garde, Internationalism and Politics: Argentine Art in the Sixties* (Durham, NC: Duke University Press, 2007)

Gradowczyk, Mario H., and Nelly Perazzo (eds.), *Abstract Art from the Río de la Plata. Buenos Aires and Montevideo, 1933–1953* (New York: Americas Society, 2001)

Greet, Michele, *Beyond National Identity: Pictorial Indigenism as a Modernist Strategy in Andean Art, 1920–1960* (University Park: Pennsylvania State University Press, 2009)

Hurlburt, Laurance P., *Mexican Muralists in the United States* (Albuquerque: University of New Mexico Press, 1991)

Indych-López, Anna, *Muralism Without Walls. Rivera, Orozco, and Siqueiros in the United States, 1927-1940* (Pittsburgh: University of Pittsburgh Press, 2009)

Joselit, David, *American Art Since 1945* (London: Thames and Hudson, 2003)

Katzenstein, Inés, and Andrea Giunta (eds.), *Listen, Here Now! Argentine Art in the 1960s* (New York: Museum of Modern Art, 2004)

Lear, John, *Picturing the Proletariat. Artists and Labor in Revolutionary Mexico, 1908–1940* (Austin: University of Texas Press, 2017)

Martínez, Juan A., *Cuban Art and National Identity: The Vanguardia Painters, 1927–1950* (Gainesville: University Press of Florida, 1994)

Martins, Sérgio B., *Constructing an Avant-Garde. Art in Brazil, 1949–1979* (Cambridge, MA: MIT Press, 2013)

McEwen, Abigail, *Revolutionary Horizons: Art and Polemics in 1950s Cuba* (New Haven and London: Yale University Press, 2016)

McKay, Marilyn Jean, *Picturing the Land: Narrating Territories in Canadian Landscape Art, 1500–1950* (Montreal: McGill-Queen's University Press, 2011)

O'Brian, John, and Peter White (eds.), *Beyond Wilderness: The Group of Seven, Canadian Identity, and Contemporary Art* (Montreal: McGill-Queen's University Press, 2007)

Olea, Héctor, Mari Carmen Ramírez, and Tomás Ybarra Frausto, *Resisting Categories: Latin American and/or Latino* (Houston: Museum of Fine Arts, 2012)

Oles, James, *Art and Architecture in Mexico* (London: Thames and Hudson, 2013)

Pérez-Barreiro, Gabriel (ed.), *The Geometry of Hope: Latin American Abstract Art from the Patricia Phelps de Cisneros Collection* (Austin: Jack S. Blanton Museum of Art, 2007)

Poupeye, Veerle, *Caribbean Art* (New York and London: Thames and Hudson, 1998)

Powell, Richard J., *Black Art: A Cultural History* (London: Thames and Hudson, 2003)

Ramírez, Mari Carmen, and Héctor Olea (eds.), *Inverted Utopias: Avant-garde Art in Latin America* (Houston: Museum of Fine Arts, 2004)

Rochfort, Desmond, *Mexican Muralists: Orozco, Rivera, Siqueiros* (San Francisco: Chronicle Books, 1998)

Sandler, Irving, *The Triumph of American Painting: A History of Abstract Expressionism* (New York: Praeger, 1970, and later eds.)

Sawin, Martica, *Surrealism in Exile and the Beginning of the New York School* (Cambridge, MA, and London: MIT Press, 1997)

Stratton, Suzanne (ed.), *Modern and Contemporary Art of the Dominican Republic* (New York: The Americas Society and the Spanish Institute, 1996)

Suárez, Osbel, and María Amalia García, *Cold America: Geometric Abstraction in Latin America (1934–1973)* (Madrid: Fundación Juan March, 2011)

Sullivan, Edward J. (ed.), *Brazil: Body & Soul* (New York: Solomon R. Guggenheim Museum, 2001)

———, *The Language of Objects in the Art of the Americas* (New Haven and London: Yale University Press, 2007)

——— (ed.), *Latin American Art in the Twentieth Century* (London: Phaidon, 1996)

Unruh, Vicky, *Latin American Vanguards: The Art of Contentious Encounters* (Berkeley and Los Angeles: University of California Press, 1994)

Index

Index

Index

Picture Credits

Laurence King Publishing Ltd, the author, and the picture researcher wish to thank the institutions and individuals who have kindly provided photographic material for use in this book. Details of collections are given in the captions. Additional information, © credits, and photo sources are given below. Numbers are figure numbers unless indicated. While every effort has been made to trace the present © holders we apologize in advance for any unintentional omission or error and will be pleased to insert the appropriate acknowledgement in any subsequent edition.

Key: ALC = ALC; ARS = Artists Rights Society, New York; BI = Bridgeman Images, London/Paris/New York; CCP = Center for Creative Photography, The University of Arizona Foundation; CI = Christie's Images, London; DA = De Agostini Picture Library; DACS = Design and Artists Copyright Society, London; DRFK = Banco de México

Diego Rivera Frida Kahlo Museums Trust, Mexico, D.F.; MFAH = Museum of Fine Arts, Houston, Texas; MMA = The Metropolitan Museum of Art, New York; MoMA = The Museum of Modern Art, New York; RMN = Réunion des Musées Nationaux, Paris; PC = The Phillips Collection, Washington, D.C.

Foreword
Page 6 & **Fig. 1** MoMA Library, NY. Acc. n.: LI238. Digital image, MoMA/Scala, Florence; **Fig. 2** MFAH/ALC/BI. Courtesy of Thiago Lupo Maluf.

Chapter 1
Page 18 & **1.12** Museo de Arte Latinoamericano de Buenos Aires, Fundación Costantini. Photo MALBA, Buenos Aires. Courtesy of Guilherme Augusto do Amaral; **1.1** Photo © Museo Nacional de Colombia/ Samuel Monsalve Parra; **1.2** Photo © Museo Nacional de Colombia (reg. 2115)/Julio

César Flórez. Courtesy of María Cristina de la Cuadra; **1.3** Private Collection/BI; **1.4** Photo Museo Nacional de Arte (MUNAL), Mexico City, Mexico. © DRFK/DACS 2017; **1.5** Photo Museo Nacional de Arte (MUNAL), Mexico City, Mexico. © Estate of Ángel Zárraga; **1.6** DA/G. Dagli Orti/BI. © Estate of Ángel Zárraga; **1.7** © DACS 2017; **1.8** Photo © CI/BI; **1.9** Brooklyn Museum of Art, New York. Gift of the Artist/BI. © The Feitelson/Lundeberg Art Foundation; **1.10** San Diego Museum of Art. Gift of the Artist/BI. © Estate of Agnes Pelton; **1.11** Reproduced from the original held by the Department of Special Collections of the Hesburgh Libraries of Notre Dame.

Chapter 2
Page 48 & **2.6** Harwood Museum, Taos, New Mexico. Gift of the Artist (1980.0275.0000). © Estate of Rebecca James; **2.2** Photo © CI/BI; **2.4** By kind permission of the Juan

Manuel Blanes, photo by Eduardo Baldizan and his assistant Nestor Pereira. © José Cuneo Perinetti/AGADU; **2.5** Cleveland Museum of Art, OH. Leonard C. Hanna, Jr. Fund with additional support from the Gill and Tommy LiPuma Fund/BI; **2.7** BI. © The family of Lawren S. Harris; **2.8** Art Gallery of Ontario, Toronto. Gift of Richard Ivey, 2008/BI; **2.9** BI. © DACS 2017; **2.10** Courtesy of the Estate of Joaquín Torres-García; **2.12** PC, Acquired 1926/BI. © Estate of Charles Sheeler; **2.13** Image © MMA/Art Resource/Scala, Florence. © MMA; **2.14** © 2017. Image © MMA/ Art Resource/Scala, Florence. © MMA; **2.15** © D.R. Rufino Tamayo/Herederos/México/ Fundación Olga y Rufino Tamayo, A.C. 2017; **2.16** Index/BI. Courtesy of Guilherme Augusto do Amaral.

Chapter 3
Page 88 & **3.20** MFAH/ALC/BI. Courtesy of Sr. Roberto Bicca de Alencastro; **3.1** Photo Isabella Matheus. Courtesy of Sylvia Malfatti R Sousa; **3.2** akg-images. Courtesy of Guilherme Augusto do Amaral; **3.3** Digital image, MoMA/Scala, Florence. © Museu Lasar Segall-IBRAM/MinC; **3.4** Photo Mariano Hernández © Francis Woss y Gil; **3.5** Photo © RMN-Grand Palais (musée d'Orsay)/Hervé Lewandowski; **3.6** © Marina Grisolía and Juan Miguel Grisolía; **3.7** BI. © Estate of Victor Manuel García; **3.8** Photo © Valerie Gerrard Browne/Chicago History Museum/BI. © The Estate of Archibald Motley/BI; **3.9** Image Courtesy of the Edna Manley Foundation; **3.10** Cernuda Arte, Miami, Florida; **3.11** Photo courtesy of Michael Rosenfeld Gallery LLC, New York, NY. © 1936 The Charles White Archives; **3.12** Brooklyn Museum Fund for African American Art and gift of Auldlyn Higgins Williams and E.T. Williams, Jr./BI. © Loïs Mailou Jones Pierre-Noel Trust; **3.13** Courtesy of Mrs. Doreen-Howell Watson; **3.14** © The Estate of Albert Huie; **3.15** Philadelphia Museum of Art, Pennsylvania, PA. Purchased with the Alice Newton Osborn Fund, 1999/ BI. © Catlett Mora Family Trust/VAGA, NY/ DACS, London 2017; **3.16** PC, Acquired 1942/BI. © Estate of Jacob Lawrence. ARS, NY and DACS, London 2017; **3.17** Minneapolis Institute of Arts, MN. The John R. Van Derlip Fund/BI. © Romare Bearden Foundation/DACS, London/VAGA, New York 2017; **3.18** Photo © CI/BI. © ADAGP, Paris and DACS, London 2017; **3.19** Cernuda Arte, Miami, FL.

Chapter 4
Page 124 & **4.5** Dallas Museum of Art, Texas. Allied Arts Civic Prize, Eighth Annual Dallas Allied Arts Exhibition, 1937/BI. Courtesy of Pat Bywaters on behalf of the Jerry Bywaters Family; **4.1** Galerie Bilderwelt/BI; **4.2** © CCP/Art Resource, NY/DACS 2017; **4.3** Photo Art Resource/Bob Schalkwijk/Scala, Florence. © DRFK/DACS 2017; **4.4** Detroit Institute of Arts. Gift of Edsel B. Ford/BI. © DRFK/DACS 2017; **4.8** BI. © DACS 2017; **4.9** Omniphoto/UIG/BI. © DACS 2017; **4.10** Photo Schalkwijk/Art Resource/ Scala, Florence. © DACS 2017; **4.11** Detroit

Institute of Arts. Museum Purchase/BI. © Estate of Hale Woodruff/DACS, London/ VAGA, NY 2017.

Chapter 5
Page 152 & **5.16** Private Collection/Photo © CI/BI. © Archivo Antonio Berni; **5.1** Photo © CI/BI. © DACS 2017; **5.2** Digital image, MoMA/Scala, Florence. © DACS 2017; **5.3** Digital image, MoMA/Scala, Florence. © The Pollock-Krasner Foundation ARS, NY and DACS, London 2017; **5.4** Courtesy of James Jones; **5.5** Bettmann/Getty Images; **5.6** © Estate of Francisco Goitia; **5.7** Photo © CI/ BI. © The Estate of Alice Neel. Courtesy of David Zwirner, New York/London; **5.8** BI. © DACS 2017; **5.9** & **5.10** © Colette Urbajtel/ Archivo Manuel Álvarez Bravo, S.C.; **5.11** Image © MMA/Art Resource/Scala, Florence. © Walker Evans Archive, MMA; **5.13** DA/ G. Dagli Orti/BI. Portinari, Candido/© DACS 2017; **5.14** Courtesy of Nitza Tufiño; **5.15** DA/M. Seemuller/BI. © The Estate of Eduardo Kingman. Courtesy of Soledad Kingman, Quito.

Chapter 6
Page 186 & **6.17** © Fernando de Szyszlo; **6.2** © Estate of Maria Luisa Pacheco; **6.3** BI. Courtesy of Carmen M. Vivas; **6.4** Dallas Museum of Art, Texas. Foundation for the Arts Collection, gift of The Ford Foundation/BI. © The Harriet and Esteban Vicente Foundation; **6.5** Digital image, MoMA/Scala, Florence. © Pettoruti Foundation-www.pettoruti.com (Reproduced in the "Pettoruti" catalog, edited by the Pettoruti Foundation in 1995, Buenos Aires, ficha Nº 48.); **6.6** Photo Mark Morosse. © Proyecto Armando Reverón; **6.7** MFAH. Museum purchase funded by the Alice Pratt Brown Museum Fund/BI. © Proyecto Armando Reverón; **6.8** DA/G. Nimatallah/ BI. © Georgia O'Keeffe Museum/DACS 2017; **6.9** Image © MMA/Art Resource/ Scala, Florence. Courtesy of Diane Rehm; **6.10** PC, Acquired 1942/BI. Courtesy of Michael Rosenfeld Gallery LLC, New York, NY; **6.11** Photo Courtesy of Mary-Anne Martin Fine Art New York. © ADAGP, Paris and DACS, London 2017; **6.12** Courtesy of Gallery Wendi Norris, San Francisco; **6.13** Photo © CI/BI. Courtesy of Lic. Oscar Roman; **6.14** © Estate of Lee Mullican Courtesy of Ryan Good; **6.15** Private Collection/BI. Courtesy of Steve Wheeler estate; **6.16** Davis Museum and Cultural Center, Wellesley College, MA. Museum purchase with funds provided by Wellesley College Friends of Art/BI/© John Michael Gerzso.

Chapter 7
Page 222 & **7.6** Davis Museum at Wellesley College, Wellesley, Massachusetts. Museum purchase, The Mary Clothier Slade Fund 2006.179. © Estate of Rosa Acle; **7.1** BI. Courtesy of the Estate of Joaquín Torres-García; **7.2** BI. © DRFK/DACS 2017; **7.3** BI. © Estate of Ramón Alva de la Canal; **7.4** BI; **7.5** BI. Courtesy of the Estate of Joaquín Torres-García; **7.7** MFAH. Museum purchase/ BI. Courtesy of Jean-Pierre Joyce; **7.8** Photo Mark Morosse/Colección Patricia Phelps de

Cisneros. © Estate of Juan Melé; **7.9** Photo Gregg Stanger. Courtesy of Sonia Henríquez Ureña de Hlito and Gabriela Hlito; **7.10** Photo Sarah Wells. © ADAGP, Paris and DACS, London 2017; **7.11** MFAH/ALC/ BI. Courtesy of the Associação Cultural "O Mundo de Lygia Clark" Ref No 00756; Archive No 586/Certificate No 000603; **7.12** MFAH/ALC/BI. © César and Claudio Oiticica Collection; **7.13** MFAH/ALC/BI. Courtesy of Walter de Castro; **7.14** MFAH/ ALC/BI. © Estate of Hercules Barsotti; **7.15** Courtesy of Martha Flora; **7.16** Digital image, MoMA/Scala, Florence. © Amelia Pelaez Foundation; **7.17** © Carmen Herrera, Courtesy of Lisson Gallery, New York; **7.18** © The Barnett Newman Foundation, New York/ DACS, London 2017; **7.19** © Ellsworth Kelly. Photo courtesy of Ellsworth Kelly Studio; **7.20** BI. © Agnes Martin/DACS 2017; **7.21** Art Gallery of Ontario, Toronto. Purchase, 1980/BI. © SODRAC, Montreal and DACS, London 2017.

Chapter 8
Page 264 & **8.8** Philadelphia Museum of Art, Pennsylvania, PA. Purchased with funds contributed by C. K. Williams, II, 1999/BI. © ADAGP, Paris and DACS, London 2017; **8.1** Photo © Gérald Bloncourt/BI. © Estate of Hector Hyppolite; **8.2** MFAH. Gift of Colonel J. W. Flanagan through Mrs. Jesse Jones/BI. Courtesy of Nora Martins Lobo; **8.3** Harry Ransom Center, University of Texas at Austin, Austin. Photo © Leemage/BI. © DRFK/DACS 2017; **8.4** Photo Courtesy of Mary-Anne Martin Fine Art New York. © DACS 2017; **8.5** Philadelphia Museum of Art, Pennsylvania, PA. Gift of Mr and Mrs Henry Clifford/BI. © Fundación Juan Soriano y Marek Keller A.C.; **8.6** BI. © Estate of Leonora Carrington/ARS, NY and DACS, London 2017; **8.7** © Estate of Remedios Varo; **8.9** Photo © CI/BI. © DACS 2017; **8.10** Photo © CI/BI. © DACS 2017; **8.11** Photo courtesy of Martha Graham Company; **8.12** Fogg Art Museum, Harvard Art Museum. Gift of Dr. and Mrs John P. Spiegel/BI. © Estate of Elie Nadelman; **8.13** Photo Daniel Giannoni. Archi, Archivo Digital de Arte Peruano; **8.14** © CCP/DACS 2017; **8.15** Photo © Boltin Picture Library/BI; **8.16** BI. © Estate of Agnaldo Manoel dos Santos.

Epilogue
Page 300 & **9.9** © Estate of Norman W. Lewis; Courtesy of Michael Rosenfeld Gallery LLC, New York, NY; **9.1** Photo Peter Newark American Pictures/BI. © Estate of Raúl Martínez; **9.2** BI. © 2017 The Andy Warhol Foundation for the Visual Arts, Inc./Artists Rights Society (ARS), New York and DACS, London; **9.3** BI. © Marisol. DACS, London/ VAGA, New York 2017; **9.4** MFAH. Museum purchase funded by the 2007 Latin American Experience Gala and Auction/BI. © Beatriz González; **9.5** BI. © Robert Rauschenberg Foundation/DACS, London/VAGA, New York 2017; **9.6** MFAH. Museum purchase funded by the 2005 Latin American Experience Gala and Auction, and the Latin Maecenas/BI. © ADAGP, Paris and DACS, London 2017; **9.8** © Artur Barrio. Photo by César Carneiro.